THE REAL OLIVER TWIST

JOHN WALLER

ICON BOOKS

This edition published in the UK in 2006 by
Icon Books Ltd, The Old Dairy,
Brook Road, Thriplow,
Cambridge SG8 7RG
email: info@iconbooks.co.uk
www.iconbooks.co.uk

Originally published in 2005 by Icon Books Ltd

Sold in the UK, Europe, South Africa and Asia
by Faber and Faber Ltd, 3 Queen Square,
London WC1N 3AU

ISBN 10: 1-84046-727-4
ISBN 13: 978-1840467-27-7

Text copyright © 2005, 2006 John Waller

Typesetting by Hands Fotoset

Printed and bound in Great Britain by
William Clowes Ltd, Beccles, Suffolk

To my mother, my wife and my daughter,
Susan, Abigail and Esther

About the author

John Waller was born in Lancashire, England in 1972. Educated at the universities of Oxford and London, he has taught at the University of Melbourne and now lectures at Michigan State University. His previous books include *The Discovery of the Germ* (Icon, 2002), *Fabulous Science* (OUP, 2002) and *Leaps in the Dark* (OUP, 2004). He lives with his wife and daughter in Michigan.

Contents

Contents

List of illustrations

Plate section

Here sighs, plaints, and voices of the deepest woe resounded through the starless sky. Strange languages, horrid cries, accents of grief and wrath, voices deep and hoarse, with hands clenched in despair, made a commotion which whirled forever through that air of everlasting gloom.

Dante, *Inferno*, canto iii

Let not Ambition mock their useful toil,
Their homely joys, and destiny obscure;
Nor Grandeur hear with a disdainful smile
The short and simple annals of the Poor.

Thomas Gray, 'Elegy Written in a Country Church-yard'

I am seeking to rescue the poor stockinger, the Luddite cropper, the 'obsolete' hand-loom weaver, the 'utopian' artisan … from the enormous condescension of history.

E.P. Thompson (1963)

Introduction

God made the country and man made the town.
William Cowper

Am I not a man and a brother?
Motto popularised by the Society for Effecting
the Abolition of the Slave Trade

Poster boy

For Robert Blincoe the memory of Saturday 25 August 1832 remained always fresh. On this extraordinary day the steam engines, mules and power looms of Manchester stood still. The city streets were thronged with working people and the air reverberated with the discordant, interwoven strains of seventeen marching bands and the sharp retorts of a thousand pairs of working-man's clogs striking cobbled streets. Since early morning, from towns and villages all over Lancashire, poor men, women and children had been converging on the greatest city of the industrial age. Made rich, famous and populous, but also filthy, diseased and dangerous by the cotton trade, on that summer's day 'Cottonopolis' buzzed with angry passions and a hint of carnival high spirits. The cradle of Britain's new wealth, and to many the most likely flashpoint for a social revolution, awaited the appearance of Richard Oastler, a brilliant orator widely known as 'The King of the Factory Children'. Somewhere amid the crowd on that unforgettable day stood Robert Blincoe.

Bent, twisted and scarred from years of gruelling labour and physical abuse, Blincoe had suffered grievously from the onset of the factory age. But on this late summer afternoon his name was on the lips of many thousands of his fellow workers. It was a remarkable feat. Born 40 years earlier into terrible poverty, raised in a workhouse, then sold into the 'white slavery' of the early cotton trade, now he stood proud. A devoted father and benevolent employer, he was committed to the cause of saving other children from the suffering he had undergone. In Manchester on 25 August he had more reason than most to applaud as Oastler made his dramatic appearance.[1]

For those who had never visited Manchester, or were now returning after a long absence, the shock must have been great. The town

3

had lost its calm rusticity long ago; in 1714 Daniel Defoe had dubbed it 'one of the greatest, if not the greatest meer village in England'. But in little more than 50 years, Manchester had been transformed into a vast confusion of slums, riverside wharfs and textile mills. Smoke-belching chimneys crowded the skyline, belittling church towers and steeples. Wharfs, warehouses and red-brick mills, many several storeys high, squatted along thoroughfares and lined the banks of the River Irwell, while canal barges penetrated deep into the city, loaded with iron, coal, cotton, finished yarn, girders, flour, fine clothes and upholstery. Everywhere, signs of the vast increase in the wealth of the capitalist classes were to be seen. And at the city's Literary and Philosophical Club, barons of industry now took tea with gentlemen of older and staler wealth.[2]

What George Eliot called the 'higher pains' of the factory age were no less evident. 'From this filthy sewer pure gold flows', conceded Alexis de Tocqueville in 1835, but it came at a heavy cost. 'In Manchester', he went on, 'civilised man is turned back almost into a savage.' 'It is scarcely in the power of the factory workman to taste the breath of nature or to look upon its verdure', remarked a like-minded Dr Bisset Hawkins. But during that August the city was paying a far heavier price for its filth and squalor. Its notorious slums were being ravaged by the first of many devastating attacks of a new malady, Asiatic cholera.[3]

Since the arrival of cholera earlier the previous year in Sunderland on England's north-east coast, Manchester had awaited its appearance with mounting dread. Now it was scything through entire families. Local doctor James Kay told of how he visited a house in the morning to inspect the corpse of a poor man. He confirmed cholera as the cause of death, and by the early hours of the night, the dead man's widow, two children and an infant had followed him into a mass grave. 'Venice hath her Bridge of Sighs,' remarked one local, 'Manchester its "Bridge of Tears".' Life in the city for the poor was desperately hard. The working classes lived on average just seventeen years. This was less than half as long as the denizens of damp, tumbledown cottages in rural England. It was barely longer than the lifespan of medieval Britons in the century of the Black Death. To aggravate matters, in 1832 Manchester was reeling from a trade

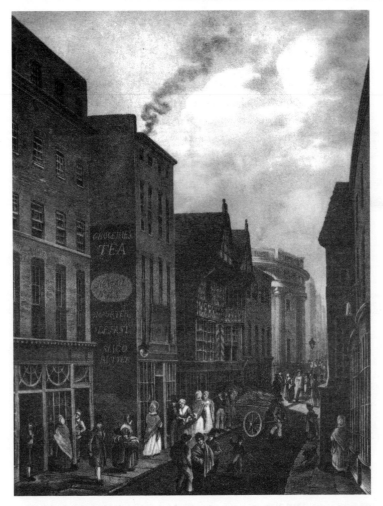

1. An image of Manchester in the early 19th century by John Ralston. Some old buildings survived, but the city had become crowded and filthy, and mills, forges and workshops belched smoke into the air.

recession. As unsold fabrics accumulated in city warehouses and orders for cottons and calicos plummeted, many were thrown out of work. Hand-outs from Friendly Societies kept the lucky going; the less fortunate had to turn to parish or private charities.[4]

To save themselves from the 'poisonous miasmas' of central Manchester, most of the city's well-to-do returned each evening to homes in the city's outskirts, upstream and upwind of the slums. In the centre, not even Manchester's magnificent new municipal buildings could escape a thick coating of soot and grime. Smoke from chimneys and furnaces covered the city in a vast grey canopy, and it was said that when easterly winds blew, the fleeces of sheep grazing 90 miles away on the Isle of Man were contaminated with the effluvia of Manchester's wealth. The city's dye works and the crudest of sewerage systems left the Rivers Irwell and Irk 'turbid' and 'black as ink'.[5]

Yet on 25 August 1832 the workers of Manchester and its outlying villages seemed to transcend the horrors of daily life. By lunchtime, a huge crowd had formed upon Ardwick Green outside the Shakespeare Inn. They had come to see and hear several of the inn's guests, leaders of the 'Ten Hours movement', radical men united in pressing Parliament to reduce the working day of factory children from as many as seventeen to a kinder ten hours per day.[6]

Among them was Michael Sadler, Esquire, a Tory economist, Member of Parliament, and son of a gentleman farmer who could trace his lineage back to one of Henry VIII's ministers. Sadler had recently introduced into the House of Commons a Ten Hours Bill, which had been shunted by its critics into a Select Committee, leading Sadler to spend months compiling a litany of damning evidence against the owners of textile factories. In a few weeks, extracts from the Sadler report would be quoted in *The Times* and fill many of its readers with a blend of shame and disgust. Although weakened by sickness and plagued with self-doubt, Michael Sadler was in Manchester to whip up public support for his Bill.[7]

Richard Oastler was also readying himself in the Shakespeare Inn. The son of a Wesleyan cloth merchant, and now the steward for an absentee Yorkshire squire, Oastler had met Sadler in Leeds in 1813 when they were both campaigning for the election to Parliament of the leader of the anti-slavery movement, William Wilberforce. The two men had subsequently joined arms in bringing spiritual and material succour to 'the filthiest and most loathsome hovels' of Yorkshire's poor in the midst of an appalling typhus epidemic. Oastler's militancy had subsided along with the typhus outbreak and he had eventually settled down to the comfortable life of an estate manager. Then, in 1826, he had been exposed to the horrors of child labour in factories operated by a mill-owning friend who had already tried and failed to convince his fellow manufacturers to reduce the hours worked by young boys and girls. Won over by his friend's earnest entreaties, Oastler had largely given up his peaceful existence in rural Yorkshire to champion the cause of the factory child.[8]

Discovering a supreme talent for public oratory on the eve of his 42nd birthday, Oastler had risen to the fore of the Ten Hours movement. Wherever he spoke, care-worn foot-soldiers of the industrial revolution flocked to hear him. It was with bitter sarcasm that a newspaper editorial had recently dubbed him 'The King of the Factory Children'. But the sobriquet, uttered reverentially by his followers, had stuck fast. Six feet tall, with a booming voice, he was, according to Tom Trollope who met him in 1837, 'the very *beau-ideal* of the mob orator'.[9]

Next to Oastler, as the Ten Hours men prepared to leave the inn, was another consummate platform speaker, the Reverend George Stringer Bull. Recently returned from the mission fields of Africa, Stringer already had a huge following. Fierce but eloquent, small in stature yet stocky in build, he had been christened 'the pugnacious parson' and 'the reverend bruiser' by hostile newspapers.[10]

Beneath these 'generals' of the Ten Hours movement were echelons of local leaders and thousands of rank-and-file supporters. Arrayed against them was the combined might of factory owners, economists, much of the orthodox Church, and large sections of the two leading political groupings, the Whigs and the Tories. What the movement really needed was such a show of force that even this mighty opposition would be bludgeoned into a new humanitarian resolve.

The 25th August 1832 was the chosen occasion. At five o'clock, Sadler, Oastler, Bull and their comrades stepped out of the Shakespeare Inn. Even for men accustomed to addressing large crowds, the sight must have been awesome. 'As far as the eye could reach', wrote one witness, 'nothing was to be seen but banners, flags, green boughs and various other emblems.' A reporter for the *Manchester Guardian* was on hand. The paper was then a friend to the capitalists, damned by one Radical as a 'foul prostitute and dirty parasite of the worst portion of the mill owners', and its representative was not inclined to overstate the scale of the day's events. But even he was struck by the number of factory children, thousands of ill-clad boys and girls, 'decorated with bits of coloured calico', carrying flags of pink, blue and white, imitations of the cotton plant made from tree branches festooned with waste cotton, and virtually anything else they could find to wave, including mops and sprays of flowers.[11]

Many different local Ten Hours organisations were also represented. Several delegations were accompanied by marching bands, giving the gathering a distinctly martial air, an impression reinforced by hundreds of tall, standard-like banners that towered over the crowd, bearing inscriptions like 'Sadler for ever', 'No white slavery', 'Sadler, the factory child's friend', 'Oastler our champion', and 'Cursed are they that oppress the poor'. One man held aloft a 'very neat model of a cotton-factory' bearing the inscription 'The infant's Bastille'.[12]

Having acknowledged their supporters, the leading Ten Hours men boarded an open-topped cart, set off up Downing Street, and went 'perambulating' around 'various parts of the town'. The crowd swelled and surged as they passed by. Hundreds reached up to the speakers to shake hands and offer encouragement. Windows en route were thrown open, the occupants leaning out to add their voices to the tumult; others clambered onto rooftops better to see the extra-ordinary spectacle below, thousands crying 'God bless Mr Oastler'. The *Leeds Intelligencer*, a Tory paper with some sympathy for the cause, also sent a reporter. Delighted and awestruck by the crowd's enthusiasm, he declared: 'It is to the honour of the females of ... Lancashire, that they seem most anxious to give their offspring the benefit of a more humane system.'[13]

It took over two hours for the cart to reach Camp Field, the day's main venue, a large expanse of open ground in front of the Church of St Matthew's imposing gothic façade. Once there, the driver struggled to clear a path through the dense crowds already assembled. The *Manchester Guardian* estimated them to number about eight thou-sand, but there were almost certainly far more – twenty thousand is much more realistic. Abandoning any attempt to reach the specially erected platform, at 7.30 p.m. the driver came to a halt near the centre of the field and explained to his passengers that they would have to speak from there.

Oastler stood up and surveyed the huge mass of people. Having 'with some difficulty procured the silence' of one exuberant drummer, he began: 'We have met together in a proudly professing Christian country, to assert the truths of the gospel – to tell those individuals who have made their profit from the blood and bones and sinews of those dear little ones, that their conduct was contrary to the law of God.' The crowd roared in approval as Oastler questioned the godliness of those who so often labelled the workers as brutish heathens. They had met in their tens of thousands, Oastler went on, 'to tell those nominal but hypocritical professors of Christianity that they should no longer degrade the gospel by practices so fiend-like'. Cheers again. 'They had met in their tens and twenties, even hundreds of thousands', Oastler roared, 'to see if there be any real Christianity left in the hearts of our governors.'

Continuing in a similar vein for some minutes, Oastler played on the crowd's mounting indignation. He had been told by 'one of his majesty's ministers', he declared, 'that when we have *proved* our case he would [still] *oppose* our bill.' Hisses filled the air. Now Oastler raced to the climax of his speech: 'If the bill is thrown out, I should dread the consequences, but as the king of the factory children I would say, "I will have it, in spite of all the political economy in the world, because my God will give it to me."' The crowd bellowed its assent.

Having worked his magic, Oastler introduced the ailing Michael Sadler. A more moderate speaker, closer in style to the preacher than the demagogue, he too was caught up in the thrill of the occasion. Mounting the driver's box, Sadler announced that 'to receive their approbation was next to the approbation of God himself, the most cheering to the human heart'. Then Sadler turned on, among others, his old political mentor, the abolitionist William Wilberforce. He denounced 'the spurious and pretended philanthropy' of those who fretted over the conditions of African slaves in the Americas while far, far 'greater crimes and suffering at home' were serenely overlooked.

Several more speeches left the crowd hoarse but exulting in a feeling of collective strength. Such was 'the buzz occasioned by the tremendous multitude' that many of those present would not have heard the orators' words. Yet tremendous excitement had been unleashed. So Oastler, exuding confidence and self-belief, sought to rein in any tendency towards militancy. Aware that wanton destruction and street brawling would be a gift to the enemies of the Ten Hours Bill, he informed the crowd: 'Your king commands that you will all go home in peace!' However much the crowd despised their factory masters, and however untouched they had been by the paternalistic concern of rural squires, they were still responsive to the stern commands of one of their 'betters' who meant them well. As the speakers drove out of Camp Field, and as the last rays of light fell, the crowd calmly dispersed. Not even the *Manchester Guardian*'s cynical reporter could fault the behaviour of the 'mob'.[14]

Disappointed at having no violence on which to vent his literary skills, the *Guardian*'s reporter could at least create a vivid impression of the day's pageantry. And one of the innumerable banners carried that day particularly caught his attention. He described it as showing 'a representation of a deformed, knock-kneed man, with the inscription, "Am I not a man and a brother?"' The *Leeds Intelligencer*'s reporter also remarked that the procession was headed by two men bearing a giant flag with a picture of a 'deformed man'. This banner was held to the fore along the entire convoluted route from Ardwick Green to Camp Field. And there were hundreds like it hanging above the vast phalanx of Lancashire's working men, women and children. The words it carried were those of Josiah Wedgwood, entrepreneurial founder of the giant Staffordshire pottery firm, and they had been coined for Britain's anti-slavery movement. Capturing the essence of the abolitionist's argument, that the difference between whites and blacks was no more than skin deep, it had appeared on countless coins, medallions, flags, posters and handbills in the years before the abolition of the slave trade in 1807, always beside the outline of an African slave brutally manacled. Factory children, the message went in 1832, are no better off than the most benighted African slave.[15]

The woodcut of a human form emblazoned on this banner manifested all the evils of naked capitalism. But it was not the product of a creative imagination. As many of those present on 25 August knew straight away, it was a true likeness of one of their own. Many had read

2. 'Am I not a man and a brother?' A medallion designed and produced at the pottery firm of Josiah Wedgwood. Reproduced on thousands of medallions, flags, pamphlets and plates, this slogan defined Britain's anti-slavery movement. By courtesy of the Wedgwood Museum Trust, Barlaston, Staffordshire

the narrative of his life in early 1828 when it was printed in weekly instalments in a twopenny working-class rag called *The Lion*. In 1832 his story had then been reprinted in an extraordinary and enduring pamphlet: *A Memoir of Robert Blincoe, An Orphan Boy; sent from the workhouse of St Pancras, London, at seven years of age, to endure the Horrors of a Cotton-Mill, through his infancy and youth, with a minute detail of his sufferings, being the first memoir of the kind published.*[16]

Since then, Robert Blincoe's story had become synonymous with the inhumanities of the factory system. Yet as the pamphlet's rather detailed subtitle indicated, his life had begun not in the slums of a manufacturing town but in the relative tranquillity of a London parish about two hundred miles south of the grime and the din of industrial Manchester. Its author was a Lancashire-born writer called John Brown. He had brought to the attention of tens of thousands the horrendous experiences of a young man whose early life had been sacrificed to the gods of Technological Progress and National Prosperity.

Brown's path crossed with that of Blincoe after he had abandoned a youthful predilection for foreign travel and begun to devote most of his time to the campaign to release young children from servitude in textile mills. Sometime in 1822, he decided that one powerful means of exposing 'the enormities of the cotton masters' was to recount the experiences of someone who had suffered grievously from their ruthless profit-seeking. Somehow, John Brown learned of Blincoe and persuaded him to retell his story. The result was a shocking narrative of appalling suffering, ill-treatment and neglect.[17]

Brown's *Memoir* is not a transparent historical document. Propagandist in nature, it turned Blincoe's story into a blunt instrument with which to beat the mill bosses and put pressure on the government. Furthermore, John Brown's heavy-handed literary style tends to obscure Blincoe's own voice. Time and again, he ascribed to his literate but unlettered subject highly improbable statements. In one passage, for instance, Blincoe describes himself as 'a moral outcast, ... a scathed and blighted tree, in the midst of a verdant lawn.' 'I dare not aver', Brown thought it prudent to add in this case, 'that such were the very words Blincoe used, but they faithfully convey the spirit and tendency of his language and sentiments.' The story's telling is at all times mediated by Brown's politics and personality; there is a clear party line throughout. As a result, while aspiring to a high level of literary sophistication, his *Memoir* often slips into a noisy verbosity.[18]

Even so, the *Memoir*'s value is quite simply profound. This is because it remains a minor miracle that the life of such an obscure working man was ever recorded at all. For every biography of a working man or woman there are ten thousand or more lives of kings, saints, generals, admirals, statesmen, master criminals or ladies of rank. Except for fragments in parliamentary inquiries, private letters, police reports and Old Bailey journals, the lived experiences of the poor in Georgian and Regency England are mostly lost to us. As the economist Adam Smith said of the pauper: 'His voice is little heard and less regarded.' The thoughts, feelings and beliefs of the majority of working people can only be guessed at. But for all the enervating effects of labour, poverty, bereavement and sickness, their lives were no less intensely lived than were those of the literate and affluent. Too often they are treated as little more than innumerable identical atoms in a homogeneous social mass. It's a sin of which even the champion of the proletariat, Karl Marx, was himself sometimes guilty; the individual French labourer, he wrote in 1856, barely differs from the rest of his class, 'much as potatoes in a sack form a sack of potatoes.' Such views are not grounded in fact, but in want of information. And it's because we have so little insight into the lives of history's poor that we wrongly imagine them to constitute a faceless, if occasionally potent, historical force.[19]

There are, of course, exceptions to this rule. The year 1816 saw the publication of William Hutton's biography. It told the story of the son of a wool-comber, born in Derby in 1723, who was sent to work in an early silk mill, ran away, and died in 1815 having become one of Birmingham's largest booksellers. There were perhaps 30 similar accounts printed in this period, mostly charting either the rise of working men to fame and fortune or their heroic triumph over drunkenness and vice to embrace Christian belief. Only a few of these said much about life and work among the poor. In contrast, Samuel Johnson's *Life of Richard Savage* had much to say about its subject's bleak early years. And Thomas De Quincey reflected at length on his disadvantaged childhood in his *Confessions of an English Opium Eater*. Moreover, the 'parish boy's progress', later the subtitle to Charles Dickens' *Oliver Twist*, was a recognised fictional genre. Like-wise Henry Fielding's 1754 novel *Tom Jones* made superb use of the ancient ploy of the poor boy turning out to be the offspring of respectable parentage. And hundreds of 18th-century books turned on the themes of social ambition, fortune hunting, and the perils of getting ideas above one's station.[20]

But only a handful of these books are anything like Blincoe's *Memoir*. For not only are biographies of the poor seldom written and even less often read; those which do reach the bookstands are invariably the memoirs of individuals who have risen from the lower ranks to achieve fame or notoriety. Hutton's biography described the strange case of a poor boy climbing out of a deprived situation. In no sense was it typical of the life-cycle of England's working poor. The vast majority of the labouring classes have lived and died if not in absolute silence, then in complete anonymity.

Blincoe's *Memoir* is quite different. It seems to be the first biographical narrative in the long history of the written language of somebody 'ordinary'. He was not, it should be said, a complete nonentity. The terrible nature of his sufferings in a cotton mill, although far from unique to himself, did attract attention. But when his *Memoir* appeared, Blincoe was still a poor working man. Though he had found plenty of solace in adult life, he had not risen to the leadership of a political movement, created a major business empire, or discovered in himself an unexpected literary genius or talent for preaching the gospel. Blincoe's story has some of the extraordinary qualities of Hieronymus Bosch's depiction of Hell, but when John Brown tracked him down in Manchester in early 1822 he was a man who had settled into quiet obscurity. As such, the odds against his biography ever being written were astronomically long.[21]

What makes the *Memoir* even more striking is that Blincoe had been born into virtually the lowest caste of the age. He was a work-house orphan, and probably an illegitimate one at that. And so, from the moment of his birth, he seemed fore-ordained to gruelling labour and an early, possibly violent, death. But, by great good fortune, Brown heard of his history and passed on to us priceless insights into the working conditions of children in the new industrial age. The *Memoir* details the cruelty of masters and overseers, the weakness of the law, and the harsh realities of a child's life dictated by the relentless rhythm of machines and the clanging of the work-place bell. And while Brown was an unashamed propagandist, inclined to exaggerate and omit, most of what he said can be corroborated from other sources. Read with due caution, the *Memoir of Robert Blincoe* is an invaluable source.[22]

Blincoe's story has another great virtue. From the very outset, this parish orphan refused to play the role of passive victim. From his earliest years, he brimmed with determination, a strong sense of self-worth, and an instinctual feeling for what was right and just. Even had he wanted to, John Brown could not have shoe-horned his subject into a clichéd drama of a powerless orphan crushed by callous and greedy masters. Robert Blincoe always fought back. And, when he reached adulthood, married and set up his own business, he laboured doggedly to raise his own children to a better situation. Although Brown's account closed around 1824, surviving records allow us to trace the outlines of Blincoe's later life and that of his eldest son. Robert Blincoe never did achieve social pre-eminence. He was remembered, if at all, as somebody who fought bravely against the cruel vicissitudes of life. But his own hard work and his devotion to his family eventually achieved for them a degree of respectability beyond the wildest imaginings of anybody who had known him as a bruised, lonely and desperately unhappy parish apprentice.

Following the *Memoir*'s publication in a radical newspaper of 1828, and then in pamphlet form in 1832, Blincoe had several other brushes with national or local fame. The pamphlet in particular made his name well known to those fighting to humanise the factory system. One result of this was the use of his story as the foundation for Frances Trollope's hugely controversial 1837 novel *The Life and Adventures of Michael Armstrong, the Factory Boy*. More tantalisingly, we can also discern traces of him in one of the early works of Britain's finest campaigning novelist. There's strong textual evidence that Charles Dickens read Blincoe's *Memoir* shortly before writing *Oliver Twist*. The parallels between the opening chapters of Dickens' novel and the story of Blincoe's life recounted in the *Memoir* are striking. Both start in a parish workhouse where the heroes are subject to the brutal authority of money-grubbing parish officers. In both books the central character narrowly avoids being apprenticed to a master sweep. And while Blincoe expressed the belief that he was a child of respectable paternity, *Oliver Twist* turns on its hero's genteel ancestry. Brown's account of Blincoe's early life can be read as the prototype for *Oliver Twist*, to which the author then applied his genius for characterisation, dialogue and melodrama. This reading is lent plausibility by the relatively short period that elapsed between the publication of Blincoe's *Memoir* and that of *Oliver Twist*, especially bearing in mind the extreme paucity of working-class biographies and the widespread interest stimulated by Brown's pamphlet. Blincoe's *Memoir* would have had a deep impact on a man who had been sent to work in a blacking factory aged twelve and never reconciled himself to his family's loss of gentility. And it would also have yielded rich background material that Charles Dickens' own life didn't provide but which the plot of *Oliver Twist* required.[23]

But Blincoe's story is more than a companion piece to *Oliver Twist*. Blincoe was a real Oliver Twist in that his was a true parish boy's progress. His experiences confirm many of the horrors that Charles

Dickens set out to expose. But if he, like Oliver Twist, struggled against abject poverty and the disdain of social betters, his life story followed a route shaped by socio-economic realities rather than the conventions of the literary imagination. Blincoe's progress from workhouse to cotton mill and after provides the story of a pauper's life stripped of the improbabilities of plot, the overly virtuous heroes and the grotesque villains which make *Oliver Twist* a great novel but not very reliable history.

The *Memoir* itself, however, is only a starting point in reconstructing Blincoe's life. John Brown told a one-dimensional story of vicious abuse at the hands of mill owners. He said hardly anything else about Blincoe's world or the people and places his hero encountered on his progress through it. By delving into the surviving records, a fuller story can now be told of Blincoe's troubled childhood and his gentler later life. And here there's another crossover between his story and the literary canon of Charles Dickens. Blincoe's life is Dickensian in its sheer descriptive scope; he saw at least as much on his travels as Mr Pickwick did on his. Through his eyes we gain a glimpse of life in London's rural hinterland; the interior of a squalid parish workhouse; a smallpox hospital at the top of Gray's Inn Road; a snapshot of Georgian Nottingham; the first generation of cotton mills perched alongside swiftly-running streams in Nottinghamshire and the Peak District; carding rooms in early spinning factories choked with dust and flue; a magistrate's parlour in rural Derbyshire; Manchester at the height of the machine age and in the midst of riots, strikes and machine-breaking; the shop of a radical bookseller imprisoned for sedition and libel; a debtors' gaol in the grounds of Lancaster's ancient castle; and the plush rooms of a hotel where Blincoe spoke to a patrician doctor appointed by the crown to investigate child labour in factories. Nor were Blincoe's experiences restricted to the grimmest aspects of capitalism's triumphant march. Through his industry, ambition and self-sacrifice, his three children, though hindered by their father's low birth, reaped some of the benefits of England's rise to economic greatness.

Few personal histories allow one to tell the story of changing worlds as effectively as Robert Blincoe's. Following his progress from rural parish to remote mill and bustling industrial city, we gain access to a largely vanished world, an England not so distant in time but another country in terms of its attitudes, practices and beliefs. In this sense, Blincoe's life illuminates an entire, fascinating age. And it's a story told not from the narrow perspective of lords, kings, generals and courtiers but from that of a working man who was on the receiving end of a period of dramatic and often violent change. This account of Blincoe's life is not, however, a straightforward biography. The life story it pieces together is as much about the world he lived in as it is about him as an individual. Through Blincoe we can chart the birth of the first industrial economy, the demise of an older, far more hierarchical society, and the cruel impact of the early factory system upon many thousands of young boys and girls. But even this most humble cog in the engine of the industrial revolution managed to make his own history. And although he was so often a victim of faceless forces out of his power to control or divert, Blincoe's life provides an outstanding example of courage, tenacity and a refusal to be downtrodden.

Part 1

Blincoe's World

Left on the world's bleak waste forlorn,
In sin conceiv'd,
To sorrow born,
By guilt and shame fordoom'd to share,
No mother's love, no father's care.

Anon. (c. 1750)

Noah was a charity-boy, but not a workhouse orphan. No chance-child was he, for he could trace his genealogy way back to his parents.

Charles Dickens, *Oliver Twist* (1837–8)

Were I asked who is the most arbitrary sovereign on earth? I should answer, neither the King of France, nor the Grand Signior, [but] an Overseer of the Poor in England.

William Cowper to Lady Hesketh (1 January 1788)

Their's is yon house that hold the parish poor, …
There children dwell who know no parent's care,
Parents, who know no children's love, dwell there!
Heartbroken matrons on their joyless bed,
Forsaken wives, and mothers never wed.

George Crabbe, from 'The Parish Register' (1783)

1

Work'us boy

Around the year 1792, somewhere in the London parish of St Pancras, Robert Blincoe made his entry into the world. Whether the parish surgeon attended, or a local midwife, or whether his mother delivered him alone in secret, we will never know. We can be fairly sure, however, that his birth was not the cause of much joy. Of his first few years Blincoe retained only vague impressions. But one thing he 'perfectly recollected'. At the age of four he was taken in a coach, accompanied by an unknown woman, and left at St Pancras workhouse.

Blincoe was later convinced, on the basis that he recalled no sorrow at their parting, that the woman in the coach bore him no relation. And his patchy memories of his first years suggested to him that he had 'passed through many hands before he arrived at the workhouse'. Who knows what series of wet nurses or impoverished relations he had been entrusted to before his complete abandonment; or what agonies a desperate mother may have suffered following his birth? There is a hint in Blincoe's description of sustained efforts having been made to keep him from the misery of the workhouse. It may also be that in these years he received the balm of a mother's love; his subsequent strength of character certainly suggests that someone had once made him feel treasured and important. But we can do no more than speculate.[1]

As a 'work'us boy', to use Noah Claypole's unendearing term, Robert Blincoe entreated the parish authorities to reveal his mother's identity. Initially, they wouldn't even tell him his full name. Fifteen or so years later he received official papers stating that he had been christened 'Robert Blincoe'. While he vaguely remembered hearing the name 'Robert' applied to himself at the workhouse, his surname came as a complete revelation. Why the parochial officials were so chary in divulging this detail is a mystery. Perhaps they were simply blind to a work'us boy's need to feel connected. Maybe they thought it best that he put all such thoughts out of his mind. And it's just about possible that they were protecting the reputation of a respectable parishioner. It's far more likely, however, that they had no reason beyond bureaucratic indifference. Blincoe was a mere ward of the parish and as such his private woes were beneath their dignity. The only parents he knew or would ever know were the master and mistress of the parish workhouse. And as far as the parish authorities were concerned, he deserved no better.

But the tongues of the resident nurses were less strictly governed. Workhouse nurses were typically not much better off than their wards; one reliable observer called them 'indigent, filthy and decrepit'. They usually slept in the inmates' beds and followed the same grinding routine. But they were often privy to parish secrets and always keen purveyors of rumour and gossip. One of these nurses informed Blincoe that 'soon after his arrival' an anonymous 'female' had inquired after him by the name of 'Saint'. She had then left a penny piece, and informed him that his mother had passed away. She apparently gave no information as to the circumstances. Although Blincoe heard nothing more of his parentage, up until his 21st birthday he went either by the nickname 'Saint' or, more commonly, 'Parson'. This appellation was enough to feed the workhouse rumour mill. For didn't it imply that Blincoe, as John Brown put it in the *Memoir*, 'owed his existence to the mutual frailties of his mother and a reverend divine'?[2]

It's hardly likely that an adulterous priest would have conferred his surname on his illegitimate child. In any case, there's no evidence of a Parson Blincoe preaching in late-18th-century England. Blincoe's father might have been a non-Anglican pastor, one of the age's numerous itinerant, non-conformist preachers. Yet the appellation 'Saint' was usually applied to members of the period's evangelical movement, men and women who rejected orthodox Anglicanism as emptily ritualistic and embraced a much more personal, vital and emotional kind of religion. Perhaps one of these clerics, entranced by a local woman, had allowed his enthusiasm to outstrip his piety.[3]

Even if Blincoe did have an ecclesiastical father who knew of the pregnancy, there would have been little possibility of a happy reconciliation. Most ministers guilty of such a lapse felt driven to suppress something so damaging both to themselves and to the outward face of the profession and class to which they belonged. To those in the know, appeasement of the parish which would now have to pay for the upbringing of the child could be bought discreetly for a one-off payment of around £10. Since the child was unlikely to live for long, having received the money, parish officers would then probably squander it in an ale-house. Just one of the perks of parochial office.[4]

Sadly, the truth of Blincoe's paternity is now lost to us. What really matters, however, is what Blincoe himself believed. And, as far as we can tell, he took the nurses' gossip seriously. Accordingly, he laid great stress on the story of a clerical lapse when speaking to his biographer 30 years later, and he then repeated it on subsequent occasions. For Blincoe, the negative side of his accepting workhouse rumour was that it entailed him bearing the odium of the bastard; but he was recompensed by the thought that he, a friendless child living among society's most degraded and desperate, was the abandoned scion of a respectable family. Like many of those raised in cruel circumstances, he seems to have clung onto a wish-fulfilment fantasy which held open the possibility of eventual discovery and his being restored to his 'proper' station in life.[5]

This aspect of Blincoe's story is the first of many intriguing parallels with *Oliver Twist*. Himself later a resident of St Pancras parish, Charles Dickens was long troubled by the declining family fortunes that had seen his father imprisoned for debt and he himself consigned to demeaning labour in a London boot-blacking workshop. *Oliver Twist*, in which the hero is ultimately recognised to be the descendant of a genteel family, is said by some to have been a sublimation of Dickens' own desire to belong to a superior social caste. If Dickens read the *Memoir* before beginning *Oliver Twist*, the suggestion that this poor boy had respectable ancestors would surely have struck a chord.

Yet in all probability Blincoe had far less lofty origins. The story of a clergyman's frailty was probably pure invention, salacious gossip rushing in to fill a void created by ignorance. Nor is there any reason to think that his birth name really was 'Blincoe'. There are no records of Blincoes, Blinkos or Blencowes living in St Pancras parish in the 1700s. It was, however, common practice for parish authorities to name orphaned children after themselves or their superiors, much as slaves were given the names of their masters. In other cases, any name which sprang to mind might be applied. So Blincoe may have been an unknown foundling who turned up on somebody's doorstep. It's even possible that he was the 'Male Child, appearing to be about four months old' mentioned by a newspaper, 'dropt at a Gentleman's Door in John-Street, Tottenham Court-Road' in 1791, protected from the elements by 'two Caps, an old Handkerchief, ... three Shirts, and old Flannel Jacket.' If so, he would almost certainly have been sent straight to a 'baby farm', and entrusted to a wet nurse employed by the parish to meet just such a need. As Oliver Twist discovered, parish-appointed wet nurses were not always motivated by a love for children. Typically starved of affection, orphaned infants were induced to drink quantities of gin, rum or the potent opiate Godfrey's Cordial to keep them quiet. This would have been the arrangement up until Blincoe reached the age of four or five. Then, along with any other contemporaries who had managed to survive the nurse's neglect, he would have been deposited at the parish workhouse.[6]

The identity of Blincoe's mother is equally mysterious. No local woman receiving parish aid had a surname anything like his. But the story of her passing away soon after Blincoe's arrival at the workhouse does ring true. The middle years of the decade were memorably harsh. The year 1795, around about the time when Blincoe entered the workhouse, witnessed one of the worst harvests of the entire century. The summer of 1794 had been so hot that wheat and corn ripened prematurely and shrivelled in their husks. Winter then struck with savage force. The third most severe in a hundred years, the temperature hardly lifted above freezing from December to March. 'Day after day the iron-grip of the frost continues unbroken', noted one Londoner; 'the milk freezes in the milk-maid's pails.' And as reserves of grain were exhausted, bread prices soared. Hungry men and women rioted in towns across the country. In St Pancras, journeymen brick-makers 'proceeded to great acts of violence', a newspaper reported, 'by destroying large quantities of bricks, & c. belonging to their employers, and even threatening to pull down their houses'. But most of the parish poor sank less dramatically into a state of misery. When epidemic fever visited over the following months, many died in St Pancras and beyond. These conditions were conducive for a poor woman, having struggled to feed both herself and her child, to finally succumb.[7]

The workhouse gossips were probably right in thinking that Blincoe's mother never married. This would account for his never having been visited or adopted by an extended family, and why rumour coalesced around his paternity. So, from the moment of his birth, Robert Blincoe was mired in shame, the guilty outcome of an act that in the eyes of the respectable could only ever be redeemed by matrimony. Many of Blincoe's contemporaries assumed that a child born of unholy lust would be already corrupted by its parents' sin. Hence during a Parliamentary debate on the savage abuse of young chimney sweeps, one noble lord said that they deserved no protection since so many of them were 'children of rich men begotten in an improper manner'. The bastard bore a lifelong curse. Unless the acknowledged result of a liaison between unmarried aristocrats, he or she was morally compromised from conception on. They lived in a state of chronic infamy, the burden of guilt increasing in proportion to their poverty. Not surprisingly, bastards died at twice the rate of the legitimate. Pitifully poor and a presumed bastard, Blincoe was to carry a heavy burden of stigma.[8]

But he was just one among thousands of poor bastards thrown, because of parental mortality, immorality or misfortune, onto the meagre charity of the parish during the later 1700s. His mother might have been a prostitute, the victim of rapacious lust, the dupe of an amorous neighbour, or a fallen lady of decent birth. We will never know the truth. What matters is that her son had been stigmatised as illegitimate and abandoned by whatever family still lived. Thereby Robert Blincoe was condemned to a childhood of profound emotional emptiness and economic exploitation.

In the handful of pages devoted to Blincoe's workhouse years in the *Memoir*, the depth of his childhood suffering occasionally breaks through John Brown's verbosity. In narrating his early life to Brown, Blincoe recalled with fresh pain the occasions on which the family members of the other work'us children, mainly parents unable to afford to care for their children themselves, were permitted to enter the workhouse gates to embrace their offspring. Never was Blincoe's name called out, though he presumably remained in hope of a visit for many months. For years after, he stood by as his peers rushed excitedly to the meeting room. It was a gruelling ritual for the parish orphan. 'When the friends, relatives, parents of other children came to visit them', the *Memoir* explained, 'the caresses that were sometimes exchanged, the joy that beamed on the faces of those so favoured, went as daggers to my heart.' We don't know if Blincoe really used this expression, but it was surely an apt description of the extreme loneliness he felt at the time.[9]

There were perhaps 30 or 40 other orphans in the workhouse; enough to prompt a parish officer's cynical remark that the work'us children weren't 'much blessed in the way of parents'. But most of the orphaned boys and girls had aunts, uncles, cousins or family friends who could visit. Blincoe's state of isolation was as depressingly complete as that of the children who had been dumped at Coram's Foundling Hospital, situated towards the southern end of the parish. Parents who left their unwanted babies there were forbidden from trying to make contact in later years. Many left trinkets and locks of hair in the hope that they would be able to do so anyway. Some perhaps tried; none succeeded. And like Blincoe, those children grew up never knowing their true names. But they did have one advantage over him. Coram's foundlings didn't have to live in the midst of hundreds of boys and girls who had parents, albeit desperately poor ones, only a short walk away. Blincoe envied the orphans of the Foundling Hospital for another reason. Over twenty years later, speaking to John Brown, with 'tears trickling down his pallid cheeks, and his voice tremulous and faltering', he explained:

> I am worse off than a child reared in the Foundling Hospital. Those orphans have a name given them by the heads of that institution, at the time of baptism, to which they are legally entitled. But I have no name I can call my own.[10]

The keenness with which Blincoe felt the absence of parental affection is clear from another of the anecdotes he told of this time. A couple of years after entering the workhouse, he was asked during a chapel service to repeat the Fifth Commandment. To the chaplain's astonishment he 'suddenly burst into tears'. Asked why, he explained: 'I cry, because I *cannot* obey one of God's commandments, I know not either my father or my mother, I cannot therefore be a good child and honour my parents.' Blincoe's tearful response might have moved the hardest of hearts, but charges of the parish weren't often pampered by their betters. Nor were the children led to expect it. St Pancras parish, in accordance with the law, was duty bound to feed, clothe and house its workhouse inmates. Few were the extra consolations it was willing to provide.[11]

Blincoe's life as a work'us orphan was dictated by an elaborate body of legislation known as the Poor Laws. These determined everything from the stale air he breathed, the food he ate and the sermons he heard, to the clothes he wore and the rules he obeyed. And they ensured that his life in St Pancras workhouse was hardly less circumscribed than that of a galley slave, a chained lunatic, or a 'powder monkey' aboard one of His Majesty's men-o'-war. The Poor Laws began with a series of Acts passed under the Tudors. They were devised to strike a balance between the need to deal firmly with the growing number of able-bodied poor and a grudging recognition that it was not right to allow humble, God-fearing paupers to starve to death. Elizabeth I's Poor Law of 1601 made a customary distinction between the worthy and the unworthy poor. The former category was made up of the old, the sick and the young, like Robert Blincoe. The 'unworthy' comprised 'wandering scholars, jugglers, tinkers, peddlers, ship wrecked seamen, gypsies, minstrels, players, discharged prisoners and fortune tellers', men and women who were apparently healthy and able to work, but who went from parish to parish harassing people for money. The worthy, the law said, were to be given food, shelter and work materials to keep them busy and alive. The unworthy were to be flogged, whipped 'until his or her body be bloody', branded and badged; such treatment reflected long practice, though its acceptability had waned by the late 1700s.[12]

The enduring innovation of the 1601 Act was its requirement that every parish follow strict guidelines in dealing with their poor. Each of the nation's roughly 15,000 parishes had to appoint officials from the 'better sorts' who were mandated to collect annual poor rates from any parishioners who could afford to pay them. These officials also had the power to billet paupers on the households of parishioners, and distribute cash, food and work materials to the poor in their own cottages. And they were responsible for 'setting to work' any pauper able to wield a hoe, spin cotton, flax or wool, use a needle and thread, or mend a shoe. The 1601 Act made control of the poor in England a largely parish affair.

Most parishioners felt the duties involved in parochial office to be onerous, not to mention detrimental to their farming or business concerns. The wealthier ranks often elected to pay fines to avoid serving. St Pancras' Robert Silk, for instance, having first claimed to be 'incompetent', agreed to pay £10 in 1795 to 'be exempted from office as constable'. (John Field dodged his parish duties by producing 'a burglar catching certificate'.) Where the wealthier residents bought themselves out, an opportunity arose for tradesmen, merchants and shopkeepers to conduct parish affairs. Predictably, those left to govern were not always the most competent or committed. Sometimes they were illiterate, or very nearly so. An overseer's record book from a Kent parish categorised one set of paupers under the heading 'hilly jittimites'. But canny parish officials could turn the situation to their advantage. When the first St Pancras workhouse was set up in 1722, one Mr Broadhead was requested to 'serve The house with Small beer att six shillings Per Barrell'. Mr Broadhead happened also to be on the board of inspectors for the workhouse, charged with ensuring that it was properly provisioned and charged the parish a fair price. In this situation, the temptations to corruption were great. In 1781, the parish decided that abuses had gone on long enough. Officials were instructed to desist from supplying the workhouse.[13]

Parish overseers were responsible for most of the day-to-day business of the Poor Law. And as an inmate of the workhouse, Blincoe's destiny fell almost entirely within the overseer's hands. His brief was a simple one: to keep the poor alive and busy while keeping the poor rates down. If he didn't, he would incur the wrath of his neighbours and set precedents that would cost him dear in later years. One obvious way of keeping costs low was to limit the number of claimants. Under the Poor Law, paupers were entitled to aid only in the parish in which they had a 'settlement', a provable claim on Poor Law funds. Most people gained a settlement in their father's parish, though wives were automatically granted settlement in their husband's parish and illegitimate offspring had settlement in the parish in which they were born. To minimise expenditure on the poor, the laws of settlement were widely and ruthlessly enacted.[14]

Anyone who entered a parish in which they didn't have settlement and lived in an abode worth under £10 a year could be forcibly ejected at any time in the first 40 days of their residence. As most cottagers inhabited dwellings worth less than 50 shillings a year, this meant that only moneyed visitors were safe from expulsion. Incomers didn't need to have appealed for parish aid, they just had to be there. In village societies, few could long remain undetected. But just in case some did slip through the net, after an Act of 1692 the 40 days began only after the stranger's name had been read out in church. Since all but poor labourers and paupers had to pay poor rates, there was a real incentive to keep migrants out. Many landowners demolished or refused to let their cottages through fear of attracting newcomers.[15]

We shouldn't be too surprised at such tightfistedness. After all, money was not easy to part with at a time when even respectable tradesmen could easily find themselves on the slow declension towards workhouse pauperism. But where the very poor couldn't prove their entitlement they would find themselves with unseemly speed heaved on a wagon, regardless of rain, snow or ice, and sent on their way to their parish of birth or last abode. For such rate-reducing antics, many a humanitarian held up the overseer as a model of unchristian brutality. The poet John Clare personified their miserliness with the names 'Father Cheetum' and 'Old Saveall'. But overseers weren't all mean – the improbably-named Messrs Spendlove and Scattergood of St Martin Vintry in the City of London were said to have lived up to their names. Even in their domain, however, young women were vulnerable, especially those pregnant out of wedlock. A third of the poor people removed from Cambridgeshire parishes between 1660 and 1834 were expectant women.[16]

This isn't surprising. As bastards gained settlement in the parish in which they were born, their birth cost parishioners dear. So overseers mercilessly expelled pregnant women who had neither a settlement nor a husband to finance their child's upkeep. In some cases, poor women in the throes of labour were manhandled to parish boundaries and left to have their children unaided a few yards over the line. In 1681 the residents of Stoke were fined by the magistrates for 'removing a woman in labour'. Where a pregnant spinster did have a local settlement, parish overseers leapt into action, bent on running the father to ground and forcing him to marry her and take responsibility for the unborn child. Since compulsion played a greater role than romance, these were dubbed 'knobstick weddings'. St Pancras had its share of coercive nuptials. In 1765 the parish vestry agreed that 'the expenses of the Marriage of John Crosier with Mary Martin, amounting to two pounds one shilling [should] be paid by Mr Sewell, the Overseer … She being pregnant by him.' Mr Sewell had done his duty in keeping a bastard off the parish list.[17]

When a bastard child was born, the parish authorities were still capable of extreme cruelty. In 1720, Mary Mann died due to their 'hard usage'. Having given birth to a child out of wedlock, she had been 'barbarously and unnaturally' torn from her lying-in bed in terrible weather and hurled before a magistrate. It was this regime of spiteful vigilance which persuaded Blincoe that his mother had a settlement in St Pancras parish. He perhaps didn't wish to reflect on the upsetting possibility that overseers from over the parish border had stealthily dumped his mother somewhere in St Pancras' fields as her contractions set in.[18]

The St Pancras overseers – there were fourteen of them by the 1790s – were assisted by the churchwardens, sidemen, constables and beadles. Mr Hutchings, the beadle, was a particularly busy man. Hardly a day went by when he didn't have to escort a poor person to their rightful parish. Mostly the incursions came from the parishes of Marylebone, to the west, and desperately poor St Giles, just to the south. But in the years after Blincoe's departure, the parish went so far as to send a pauper back to Scotland by boat. St Pancras had a particular problem due to the location of the Foundling Hospital. Some mothers, too tired to await the Hospital's morning opening, too ashamed to speak to its staff in person, or having been turned away when all the beds were filled, left their infants at its gate. In such cases, the parish was obliged to accept responsibility for the welfare of the child. It cost them dearly. Hence, in 1793 the vestry placed an advertisement in local newspapers offering a reward for information leading to the 'Conviction of the Person guilty' of leaving an infant at the hospital gates.[19] No one came forward.

Such children were bundled up and then transferred to baby farms. The adult poor were more likely to receive 'outdoor relief', charity given to them in their cottages and hovels. 'Blind William Beck', 'widow Galopine', 'widow Crew' and 'widow Rust' received regular aid in their cottages. In all, the parish always gave money to 60 or so paupers, but this form of parish relief had plenty of critics. Many considered the system ripe for abuse by sturdy, work-shy beggars who wanted something for nothing. Far better, they said, to set up a place in which the poor could be put in the halter and the lazy habituated to hard work. The Quaker philanthropist John Bellers spoke of the poor as 'a treasure that lies hid in our bowels'. And this kind of sentiment, if not always couched in such colourful language, led to the creation of the nation's earliest workhouses.[20]

The first was set up in Bristol in 1696 by John Cary, who considered the existing Poor Laws to be ineffective, not least due to the 'idle tippling' of the city's poor. The able-bodied, the young and the infirm were herded into a purpose-built house and set to work on menial tasks. Cary boldly claimed that the poor rate in Bristol parishes had been slashed by his new approach. As word spread, dozens more workhouses were set up. St Pancras entered the field in 1722 when it bought a house on the main road between Battle Bridge and Kentish Town in which to 'lodge and imploy the poor'. A dozen or so paupers were shepherded inside. This property was soon outgrown and the parish had to find a new, larger site. It was its replacement, opened in 1787, that became Robert Blincoe's home. John Brown had virtually nothing to say about Blincoe's workhouse and his time there – he gives us a mere handful of anecdotes and a couple of brief descriptive passages – but from fragments of surviving parish records we can build up a fair idea as to the quality of his life inside.[21]

2

Blincoe's alma mater

St Pancras workhouse stood in Camden Town, at a junction where the main coaching way from London divided. One fork led up to the bosky heights of Hampstead, the other, subject to frequent flooding by the River Fleet and fittingly called Water Lane, led on to Kentish Town. To those not incarcerated within, the workhouse formed part of a pleasingly bucolic scene. A small soap manufactory and a plant nursery stood close by, but for the most part the inmates looked out onto meadows stretching for several acres, sprinkled with barns and grazing cows. A hundred yards up Water Lane lay the Castle Tavern, with its attractive gardens and a tea room. Diagonally opposite the workhouse stood another inn, known variously as the Halfway House or Old Mother Red Cap, said to be 'the resort for all Country Carts and Waggons who came to and fro from the north' of England. This famous inn's extensive gardens were a favourite out-of-town retreat for Londoners. Less quaint, but rather more apposite, were the prison cage and the village stocks which stood alongside the workhouse's southern wall, purposely placed in full view of the village and the hundreds of travellers passing by.[1]

The workhouse building itself, once a gentleman's mansion and later an inn, was described by a local artist as 'a handsome brick edifice'. The one surviving image shows an engine room, a fair-sized chapel with two small buildings either side, and a stately, four-storey main structure. A wall, six feet high, enclosed the site, this alone hinting at the building's custodial role. Inside, the atmosphere was gloomy and sullen. One contemporary, Arthur Young, described workhouses as 'gaols without guilt'. He was only half right. Innumerable poor families struggled, wracked by hunger and sickness, before they would consent to enter one of these degrading institutions. Pride kept many out.[2]

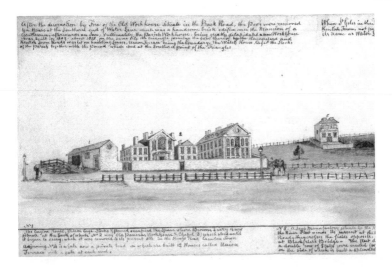

3. The building to the left, surrounded by a high wall, is the St Pancras workhouse. It was drawn from memory by James Frederick King around 1850. Here Robert Blincoe lived, bereft of affection and amid growing squalor, from 1796 until August 1799. The Camden Town stocks are visible to the extreme left of the workhouse complex. © Camden Local Studies and Archives Centre

4. Old Mother Red Cap, or the Halfway House, a famous coaching inn diagonally opposite from the St Pancras workhouse, drawn by James Frederick King around 1850. King under-estimated the number of dwellings built alongside the inn, but fields did stretch for acres around. © Camden Local Studies and Archives Centre

In its days as a gentleman's residence and coaching inn, the workhouse building had been roomy and airy. Now it was anything but. By 1787, nine years before Blincoe arrived, the wards were so congested that five or six people had to sleep in each bed. Roughly half of the 450 inmates were children, and the remainder were mostly elderly men and women. There were also ten or so resident 'lunatics'. Since there were only a handful of public asylums in Georgian England, the mentally ill were often confined in workhouses, prisons or Houses of Correction. 'Lunatics' often took a lot of looking after. Records from St Marylebone's workhouse show that inmates were bribed to cut the toenails and corns of the mentally troubled. And one obliging resident was given a hunk of gingerbread for washing another's 'nasty' bedclothes. Yet many of the sane workhouse inmates were themselves depressed, querulous and abusive. Broken by the vagaries of life, few of the more elderly residents made for congenial company. And doubtless many of the children could, like Robert Blincoe himself, be sullen, lonely and withdrawn.[3]

The beds at St Pancras workhouse, already overcrowded, were also shared with millions of bugs. The parish overseer's account book of 30 May 1775 records the hefty sum of eleven shillings and twopence paid to 'Thos. Endes for Druggs to kill Buggs at 4 sevl times'. When a new workhouse was set up in 1809, a report on what items were fit to be transferred to the new premises noted: 'On examining the bedsteads the number is 224, fifty-two of which are single and ninety-seven double bedsteads, all of which may be fit for use if they be cleansed from vermin.' Another 75 were deemed fit only for being taken outside and incinerated. In such conditions young Robert Blincoe snatched what sleep he could. But over and above the cramped sleeping arrangements and constant itching, he was forced to endure the revolting stench of hundreds of unwashed bodies claustrophobically crowded into a single house.[4]

This was, of course, an age accustomed to rank odours. To the dismay of early public health reformers – who equated disease with foul smells and wandered city streets calibrating the quality of air with their noses – the lower orders frequently lived amid stinking tanneries, slaughterhouses, grave pits and open drains. They also shared rooms with pigs, dogs, cats, and assorted vermin. The well-to-do generally avoided the poorer areas of town, and when they came into contact with the lower orders they reached instinctively for heavily perfumed nosegays to conceal the ordure and to combat typhus. Dwellings for the labouring classes in the metropolis hadn't always been as bad as they were in the 1790s. But as population pressures escalated, old houses were repeatedly subdivided into more and more cramped, airless tenements, and new ones were squeezed into narrow medieval courts and alleys. Sewerage frequently had to be drained down into basements from where it was collected, once in a while, by night-soil men. And the stench of gallons of faeces inevitably wafted up through the houses of the poor. Nor were the social elites always fragrant. Standards of personal hygiene were wretchedly low among all classes in the 18th century. Few could afford baths, or took them even if they could. Francis Place, a London tailor and therefore knowledgeable about these matters, recalled how even 'the wives and grown daughters of tradesmen and gentlemen … wore petticoats of camblet, lined with dyed linen, stuffed with wool or horsehair and quilted … [which were] worn day by day until they were rotten, and never were washed.'[5]

Even people raised amid such filth would have found it hard to stomach the smell of 450 dirty inmates crowded into a building designed to house less than a tenth of that number. To make matters worse, water splashed up between the floorboards from a basement cellar into which effluent flowed. Shortly after Blincoe's departure from the workhouse it was declared to be 'decayed and ruinous'. Inspections revealed that supporting walls had been knocked down, leaving the building perilously unstable, and the timbers were seriously decayed. As always, however, it was the close atmosphere and filth that most upset the parish inspectors. For decades they had nervously awaited outbreaks of fever. After all, it was only a little over a decade since John Howard had exposed the wretched conditions in England's prisons and shown how cramped, ill-ventilated quarters bred what we know as typhus and they called 'gaol fever'. But if workhouse mortality had raised worried comment, there had not been much in the way of action.[6]

Quite apart from smells, bugs, the gloom and overcrowding, Robert Blincoe had to tolerate a tedious daily routine, a monotonous regime of work, basic schooling and religious service. As workhouses were intended to be schools of industry in which the poor were made self-sufficient, masters were hired on the basis that they would keep a percentage of the profits brought in by resident paupers. The system seldom, however, lived up to John Cary's bold promises. Work wasn't always available, since there were lots of unskilled labourers outside the workhouse who seized on what little was going. But when the master did secure a contract, Blincoe and his fellows were set to labour from 6 a.m. to 6 p.m. in the summer and autumn, and for 'as long as [they] could see' in the winter and spring. Oakum picking was one of the few jobs they could get. It entailed picking heavy old ropes apart so that their fibres could be mixed with tar and used to seal gaps and splits in ships' timbers. Spending long hours in this manner would have left Blincoe with raw and bleeding fingertips.[7]

A few hours every day were set aside for learning the rudiments of reading, writing and arithmetic. Blincoe also had to attend religious services given by the workhouse chaplain every Sunday, as well as the Lord's Supper, catechism and evening service on the first Sunday of every month, and an evening sermon every Thursday. The routine had been carefully devised. Its objective was to leave the children no time for idleness or play. Romantic poets like William Wordsworth and Enlightenment thinkers like Jean-Jacques Rousseau saw childhood as a unique time to be valued and indulged. But to most who wrote on the matter, children, and especially those of the poor, were difficult, unruly and burdensome creatures who had to be habituated to hard work and obedience. Nor was child labour in any sense unusual. Travelling around the country in 1714, Daniel Defoe was delighted upon arriving in Taunton to find that 'there was not a child in the town, or in the villages round it, of above five years old, but, if it was neglected by its parents, and untaught, could earn its own bread.' It was surely best for the children of the labouring classes, people said, to be bred up to the lives of unremitting toil for which they had been born. In all seriousness, Thomas Firmin wrote in 1678: 'if whilst they are young they are taught to work they would fall in love with it.' Indolence was a sin, explained a pious Mrs Sarah Trimmer, and it was 'a disgrace to any Parish, to see the Children of the Poor, who are old enough to do any kind of work, running about the streets ragged and dirty.' The young had to be disciplined early to subordination and industry.[8]

Poor parents tended to agree. Until their mid-teens, children were an economic burden on their families which could be reduced only by finding them work to do. And when they weren't labouring, young boys were liable to get into trouble, having fist-fights, swimming along reedy river banks, climbing trees and stealing from orchards and hen coops. So thousands of parents gladly sent young children to work. They did various jobs: scaring away crows, shovelling dung, feeding cattle, assisting with harvesting and fruit-picking, carding wool, flax or cotton for spinning, running errands, or sweeping chimneys. Some child workers were very young indeed. Lancashire's George Crompton recalled starting work aged four, helping his mother prepare cotton bails for spinning on a wheel. 'My mother then tucked up my petticoats about my waist', he said, 'and put me into the [soapy] tub to tread upon the cotton at the bottom.' In the town of Berkhamsted, four- or five-year-olds were started on lace-making careers. And in Dunstable boys and girls began 'to pick the straw' for straw-plaiting at the tender age of four.[9]

Making children like Blincoe work was almost universally agreed to be a good thing. Schooling, on the other hand, was seen to have its dangers. Juvenile, sweated labour inured poor children to their 'inferior offices in life', but education threatened to give them ideas above their stations. This was a real concern in the highly-stratified world of 18th-century England, in which everyone was meant to have their place upon a vast hierarchical chain stretching from the most degraded humans – beggars, actors and minstrels – on to artisans, shopkeepers and tenant farmers; next to bankers and merchants; and finally arriving at the dizzy heights of squires, barons, earls, dukes, archbishops and, at the very top, monarchs. The gradations in this linear taxonomy were many and subtle. They were also instantly recognisable. All but the most clumsy or socially inept instinctively appreciated the social cues telling them the right amount of defer-ence, familiarity or condescension they were expected to show. Most people were reconciled early on to their place in the chain and told that inequality was all part of God's plan.[10]

Herein lay the danger of pauper schools. Some conservative

thinkers argued that, having been schooled, the poor would think too much, read seditious books, and crave honours reserved for their superiors. Ignorance, in contrast, was a basis for social bliss. 'There must be in society hewers of wood and drawers of water', warned the magistrate Thomas Ruggles; 'if all are good penmen where are those who will contentedly live through a life of toil?' Ruggles believed that putting pen to paper was potentially more subversive than reading alone. But education of a sort *was* introduced for many poor children. This happened not because the ruling classes saw a learned population as a national asset, but because education proved to be a potent means of social control. The leaders of the Sunday School movement, for example, saw their primary role as imbuing children with the virtue of servility by teaching Christian doctrine. Poor children, the Sunday School pioneer Mrs Trimmer primly remarked, must receive instruction 'suited to their capacities and conditions'.[11]

The education dispensed by Trimmer's followers to young boys like Robert Blincoe used revealed religion to powerful effect, teaching that God loved hierarchy and would punish any hint of insubordination. The true Christian labourer, generations of chaplains and Sunday School teachers intoned, is obedient, respectful, hard-working and long-suffering: not coincidentally, the virtues that promised to make the respectable classes richer and securer in their wealth. And in an age when the reality of God was seldom doubted, He served as a powerful co-signatory. 'Imparting good education to the poorest classes', later proclaimed a Poor Law inspector, 'is equivalent to an insurance on our property.'[12]

So when St Pancras' vestry met on 22 September 1775 to discuss building a charity school, the themes of education, religion and subordination were tightly woven together. To a lack of proper Christian education the vestry put down 'all Vice, Idleness and Debauchery'. And its members agreed that by being 'instructed in the Principles of the Christian Religion', the parish's poor children would be 'taught true Humility and Obedience to their Superiors and such other Education as may be really necessary to make them of Benefit to the Community as honest and useful Servants.' This, in short, is the pious spirit in which master and chaplain conducted Blincoe's education.[13]

In both schoolroom and working areas, he was also subject to strict discipline. Masters oversaw the labour carried out and punished infractions. In 1776 Marylebone's work-shy inmate Johanna Parry had a wooden log affixed to one of her legs. When two female inmates left the workhouse a few years later without permission, they were retaken, stripped naked to the waist and flogged 'until their backs [were] bloody'. They were then put in solitary confinement and restricted to a bread-and-water diet for a week. The same punishment was meted out to 'Henry Wagstaff and others' of the St Pancras workhouse in January 1798, 'as the most likely means of reforming their conduct.' Blincoe said nothing of whipping, but in a house containing nearly 200 unhappy children one imagines that the birch put in an appearance. Thrashing was customary for children in the 1790s. Even so, parishes often had to make do with unscrupulous masters who flogged over-zealously even by the standards of the day. Some were patently unsuitable. Francis Parent, master of Marylebone workhouse in the 1780s, was typically drunk, absent, or both. Scandal erupted when his son was caught in bed with a female inmate, with every prospect of adding a bastard to the parish list. Marylebone wasn't an isolated example. The master and mistress of Hampstead's workhouse were booted out for neglecting the poor and insulting the overseers, though one suspects the latter was the more grievous sin.[14]

Yet the 18th-century workhouse, though it could be filthy, cramped and humiliating, typically lacked the efficient brutality of the institutions railed against by Dickens in *Oliver Twist* in the 1830s. Indeed, in later life Blincoe looked back fondly on the workhouse diet. His breakfast there comprised a pint of milk porridge and his supper bread and cheese. For lunch there was a set menu with boiled beef three times a week and mutton once. On the meatless days, Blincoe could reliably predict that lunch would consist of bread and cheese, barley broth or gruel, or a pease soup with a meat base. This might sound dull, but in the hungry 1790s many an agricultural labourer would have thought this rich living indeed. And while no epicure would have relished the St Pancras workhouse diet, it was relatively tasty and nutritious, and the helpings were generous. Set meals were also bulked out with servings of bread, potatoes, sugar and butter, and the inmates had allowances of 'Soap, Candles, Coals, Salt, Vinegar, Oatmeal, [and] Chamber Oil'. So even if Blincoe's meals lacked some nutrients (local physicians complained of a shortage of 'animal food'), in St Pancras he experienced few of the privations that spurred Oliver Twist to ask for more. And when Blincoe and many other of the children were sent to a textile mill in Nottinghamshire in 1799, the local workers cooed over their 'fine, clear complexions'.[15]

Moved by seasonal sentiments, at Christmas the parish also supplied a treat of roast beef and plum pudding, plus an ounce of tobacco for the men, an ounce of tea for the women, and twopence each for the children. No doubt the price to be paid for this bounty was an impressive display of deferential gratitude. A person's worthiness for charity had to be proved by their showing proper humility and reverence towards parochial officials. Those who didn't could expect bread and water or, in extreme cases, expulsion from the workhouse.[16]

Blincoe and his colleagues were also entitled to a modest share of the proceeds from their tedious labour. Every so often he received a few pennies to be spent on sweet cakes or other luxuries. But here we know there was extensive abuse. When the Reverend William Bromley conducted an investigation into St Pancras workhouse affairs in 1803 he found evidence of systematic fraud going back years. The twopence in every shilling earned, to which the inmates were entitled, seldom reached their pockets. When it did, they were taxed a 'poundage' of ten pence in the pound and were illegally charged for the washing of 'their own Caps and Handkerchiefs'. (Not that they had many items to wash, because as Bromley's investigation also revealed, the master and mistress were selling on the sly nearly all the clothing fabric they got from the overseers.) An enraged vestry warned the master that he must 'strictly conform to the rules and advice afforded by the Committee ... on pain of being dismissed.'[17]

But the abuses weren't entirely one-way. The Reverend Bromley's sleuthing revealed that many of the inmates were regularly tipsy from the 'great & improvident abuse' of porter beer. Initially allowed only as an indulgence for nurses attending sick inmates, by 1803 the house was consuming £200-worth of porter a year. Children were entitled to three-quarters of a pint daily. If the workhouse was overcrowded, gloomy and stinking, and schooling and religious services tediously didactic, life did have its occasional pleasures.[18]

In others ways, too, the workhouse that Blincoe experienced was far better than it had been even 30 years before. Mortality rates, especially for children, had then been disgracefully high. It took one Jonas Hanway, lately the agent of a merchant company in St Petersburg in Russia, to make plain just how lethal workhouses were.[19] Having visited most of the city's workhouses in and around 1762, he calculated that nearly half of infants died before their second birthday. Nobody's fool, Hanway realised that parish officers shed few tears over this terrible statistic. For every year that an abandoned child like Blincoe managed to survive, the parish had to stump up another £6. 'Parish officers', he wrote, therefore 'never intend that parish children should live'; at least in part, workhouses were institutions for tidying away sexual errors. But Hanway caused acute embarrassment by bringing the mortality rate of parish children into the open. Parliament's stiffened joints moved slowly into action, and after 1762 each parish had to keep a register of orphans and their fates. Then an Act of 1767 laid down that children under six be sent to a wet nurse not more than three miles from London. The nurses were to be reasonably paid and provided with cash incentives for keeping their wards alive. The result was that by the time Blincoe arrived at the St Pancras workhouse, life expectancy for poor orphans had risen. Of boozy and negligent baby-farmers there were still many. But fewer orphans were 'summoned into another world' having 'sickened from want and cold' than Dickens' *Oliver Twist* implied.[20]

Despite Hanway's efforts, living past early childhood in the late 1700s was among the greatest of life's challenges. Edward and Judith, the parents of the classical scholar Edward Gibbon, were said to have named six of their sons Edward so as to ensure that the name would descend from father to son despite the best efforts of diarrhoea, measles, smallpox, sweating sickness, typhus, typhoid and influenza. But bubonic plague had, at least, receded.[21]

By Blincoe's time, the pesthouses were largely abandoned. Nonetheless, fear of plague still haunted the imaginations of St Pancras parishioners. This dreadful, ill-understood killer had not scythed through England's counties since 1665. It had, however, laid waste to Marseille in 1722 despite a raft of quarantine procedures. Fearing its return in 1781, the vestry told locals to remove any fresh twigs from hedgerows that carried an unspecified 'insect' said to have appeared before previous onsets of that 'dreadful Calamity'. It gives some sense of the low value still attached to the lives of workhouse inmates that on 24 November 1796, when two men died from suspected plague after unpacking cotton captured from a Spanish vessel, one of them was carried straight to St Pancras workhouse. There he lay, as Robert Blincoe and the other inmates panicked and prayed, until the next day, when a Dr Smyth assured everyone that pleurisy, not plague, was the true cause of death.[22]

However, some attempts were made to prolong life in the workhouse. A surgeon called Mr Ince received 30 guineas a year to treat the poor. He would bleed and cup them in order to prevent dangerous build-ups of humours, bandage damaged limbs and, if necessary, perform amputations. Ince was supplanted in 1799 by the more cost-effective Mr Barnett, one of a new breed of surgeon-apothecaries, precursors of the general practitioner, who prescribed remedies in addition to performing surgery and letting blood. The church-wardens also paid for the very sick to be moved from the workhouse to St Thomas's Hospital. But the parish took careful precautions to keep medical costs low. New applicants to the workhouse were subject to a searching medical examination by physicians. They would have looked closely for evidence of anything deemed contagious, especially the blister-like genital eruptions called 'chancre', the first indications of syphilis.[23]

The workhouse children were also given smallpox inoculation 'at the Small Pox Hospital' south of St Pancras Church at Battle Bridge. Before it arrived in Europe in the 1730s, inoculation had been practised in the Far East and the Arab world for centuries. If the recipient recovered, as they generally did, lifelong immunity was conferred against a terrifying malady. Deaths did, however, occur. Samuel Bagster, a contemporary of Blincoe and one-time resident of St Pancras parish, saw his brother die following an inoculation. But with smallpox routinely afflicting as many as one in twelve people, the risks of inoculation were acceptably small. Naturally, the workhouse children weren't given the choice. And so, sometime in 1797 or possibly 1798, Blincoe and a motley crew of workhouse children were rounded up and escorted down the coaching road to the St Pancras inoculation hospital.[24]

3

'All for a naughty orphan which nobody can't love'

The smallpox hospital lay just two miles away. For Blincoe it was probably the first time he had escaped the stultifying atmosphere of the workhouse since being brought there in 1796. He was to see much of the parish of his birth for the very first time. In the late 1790s, St Pancras comprised a ragged oblong of land. In addition to Highgate's fish ponds and Lord Mansfield's opulent Kenwood Estate, it encompassed the hamlets of Kentish Town and Camden Town and the Old Church just north of Battle Bridge; it then swept downwards, across the New Road (now Euston Road), to include Coram's Foundling Hospital and the open meadows of what would later be Bloomsbury and Holborn. Comprising both town and country, the parish had a decidedly mixed character. The one element of continuity was the River Fleet which eased through the entire length of the parish. Victorian writers conjured up elegiac scenes of carp fishing in the Fleet's 'clear and running' waters. Blincoe had a rather more realistic view. The river flowed within a hundred yards of the workhouse, and he knew that it was prone to flooding and, as *The Tatler* recorded, that it carried along:

> Sweepings from butchers' stalls, dung, gut, and blood,
> Drowned puppies, stinking sprats, all drench'd in mud.[1]

The upper-storey windows of the workhouse afforded impressive views of the immediate locality. Blincoe later recalled how he had spent long hours gazing out, coveting the liberty of those outside and making wildly unrealistic plans of escape over the 'too well guarded gates'. We can make a fair guess as to what he observed below. From the top of the coaching road running north from the city, he could see the ever-growing bustle of the parish. Throughout the day there were farmers transporting crops and driving their cattle to market, chimney sweeps plying their trade from house to house, wagons rumbling past carrying coal, timber, and industrial wares from the Midlands, day-trippers passing through on their way to the watering-holes of Hampstead and Highgate, pinched-faced paupers coming to the workhouse to collect their parish pensions, an array of local tradesmen, and several times a day, the parish beadle walking by, complete with lacquered staff, 'Brown Great Coat, with a Red Cloth Collar and Gold Lace Hat' on sharp-eyed patrol.[2]

Had Blincoe been permitted to leave his dormitory at night, he would have witnessed a very different scene. After sundown, the streets became the domain of packs of wild dogs, drunken revellers boozing late at the Halfway House, and night-soil men emptying cesspools into carts. On occasion he might have witnessed footpads and highwaymen at work. The coaching road was a favourite among thieves. Not far from the workhouse, in November 1787, a Mrs and Miss Perry were stopped by a 'highwayman well mounted' who, 'in a very polite manner, asked the ladies to lend their purses.' Conforming to the romantic stereotypes that had already made Dick Turpin a popular hero, he coolly apologised and told the ladies to blame his 'spiteful master'. But most thieves were charmless, desperate thugs. Nearby in 1792 a Mr Hoyt was robbed and slashed with cutlasses by 'three boys'. Soon after, footpads cut a Mr Mayer in 'a terrible manner'. Having seen trade suffer, in 1790 the inhabitants of Kentish Town got up armed foot patrols to escort visitors back to the city.[3]

The St Pancras upon which Robert Blincoe gazed remained part of London's rural hinterland into the 1800s, with blackberry hedgerows continuing to thrive along Tottenham Court Road. But in the 1790s this was already a parish on the move. Camden Town itself had lately been an obscure hamlet comprising just three inns, a dairy, a couple of chapels, a Charity School, and a few modest dwellings. By the time Blincoe moved into the workhouse it was fast becoming a thriving village. From the workhouse windows he would have had a clear view of the gangs of house builders, the intricate frames of wooden scaffolding, the dense clouds of brick dust, and dozens of new residents moving in. Blincoe could have had no conception of the

5. A plan of St Pancras parish in the late 1700s, prepared by R. Percival for his two-volume compilation of material relating to the history of the parish. Plenty of building is under way in Camden Town, but the parish retains its rural character. © British Library

profound social and economic forces that were transforming this small section of his parish, and virtually every other village, town and city in the kingdom. But he was witnessing some of their effects. As he watched, the parish's pastoral flavour ebbed away as the girth of the metropolis expanded outwards. New buildings were being hastily constructed as the profits of England's vast trading empire, built first on wool exports, then on the slave trade, but increasingly on iron, tin, pottery and textiles, filled the pockets of town labourers and their capitalist masters.[4]

The parish was also expanding to accommodate more people. In St Pancras, a population of 5,000 in the early 1780s rose to over 30,000 by 1801. For the first time in centuries, Londoners were having children faster than they were burying their dead; no longer were migrants from other counties needed to top up the population. Indeed, for reasons that still aren't fully understood, the population in most parts of England was rapidly on the increase in the century's final quarter. Only a decade before, writers had predicted national decline due to depopulation. Deaths to fever, deprivation and poisonous liquor were said to be depleting the nation's finite life force. New houses were built, people argued, only because a pampered populace wanted to luxuriate in spacious dwellings. In 1801 the 'luxury thesis' died a sudden and deserved death. The state ordered the first full-scale census, coupled with a systematic study of parish birth and death records going back decades. Its findings were unequivocal. There were more English people alive than ever before.[5]

Colonel Charles Fitzroy, first Earl of Southampton, didn't need to be told that new homes were in urgent demand. Seizing the main chance, in the 1780s he ordered the construction of a ribbon of houses, christened Southampton Row, Warren Place and Pleasant Row, on his land fringing the western side of the main coaching road heading north from the New Road. In 1791, following the Kentish Town Act, the Earl of Camden set about building up the eastern side of what would shortly be christened, in honour of his political services, Camden Town.[6]

Into these first houses moved men like the artist George Morland. He later claimed to have lived 'in genteel style' at the end of Warren Place. But neither Camden nor Fitzroy had set out to create the kind of resort that would rival Hampstead's elegant mansions or the stylish classical villas built in Kentish Town just to the north. Both noble developers were unconvinced that people of their own station would want to reside in Camden Town, in part because the area still had a dubious reputation to shake. Its image wasn't improved by the government recently having considered setting up a public gallows there to ease the demand on hard-pressed Tyburn. So the houses were built to appeal to a low-to-middling class of resident; one less-than-impressed visitor described them as 'miserable, modern erections'. From the start, Camden drew the better sorts of artisans, tradesmen and craftsmen – shopkeepers, carpenters, printers, cabinet-makers, tailors and shoemakers – escaping the squalor of the metropolis. Some hoped to find in St Pancras an idyllic world of comely milk-maids and poetic swains. In this they may have been disappointed, but their rear windows did face onto meadows and barns.[7]

The new buildings of Camden Town were all familiar to the work'us children. But just south of there, en route to the smallpox hospital, Blincoe and the rest of the bedraggled coffle of infants entered what was for them uncharted territory. Here the heavy clay soils favoured brick-making. Vast quantities were baked in honeycomb-shaped kilns which one contemporary said formed a 'ring of fire' around the New Road. These kilns supplied the materials for London's rapid expansion. But dust from them gave the surrounding air an acrid flavour, polluted the Fleet, and turned much of the land near the New Road into 'a frightful wasteland of pits, ponds, dust and heaps'. The novelist Oliver Goldsmith wrote scathingly about the towering dust heaps, the open drains and the barren ground; this was no rural idyll. Fittingly, press-gangs were known to harass those who toiled in the kilns, occasionally catching those too slow or naive to flee. But the clay soil in the southern section of the parish also encouraged cattle farming; hence the acres of lush meadow separated by ancient hedgerows. Milk and meat produced from hundreds of grazing cows nourished London's fast-growing population.[8]

To Blincoe's left as he headed south, approaching Battle Bridge (the area now known as King's Cross), both road and river curved towards the site of the parish's principal place of worship. St Pancras Church was a plain Gothic structure with a square tower, capped with a bell-shaped roof and weathervane. Built in the Middle Ages on the site of a Saxon place of worship, it derived its name from that of a young Phrygian noble, Pancratius, who was executed by order of the Roman Emperor Diocletian in 304 AD.[9] Once at the centre of the parish, the church had long since been abandoned to cow grazing, ancient trees, a vicarage, and to the lovers of bucolic pursuits. Samuel Bagster, who stayed near the church as a boy, described it as 'fine, open country', famous for its 'stately row of full grown unlopped elms'. Over a century earlier, the chronicler John Norden wrote that when a corpse was buried within this 'forsaken ... church-yard ... it resteth as secure against the day of resurrection, as if it laie in stately Paules'. By 1830, the graves had been pushed aside by the London–Midlands railway line terminating at Euston station (as a young surveyor, the novelist Thomas Hardy later had the job of stacking the gravestones up against a giant oak away from the tracks). But Norden was right about the church's isolation. This made it a favourite among grave-robbers. Jerry Cruncher in *A Tale of Two Cities* went there to dig up bodies to sell to corpse-hungry anatomy instructors.[10]

Immediately below the church, towards the eastern corner of the parish, Blincoe and the other children were led past the St Pancras Wells. This was one of many spa resorts that made the parish a popular weekend destination for hard-working Londoners. Those who lacked the leisure time or the extra sixpence coach fare to reach the more prestigious Hampstead wells alighted and spent the day among the resort's shaded avenues of trees. Throughout the day, they would imbibe the spa waters in the promise of a cure for such maladies as 'Leprosy, Scurvy, King's Evil, [and] Cancers of the most Corrosive Ulcers'. And in handbills referring to cures for 'the most Stubborn Weakness of either Sex, from what Cause soever proceeding', contemporaries recognised – couched in suitably coy terms – a pretended cure to syphilis, gonorrhoea and warts. Local historian William Maitland described it as 'a good spaw, whose water is of sweet taste, very clear and operates very gentley by stool.' Not all were so approving. For most guests had something a little stronger than water. And a London newspaper report of 1789 enumerated 'the returning situation of these persons' as follows: 'Sober, 50,000; in high glee, 90,000; drunkish, 30,000; dead drunk, 5,000.' All respectable people, this rather humourless journalist concluded, should have felt 'degraded' to be among such company.[11]

St Pancras Wells wasn't the only site of dissipation in the southern end of the parish. Aside from several other wells and dozens of public houses like the Adam and Eve, once a year rowdier parishioners could indulge themselves at Tottenham Court and Gooseberry fairs. At such venues they gathered in makeshift amphitheatres and bet over both male and female boxing, bear-baiting, cock-fighting and sundry other forms of 'wild debauchery'.[12]

To his right, as he headed south towards the New Road, Blincoe could make out the new developments of Somers Town. Here, gentrification was well under way. The depredations of thieves, vandals, and packs of wild dogs had once deterred local farmers. In late November 1789, a 'decent-dressed woman' was found murdered 'in a ditch adjoining Somers-Town'; she had a 'violent contusion on the back part of her head' and 'a deep cut' in her neck inflicted by a heavy stick. But in the 1780s, Lord Somers, a descendant of one of Henry VIII's jesters, began developing the area. Passing close by in the late 1790s, Blincoe may have noticed exotic accents and unusual fashions. For here lived hundreds of French clerics, lesser nobles and loyalists of many stripes, émigrés from a Revolution which had threatened to consume them. Somers Town now provided a haven where homesick monarchists, disavowed by their native land, spun out declining fortunes, upholding a semblance of gentility by pawning whatever valuables they had been able to smuggle out of France.[13]

Having passed the wells, the parish children met the New Road and then headed east for Battle Bridge. This part of the parish had an especially raffish character. London streets had been gas-lit since the 1760s, so illicit lovers and unsavoury characters now went to St Pancras for the luxuries of privacy and an easy escape. One section of derelict ground, Lamb's Fields, earned the sobriquet 'Forty Paces' since it was popular as a site for duelling, illegal after 1790 but still practised for the dubious sake of honour. City broadsheets recorded at least a dozen duels in the seven years that Blincoe lived in St Pancras parish; one of them between an army lieutenant and a 'gentleman' over 'the moving of a peg at a game of cribbage'. Just south of the New Road, 'pitched battles' were said to be fought by rival gangs of youths.

And as late as 1807, John Middleton fretted, 'the fields are never free from men strolling about in pilfering by day, and committing greater crimes by night.'[14]

It was in the southern section of the parish that many of the poorer inhabitants lived. Bagster recalled swimming as a boy in a pond close to what would become Judd Place. Nearby was a ditch serving as 'a receptacle for the bodies of domestic animals – a canine and feline cemetery, and a variety of other filth.' The parish's poor women, Bagster explained, converged there to remove the animals' teeth, which they then sold to bookbinders for burnishing the edges of books. As this suggests, for all its rural charm, St Pancras had plenty of chronically poor parishioners who fell within economist Patrick Colquhoun's description of 'Grubbers, gin-drinking women, and destitute boys and girls, wandering and prowling about the streets and bye-places after chips, nails, old metals, &c.' Life for those at the bottom was brutish, but usually short. Saunder Welch, a magistrate, estimated that as many as twenty Londoners died indirectly of hunger each week: weakened by malnutrition, they were knocked down by the gentlest epidemic breeze.[15]

The smallpox hospital, erected at the heart of Battle Bridge, lay close to the Fleet amid dairies and meadows. Fronted by neat lawns, three storeys high and topped off with a clock tower, it was an impressive edifice. The hospital was an object of civic pride to the parish at a time when the ruling elites were slowly beginning to see Hanway's point that commercial and military power depended on the health and well-being of the citizenry. It also reflected a traditional sense of duty – although not always fulfilled – on the part of the aristocracy, to act as stewards towards the poor. Set an example by such lordly sponsors as the Duke of Devonshire, the Earl of Upper Offroy, and the hero of campaigns in the Indian subcontinent, Lord Clive, thousands of Londoners donated money so that 'All poor persons (not being paupers or domestic servants of non-subscribers)' could turn up and receive free inoculation.[16]

Dr William Woodville, who ran the hospital, was soon to make his name as the first physician to conduct large-scale trials of the cowpox vaccine announced in Edward Jenner's famous *Inquiry* of 1798. Woodville obtained his cowpox sample from the blistered hand of a

The Small Pox Hospital

6. The smallpox hospital at Battle Bridge run by Dr William Woodville. Here, Robert Blincoe was inoculated with smallpox matter some time before August 1798. © Camden Local Studies and Archives Centre

milkmaid working in a dairy on Gray's Inn Road. By May of 1799, Jenner's handful of successes paled against the 600 achieved by Woodville and his assistant Dr George Pearson. It was perhaps inevitable that Jenner and Woodville would clash over who had made the greater contribution to the advent of cowpox vaccination. When some of Woodville's patients developed complications, Jenner accused him of accidentally infecting them with smallpox. Woodville responded with sharp invective, prompting Jenner to damn him and Pearson in return as 'snarling fellows and so ignorant withal that they know no more of the disease they write about than the animals which generate it.' So was another great scientific breakthrough sullied by vainglory.[17]

But when Blincoe arrived in 1797 or early 1798, Dr Woodville was still using smallpox matter. From his own published books, we know pretty much exactly the process that Blincoe and the other children underwent. Woodville first identified 'a young subject' who had 'the Small-pox in the most favourable [i.e. mild] manner'. When the child's pustules were 'perfectly matured' he ripped two or three of them open with 'a glover's needle or small lancet' and then wiped across them 'a couple of small [moistened] pledgets of lint or cotton'. He placed these in a vial and carried them to the workhouse children. Incisions were made with a lancet in the 'brawny parts of both arms' of the recipients, and the pledgets were then laid upon the cuts and kept in position for a day, after which the incisions were dressed with warm cabbage, or something similar. A few days after, Blincoe would have developed pustules near his incisions, possibly accompanied by fever and 'flushing heats'. By about a week later these pustules would have started to 'run with a thick purulent matter' as his wound enlarged before beginning to scab and heal over.[18]

John Brown recorded that Blincoe was made to drink a 'copious dose of salts' immediately after Dr Woodville or one of his assistants had made incisions in his arms. These would have been Glauber's salts, a laxative draught given in the belief that health required one's body to be free from excess fluids or noxious humours. Their only real effect was to add a few bouts of diarrhoea to the disagreeable symptoms of a mild smallpox infection. They also had an unpleasant taste. Blincoe gagged as the salts touched his lips and his hand shook as the acrid solution was poured into his mouth under the imperious gaze of a workhouse nurse. Such an overt display of discomfort offended the nurse's keen sense of the duties of the humbler ranks. A 'pauper child', she barked, ought to 'lick his lips' and 'say thank you, for the good and wholesome medicine provided for him at the public expense.' The workhouse boy's prerogative, Blincoe learned (if he hadn't already), was to suffer in silence. Histrionics were a luxury reserved for the higher ranks.[19]

Blincoe made a full recovery from the inoculation. But it stands as eloquent testimony to the horrors of his later life that he told John Brown that, having received it, he later felt cheated of an easy escape from life's torments.[20]

4

The master sweeps call

John Brown recoiled in shock. Reaching back in his mind to his painful years as a work'us boy, Robert Blincoe had recalled gazing out of the upper-storey workhouse windows and yearning after the life of the 'sweep's boy'. An astonished Brown listened as Blincoe told him that he had dearly wished to tramp alongside those children of eight, nine or ten who walked the streets in search of business, in all weathers, scantily clad, and who returned to damp cellars after long days of clambering up dangerously narrow flues. If Charles Dickens did draw inspiration from the *Memoir*, then he too must have flinched at this point in the story, for he had Oliver Twist reduced to a state of horrified panic when Mr Gamfield, the master sweep, tried to take him on as an apprentice. Brown put Blincoe's misdirected aspirations down to a 'diseased imagination' and 'perverted feelings'. Perverted or not, they had been sincerely felt.[1]

If Brown was shocked at the object of Blincoe's envy, the parish overseers would have been thrilled. For having collected the poor rate, expelled any paupers without settlement, and tracked down the errant fathers of bastard children, the overseer's next priority was to ensure that every workhouse child was apprenticed into the care of somebody else.[2]

Apprenticeship was central to the organisation of labour in 18th-century England. A practice enshrined in Tudor statutes and sustained by self-interest, it forbade anyone from practising a trade who had not first completed a certain number of years' training under a qualified master. During their apprenticeship, spanning from seven to sixteen years, young men and women learned the 'arts and mysteries' of their future trade. Parents or guardians paid the master a negotiated sum, from £3 in the case of low-status trades like farm labour, hat-making, chimney-sweeping, cat gut-dressing and the like, to as much as £200 in respectable kinds of work, such as the law, surgery and types of skilled weaving. According to the standard apprenticeship contract (or indenture), the master was responsible for the apprentice's board, lodging and clothing. Some apprentices also received a wage, but they didn't expect to become independent until they had completed their apprenticeship, become journeymen, and taken on apprentices of their own.

Many parents took great pains to find a decent and reliable master. After all, if well taught, their children would tend to stick with the trade they had learned and this would determine their future prosperity. Others were less fastidious; Francis Place was marched into the parlour of his father's public house and offered to the lowest bidder. Children of the middle and lower orders usually started their apprenticeship in their mid-teens. Before then they were deemed to lack the strength and mental agility to perform their tasks. Not so for pauper children. Well before they reached puberty, boys like Robert Blincoe felt the tap of parish charity run dry. They were often indentured as young as seven or eight years old under a contract which bound them to their masters until they reached the age of 21. In fact, the title of 'apprenticeship' was a mockery when applied to the back-breaking, tedious, mindless, and often dangerous and unhealthy work they were fated to perform.[3]

Unfortunately, parochial authorities were among the most ardent admirers of this bastardised apprenticeship system, for it had the great merit of allowing them to shift the expense of feeding, clothing and lodging poor children on to a third party. '[T]o save Expense,' it was said of overseers in 1732, '[they] are apt to ruin Children, by putting them out as early as they can, to any sorry Masters that will take them … on account of the little Money that is given with them.' The practice of indenturing parish orphans went back centuries. In 1618 the City of London had sent 100 boys and girls to work on Virginian plantations. And an Act of 1691 gave an even greater incentive for adopting this strategy. It stipulated that a child gained legal settlement after just 40 days of apprenticeship in another parish. In a book of 1764, Richard Burn described the abuses that this Act accidentally unleashed. 'Overseers', he wrote, 'bind out poor children apprentices, no matter to whom or to what trade, but to take especial care that the master lived in another parish.'[4]

After 1691 the overseer's express duty was to get more children bound in other parishes than rival parishes could bind to their own. And so keen were parishes to shed the burden of poor children that they happily paid masters to take them away. The typical fee was around £5, a fine investment when it cost at least £6 to keep a child for a year in a workhouse. During the 1700s, the Foundling Hospital bound thousands of girls to domestic service and boys to textile mills or the merchant navy. And as Blincoe was soon to learn, in striving to reduce the poor rates, magistrates and overseers seldom did much reflecting before affixing their signatures to parish children's indentures.[5]

The overseers of St Martin in the Fields, in London, were past masters at invoking the 1691 Act. As many as 91 per cent of their pauper children were bound to masters domiciled in other parishes. The savings they made were immense. It's unlikely that St Pancras parish was quite as successful, but its overseers did form useful ties with the agents of northern manufacturers to send cartloads of children to work in factories, often in declining trades and under unknown masters. In 1799 a Mary Howard was sent to the Isle of Skye, off the western coast of Scotland, to be trained in the 'business' of 'household work'. The system of parish apprenticeships, as eagerly exploited by these overseers, was no more than legalised child slavery.[6]

In all this manoeuvring to save money, the welfare of children came nowhere. Everyone involved knew that masters had little to impart in terms of skills, but children were still forced to sweat for a paltry wage for as many as sixteen years. At the end of this gruelling term they were left with few, if any, useable talents. This suited their masters fine. Those who took on pauper apprentices usually worked in over-stocked trades with insufficient work to go round. They needed the cheapest labour available, and they certainly had no wish for their apprentices to set up on their own account. Some wanted only the cash fee from the parish. Mr Gamfield, the impecunious master sweep in *Oliver Twist*, sought to indenture Oliver having noticed a sign on the workhouse gates advertising apprentices, just as he had been 'deeply cogitating in his mind his ways and means of paying certain arrears of rent, for which his landlord had become rather pressing.' Masters often smartly absconded having received the apprentice fee. And even to those who could find their apprentices work, the boys and girls were cheap labour, nothing more.[7]

It was also an open secret that many masters severely maltreated their apprentices. Those worn down by privation, drink and the sapping insecurities of life in a low-skilled trade were often careless or cruel. 'The master may be a tiger of cruelty,' wrote one authority in 1738, 'he may beat, abuse, strip naked, starve or do what he will to the poor innocent lad, few people take much notice.' In 1767, a law was passed to make it easier for abused children to have their indentures cancelled. But few apprentices had the temerity to appeal to the authorities. Too often, those who did so were sent chastened back to their masters. In 1802, when the St Pancras overseers received a letter from a young apprentice sent to a mill in Lancashire complaining of ill-treatment, they refused to allow her to return because of the 'further Terrible expense [that] would ensue by [their] consenting to the measure.' She was left to the mercy of her master.[8]

But there was at least one trade which seemed so ineffably cruel and hard that even parish overseers of the poor were reluctant to apprentice their wards to it. Master chimney sweeps had to procure apprentices from the lowliest families in London's wretched East End, the offspring of parents who were out of work or engaged in mean trades such as hawking fish and the flesh of dog or cat. Those with a taste for hard liquor were especially good suppliers of young lives. For their part, master sweeps usually preferred to keep overseers and churchwardens out of the picture, for there was always the chance that they would protest when a child returned to the workhouse badly bruised or singed, or complaining of being loaned out to anyone able to pay.

Then, to the horror and consternation of the St Pancras workhouse children, sometime in 1798 one of the nurses brought them startling news. A party of master sweeps had arranged to visit the workhouse and would indenture any parish children of suitable dimensions for ascending chimney stacks. In spite of the long-standing aversion of parish authorities to masters of the 'sooty tribe', the rumour turned

7. George Cruikshank's depiction of the parish overseers asking the magistrates to apprentice a young Oliver Twist to a vicious-looking Mr Gamfield, the master sweep. Oliver trembles at the prospect.

out to be well grounded. And it says much about the priorities of St Pancras' overseers that they were prepared to do business with such men. A decade earlier they might have scrupled. But now things were different. The parish was in heavy debt and all qualms had melted away.[9]

On 15 July 1795 the parish had convened a vestry meeting, with the proceedings as usual starting in a chapel and ending more agreeably at a local inn. On this particular evening, many parishioners expressed their alarm at a sudden increase in the numbers of parish poor. Everyone knew that rising bread prices, caused by severe harvest failures, were making the situation acute. This staple of the poor family's table had more than doubled in price from 43 shillings and twopence per quarter in January 1792 to an incredible 108 shillings in August 1795. A local baker called Samuel Wallis rose to his feet and explained that he had contracted to supply bread at a fixed price, but due to 'the prodigious rise' in prices he was supplying the parish workhouse 'at a discount price'. On 10 March 1796, at another vestry meeting, the same problems forced aside all other business. Parishioners now heard that the workhouse population had swollen. New premises had had to be taken on the Hampstead Road to house the overflow. And evidence of distress was everywhere to be seen.[10]

While the workhouse inmates shivered through the winter of 1794 and the following spring, they could see the queues of applicants for parish relief lengthening every day. Hunger and desperation now took hold of the parish poor. Pinched-faced labourers begged for work. Pawn shops were crowded with wares, as furniture, clothes, and then tools were sold to buy bread. And the situation went on deteriorating. The £148 spent on the parish's poor in 1791 almost doubled to £285 in 1792. From then on, the gradient of increase became steeper each successive year. By 1799, the parish was paying £790. Come the year 1815, even this alarming figure had doubled.[11]

Yet St Pancras had been anything but gratuitous in doling out relief. Its £148 a year in 1791 hardly compared with St Giles Cripplegate's huge Poor Law bill of £2,912 in the same year. St Giles did contain the rookeries of Gin Lane and the liquor palaces, brothels and foetid tenements of Seven Dials, but St Pancras had its poorer quarters and down-at-heel labourers, and it had kept going on a budget. Then a system able to tick comfortably along for generations despite plenty of waste, abuse and incompetence had begun to buckle. A sudden rise in pauperism hit the ramshackle structures of parish relief with terrible force.[12]

The workhouse continued to be supplied with food, and Mr Wallis was placated with a £10 donation, but life there steadily worsened. Throughout the 1780s, the inmate population had fluctuated around the 150 mark. By the time Blincoe arrived, it had jumped to an extraordinary 450 souls. A high water mark of 623 inmates would be reached in 1802. It wouldn't have taken Blincoe long to sense that things were getting worse. Every year he spent in the workhouse, his strip of mattress narrowed as he had to move over to make room for more. Even for a very young boy, it was a telling indication that all was not well.[13]

With the recent horrors of the French Revolution in mind, the more nervous members of the propertied classes hastily refined their arguments in favour of social inequality. Writing to some wretchedly poor women in the Mendips, the evangelical Hannah More waxed lyrical on the virtues of the 'scarcity'. The terrible harvests had been 'permitted by an all-wise and gracious Providence', she explained, in order to show the labouring poor 'how immediately they are dependent on the rich', and the enormous advantages they derived 'from the government and constitution of this country.' William Paley, theologian and prebend of St Pancras, went even further. He argued that the poor were far more fortunate than the wealthy, that their hardships were really 'pleasures'. His reasoning was that the rich have so much that they are unable to appreciate or enjoy what they have. The poor, in contrast, are able through deprivation to value every mouthful of food or drink they can procure.[14]

Something had clearly gone wrong, however, and Hannah More was quick to blame the usual suspect. Pauperism, she declared, arose from that 'silent murderer, sloth'. In fact, during the 1790s, things were so bad that the industrious, the prudent and the sober struggled and starved alongside the idle and the drunken. But More's point of view had growing appeal. Some people had always baulked at the suggestion that they give up a slice of their hard-earned income to the jobless, the friendless or the homeless. Sunday sermons extolled charity, but their instincts advocated the reverse. And to those who preferred not to give, it was tempting to imagine that the poor were lazy and immoral and therefore undeserving of parish relief. Only slightly more generously, many others insisted that the poor had been rendered indolent and vicious by the generosity of the Poor Laws. This last claim had a long pedigree.[15]

Earlier in the century, Daniel Defoe stated that 'No man in

England, of sound limbs and senses, can be poor, merely for want of work'; ergo those who beg or steal do so because the Poor Laws give them something for nothing. In support of his controversial thesis, Defoe boasted of how he had had two 'lusty fellows' shackled in the town stocks for rejecting nine shillings for a week's work. By the 1790s a cruel paradox had arisen. Never had Defoe's analysis been less applicable, but at no time in the preceding two centuries had it been so widely embraced. Several factors had converged to make life grimly hard for the rural poor in particular. The harvest failure of 1795, a costly war with France, and the enclosing of common lands all hit hard. One factor, however, caused more hardship than any other – the explosive increase in the number of people alive. The population of south-east England alone had jumped by nearly a quarter between 1750 and 1780. This dramatic surge in fertility intensified competition for work and drove down the wages of those lucky enough to get it.[16]

There were lots of suggestions as to how to reduce pauperism. Edmund Gillingwater recommended making workhouses more wholesome institutions for engendering good morals. Others, like Sir Frederick Eden, advised setting up hundreds of Friendly Societies and encouraging the poor to put money away for times of need. A good number targeted ale-houses as increasing the 'wickedness and profligacy of the poor'. But for many, something more heroic was required: the slimming down, even the wholesale abolition, of the Elizabethan Poor Laws.[17]

Cue the Reverend Thomas Malthus and his 1798 *Essay on the Principle of Population*. Malthus, although a humble village curate, had a reputation for liking 'fighting for fighting's sake'. But his famous essay, while in fact the most vigorous polemic, seemed to many as dispassionate, logical and straightforwardly true as Euclidean geometry. Malthus explained that humans were condemned to suffering, starvation, war and want because in every generation there are more children born than there is food to support them. Misery, hunger and distress were regrettable but inevitable. From this point of view, the Poor Laws were a dreadful mistake, for they kept paupers alive, allowing them to breed and entail on future generations yet more suffering. For the Malthusians, accepting parish aid was the equivalent of the shipwrecked sailor drinking sea-water: momentary relief was far outweighed by subsequent harm. Many read Malthus as saying that to withhold poor rates was both virtuous and wise, and in this way his ideas flowed into a torrent of criticism directed at the Elizabethan Poor Laws. Kindness was pernicious since it removed the incentive for the jobless, homeless, drunken and unproductive to mend their ways.[18]

Poor relief had been attacked before. But experienced magistrates and overseers knew that depriving the poor of their age-old dues was likely to lead to nocturnal attacks on property and person. From an instinct of self-preservation, as pauperism grew, many decided to give more, not less, and an Act of 1795 repealed all restraints on the granting of outdoor relief. Yet when, in 1796, several JPs met at the Pelican Inn at Speenhamland near Newbury, and agreed to make up from the poor rates any shortfall between the costs of living and the wages labourers received, they were upbraided from pulpit to podium for making matters worse. Rather than going out to find extra work, a legion of critics objected, labourers now saw that they could slack off whenever they liked, spending time in the ale-house with the comforting thought that as they drank, their hard-working and prudent neighbours were subsidising their free-and-easy lifestyle. The fact that rural labourers were starving no matter how hard they worked seemed to pass these critics by. Few wished to find the poor blameless when doing so implied the need for greater sacrifices from their social betters.[19]

However, the haemorrhaging of parish funds aggravated the nation's cynical view of the Poor Laws, and the parishioners of St Pancras fought doggedly against attempts to increase the amount of relief money collected. Fear also grew of the presence in their midst of so many paupers. With the circulation of seditious doctrines from France, some perceived the potential for violent political revolution – the overthrow of the propertied by the *sans culottes* – as had happened only 22 miles across the Channel. It hardly helped that William Godwin, an energetic purveyor of radical political ideas, had moved into the polygon, one of Somers Town's elegant new buildings. Its architect, Jacob Leroux, had chaired a public meeting in 1792 imploring parishioners to seek out 'all private enemies' and 'suppress seditious pursuits'. In 1795 the parish priest, Weldon Champneys, again rallied them to the flag. We are living through an 'awful crisis', he proclaimed. And, with his encouragement, they formed the St Pancras Volunteers, a motley squad of local men armed to defend the parish. These were extremely tense times. With the political temperature rising, leading parishioners decided that action against pauperism had to be taken. Desperate measures were required to drive down the parish debt and make existing funds spread further.[20]

To this end, they set about doing whatever possible to offload the workhouse's children. This included breaking with long tradition and inviting the master sweeps to come and inspect them. Old scruples no longer had a place in the overseer's worldview. After all, according to the wisdom of Defoe, it was just such lily-livered generosity that had caused the parish to be overwhelmed with paupers in the first place. The overseers were under no illusions, however, as to the degradation this meant for any of the children selected.

As Charles Dickens made clear, the Mr Gamfields of the world were rarely among the benefactors of mankind. It gives us some idea of the mindset of the master sweep that in 1795 a three-and-a-half year old boy was articled to one of their number at a London inn. His desperate parents accepted, in return, some immediate refreshments. When parliamentary inquiries were made into the trade, sweeps told MPs of masters who thrashed their young apprentices for any sign of timidity, set fires in the grates beneath them or held sharp sticks under the seats of their pants to hasten their ascent of chimneys, and sent up novices with bruised and bloodied elbows and knees. Committees of inquiry also heard of chimneys so convoluted that sweeps got lost inside and could be retrieved only by the brickwork being dismantled. There were dozens of stories of children being asphyxiated having cleaned upright sections, only to find the way back blocked with soot.[21]

Most chimney sweeps did survive into adulthood, but long before their twenties they were 'turned out upon the world'. By then too large to shimmy up slender flues, they found themselves entirely 'without education, without information, without any means of supporting themselves'. Hence, remarked one witness to a parliamentary committee in 1818, 'they must have recourse to robbery and plunder'.

About the only thing climbing flues did qualify sweeps for, aside from chimney-sweeping, was house burglary; hence they were well represented in the lists of those whose lives ended at Tyburn or in the prison colony of Botany Bay.[22]

The sweep's woes were, however, as much the result of deforestation and new building styles as of vicious masters. By the late 1600s, England's forests had shrunk to a tiny fraction of what they had been at the time of the Norman Conquest. This shortage of timber made coal mining economical, but because coal doesn't burn as readily as wood, it needs the good draught supplied by a narrower flue. The constricted chimneys of the newly-built coal-burning houses were far more prone to blockages, and if they weren't regularly swept the house was at high risk of burning down. The situation for sweeps was made still worse by the rising demand for modestly-sized townhouses. Smaller rooms demanded yet smaller chimneys, and a total disregard for the children who had to clean them meant that buildings were constructed with the most convoluted flues. Some turned at right angles, ran horizontally or diagonally, even zig-zagged or plunged downwards before rising up towards the stack. One London chimney switched direction an amazing fourteen times. Only small boys could wriggle up such chimneys, and master sweeps took to printing handbills advertising 'small boys for small flues'. The smaller the boy, remarked Dr Lushington, physician and philanthropist, 'the larger the price he fetches'.[23]

A sweep's boy generally slept on the floor of his master's cellar with only his soot bag and tattered clothing to keep him warm. Few were well dressed. The German writer and diarist Sophie de la Roche noted on 6 September 1786: 'I was dressed when I saw the first workman passing and heard a young voice calling: "Chimney-sweep! Chimney-sweep!" and perceived a tiny chimney-sweep boy, six years old, running along barefoot at his master's side, his soot bag on his back, and shouting for all he was worth.' Dr William Buchan commiserated with young sweeps in his *Advice to Mothers*, painting a bleak image of their daily grind: 'Half naked in the most bitter cold, he creeps along the streets by break of day, the ice cutting through his feet, his legs bent, and his body twisted.' But perhaps the greatest misery was reserved for those who developed scrotal cancer, a condition to which chimney sweeps, in constant contact with soot, were terribly prone. In a pioneering study of occupational health, the physician Percivall Pott explained in 1775 how 'a warty excrescence' appears on the testicles and 'discharges a thin acrimonious ichor, which excoriates the surrounding skin'. Pott thought it was caused by blocked perspiration, but the salient facts were that scrotal cancer was very painful and that 'the scalpel [was] the only resource'.[24]

In the 1770s, Jonas Hanway, once more stung into action, fired off dozens of letters to statesmen, churchmen and master sweeps bemoaning the chimney sweeps' condition. These were the opening salvoes in a century-long campaign to improve their lot. Horace Walpole, one of few converts, complained in 1784: 'I have been these two years wishing to [alleviate] the woes of chimney-sweeps, but never could make impression on three people; on the contrary, have generally caused a smile.' When Bills were introduced to provide them with some protection from their brutal masters, the House of Lords laughed them off the stage as gross impertinences. One noble lord blithely declared young sweeps to be 'gay, cheerful, and contented'.[25]

It was to this 'right pleasant trade', as Dickens ironically called it, that several of the St Pancras workhouse children were to be indentured. Most children knew enough to be alarmed. They understood that falling into the hands of a master sweep meant long years of frightening servitude. Oliver Twist begged that the parish beadle 'would starve him – beat him – kill him' rather than abandon him to the malign care of Mr Gamfield; but the parish wanted rid of him, and Gamfield needed the £5. Blincoe's contemporaries feared the master sweeps with the same fierce intensity as Oliver.[26]

Not so Robert Blincoe. The news of the master sweeps' impending visit filled him with hope. And nothing he heard could persuade him to alter his attitude. The nurses, Brown recorded, 'told him how bitterly he would rue the day that should consign him to that wretched employment, and bade him pray earnestly to God to protect him from such a destiny.' Blincoe treated their opinions with 'silent contempt'. The only difficulty was his age. Only six, he was fairly tall for his years, but unmistakably puny. Smallness was a virtue in this trade, but one also needed some muscle to climb, sweep, and carry heavy bags of soot. Even were he selected for the master sweeps' muster, he risked being turned away because of his youth and diminutive limbs. So, foreshadowing his later determination, Blincoe took to walking on tip-toe to accustom himself to the taller posture he would need to assume on the appointed day. He even tried to elongate his body by hanging down from rafters and balustrades.[27]

Despite his perverse enthusiasm, on the day of the master sweeps' visit Blincoe found that he wasn't among those selected to stand before them. Too slight and immature for the job of clambering up flues, he was told to keep away. Blincoe did not, and never would, give up so easily. Somehow, as the line of sad-faced youths marched to a room to appear before the masters, he sneaked into their company. There followed a tragi-comic scene in which Blincoe, straining with every sinew to look taller and older than he really was, stood alongside several other boys, their unhappiness and looks of desperation contrasting absurdly with his own expression of innocent enthusiasm. The masters proceeded to select several boys of what Mr Gamfield would have considered 'a nice small pattern'. They all rejected Blincoe. 'Some of the sweeps complimented him for his spirit', the *Memoir* says, 'and to console him, said, if he made a good use of his time, and contrived to grow a head taller, he might do very well for a fag, at the end of a couple of years.' As the master sweeps laughed, Blincoe felt his first chance of liberty slip away.[28]

The children were led back to their quarters, those selected as sweep's boys in a disconsolate state. They now had to wait for the negotiation and payment of the apprenticeship fee. After that, the case would be put to a couple of local magistrates and then they would place their signatures on the indentures just beneath where the master agreed, as a legal nicety rather than an expression of serious intent, that he would treat his ward 'with humanity and care'. It was at this juncture that Oliver Twist secured his reprieve. Having elicited the rare sympathy of two elderly and 'half childish' magistrates by his terrified expression and plaintive appeals, Oliver was relieved to hear the overseers admonished and told to take him 'back to the workhouse, and treat him kindly'. Since the St Pancras magistrates also sat on the vestry, and were at that very juncture agonising over the parish debt, there would be no stay of execution for these boys.[29]

They knew all too well what a life of wretched misery being apprenticed to a master sweep entailed. When they returned to their sleeping quarters, 'weeping and wailing', they gave full vent to their anxieties, a collective catharsis hardly helped by Blincoe vocally wishing that he was among their number. That he should have looked back and envied the sweeps is more understandable, given the traumas of his eventual apprenticeship. But that he felt envy at the time speaks movingly of his acute unhappiness in the workhouse. If Blincoe's *Memoir* did inspire the scene with Mr Gamfield in *Oliver Twist*, Dickens must have realised that few readers would find it credible that any child could be desperate enough to want to become a sweep's boy, still less one who sank into a fit of deep despondency upon finding that he could stay in the workhouse and avoid the extreme privation of the chimney sweep's existence. John Brown noted that confinement in a workhouse was more 'irksome' to Blincoe since 'all his comrades had friends, parents, or relations', whereas he

> ... stood alone, no ties of consanguinity of kindred bound him to any particular portion of society, or to any place, he had no friend to soothe his troubled mind, no domestic circle to which, though excluded for a time, he might hope to be reunited.[30]

Yet in his desire to join the 'sooty tribe', Robert Blincoe also displayed a more positive side to his character, an irrepressible belief that, given a modicum of freedom, he could change his life for the better. It wasn't just melancholy that impelled him to seek an escape from the workhouse. At this early age he had the same determination and self-respect that would one day enable him to pull himself clear of callous overseers and unscrupulous masters. Doubtless, he also imagined that as a chimney sweep, walking the streets day after day, he would be able to search every house, hovel, barn and lean-to shed in St Pancras parish in the hope of finding some surviving family.[31]

With the departure of several boys in 1798, the parish had made a fair saving. But it wasn't out of trouble. On the contrary, its financial state was more parlous than ever. Early in 1799 the overseers and churchwardens had painfully to admit that their parish was limping under an immense debt of 2,000 guineas. Before too long, Blincoe's prayers of leaving the workhouse were bound to be answered. His surrogate parents, the overseers of the poor, were as desirous of getting rid of him as he was to leave.[32]

5

A promise of roast beef
and plum pudding

In early summer 1799 another rumour reached Blincoe's ears. It inspired him with 'new life and spirits'. The churchwardens and overseers were apparently in talks with the 'owner of a great cotton factory, in the vicinity of Nottingham' who needed plenty of young apprentices. A certain Mr William Lambert, resident of Southampton Place, a few hundred yards south of the workhouse, had made contact with the parish authorities on behalf of two of his relations. William Charles and Francis Lambert were the proprietors of a cotton and hosiery mill on the banks of the Dover Beck in Lowdham village, a few miles outside Nottingham. They needed child apprentices, and William had agreed to use his local connections to procure some from the St Pancras authorities.[1]

Debt-ridden, the parish was only too ready to oblige. They had already sent dozens of pauper children north to the Midlands and Lancashire. The overseers and churchwardens were by now cosily familiar with Messrs Gorton and Haslam, who acted for northern manufacturers and received a commission for every child they took off the parish's hands. Children were hustled aboard wagons and sent north in batches; if they weren't returned within six weeks, their settlement in St Pancras lapsed and the overseers could rest content that they were no longer responsible for them. And such was the incentive to dispose of the burden that nearly two-thirds of the children apprenticed by the parish while Blincoe lived in the work-house were sent into the textile industry, many of them hundreds of miles from their place of birth.[2]

Even having paid a generous commission to the manufacturers' agents, parishes were still in pocket. It cost St Pancras just 30 shillings for each apprentice indentured to cotton spinners, but over four times as much per year to support a child in the workhouse. Small wonder that apprenticing children to northern textile mills was standard practice among London's parishes. In 1790 the overseers of Hanwell in Middlesex threatened the local poor that if they didn't 'avail themselves' of the 'offer' of sending their children to the Nottinghamshire textile mill of Messrs W. Toplis and Co. Ltd., then they would be struck from the parish pension list. St Martin in the Fields, St Luke's, Chelsea, St Botolph without Aldersgate, St George's in Southwark, St Clement Danes, St Margaret's in Westminster all sent consignments of children to mills in Lancashire, Derbyshire or the Midlands. In 1794 St Margaret's sent 50 in a single batch. Several advertised their workhouse or vagrant children in provincial newspapers. And at least one overseer boasted of working an 'idiot' in with every twenty children, though agents were usually relied on for rejecting the obviously unsuitable. When the cotton master Samuel Oldknow obtained 70 children from Clerkenwell in 1796, he wisely took the precaution of having a doctor examine them before signing any paperwork.[3]

Sending workhouse children hundreds, even thousands, of miles away from the parish of their birth was by no means novel. What was new during the 1790s was the scale of the forced migrations. St Pancras sent only two or three children per year into the cotton trade before 1795. Thereafter supply and demand soared in unison. As the parish sank into debt, the overseers contacted masters as far away as Stockport and Bury in Lancashire. It was a classic coincidence of needs. Demand kept pace with supply as the northern counties were undergoing nothing short of a technological revolution. As the Derbyshire surveyor John Farey wrote, 'in most newly-erected cotton-spinning mills ... the demand for children's labour ... exceeds even the inordinately excited increase of population in the place, and children are not only sought for through adjoining districts, but in many instances have been imported by scores at a time ... from London, Bristol, and other great towns.'[4]

Mill owners hungered for parish apprentices. They knew that, without them, their enterprises would rapidly cease to be viable. As employees, children were not always the natural choice. But freeborn adults usually recoiled at the prospect of entering the new textile mills. Labouring men were accustomed to working for a few days every week until they had sufficient cash to meet their immediate wants. Then many adjourned to the parlour of the local inn to celebrate Saint Monday or even Saint Tuesday in an atmosphere of tipsy conviviality. Most preferred the relative liberty of traditional patterns of work and scoffed at being 'tee'd to a bell' in factories, subjected to what the mill owner's friend Andrew Ure admiringly called the 'unvarying regularity of the complex automaton'. And while trade was good, there was little incentive to give up another job to enter the mills. The Lancastrian weaver William Thom later recalled how 'four days was a week as far as working went – and such a week brought the skilful worker forty shillings.' This was a fine income, enough to buy plenty of meat, plus watches for the men and fashionable dresses for their wives and daughters.[5]

This gave the mill owners a serious problem. Before the advent of steam-powered mills, they had to set up alongside fast-flowing streams which could drive their waterwheels. Mill surveyors looked out for the frothy white waters of streams compressed by sheer gorges and steep-sided valleys. But finding any labourers at all in these typically remote areas required creative hiring practices. Some mill owners tried to get entire families to work for them by offering inducements. The more astute provided schools and markets to entice workers, and 'factory villages' often had chapels for inculcating habits of industry and subservience. Richard Arkwright, a pioneer of mechanical spinning, was among the few to yield to the labourers' more prosaic wants – in Cromford, Derbyshire, he had an inn built for their gratification.[6]

Parish apprentices were an alternative, if only partial, solution. To the more ruthless employer they had many virtues. Easily obtained, legally bound to their master, and hundreds of miles from home, they had few means of redress if badly treated or overworked. They could also be very cheaply fed and housed, and paid a mere pittance. Furthermore, for certain jobs they were physically highly adept. Children had two main roles in textile mills. They worked as scavengers, retrieving cotton waste from beneath and upon moving machines, and as piecers, repairing splits as the yarns were drawn out and spun. Their slight bodies and delicate hands made them far superior at these tasks to their elders. 'Their fingers are more supple', explained the owner of a Cheshire silk mill. They were also, he added, 'more easily led into the habit of performing the duties of their situation'. In other words, children were more pliant; they could be bullied and cajoled in a way that only the most broken adults would tolerate. This was the subtext to Andrew Ure's later remark that 'it is found nearly impossible to convert persons past the age of puberty ... into useful factory hands.' And this was the background to William Lambert's arrival at the St Pancras workhouse in August of the year 1799.[7]

One might imagine that his brief was a difficult one. Tales abounded of the maltreatment of parish orphans in northern textile mills. So many young apprentices ran away from the mills of Nottingham that local owners had clubbed together and set up offices at the Bear Inn to reclaim them. They ruthlessly prosecuted anyone who harboured an apprentice on the run. In 1784 the Lancashire magistrates had drafted in a panel of physicians, led by Dr Thomas Percival, to inquire into an outbreak of putrid fever at a mill owned by the Peel family. They condemned the building as stuffy, malodorous and filthy. But they reserved most of their ire for the excessively long hours the children were made to work. The physicians concluded that the length of the working day was excessive and that more breaks were 'essential to the present health and future capacity of those who are under the age of 14.' Horrified at the inhumanity of the mills, though no doubt disdainful of *nouveau riche* capitalists as well, the Lancashire magistracy promptly took steps to prevent local children being made to do night work in the county's spinning mills.[8]

The complacency of the London parishes was less easily disturbed. The parish vestry of St Clement Danes decided in 1791 to send three of its members to inspect children whom it had sent to a cotton mill; but it was six years later, following an unsettling visit to Messrs Middleton Wells and Co. of Sheffield, that the parish finally resolved to send no more children to work in textile factories. Not long after, the magistrates of the Middlesex Quarter Sessions said that overseers were making too little effort to ascertain the quality of the masters to whom they entrusted parish children. Utterly regardless, the St Pancras parish officers went on sending children to the mills of the north and the Midlands. (Concern for the local rate-payers wasn't their only consideration. Some parochial officials were on the make. For example, William Pepall, one of the parish's beadles, was much later discovered to have invoiced both the parishioners and the mill owners for the same personal expenses.)[9]

It may be that reports of the cruelty of certain cotton masters had not penetrated the closed world of the workhouse. But as Lambert's overtures became public knowledge, children and parents must have felt some foreboding at the prospect of their being sent hundreds of miles from their parish. So in order to appease gullible adults and to enthuse the workhouse children, the overseers resorted to an expedient of the most brazen cynicism. The children were unblushingly told that upon arrival at the Lamberts' cotton mill they would be 'transformed into ladies and gentlemen'. The lie was perfectly tailored to the limited knowledge and experience of the workhouse children. As the *Memoir* records, they were informed that

> They would be fed on roast beef and plum-pudding, be allowed to ride their masters' horses, and have silver watches, and plenty of cash in their pockets.[10]

It was consummately done. Within their limited frames of reference, here were all the embodiments of comfort, wealth and refinement. Roast beef and plum pudding were the workhouse's Christmas treats, and their very mention was guaranteed to thrill children accustomed to bread, cheese, cheap mutton and potatoes. While the English could afford to eat much more flesh than their French or German counterparts, for poor cottagers and labourers this was largely restricted to cured bacon, tripe, offal, trotters and hogg's puddings, all derived from the family pig, itself reared on food waste or whatever else could be found. Only the likes of the yeoman farmer, physician, merchant, and all those above them in the social scale could afford red, fleshy meat more than once or twice a year. And not least because it reaffirmed their place in society, as a French traveller noted, 'People of good Substance … have a huge Piece of Roast-Beef on Sundays, of which they stuff till they can swallow no more, and eat the rest cold, without any other Victuals the other six Days of the Week.' It was, literally, an exercise in conspicuous consumption. Ready access to roast beef was as much a mark of high social status in Georgian England as owning horses, silver watches, and purses full of money.[11]

Roast beef had strong cultural significance as well. It was the kind of no-nonsense fare said to be suited to sturdy, brave, free-born Englishmen. 'When mighty Roast Beef / Was the Englishman's food', ran the popular ballad 'The Roast Beef of Old England':

> It ennobled our brains
> And enriched our blood.
> Our soldiers were brave
> And our courtiers were good.

'Beef is a good meate for an Englyssheman', boldly asserted the writer Andrew Boorde in 1542. Nothing happened in the interim to alter this view. Indeed, by the 1790s, infantry regiments would hang lumps of roast beef above their recruiting stalls, drawing in hungry youths with the promise of the tastiest victuals.[12]

The prospect of regular servings of roast beef would make any poor child's head swim. And in Georgian England, plum pudding was the natural accompaniment to an entrée of roast beef. 'The art of cooking as practised by Englishmen', scoffed the Swedish traveller Pehr Kalm in 1748, 'does not extend much beyond roast beef and plum pudding.' But such contempt among foreigners was the exception. Frenchman Henri Misson, not easily provoked into praising English cuisine, enthused: 'Ah, what an excellent thing is an English pudding! To come in pudding-time, is as much to say, to come in the most lucky moment in the world.' This heady blend of currants and raisins soaked in brandy disgusted the Puritans of the 1600s, who are said to have had it outlawed as 'sinfully rich'. The same richness would have thrilled the taste buds of a young Blincoe.[13]

It may seem surprising that Robert Blincoe and the other work'us children fell for such wildly improbable promises. That they did so speaks of their intense need to believe that life had more to offer them than the meaningless existence they had so far endured. It was a case of hope triumphing over experience. Who actually sold them the false prospectus we do not know. The overseers and William Lambert were certainly involved, and they perhaps put some of the nurses up to disseminating their falsehoods. Either way, it's clear that the practice of promising workhouse children wealth and status was not unique to St Pancras. John Brown was aware of many similar cases, and a certain 'Orphan John' of Bethnal Green workhouse later wrote in the *Ashton Chronicle* of how he had been told by parish officers that if he agreed to go to a Derbyshire cotton mill, he would have 'fine sport' among the hills, abundant time for 'play and pleasure', plenty of roast beef and money, and that he would come back a seasoned gentleman. It was a tried and tested ruse.[14]

When Lambert arrived at the workhouse he couldn't have found a more pliant or excited collection of boys and girls assembled in the committee-room. The master had them lined up so that the honoured guest could examine both their physical state and, as John Brown noted with disgust, 'their *willingness* to go and serve as apprentices, in the way and manner required.' Although he hadn't known it, Blincoe had been lucky to disappoint the master sweeps. Now his good fortune ran out. He was selected along with 31 others to serve the Lamberts until the age of 21. The surviving parish registers record the children's names, ages, and destination. At seven years old, Robert Blincoe was equal youngest; but the average age of the children was only eleven. The official indentures stated that in the last years of their apprenticeships, the boys were to be taught stocking-weaving and the girls lace-making. It seems unlikely that William Lambert ever believed that these children would be taught such marketable skills. He must have realised that he was in the business of securing cheap labour, and nothing more. But the charade completed, the poor children were dismissed.[15]

It's sometimes hard to imagine why the lower orders in times of extreme distress, or when ruthlessly exploited, didn't rebel more often against their social 'betters'. Rather than rising up in arms, they more often accepted appalling hardships with resilience and resignation. Part of the reason for this lies in the outlooks and attitudes associated with the hierarchical structure of the old society. There was a solidity to England's caste system built on the fact that those at every link in the social chain more often envied and admired than resented or despised those higher in the scale. And in striving to be like their superiors, they actively reinforced the hierarchy itself. At the level of the individual, this was no more than sound good sense. One naturally sought what one's betters had, and while movement through the ranks remained possible, it was usually wiser to work hard to improve oneself than to rail vainly against the system; Adam Smith called it 'the natural effort of every individual to better his own condition.'[16]

Moreover, anyone who preached the gospel of equality ran the risk of jeopardising whatever privileges they themselves had. The duke who denied the sanctity of kings risked dispelling the mystique of ducal houses; the village curate who denied that the flock needed the ministrations of the bishop begged the question of why God needed middle-men at all; and the owner of a tumbledown cottage usually sensed, however vaguely, that to condemn the Palladian grandness of the squire's hall might lead his poorer neighbours to challenge the idea of property ownership itself. It also helped, of course, that nearly everyone had someone else to look down upon. Noah Claypole, Dickens' charity boy, relished the arrival of the mere work'us boy, Oliver Twist. Noah exulted in the same sense of social superiority that a duke felt next to a baronet, or a wealthy merchant to a humble shopkeeper. The links in the social chain were held intact by the powerful emotions of envy and snobbery.

Even Dickens' master sweep, Mr Gamfield, could disdain the poor 'prentices who swept chimneys for him, and landing blows on his hapless donkey's skull and flanks also afforded a modest sense of social mastery. Rank was there to be pulled, but it had to be visible to have its intended effect. For the upper class, this meant investing in spacious estates, patronising talented artists, drinking French and Rhenish wines, dressing in the clothes of the moment, and arbitrarily redefining table manners in ways that made the lower orders seem rude and uncouth. Power was as much about show as about the implicit threat of force. Merchants, lawyers, physicians and peasants all knew that they belonged to decidedly lower estates when a noble lord galloped by in a luxurious coach, its sides emblazoned with his coats of arms, and with two liveried servants perched at the rear.

At every level of society, rank was cultivated and asserted with equal assiduity. The middling orders keenly emulated their betters.

Those who made fortunes in manufactures bought manor houses, stables and classical educations for their heirs. And, keen to distance themselves from mere arrivistes, many put together spurious family trees tracing their lines back to Saxon kings or soldiers who had fought on the right side at Agincourt. Sir Robert Peel, who made a vast fortune from the manufacture of calico cloth, contrived a coat of arms and Latin motto to give his heirs the mark of gentility. For their part, labourers and servants spent their spare cash on fine clothes and household wares, silver shoe buckles and pricey watches. There was no such thing as English peasant dress by the late 1700s, since virtually all sections of society were involved in the great game of social catch-up.[17]

The same close attention to birth, place and the conspicuous display of rank which underpinned the strict protocols at the Hanoverian royal court were reproduced in every inn parlour, parish vestry, drawing room and salon of the kingdom. Beyond court society, the subtle arts of emulation and condescension were played out in less ostentatious fashion, but parochialism implied no lack of earnestness. Even in the St Pancras workhouse there was a strict hierarchy. The inmates deferred to masters and nurses; older children looked down on the younger; and those with parents lorded it over orphans. Bastards were disdained by all. In this context, however, Blincoe probably clung doggedly to the nickname 'Parson', for the illegitimate son of an educated clergyman could claim more respect than a run-of-the-mill bastard. He might even have made the case that illegitimate offspring of gentlefolk deserved greater esteem than the legitimate children of hardened parish paupers. Charles Dickens certainly held this view. An implicit moral of *Oliver Twist* was that Oliver had been fortified against the immorality of Fagin's thieves' den by his respectable ancestry. He was a born gentleman in spite of his mother's lack of a wedding ring. Along the same lines, Blincoe perhaps felt that, whether he was legitimate or not, his veins coursed with a bluer blood than those of his fellow inmates.

Following the signing of their indentures by the magistrates, the boys and girls accepted by William Lambert all decided that they had suddenly risen several places in the social hierarchy. And, as Blincoe explained in May 1822, they now began to assume the airs of the gentlemen and ladies they expected to become. 'They strutted about', he recounted, 'like so many dwarfish and silly kings and queens.'

> We began [he continued] to treat our old nurses with airs of insolence and disdain – refused to associate with children, who, from sickness, or being under age, had not been accepted; they were commanded to keep their distance; told to know their betters; forbidden to mingle in our exalted circle.

The indentured girls even 'began to feel scruples, whether their dignity would allow them to drop the usual bob-curtsey to the master or matron of the house, or to the governess by whom they had been instructed to read, or work by the needle.'[18]

This tragic farce deepened as the day of departure neared. Having reassessed their status within the workhouse, in their own estimations the selected children had vaulted over all their peers, elders, nurses, even the master and his wife. Now the children began fighting for position among themselves, jostling to be considered the most genteel. Being a gentleman or gentlewoman was no longer enough. Everyone knew that there were gradations of gentility, and each child wanted to be more refined than the next. So the boys wrestled over who was entitled to have the first ride on their master's horses, and 'violent disputes' arose among the girls 'on subjects equally ludicrous'. The children's behaviour seems a gross and pathetic parody, but they were merely imitating the obsession with rank, hierarchy and the display of social status which occupied so much of their elders' time and money. As with most juvenile play, although in their case built on a lie, their games were rehearsals for adult life. Blincoe made no secret of his involvement in these squabbles over rank. But for him, the stakes were very high. The others were now expecting a change in circumstances far beyond their previous hopes. He almost certainly felt that Messrs Lambert were about to restore him to his proper station as the offspring of a respectable family.[19]

Nothing happened immediately to disabuse the children of the overseers' lies. In fact, the subsequent behaviour of the overseers only confirmed them in their delusion. The overseers congratulated themselves on their success in divesting the parish of so many hungry mouths to such a distant location. And their self-satisfaction led them into a rare fit of generosity. Each of the children received new clothes, a suit for working in and another for 'holiday dress'. In a show of still more unusual munificence, the children were also each given a shilling, a pocket handkerchief and a chunk of gingerbread. Such uncommon kindness on the part of the overseers might have aroused suspicion in older children. But, gulled into believing that they were a few days away from being made into ladies and gentlemen, the children saw it as only fitting that they should be lavished with special treats.[20]

On the appointed day in early August, two covered wagons rolled up to the workhouse gates. Within hours, innocent imaginings would be en route for a cruelly bruising encounter with reality.

PART 2
Into the Fire

Scores of poor children, taken from workhouses or kid-napped in the streets of the metropolis, used to be brought down by ... coach to Manchester and slid into a cellar in Mosley Street as if they had been stones or any other inanimate substance.

Feargus O'Connor (1836)

It is happy that these little aliens to kindred affection should, by the bounty of the good and opulent, be made such useful members of society and ornaments of philan-thropy.

John Throsby (1795)

Nowhere does man exercise such dominion over matter.
T.B. Macaulay on the factory system (1831)

Nowhere does matter exercise such dominion over man.
J.L. Hammond and Barbara Hammond (1917)

6

Cartloads of lumber

Robert Blincoe was desperate to put distance between himself and the workhouse. Tearful scenes as his fellow inmates embraced parents and relations before departure only reinforced the sense of alienation he had experienced there. But the parish was keen to create a carnival atmosphere. To this end they dressed the children in brightly coloured clothing, and the beadles arrived sporting full regalia. Even so, Blincoe must have been in the minority seeing it as a jolly occasion. Surely at least some of the children's parents felt serious reservations. A few had probably read letters from those already sent north telling of the hardness of the labour and the gruelling length of the working day. When the parish of Clerkenwell informed parents that about 40 workhouse children would be sent to work in Samuel Oldknow's cotton mill in Mellor in 1796, Oldknow's representative wrote to him of how parents had 'come crying to beg [to] have their children out again rather than part with them so far off.' Some of the St Pancras parents would have been no less distraught. It's telling that two children had already been scrubbed off the list of those indentured to the Lamberts, reprieved at the eleventh hour. Presumably their parents had promised that they would be able to pay for their up-bringing after all.[1]

Any parents who were overtly uncooperative on the day of departure could easily be silenced by a threat to cut off their parish pensions. They could either acquiesce or starve. But there was always the risk that some would attempt to seize their children at the last minute. Perhaps so as to avoid ugly scenes, when the children were led to the wagons they were flanked on either side by beadles holding aloft their gold-topped staves. According to Blincoe, these cruelly deluded children simply assumed that the beadles were forming an official guard of honour.[2]

The children clambered onto the two large wagons. Those who knew anything at all about transport – and the children had seen hundreds of horse-drawn vehicles from the workhouse windows – would have realised that these were not the preferred conveyances of gentlemen or ladies. Like nearly everything else in Georgian life, mode of transport reflected wealth and status. The stately carriage drawn by four plumed and liveried horses was the hallmark of the extremely rich. Those without their own stables but with plenty of money tended to travel by post chaise; faster than stagecoaches, these held two passengers, and a post-boy rode one of the two horses. Next came stagecoaches, or diligences. These were pulled by two or four horses and had internal seating for four or, less comfortably, six passengers. The coachman perched on a box in front with the guard alongside him.[3]

Travellers on a budget generally went by stage wagon. This was the type of vehicle that picked up Blincoe and the 29 other work'us apprentices. Covered by canvas or leather hoods, with long benches either side, and pulled at a lethargic two miles per hour by around eight horses, stage wagons were no more than large carts. Their one advantage, aside from cheap fares, was that highwaymen kept away, most of them assuming that the passengers would be too poor to be worth fleecing. But as Blincoe and his comrades were soon to discover, stage wagons were rarely blessed with suspension. The only peculiarity of the wagons sent down by the Lamberts was that they had wooden hoods and lockable entrance doors. Once these doors had been closed and bolted from the outside, the children were held within like cattle.

Farewell tears crescendoed as the apprentices' eyes adjusted to the darkness of the wagon. Most of these children would never see their parents again. But their sadness was at least tempered by the dizzying prospect of all the accoutrements of respectability that were soon to be theirs. The indentures handed over, and the horses properly harnessed, the convoy was finally ready to depart.

On late-18th-century roads, a journey to Nottingham was no light undertaking. Even for those able to travel in style, road journeys could be wretchedly uncomfortable. Many turnpikes remained deeply rutted and impassable in heavy rains. Surveyors of the highways were

8. An 18th-century stage wagon similar to the one in which Blincoe and the other St Pancras pauper children were sent to Lowdham Mill.

usually parish appointees, often utterly ignorant of the science of road construction and negligent in their duties. Arthur Young described travelling along turnpike roads in the north country in 1770 as 'execrable' and fit to 'dislocate his bones', his carriage having to contend with ruts four feet deep and 'floating with mud'. Although not as bad as those experienced by Arthur Young, the main coaching roads in St Pancras drew repeated criticism in vestry meetings. Early in the century, the slack surveyors of the highways were fined for not doing their jobs.[4]

The road to London from Nottingham was described as being 'as firm and good as any turnpike road in England', but by modern standards that meant little. The constant jolting as the heavy wheels passed over ruts and rubble induced nausea among the workhouse children and caused severe bruising as they were flung repeatedly from bench to floor. Then, in the limited light that penetrated the wooden hood, they had to struggle to regain their place. John Brown coyly observed:

> The motion of the heavy clumsy vehicle, and so many children cooped up in so small a space, produced nausea and other results, such as sometimes occur in Margate hoys.[5]

Few of the children had travelled in a coach before, but the sense of novelty would not have long survived the hours they spent crammed inside. In large towns, at least, they were turned out to walk. They had no difficulty in keeping up with the lumbering pace of the wagon. Blincoe remembered passing through St Albans and then Leicester, which means that they started off along Watling Street, the old Roman road. In Leicester, in confident expectation of soon receiving bags full of cash, Blincoe rushed over to a market stall and spent his entire parish shilling on a large bag of apples. One imagines that he had seldom experienced such complete happiness. For all the discomfort of the journey, he was more than a day's ride from the workhouse, destined for a far better place, and savouring the rare joy of being able to buy fruit and consume it in the open. The apples must have tasted simply wonderful, for Blincoe still remembered eating them in 1822.[6]

Yet by Blincoe's account, doubts were already beginning to creep into the minds of a few of the indentured children. Being tossed around the insides of a bare wagon was not what they considered correct protocol for the transportation of ladies and gentlemen. Some of the more tired and bruised children, presumably those who had one or both parents back in St Pancras parish, went so far as to inform the wagon drivers that they would like to return home. Blincoe later said that he was profoundly annoyed by these 'back-sliders'. He and most of the other orphans had everything staked on the Lamberts being true to their words. With hope such a rare and precious commodity, they had no time for cynicism. As it was, the wagoners managed to placate their mutinous cargo, reassuring them that all would be fine when they reached their final destination. Blincoe's excitement continued to mount.[7]

Although sleep was taken on the move, it still took three long and excruciating days to reach the town of Nottingham. This must have been an exhausting odyssey for children unused to anything but a sedentary workhouse life. But their spirits rose during the last few miles of the journey. The mile or so of road stretching between the Trent Bridge and Nottingham town centre was widely regarded as among the most scenic in the entire country. Nottingham, wrote local historian John Blackner fondly but not too fictitiously in 1815, rivalled in appearance the city of Genoa and was surrounded by scenery which 'almost beggars all description'. Many others, not all proud locals, enthused about the extensive fields and meadows that lay either side of the London road, much of it common grazing land held by the town burgesses. These meadows, Blackner added, 'spread open their flowery bosom to welcome' travellers to the town, crocuses carpeting the fields during the spring.[8]

The road from London also wove past two large pools, Chainey Pool and Chainey Flash, both well stocked with fish. Blackner deemed fishing 'a cover for idleness', but he strongly approved of 'mechanics and artisans' spending their evenings among these 'delightful meads' to brace their 'toil-relaxed nerves' and ward off 'rheumatisms, asthmas, and consumptions' by keeping 'their animal juices in good order.' At this time, as Blackner boasted, Nottinghamshire was still a largely rural county. In 1769, Sir George Savile had jokingly observed: 'four Dukes, two Lords and three rabbit warrens, … takes in half the country in point of space.' Nottingham was the largest of only a handful of decent-sized towns. But times were changing. Canals, much more economical than road transport for the movement of goods in bulk, were opening provincial towns to trade as never before. And for some distance the London road ran adjacent to a canal, begun in 1793, that linked Nottingham to Lord Middleton's nearby coal mines.[9]

Having gazed on this new wonder of the entrepreneurial age, the children would have started to catch their first glimpses of Nottingham. In 1799, it was an elegant Georgian town. Cheap back-to-back housing was making an appearance, but most of the streets were broad and well paved, and the expansive market square was the boast of the Midlands. Windmills and church spires stood out against the skyline, and at ground level the houses in the centre of town were well spaced, with fine gardens and orchards. For centuries, Nottingham had been a prosperous market centre. Only now was the economic balance starting to shift in favour of the textile industry, and especially the manufacture of stockings and lace. Reflecting their new status, wealthy hosiers ranked high in the local corporation that governed the town. Among their number were William and Francis Lambert, the men to whom Blincoe and the other St Pancras children were indentured until the age of 21.[10]

The Lamberts were brothers, the sons of Richard Lambert, who had built up a hosiery business in Nottingham centred on a large warehouse in St Mary's churchyard. As Lambert senior's career showed, hosiery could be a lucrative business. It also seemed a highly secure one, given that stockings had been staples of both male and female dress for more than three centuries, and there was no reason to expect things to change. Blincoe's indentures stated that in due course he would be educated in the mysteries of the stocking trade, though it wasn't explained why a gentleman would need to spend long hours bent over a mechanical contraption for knitting stockings.[11]

The wagons drew up outside the Lamberts' warehouse. Almost as soon as the children had disembarked into the purer air outside, the back-sliders again began to voice their concerns. This time even Blincoe had to admit that first impressions weren't favourable. John Brown plausibly recorded that a number of townspeople soon gathered around the knot of confused-looking children, openly pitying them as 'live stock' imported from London, and 'lambs, led by butchers to slaughter'. There was a cynical edge to these expressions of sympathy which stuck firmly in Blincoe's mind. The outspoken locals evidently had a grudge against the Lamberts, and its cause isn't hard to identify. For much of the 1700s, Nottingham's hundreds of adult stockingers had thrived. In fact, Blackner calculated that nearly a third of all the stocking frames in the country were in the town, more than in the entirety of France. But adult stockingers were now beginning to feel the pinch as their efforts came under pressure from cheap labour in the form of hundreds of young parish apprentices.[12]

In 1779, skilled stockingers had petitioned Parliament to impose fixed wages and frame rents, and to curtail the practice of hosiers taking on cheap apprentices to do adults' work. Parliament refused. MPs were now guided not by Tudor protectionism but by political economists of the Adam Smith school. In 1734, the English essayist Bernard Mandeville had expounded the view that 'private vices are public virtues'. Adam Smith, the Scottish philosopher and economist, had a similarly pithy formula: 'virtue is more to be feared than vice, because its excesses are not subject to the regulation of conscience', an idea which he developed in *The Wealth of Nations* (1776). His central argument was that government interference in the economy was nearly always harmful. Individuals were the best judges of their own interests, so free-acting individuals should be left to their own selfish devices. Only by leaving them to pursue their self-interest unhindered would a nation's wealth increase.[13]

Applied to the stockingers' situation, the logic of political economy absolutely demanded that their appeals be turned down. When news of this reached Nottingham, rioting engulfed the town. Over nine turbulent days, at least 300 stocking frames were wrecked and the houses of leading hosiers had their windows, doors and tiles smashed. By an Act of 1777, smashing stocking frames was a capital offence, but the magistrates took pity on the rioters. While never openly condoned, rioting was seen by many as an acceptable response to dire need among the lower orders. And in 1779, once Nottingham's squires had stepped in, the city's hosiers agreed to take no action against the offenders beyond telling a press gang where they could find one of the riot's leaders. When he escaped, the hosiers pledged never to hire him again.[14]

By bringing a large batch of apprentices from London, the Lamberts were bound to excite the displeasure of local stockingers. Their sympathy for the St Pancras children ran less deeply than their loathing for hosiers like William and Francis Lambert. And in the summer of 1799 they were in no mood for further insults from the town's wealthy merchants. Suffering among the labouring classes was mounting daily. The dreadful harvest of 1795 had caused severe distress across much of the country, but the consecutive failures of the 1799 and 1800 harvests produced shortages and inflated prices that would be remembered for generations. In the spring and summer of 1799, frosts and rain had already ruined crops, hampered harvesting and delayed the sowing of seeds. Many poor labourers were now very hungry and increasingly embittered. And this terrible hardship was soon, in John Blackner's words, to rouse 'the vindictive spirit of the people to an almost ungovernable pitch'.[15]

Presumably having sensed the ill-tempered demeanour of the crowd, the Lamberts' coachmen quickly hustled the new apprentices inside the warehouse. There they were made presentable, their hair combed and faces scrubbed, and given refreshments, though neither roast beef nor plum pudding were anywhere to be seen. The children's thirst having been quenched and the edge taken off their hunger, the apprentices finally met their masters. Mildly troubled by the hardships of the previous three days, and the unemphatic reception so far received, Blincoe now looked to them for deliverance.[16]

When William and Francis Lambert arrived to inspect the children, already lined up in rows, Blincoe thought them 'stately sort of men'. This is understandable. As local worthies and High Church Anglicans with plenty of clout, the Lamberts didn't typically condescend to address mere apprentices. Accordingly, rather than welcome the children like long-lost sons and daughters, the Lamberts gave the children a harsh, improving lecture on the sin of idleness and the duty of hard work. John Brown recreated the scene, entirely realistically, with the Lamberts browbeating the children:

> To behave with proper humility and decorum ... [and] pay the most prompt and submissive respects to the orders of those who would be appointed to instruct and superintend them.

It was a harangue designed to 'inure them to the lowest and most early labour' – not the kind of reception fitted to those marked out for gentility. To the Lamberts, it was just a question of starting as they intended to go on. Quite apart from the fact that parish children could be extremely unruly, in the minds of the Lamberts they had to be readied for the lives of drudgery assigned to them by providence. The children were then briefed on the sorts of work that they would be doing, and how much was expected of them. By the time that they settled down to a fitful night's sleep on the warehouse floor, they had been partially undeceived.[17]

The next day brought some respite, as the apprentices were taken on a tour of local sites of interest. They passed under Nottingham Castle's ancient gothic arches and proceeded to the stocky mansion perched on a 'craggy, misshapen rock'. Long since stripped of its martial function and having slipped into a state of decrepitude, in 1795 the Castle's capacious rooms had been renovated and then subdivided into swish tenements for wealthier residents. Once the sightseeing had come to an end, all the bonnets, shoes and items of apparel lost during the journey were then replaced at local haberdasheries.[18]

Despite this show of liberality, Robert Blincoe had the unpleasant feeling that he was being treated with the hauteur reserved only for the lowest social ranks. He comforted himself with the thought that at Lowdham things would be different. This idea was soon to be put to the test, for early the following morning they boarded carts and were pulled through the four miles of open countryside separating Nottingham from Lowdham Mill.

7

King Cotton

Lambert senior had made his fortune as a hosiery merchant. No doubt he was an able businessman, but the wealth he had accrued derived from a brilliant invention made two centuries before he embarked in business. Traditionally, stockings had been knitted by hand. Then, in 1589, the Reverend William Lee, the rector of Calverton near Nottingham, devised a machine that could reproduce the delicate hand movements of the practised hand-knitter. Not surprisingly, the contraption was hugely complicated, requiring more than 2,000 separate pieces of steel and lead. Lee's machine so impressed those who witnessed it in action that it was demonstrated before no less a personage than Queen Elizabeth I. Its very virtuosity, however, drew from her a stern rebuke. Elizabeth is said to have remarked: 'My Lord, I have too much love for my poor people who obtain their bread by the employment of knitting, to give my money to forward an invention, that will tend to their ruin by depriving them of employment, and thus make them beggars.' Her response was fully in keeping with the age's economic rationales, but the Queen's dislike for innovation had regrettable consequences for the Reverend Lee. Having lost his sponsor, he emigrated to France where his ideas were well received by King Henry IV. Unfortunately, religious persecution and the King's assassination wrecked his chances there. He died in Paris, a broken man.[1]

In the same century, gig mills for finishing woollen cloth were invented. Wool-finishers could now complete in twelve hours what it had taken highly skilled workers 80 hours to do. But the Tudor state, anxious lest skilled workers become paupers, again ruthlessly suppressed the new machines. More often, however, such protectionist policies were designed to safeguard the wealth of the landed elites. In the early 1700s, when the East India Company began importing cotton goods in large quantities, the government once more stepped in. So as to protect the domestic wool industry, and in particular the wealth derived from sheep by the great landowners, they passed a statute banning the use, wearing and sale of finished cottons. Only raw cottons were permitted to enter England's ports.[2]

But in the case of Lee's stocking frame, so great was the economic advantage it offered that not even government policy could hold it back for long. Over a number of generations its use grew until, by 1782, there were over 20,000 in operation in England. Often employed by men of good family, they produced high-quality stocking nets that were then hand-embroidered by thousands of women and children. Most knitters carried out their trade in their own parlours or purpose-built sheds. But anyone with a little capital could buy a frame and hire wage labourers to operate it. This was the 'putter-out' system. The capitalists charged a frame rent, supplied their knitters with thread, and paid by the finished stocking. By the late 1700s, capitalist hosiers would typically hire out 100 or more frames, scattered over dozens of villages. The more successful had each knitter make a slightly different style, so that they would always have some stock to meet 'the caprice of fashion'. The same principle also applied in the manufacture of cotton and wool cloth. Capitalists would supply domestic hand-loom weavers with thread and frames, and then pay a piece rate. Some 'manufacturers' made vast fortunes. Blackburn's Henry Sudell employed 2,000 weavers in homes spread across miles of countryside. Emulating the local peers in ostentation if not taste, Sudell built a large mansion, replete with deer and wildfowl, and rarely entered Blackburn except in his stately carriage and four.[3]

The Lamberts had neither Sudell's showiness nor his huge wealth. But William and Francis were ambitious. Their father had made money on the old putting-out system, but they reckoned that larger profits were now to be made in setting up a mill where machines were gathered together and worked by relatively unskilled journeymen and apprentices. The first of these mills had been set up by Samuel Fellows, one of a number of masters in London who enraged adult stockingers and fell foul of the law by hiring dozens of apprentices.

Fellows saved a large sum on wage bills, but incurred the odium of the journeymen to such an extent that he had to transfer his business to Nottingham. He then quickly endeared himself to the wealthier section of his host town by taking children from the workhouse.[4]

Masters like Fellows pioneered the concentration of production in single sites. The early factories, usually converted barns, corn mills or sheds, had definite advantages. They facilitated the employment and close supervision of child workers, and they slashed transport costs. They also allowed masters to guard the secrecy of new inventions. The first important innovation was the 'Derby rib' devised by a Nottingham farmer, Jedediah Strutt, in 1758. Attached to the front of Lee's frame, this device allowed a ribbed web of looped fabric to be produced, which soon graced the legs of the most fashionable men and women of the day. But for all Strutt's efforts to conceal his machine, his rivals soon caught up. To frustrate prying eyes, the first rib frames were housed in factories with only skylights to illuminate the work below. Competitors bought spyglasses and climbed the roofs to peer down, notebooks in hand.[5]

In this fast-moving industry, Lee's original frame underwent constant refinement. With new adaptations, hosiery was shaded, brocaded and flowered with gold and silver thread, and skilled operatives made gloves, hoods, aprons, mitts and rich waistcoats in everything from knotted hose to twilled fabrics. For centuries, most of this work had been done in silk, but by the late 1700s cotton thread was of sufficient quality to be used in the stockingers' machines.[6]

The introduction of cotton yarn was the cue for Messrs Lambert. In 1784, having taken over the family firm, they were being described in *Bailey's Western and Midland Directory* as 'Merchants & manufacturers of Hose'. In the same year they obtained capital from one Robert Almond, a Nottingham linen-draper and fellow hosier, and purchased an old water-corn mill on a quiet bank of the Dover Beck near the village of Lowdham. There they installed machines for producing cotton yarn to supply their own stockingers and to sell to other local hosiers. It wasn't a new idea. Over the previous years, spinning mills had been established all along the banks of the Leen, the Meden and the Dover Beck. The Lamberts now wanted a piece of the action.[7]

Cotton-spinning, the industry on which the Lamberts were about to risk their capital, had traditionally been done by hand. Bales of fleecy cotton would be delivered on Monday mornings by bag merchants hired by town suppliers. Children from the age of four or five then got straight to work cleaning the bales, removing seeds, dirt, and the remnants of the husks from which the cotton burst forth. Next they carded the cleaned cotton. This involved running it across hand cards, out of which small teeth protruded. Doing so produced slivers of cotton in which the individual threads were roughly aligned. At this stage the mother or grandmother usually took over. She attached the slivers from the children's hand cards to a length of thread and wound it onto a spindle connected to a spinning wheel. Turning the wheel made the spindle revolve. At the same time she drew out the sliver, which received a slight twist from the spindle, and thus formed threads, called rovings. These were drawn until they formed a tightly-wound length of yarn. This finished yarn was passed to the menfolk who wove it into cloth on hand-looms, driving shuttles containing yarn at right angles across vertically suspended threads; the former was known as the weft, the latter the warp. The whole operation was a family affair. Without the cash income derived from selling cloth, many labouring families couldn't afford decent clothes, butter for their potatoes or sprouts, salt, tea, beer, decent bread, or tobacco. Spinning bought them comfort, security, even the odd trapping of gentility.[8]

Yet textile production in the early 1700s faced a real problem that stimulated efforts to mechanise. Since spinning yarn took longer than weaving, the menfolk often had to sit idly waiting for yarn to be delivered. In 1738 John Kay exacerbated the difficulty. His flying shuttle mechanised the passing of the shuttle across the warp yarn, so that in the same amount of time a weaver could complete twice the amount of cloth. The bottleneck was begging to be broken. And this is where James Hargreaves made his great contribution. An illiterate weaver with a penchant for mechanics, in 1741 he invented the spinning jenny. Old-fashioned spinning wheels spun only one roving at a time. The spinning jenny had eight or more spindles, each of which spun a length of yarn in parallel, and required hardly any more physical effort on the part of the spinner.[9]

9. A woman spins yarn using the traditional single-wheel apparatus.

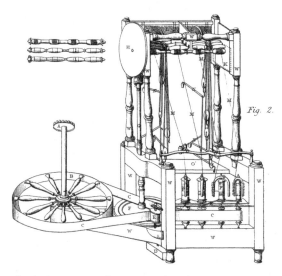

10. The mechanical contraption for spinning thread that made Arkwright rich and famous: the water-frame. Its key design feature was the set of parallel rollers at the top of the machine.

Hargreaves' jenny was effective, but something better had already been invented. In 1738 a patent had been taken out under the name of Lewis Paul for a machine made by John Wyatt of Birmingham. It worked according to a simple principle. The best cotton yarn is drawn out of the initial sliver in such a way as to ensure that the fibres are taut and straight before they are twisted together. This way the yarn comes out strong and fine. Wyatt's genius lay in producing a machine that would do this automatically, and it worked by passing slivers or rovings through pairs of rollers rotating at variable speeds. The first models were set up in 'pleasing but trembling suspense', but all his business ventures failed. It was Richard Arkwright who reaped the glory and the rewards.

Arkwright's water-frame, a device employing all the same principles as Wyatt's, revolutionised the production of cotton yarn. The youngest of thirteen children, born into a poor Lancashire family, Arkwright was the self-made man par excellence. Starting out as a lowly apprentice barber, he soon turned to bigger things. Having made a decent sum by refining a method of dyeing hair for wigs, Arkwright met a clockmaker, John Kay, who shifted his attention to mechanical design. Almost certainly, Kay told him of a spinning machine devised by an impoverished reed-maker called Thomas Highs. In Preston's Free Grammar School, the two men then secretly constructed a spinning machine employing rollers. Arkwright insisted that the invention was his alone, but it's hard to believe that he knew nothing of the work of either Wyatt or Highs.

Word eventually got out of a strange contraption operating in the local grammar school. The real threat of mob violence from local workers, terrified lest machinery wreck their principal source of income, now forced Arkwright to flee to Nottingham. There he attracted investment from Samuel Need and Jedediah Strutt, by then among the town's most successful hosiers. In 1769 Arkwright lodged a patent for a horse-driven assemblage of rollers, bobbins and spindles, essentially the same as that invented by the ill-starred Wyatt, and in all likelihood identical to the one developed by Highs.[10]

At about the same time, the process of carding with hand cards was rendered obsolete with the patenting of the first carding engines by Lewis Paul, Richard Arkwright, and others. This was a vital breakthrough. Now operatives could feed 'an entangled and knotted mass' into the carding machine, and retrieve from the other end 'a uniform and continuous sliver, ready for the spinner'.[11]

Arkwright set up his first factory in Nottingham, but shortly after he decamped to rustic Derbyshire. Alongside the turbulent streams of the Peak District, Arkwright constructed a series of mills, in Cromford, Matlock and Masson. There he acquired the genteel mansion, horses and liveried staff characteristic of the squirearchy to which he so keenly aspired. But the local gentry found plenty to fault in his manners, deportment and elocution. 'His mind was as coarse as it was bold and active', recalled one; 'his manners were rough and unpleasing.' A snobbish John Byng condemned his mansion at Willersley as 'an effort of inconvenient ill taste' and mocked its tiny library and music room. Single-minded mechanical geniuses don't always mix well, and Arkwright made it easy for the local squirearchy to look down on him through his ostentatious displays of wealth. Not that he didn't try to conform to their standards: despite working from 5 a.m. to 9 p.m. until he was over 50, Arkwright still found time to study English grammar.[12]

Arkwright's water-frame continued to be refined into the 1800s, but it soon acquired a serious competitor. By 1779 Samuel Crompton, of Hall-in-the-Wood near Bolton, had developed a 'mule' jenny, so named because it was a hybrid that combined features of two different machines: Hargreaves' jenny and Arkwright's water-frame. In this machine the rovings were attached to spindles on a moving carriage. As the carriage moved out to around four feet from the stationary frame, the rovings were drawn through a set of spinning rollers. These lengthened and stretched the threads just as in Arkwright's water-frame; but the mule produced better yarn, as the action of drawing out the carriage stretched the rovings even finer. Meanwhile, the rotation of the spindles gave them the necessary twist. When the carriage reached its maximum extent, the spinner carefully pushed it back, and this had the effect of winding the thread on the spindles in a spiral. The mule was a first-rate machine, and it was the basis for most subsequent refinements of the spinning process. In 1790 William Strutt invented the self-acting mule, which required virtually no manual labour aside from children joining broken threads as the slivers were drawn out. Not until the 1830s, however, were self-actors reliable enough to attract many orders.[13]

In the mid-1780s the Lamberts invested in machines constructed according to the latest Arkwright designs, and converted Lowdham Mill into a cutting-edge spinning factory. Then they approached at least one London parish to procure apprentices. In doing so they made few friends among the Nottinghamshire labouring classes. It was obvious to many poor families that their livelihood would be at risk if yarn-spinning were transferred from cottages to factories. Water-frames simply couldn't be operated without power far in excess of what a single arm could supply. They were also very expensive, so instead of poor women spinning at home, production had to be concentrated in large open buildings. Arkwright didn't deny the fact – on the contrary, he boasted as much in his water-frame patent. It would, he explained, 'be of great utility to a great many manufacturers … by employing a great number of poor people' in purpose-built factories. Some workers, however, did very nicely out of the invention, as the sudden rise in the quantity of finished yarn ushered in a golden age for weavers. The bottleneck which had held them back for decades now ceased to exist. Yet, during times of dearth or trade recession, the new spinning factories were always targets for angry mobs. Hargreaves had several jennies reduced to kindling. Those of Robert Peel, father of a future Prime Minister, were hurled into a river. And in 1779 Arkwright was forced to place his mill in Cromford in a state of siege, arming his terrified workers with a 'great Battery of Cannon … with plenty of Powder and Grape Shot', plus '500 Spears' and more than 1,500 'small Arms'.[14]

For Richard Arkwright, however, the law lords were more menacing as adversaries than poor men and women roaming the moors wielding axes and staves. Before long, other manufacturers were challenging his right to royalties for the invention of the water-frame, and they took him to court. In a ruling of 1785, Arkwright's most lucrative patent was quashed, once judges had accepted the superior claim of Thomas Highs as the original inventor. It was an opportunity that hundreds of budding capitalists had been waiting for. Within just two years, as many as 143 replica factories had been set up, housing row after row of water-frames. As scores of mansions in Nottinghamshire, Derbyshire and Lancashire were proving, cotton could be turned into gold. William and Francis Lambert were among those who intended to profit from Arkwright's legal setbacks. They now expected to make their fortunes.[15]

8

'Spotted as a leopard with bruises'

The Lamberts' cotton mill was a far cry from the huge multi-storey structures that symbolise a later stage in England's industrial revolution. Seeing a modest building surmounted by a large dome, Blincoe at first mistook it for a church. The Lamberts' new enterprise occupied what had originally been a water-corn mill, producing flour for bread. There had been water mills on the site even before the Norman assessors included one in the Domesday Book, their vast inventory of conquered lands. Known variously as Clive Milne, Cliff Mill, and now Lowdham Mill, it had always made use of the Dover Beck's fast-running waters. These surged through a brick tunnel under the mill and drove a waterwheel, its shaft connected to dozens of water-frames and carding engines. Approaching the mill on a jolting cart, Blincoe felt instantly reassured. Its situation, amid fields and coppices, excited anything but dread.[1]

The cart didn't stop at the mill. Instead, its drivers prodded the horses on towards the apprentice house, half a mile away. As they approached, Robert Blincoe's peace of mind rapidly ebbed away. This building, which was meant to be his home for the next fourteen years, looked unpleasantly similar to the parish workhouse he had just escaped. The one consolation was that there were neither high walls nor heavy gates. But just as in Nottingham, when the carts came to a halt, several locals approached to inspect the foreign cargo. Blincoe later recalled pitying remarks: 'God help the poor wretches'; 'what a fine collection of children, little do they know to what a life of slavery they are doomed'; 'The Lord have mercy on them'; and 'They'll find little mercy here.'[2]

These are, of course, John Brown's words. It's hard to say if a seven-year-old Blincoe really did remember what the villagers said in 1799, or even if Brown faithfully transcribed his recollections. But some of the remarks do have a strong ring of authenticity. 'Ah! What fine clear complexions!' said one, to which another replied: 'The roses will soon be out of bloom in the mill.' In comparison to those working in surrounding fields, or the scores of boys and girls already hard at work in Lowdham Mill, the workhouse's diet and daily lives of comparative ease had produced a crop of parish children healthy and ruddy-cheeked. Nor is it unlikely that the arrival of the carts caused locals to down tools and come running. At the very least these anxious children with their strange accents and neat clothes made a curious spectacle. But the villagers also had much to fear. They too resented the havoc wrought to the domestic economy by spinning machines. They also knew that if the Lamberts' venture failed, these children would be chargeable to their own parish.[3]

The children were marched directly into a large dining room in the 'prentice house and told to sit on long wooden benches alongside narrow deal tables. It was reminiscent of a similar room at St Pancras workhouse. But the air here was filled with a strange, sickly smell. The children would soon learn that this was the scent of hot oil, used to grease the mill's several thousand bobbins, spindles, levers and rollers. The odour permeated everywhere and everything, and was carried to the 'prentice house on the clothing, skin and hair of those who lived there. The apprentices were then served dinner, which consisted of milk-porridge and rye bread. Neither satisfied the expectations of even workhouse children. The bread, black and spongy, stuck to their palates and almost defied swallowing. It's unlikely that the children would have seen rye bread before. Arthur Young remarked in 1771 that the English had a repugnance to anything but white, wheaten bread, and that even the poor 'in many parts of the kingdom, eat the whitest and best'. Rye and barley bread, he added, 'are looked upon with a sort of horror even by poor cottagers.' The bread served at the mill was just about the lowest one could reasonably get on the prevailing culinary scale. The porridge wasn't much better: it was so watered down, Blincoe says, as to have a 'blue complexion'.[4]

Out of displeasure or mirth, one of the St Pancras children hurled a lump of bread into the air. It stuck fast to a wall. Instantly, the mill's governor of apprentices wheeled round in a blind fury. With a terrible, reverberating crack his horsewhip went crashing to the floor. The workhouse children froze in meek submission. John Brown described the governor as 'a huge raw-boned' ex-drill sergeant, with a giant 'carbuncled nose'. The description is surely too clichéd a portrait to be credited, and probably owed much to Blincoe's imaginative reconstruction or to Brown's literary excess. But governors of apprentices invariably ruled through terror and the liberal use of the whip. That the Lowdham one was brutal is doubtless true.[5]

Just then, Blincoe heard the babble of many voices and the scraping of feet. Within moments, the dining room had filled with mill workers. They were mostly women and children. Blincoe was taken aback at their wretched appearance. In the workhouse, they had been supplied with soap, shoes, stockings, jackets and hats. These workers were filthy, unkempt and smelled revoltingly of oil. Their hair and clothes were thick with dust and grime, and wispy trails of cotton fibre, known as flue, hung from their 'greasy locks'. The boys wore coarse shirts with neither shoes nor stockings, and the girls had on rough pinafores made from the very coarsest of linen. Scarcely stopping to examine the recent arrivals, the workers rushed to a hatch door, lifted up their greasy clothes to form pouches, and received ladlefuls of steaming hot potatoes. Until they had consumed the meagre portions they had been given, they paid no attention to the new apprentices. In exchange for answering the newcomers' questions in monosyllables, the old hands then proceeded to gulp down the many scraps of bread and porridge that the new arrivals had left uneaten.[6]

Shortly after, a bell rang out. It was a signal that it was time for the children to retire. The governor escorted the boys upstairs, while his wife, a 'large grown, robust woman, remarkable for a rough hoarse voice and ferocious aspects', led the girls to their quarters. The children, boys and girls in different rooms, were installed in double-tiered cribs, two sharing each bed. The governor wisely ensured that each newcomer bedded down with a veteran. Blincoe's bed-mate jumped straight into the crib and fell asleep, appalling his innocent companion by failing to say even one prayer. As Blincoe and the other children lay in bed that night, they must have realised that they had been lied to, and that their lives were about to take a dramatic turn for the worse.[7]

They could have no conception of quite how tough it would be. The workhouse regime at St Pancras, following John Cary's teachings, was supposed to have inured them to hard work; they were meant to thrive on – even love – long hours and repetitive labour. But there had never been much for them to do, and even when they did work long hours they could expect a good meal in the middle and at the end of the day. This, moreover, would be presented on table cloths, with salt and butter provided. At Lowdham, Blincoe noted with disgust, they didn't even have plates, and in place of salt cellars 'a very stingy allowance of salt was laid on the table'. Never before had the parish workhouse seemed so desirable an abode. Unsurprisingly, sleep didn't come easily that night. All the children, including Blincoe, were back-sliders now. He lay awake into the early hours, praying with frantic intensity and brought close to vomiting as a result of the stench of the 'oily clothes and greasy hide of his sleeping comrade'.[8]

Far greater disappointments were in store for the new arrivals on the following day. It started early. At five in the morning the bell rang out and the menacing apprentice governor appeared at the dormitory door. Within minutes, encouraged by the velocity with which the older boys leaped from their beds and by the governor's dark looks, they were back in the dining room trying to eat bread and porridge. Still half asleep, on the way downstairs Blincoe later claimed to have said: 'Bless me, have you *church-service* so soon?' 'Church-service, you fool,' responded one of the older apprentices, 'it is to the *mill service* you are called, and you had better look sharp, or you'll catch it!'[9]

By half past five they were entering Lowdham Mill for the first time. Before they had reached it, they were greeted by the stupefying roar of water driving the wheel and innumerable machines carrying forward the Lamberts' ambitions. From far off they could hear the constant clamour of hundreds of heavy rollers, shafts and flywheels, and dozens of overseers' voices raised over the din of the machinery, barking orders, warnings and rebukes. It made for a deafening cacophony, a vast mechanical orchestra with human overtones. Brutal and discordant, the sound filled the air of an otherwise still morning. As they entered the mill, the odious stench of the hot oil next assaulted their senses. Quickly brought close to vomiting, Blincoe found it 'intolerable'. Taking a deep breath, his mouth and nostrils then drew in a lungful of the dust particles and cotton flue which danced erratically in the air. It made the children cough and, unused to the harsh atmosphere, their throats were soon parched and sore.

Numbed into compliance, the children were divided into groups by the head manager, a Mr Baker, and sent into different parts of the mill to begin their fourteen-year apprenticeships. Blincoe was hustled into a room presided over by one Mr Smith, a cotton-spinner. The job assigned to him was not in itself difficult. He was made a 'scavenger', meaning that he had to pick up any loose cotton that fell onto the floor from the drawing and roving machines so that it could be passed through again. Cotton that had been shipped thousands of miles from plantations in India, America or the West Indies and then carried by land or waterway from Liverpool wasn't to be lightly wasted. Stray cotton could also interfere with the functioning of the machines, so it had to be regularly cleared away. Under Smith's unfriendly gaze, Blincoe set to work at once. Pulling flue from nose and mouth, and crouching low so as to avoid the machinery's fast-moving parts, he formed piles of waste cotton. Soon his back began to ache from constant stooping and squatting. Feeling nauseous, tired and uncomfortable, he decided to sit down for a rest. Smith made it brutally clear that there was to be no sitting down. He must keep going continuously until twelve o'clock.[10]

Finally, after five-and-a-half hours of unremitting toil, the bell sounded. Blincoe raced to get out of the mill, gulping in the cool, fresh air. Respiration had never felt so good. Then, with the other mill workers and St Pancras children, he jogged to the 'prentice house. There was much talking and commiserating to be done; but Blincoe would have realised before too long that several of the other children had it worse. He was fortunate not to be assigned to the carding room, where the ubiquitous cotton flue hung with suffocating thickness in the air. Women and children operating carding engines almost inevitably developed lung disorders. They were sometimes prescribed emetics in a futile attempt to get rid of stubborn build-ups of cotton flue in airways and throats.[11]

Back at the 'prentice house, lunch was served. After another meal well below the standards of the parish orphan, it was back to the mill, crawling from machine to machine, gathering up waste. By nightfall

Blincoe's back and ankles ached terribly. His first working day went on until eight o'clock in the evening. Excluding the time allowed for breakfast and lunch, this was a fourteen-hour day. It left him 'at night with a very great weariness', but it wasn't unusual. In future, they were often worked even longer hours. And for a paltry halfpenny extra, they were frequently induced to work during the dinner hour, their rations brought to them in the mill, cold and covered in the flue that constantly insinuated itself into eyes, mouth and lungs. At least once a fortnight they were also kept at the mill for fifteen or sixteen hours at a stretch to dismantle and clean the machinery. Only on Sundays were they excused work. Then they were expected to attend church services in Lowdham, giving thanks to a benevolent God.[12]

Blincoe's life was one of abject exhaustion. Scrabbling about for so many hours, he was in motion as constantly as the machines under which he crawled, every second fearful lest his hair, clothes or limbs become caught in the machinery. On many occasions, to make up for lost time or to fulfil rush orders, Smith drove him on late into the night and denied him permission to eat his dinner, which stood by the spinning machine in a tin can, cold, congealing and covered in flue. Having scraped off its thick coating of dust and flue, weak with hunger, he would bolt down his food in the dark on his weary walk back to the 'prentice house. After just a few days, he had become less particular about his diet.

When Parliament set up a committee in 1816 to inquire into the 'State of Children Employed in the Manufactories of The United Kingdom', it was revealed that few mills worked their child apprentices for less than eleven-and-a-half hours. Many forced them to labour for fifteen hours, with minimal breaks for refreshment. John Moss, when the apprentice master of Backbarrow Mill in Lancashire, would awake its 100 child apprentices well before five in the morning. By the stroke of the hour they were in the mill, and apart from a brief breakfast stoppage, they weren't released from their toil until eight o'clock at night. Lunch was eaten next to the machines. And the Backbarrow mill children also worked on Sundays. Moss often found children asleep on the factory floor, bent over the machinery, long after they were supposed to have retired to the apprentice house. At many other cotton factories, the children were put on shifts, some working all day and the remainder all night, so that the machines could be kept running almost continuously.[13]

Yet fatigue was the least of Blincoe's woes. Only the most unruly and work-shy at the workhouse had been subjected to corporal punishment. Here, beatings were commonplace. 'The strap or the stick, the cuff or the kick', as John Brown summarised, were freely meted out to the Lowdham children. Blincoe's overlooker, Mr Smith, cured any tendency to slack off with his boot or fist. After only weeks at the mill, Blincoe was 'spotted as a leopard with bruises'. But it was a source of great personal satisfaction to him in later life that he had refused to submit meekly to his daily beatings. 'I cannot deny', Brown quoted him as saying, 'I feel a glow of pride, when I reflect that, at the age of seven years and a half, I had courage to resent and to resist oppression.' No ordinary work'us boy, at Lowdham Mill as at St Pancras, Blincoe soon began plotting an escape. Here, at least, there was no gate to impede his flight.[14]

Throughout these early months, Blincoe nursed a deep hatred for the Lamberts and the mill's overseers. He persisted in believing that the St Pancras overseers and churchwardens had been deceived by the Lamberts. And so he decided to flee, begging his way back to London where he would alert the parish authorities to the Lamberts' duplicity. Then he would return to the far gentler workhouse regime. The *Memoir* tells us that Blincoe beseeched some of the other St Pancras children to run away with him. Surely, he reasoned, those with 'parents and relatives, to whom to flee for succour' would undertake the expedition with him, fortifying each other's courage. Yet, beaten and laboured into a state of learned helplessness, they all turned him down flat; not one of them 'durst venture to share the peril of the enterprise'.[15]

Blincoe schemed away regardless. He knew that, so long as he could get onto the London road without being observed by anyone who knew the Lamberts or who was connected to the Bear's Inn society for recovering runaway apprentices, his mission would stand a fair chance of success. The greatest danger, however, would be on the road stretching from Lowdham to Nottingham, where strange boys with fear in their eyes would excite immediate suspicion.

But he knew no other way. A few months into his period of

servitude, having waited until Baker and Smith were looking away, he ducked behind some machines, slipped out of the mill door, sprinted across the courtyard, and raced down the road into Lowdham village. Then he veered west onto the Nottingham road. It was all straight ahead now, but cottages, inns, shops and farmhouses were sprinkled along the way. And Blincoe knew that Baker would soon notice his absence and send out a search party. Despite exhaustion and hunger, he kept up a rapid pace, constantly looking over his shoulder for any sign of pursuit. He saw nothing. And before long, Lowdham Mill lay two miles behind him. It was only two more to Nottingham. From there on, the busy road south would bring a protective anonymity.

Then from behind a shop-board appeared a tailor. He instantly recognised Blincoe, stood directly in his path, and addressed him using the only name by which he was known: 'Oh! Young Parson, where art thou running so fast this way?' It's entirely probable that the tailor knew Blincoe by name, since it's likely that he purchased his yarn, at a discount price, direct from Lowdham Mill. Seizing the boy, the tailor dragged him into his cottage, sat him down, and stood in front of the door to prevent an escape. Blincoe was too tired to struggle and he gladly accepted the oaten bread and butter milk proffered by the tailor and his wife. The delicious food combined with the apparent generosity of his hosts put him in the mood to confess. He unburdened himself of his plan to reveal the Lamberts as low-down tricksters and to expose the plight of the children slaving in their cotton mill. 'Aye, I thought so', he remembered the tailor replying. But if he expected outraged sympathy he was sadly disappointed. The tailor went on: 'Young Parson, I thought so – I saw Satan behind thee, jobbing his prong in thy arse! I saw thee running headlong into hell, when I stept forth to save thee.'[16]

The tailor's talk of the devil wasn't necessarily metaphorical. While few among Georgian England's educated classes believed that Satan was active in the world, superstition was still rife among the less enlightened. As late as 1799, a supposed witch was ducked at Stanningfield in Suffolk. And in 1819, when desperate Nottingham stockingers rose in rebellion against the government, even the magistrates who tried and sentenced them claimed that they had 'been seduced by the instigation of the devil'. Devil or no devil, the tailor and his wife reassured Blincoe that they would let him continue his flight once properly refreshed.[17]

But if a belief in dark forces remained widespread, the habit of victualling comparative strangers most certainly was not. From the very moment that the tailor had spotted young Parson, perspiring heavily and with his eyes furtively scanning the road behind, he had been calculating how best to spend the reward that would be his for catching a mill escapee. Even with the cost of the oatcake and butter-milk, his capture would leave the couple with a handsome profit. And they knew that a famished boy, once stuffed with food, would be in no position to run. The tactic worked a treat. As John Brown put it, 'his gluttonous appetite had disabled him for flight'.

Glutted with drink and food, Blincoe made no attempt to rush the tailor when informed that he was to be taken straight back to the mill. He only begged his captor to use his influence to lessen the severity of the retribution that awaited. The tailor agreed, probably just to keep the boy quiet and co-operative. If he did say something, it was ignored, for as he had expected, Blincoe was severely beaten on his return. And having been thrashed as a punishment to himself and a deterrent to others, Blincoe was left smarting by the cruel jeering of Smith.

That evening, over dinner, Blincoe was admired by some, mocked by others. He learned that he was by no means the first apprentice netted by the tailor of Burton Joyce. It seemed that ensnaring runaway apprentices was for him a profitable sideline. And the day ended on a familiar note, with 'a hearty kick on his seat of honour' by a livid apprentice governor. Blincoe now abandoned all thoughts of escape. He settled down into a life of weary and depressed drudgery.[18]

9

A violent age

Smith's blows were only a foretaste. After a few months as a scavenger, Blincoe was made 'a roving winder', operating one of Arkwright's patent machines. Fleecy slivers were taken from the carding room and passed through a 'drawing frame', essentially a water-frame, which drew out the threads without twisting them. The slivers, still thick and loose, were then collected in iron cans and taken to a roving frame. Here they were fed through sets of rollers and dropped slowly down into a fast-revolving can, giving the rovings a twist. Blincoe's job was probably that of carrying heavy cans of rovings to the roving frame and transferring them onto bobbins ready for the next stage in the process. Perhaps he had shown unusual aptitude working under Smith, for children weren't often given this much responsibility. More likely, the Lamberts couldn't find enough male spinners to do the work on the money they were paying, so likely-looking children had to be drafted in.[1]

Blincoe, not yet eight years old, was too short to operate the machinery properly. The overlookers had him stand on a box, his body arching perilously over rotating spindles and flywheels. But this solved only part of the problem. So positioned, he couldn't move fast enough to keep pace with the machine. Blincoe complained to his overseer, asking to be moved to a different task. The reply took the form of a tirade of verbal abuse, pulled hair and a flurry of body blows. The *Memoir* tells of Blincoe's hard treatment as a roving winder:

> In vain, the poor child declared it was not in his power to move quicker. He was beaten by the overlooker, with great severity, and cursed and reviled from morning till night, till his life became a burthen to him.

Over and over again, Blincoe fell behind and was hit until his body was blotched and 'discoloured' with bruises. 'In common, with his fellow apprentices', the *Memoir* explained,

> Blincoe was wholly dependent upon the mercy of the over-lookers, whom he found, generally speaking, a set of brutal, ferocious, illiterate ruffians, alike void of understanding, as of humanity.[2]

But Blincoe wasn't being singled out. Before long, the complexions of all the St Pancras children, once comparatively healthy, were sallow and their spirits depressed by the routine of hard labour and physical abuse. Left hungry by the dismal diet, some took to raiding fields at night. But perhaps the gravest danger to the children arose from the machines themselves. Their moving parts fully exposed, flywheels often rotated at lethal speeds. Machinery was a constant peril, espec-ially to underfed children prone to collapsing with tiredness where they stood. Many of the mill apprentices, Blincoe's *Memoir* explains, had 'the skin scraped off the knuckles, clean to the bone'. Others had their fingers crushed, or the last two joints of their fingers torn off when they became caught in the wheels or rollers of spinning frames.[3]

During one unforgettable lapse of concentration, Blincoe's fore-finger on his left hand became trapped between the rollers of a roving frame. In extreme agony, he screamed for help, but 'his lamentations excited no manner of emotion in the spectators, except a coarse joke'. So he 'clapped the mangled joint' together, as blood streamed to the floor, and raced once more to Burton Joyce, this time in search of the local surgeon. Well practised in stitching machine-inflicted wounds, he sutured the raw and bleeding skin and sent Blincoe back to the mill. But there was to be no period of gentle convalescence. Almost immediately he was returned to his frame, on pain of being thrashed again by his 'brutal, ferocious' overlookers.[4]

This kind of ill-treatment did not always go unnoticed by the upper classes. In 1812, the Romantic poet Robert Southey fulminated against the cruelty and dehumanising force of the factory system. 'It is a wen,' he fumed, 'a fungous excrescence from the body politic.' Visiting a Manchester cotton mill, he wrote in disgust: 'if Dante had peopled one of his hells with children, here was a scene worthy to have supplied him with new images of torment.' Southey looked back wistfully to a vanishing world in which everyone knew their place – what Samuel Taylor Coleridge had aptly called a 'community of subordination'. Instead of the rich acting as trustees over the rural poor, Southey saw society now resolving itself into masters and slaves, capitalists and wage-labourers, who formed mutually antagonistic blocs, their simmering ill-will destined for a violent explosion. 'The bond of attachment is broken', he warned.[5]

John Byng, Viscount Torrington, arrived at the same view, although in his case the main concern seems to have been the substitution of impudence for simplicity. The 'simple peasant', Byng wrote, 'is [being] changed into the impudent mechanic.' To some extent, Southey and Byng were both right to regret the demise of the old relations of deference and dependence. Landowners, in their capacities as Justices of the Peace, had often stepped in during times of dearth to ensure that bread was affordable and available to the poor of their district. On occasion, dukes, earls and squires had also doled out bread to the needy, built almshouses for the worthy poor and patronised infirmaries, soup kitchens and, as in St Pancras, inoculation hospitals. The same tradition of stewardship inspired many a squire to treat machine-breakers with an indulgence that infuriated the mill owners. When an angry mob destroyed a mill near Chorley in Lancashire, containing new spinning frames, the magistrates left the police and military to look coolly on. Similar incidents took place in manufacturing towns and villages across England. Rarely did JPs track down the perpetrators with much resolve. In contrast, many of the new class of mill owners, ideologically wedded to the principles of political economy, felt little or no moral responsibility towards those labouring for them.[6]

Yet for many, Southey's paternalistic view of society was no more than self-serving fantasy. To those properly acquainted with rural England, the life of the poor had always been ungenerously paid and unremittingly hard. Husbands and wives stayed at home on Sundays because they couldn't afford decent clothes for church; women who worked in the fields had to go to bed early to give their clothes time to dry; and entire families were destroyed by lung disease after living in

the subject of severe penalties including, after 1803, death or transportation. This was crass class legislation which placed a higher premium on an elite's entertainment than on the welfare of its tenantry. In times of scarcity, as the bellies of rural families ached, squires sentenced thousands to flogging, prison or death for trying to feed their families. Nearly a quarter of those sent to prison in the early 1800s were poachers. The English countryside was no haven for kindly paternalism.[10]

In setting Blincoe's treatment in context, it also needs to be appreciated that he was living in a conspicuously violent age. Most people were inured to sights of suffering: bears worried to death by dogs; horses collapsed through overwork having fires lit against them to force them to their feet; emaciated donkeys with bloody, fly-blown flanks whipped through the streets; crippled soldiers and sailors begging along thoroughfares; mothers, drunk on cheap liquor, paying little heed to their young; and countless street-children sleeping rough or falling into the hands of procurers. Nor was harsh treatment the sole preserve of the poor. Obedience to paternal authority was said to be among the highest and most necessary virtues in the child, and was inculcated at all levels of society with the fist and the rod. Simon Place, the proprietor of an inn near the Strand in London, regularly beat his son Francis with a stick or a length of sailor's rope with a knot at one end. His maxim was 'a word and a blow but the blow always first.' Liberal thinkers weren't necessarily any kinder to their offspring. The prison reformer John Howard would proudly demonstrate his son's obedience by instructing him to walk shoeless over rough ground or to sit motionless for hours without speaking. This was considered extreme but not disgraceful. Jack Howard finished up in an asylum, but Simon Place's son emerged as a successful artisan and influential city politician.[11]

Not even schools offered respite for the bullied child. Schoolmasters, even at elite public schools, thrashed for the most trivial infractions. The gentleman's son Henry Ricketts jotted in his diary in 1813: 'Jones got a flogging for New Testament. Heysham flogged for lessons. Jessel got a flogging for not marking the ablative case in his verbs.' Gratuitous violence in public schools was self-perpetuating. Football was played with such ferocity as to be virtually a blood sport, and children died or were left scarred as a result of fagging and brawling. The parents of children attending Nottingham's Blue Coat Charity School in Blincoe's day were instructed that they must 'freely submit to their children undergoing the discipline' of the establishment. The school, wrote Blackner, was well known for the 'broad and sanguine stripe' and the 'whip-inflicted weal'. Beating was deemed conducive to learning. In any case, no statesman would gladly come between father and child or between master and pupil, since unthinking subordination to one's betters was the touchstone of a hierarchical society. As a result, the implicit threat of physical force acted as a central prop of Georgian society.[12]

But despite this widespread violence, children apprenticed to work in textile mills really were among the age's most pitiable group. Chimney sweeps and juvenile miners experienced privations at least as great, but few of those sent out to labour in fields, barns or orchards worked the hours or suffered the tyrannical abuse of factory children. To them, the passing of the seasons also offered variety, if not always relief. Those who laboured in fields from daybreak to nightfall in harvest season were usually allowed some freedom to play or otherwise amuse themselves; and at other times there was little work to be done. And rural children worked in the nurturing company of parents and siblings.[13]

So too did the thousands of boys and girls who cleaned and carded cotton at home, a few yards from their spinning mothers and weaving fathers. Marx's collaborator and patron, Friedrich Engels, wrote that before the coming of the factories, 'young people grew up in idyllic simplicity and intimacy with their playmates'. This was overdoing it. But they did have opportunities to develop strong bones and cheerful countenances in a way not open to apprentices in the early textile mills. Even the manner of discipline differed. Except for the unfortunate, a child's parents were far more likely to exercise proper restraint than a factory master or hired hand. In factory communities like Lowdham, set in remote English villages, masters had licence to tyrannise their apprentices.[14]

But the rhythm of life was dictated by the machines themselves. As J.P. Kay put it: 'whilst the engine runs the people must work – men, women, and children are yoked together with iron and steam.'

Carding engines, drawing frames and winding rovers didn't stop for impromptu breaks, and nor could the operatives. For the factory child, there was no time for sitting down, bantering or playing. And when the day ended, there was neither energy nor sunlight left for recreation. In this brave new world of water-driven machines, labour lost its consolations. The factory age had seriously upped the ante of child suffering.[15]

Robert Blincoe instinctively felt that his treatment at Lowdham Mill was indefensible. No doubt his sense of moral outrage was sharpened by the fact that he always felt cheated of a promised gentility. But he seems to have had an almost visceral awareness that no overlooker should strike, kick or flog a child too tired to concentrate or too young to do the job despite their hardest efforts. With rare courage, not long after being promoted to the job of roving winder he challenged the mill's manager, Mr Baker, about his treatment. Baker's response was nothing if not pragmatic. 'Do your work well', he said to the impudent boy, 'and you'll not be beaten.'[16]

In time, Blincoe came to understand the system that made beatings an hourly occurrence. Spinners like Smith were expected to produce a certain quantity of thread each week. If they fell short, their wages were docked or they were fired. If they produced more, then they received a bonus. Having the dual roles of operative and overlooker, the spinners felt the need to beat and bully the boys and girls working beneath them so as to fulfil the demands of Messrs Lambert. So it wasn't simply a case of greedy capitalists directly abusing children for profit. For the Lamberts had little part in the day-to-day running of the mill. This fact was later used to insulate many such owners from responsibility. Andrew Ure argued that, since the spinners managed the children, it was 'absurd' to blame the mill proprietors for any cruelty to them.[17]

This kind of whitewashing, crude and disingenuous, cannot be credited. As seasoned manufacturers, the Lamberts knew perfectly well how much labour was required to produce a certain quantity of yarn. It might be that they seldom raised the whip hand themselves, but they were certainly aware that child apprentices at Lowdham Mill were being worked very long hours and were subject to routine thrashings. They must also have known of the high injury rate. It was their business to know, for they had sunk a lot of money into new machinery and they needed to make it pay. They were also familiar enough with the hardships of mill life to take the precaution of offering sizeable bounties to local people, like the Burton Joyce tailor, for capturing errant apprentices. Looking back to this period, one overlooker, Thomas Bennett, explained that he had beaten his young piecers and scavengers because, if his machine 'was getting behind-hand compared with what another man was doing', he would be 'called to account on Saturday night [because] the work was not done.' And if the overlooker lost his position, and thereby got a reputation for sluggishness or unreliability, his family went without. In effect, the factory masters exhausted, beat and threatened apprentices by proxy.[18]

Blincoe's treatment at the boot and hands of Smith and subsequent overlookers also reflected 18th-century ideas about the intractability of the child. It would have taken a lot of patience, confidence, and ideally a touch of charisma, to win the willing obedience of no-doubt resentful workhouse children. In some mills, a token effort was made in this direction by having the children sing hymns towards the end of a long day to keep them from flagging. But as the overlookers were themselves tired and struggling to feed their families, it was far easier to resort to the one strategy that was sure to provide an immediate cure for slackness and defiance – a cuff to the head or body.

And yet, the treatment of apprentices at Lowdham Mill was severe, even by prevailing standards. It was also short-sighted. Some mill owners, if only a small minority, recognised the value of carrots as well as sticks. They understood that routinely abused children, rather than improving over time, often either withdrew into themselves or sought sly means of avenging their oppressors. Thomas Percival, the physician who indicted Robert Peel's Radcliffe Mill, reminded them: 'Love of money stifles the feelings of humanity, and even makes men blind to the very interest they so anxiously pursue.' Few grasped this as well as Sir Richard Arkwright.[19]

At his giant mill in Cromford, Arkwright held an annual festival of candle-lighting, when hundreds of workers, primed with buns, 'strong Beer', nuts and fruit, danced and paraded all afternoon and evening. There were also balls twice a year for the workers and their families, and regular prizes of money or fine clothes for the best and hardest workers. Sylas Neville, the gentleman doctor, thought Arkwright a 'man of great understanding' because he knew 'the way of making his people do their best.' Free grog a couple or so times a year, he said, kept them loyal and 'industrious and sober all the rest of the year.' Arkwright's erstwhile partner, Jedediah Strutt of Derbyshire's Belper cotton mills, strictly forbade corporal punishment. Another relatively benevolent operation was run by Samuel Greg, at Quarry Bank in Styal, Cheshire. His apprentices were lodged decently, fed adequately, vaccinated, and looked after when sick. Their treatment when ill included bleeding and blistering, plus the prescribing of rhubarb, calomel and senna purgatives. These may not have been enjoyable or conducive to recovery, but the doctor and the master meant well. The provision of apple tea, buttermilk and daffodil root tea for sick children unquestionably did good, as did the waistcoats provided for those with bad coughs. And convalescents were even put on light work. Samuel Greg's apprentices worked long hours, but time was always set aside for play – and at the sound of a whistle they would return to the machines.[20]

Robert Owen was the most famous of the benevolent mill owners of the period. By the standards of the day, his New Lanark mills in Scotland were without parallel. Owen coupled philanthropy with an acute business sense. A militant believer in the possibility of mutual co-operation between social classes and of the ability of wise teachers to reform the morals of the lower orders, at New Lanark he introduced a regime of astonishing enlightenment. He rewarded high moral standards, banned corporal punishment, gave apprentices a proper education, helped workers save for sickness and old age, created self-contained communities for the workers near the mills, and empowered his labour force by having them elect 'jurors' to take up problems in their communities with the management. This isn't to say that stern discipline wasn't practised by these gentler mill masters. As a surviving record from Belper Mill indicates, workers were regularly punished for such infractions as drunkenness, lateness, 'idleness & looking thro' the window', 'Riding on each other's backs', 'Being saucy', 'Sending for ale' and, more bizarrely, 'Rubbing their faces with blood and going about the town to frighten people.' Evidently, the exercise of no-nonsense authority was sometimes essential. But if mill owners were often hard-bitten men, not all acted the martinet. When several girls were fined over twelve shillings for 'Dancing in Room' at Belper Mill, a good-humoured Jedediah Strutt cancelled the forfeit.[21]

The Strutts, Greg, Arkwright and Owen realised that it sometimes paid to be nice. In fact, they considered humanity a precondition for success. Bosses who assumed that a good spinner could be easily replaced were sadly mistaken. In remote mills like those operated by the Lamberts, the Strutts, Greg and Arkwright, it could be very hard to replace adult male operatives. Those with an experienced eye for the quality of cotton fibres had real value, and driving them to move on could cost an owner dear. Most proprietors took a long time to learn this simple lesson; the best that Robert Owen felt he could achieve was to get his fellow capitalists to treat their workers as well as they did their machines. Even education could pay dividends. At Belper the Strutts educated their child workers not only in the Three Rs, but in the evil of Luddism and trade unions as well. As a result, it was said, 'they mostly understand that the masters' interest is their own.' Mill owners weren't kind just because they could afford to be, but because they gained by being so. As long as bosses maintained an air of studied superiority and meted out punishment fairly and appropriately, brutality was not necessary for managing child workers.[22]

Even Messrs Lambert once in a while allowed a little time for play. They also carted the workers into Nottingham once a year to celebrate Goose Fair day. But none of the parish apprentices employed by Robert Owen and those of similar disposition were treated with the same contempt as the children at Lowdham Mill. The regime tolerated by the Lamberts and inflicted by their overlookers was exceptional for its gratuitous nastiness. The St Pancras children had drawn a short straw. It would later come as an ugly surprise that there was at least one that was even shorter.[23]

10

Welcome visitors

Sometime in 1801, Mary Richards, a 'remarkably handsome' ten-year-old girl brought from St Pancras workhouse alongside Blincoe, was pulverised by a water-frame. It was the end of the day and Mary, tired and hungry, was preparing to leave. Then it happened. Her apron became stuck fast in the heavy horizontal shaft that ran beneath the frames transferring power from waterwheel to individual rollers. In vivid and terrible detail, Blincoe's *Memoir* explains what happened next: 'In an instant the poor girl was drawn by an irresistible force and dashed on the floor. She uttered the most heart-rending shrieks!' Blincoe happened to be working nearby and raced over to Mary's machine. Both he and Mary were among the youngest children sent from the workhouse, and so it's possible that they had developed a friendship. But by the time he reached her it was already too late:

> He saw her whirled round and round with the shaft – he heard the bones of her arms, legs, thighs, etc. successively snap asunder, crushed, seemingly, to atoms, as the machinery whirled her round, and drew tighter and tighter her body within the works, her blood was scattered over the frame and streamed upon the floor, her head appeared dashed to pieces – at last, her mangled body was jammed in so fast, between the shafts and the floor, that the water being low and the wheels off the gear, it stopped the main shaft. When she was extricated, every bone was found broken – her head dreadfully crushed. She was carried off quite lifeless.[1]

Blincoe tells us that he screamed for the waterwheel to be stopped. But as her blood was 'thrown about like water from a twirled mop', he fainted in horror. Injuries like this weren't uncommon in cotton mills of the period. The slightest lapse in concentration could be lethal. When Robert Owen went on a tour of factory districts around Manchester in 1817, he found that as many as a quarter of children were burdened with 'work-related injuries or deformities'. Knock-knees from excess strain placed on immature limbs were frequent, but missing limbs, broken joints and crooked backs were also widespread. Few of those mangled by machinery as seriously as Mary Richards survived. Remarkably, she did. Her spine and skull were bruised but intact, and the surgeon was called in to stitch what he could. But it wasn't much of a life that she was left with. A permanent cripple, with little chance of a pay-out from the Lamberts and no possibility of returning to St Pancras now that she had been apprenticed in Lowdham for more than 40 days, she would have to fall back on the forced kindness of strangers in a parish that resented her presence.[2]

Tragedies like Mary's were sufficiently frequent for a movement to be gathering pace in far-off London to extend some degree of protection to parish apprentices. After a series of complaints, the parishes of St Clement Danes and St Anne in Westminster had resolved that 'no more children ... be sent to cotton mills'. The magistrates of the West Riding of Yorkshire also refused to sign the indentures of parish children destined to work in parishes other than their own. And a formal inquiry by the Birmingham parish vestry concluded that cotton mills were inappropriate places for children to work in.[3]

The Birmingham vestry had been struck by one exposé in particular, the Manchester physicians' drubbing of Robert Peel over the conditions in his Radcliffe mill. As at Lowdham, parish apprentices at the Radcliffe mill were viciously treated, underfed and overworked. Peel later acknowledged that cruel usage had stunted the growth and ruined the constitutions of many, but defended himself by saying that business demands in London and elsewhere had obliged him to leave the children in the hands of unscrupulous overlookers. Peel also mentioned a more plausible reason for his lack of attention to the health of apprentices: he feared being undercut by competitors if he insisted on the introduction of a kinder regime. Yet it's too simple to see Peel as a classic villain and his critics as all on the side of the angels. The sympathy that physicians and county justices expressed for the humble parish apprentice was not a simple matter of old-world virtues prevailing over capitalist avarice. Peel admitted that there was much wrong with his mills, and there can be little doubt that the children employed there fared worse than those working at home with their parents, cleaning and carding cotton, flax or wool. Yet, there's a revealing duplicity in some of the charges laid against him.

Peel's mills came under scrutiny in 1784 after several of his employees succumbed to typhus. But few of his critics admitted that the disease had been raging for several weeks beforehand in many parts of Lancashire. While the Manchester medicos issued a series of directions for the cleaning up of his mill, rates of typhus were considerably higher in some of the county's workhouses, houses of industry, infirmaries and prisons, institutions which typically had squires and physicians on their boards. So why were these Manchester elites so keen to make a scandal out of the quite unexceptional level of disease in Peel's mill? As the consummate self-made man, Peel excited jealousy from all quarters and snobbish disdain from his social betters. We get a sense of the envy his success inspired from the diary of the founder of the Methodist movement, John Wesley, who breakfasted with Peel in 1787. 'A calico printer who a few years ago began with five hundred pounds and is now supposed to have gained fifty thousand pounds. Oh what a miracle if he lose not his own soul!' Peel was also despised by local weavers who disliked mills and feared the spread of mechanisation. A genuine abhorrence of the plight of parish apprentices played an important supporting role, but less noble considerations eventually spurred the authorities into action.[4]

The Westminster ruling circle now became involved. The motivations of peers and squires were also mixed. Some were driven by compassion, others by a hatred of gaudily ostentatious factory millionaires. And many among the landed classes were troubled by the fact that the new men of industry were undercutting their own social primacy and coveting a role in statecraft. In a letter of 1802 to Lord Stanley, the Oxfordshire clergyman Sir William Henry Clark starkly warned his noble correspondent about those rich manufacturers 'whose weight in this County seems to tread fast on the Heels of yr. Lordship's Ancestors.' Robert Peel did nothing to placate these fears, standing and being elected as the MP for Tamworth in 1797.

There he recast himself on the model of St Paul. Having achieved notoriety as an abuser of apprentices, he drove forward the first piece of humanitarian legislation for protecting children like Robert Blincoe. He was determined to redeem himself in his own mind and to shake off his reputation as a callous industrialist addicted to money-making. It's possible that Peel also hoped to head off any attempt to prohibit the use of parish apprentices altogether. After all, in his calico mills around the north country he still had a thousand in his employ.[5]

But whatever the motives involved, Peel's Health and Morals of Apprentices Act passed both Houses of Parliament in 1802. And although it applied only to parish apprentices in cotton and wool factories, and so not to 'free' children working in factories or anywhere else, in principle the Act packed some punch. It specified that mills must be clean and well-ventilated, that boys and girls be housed separately, that no more than two children share a bed, that two suits of clothing must be provided for each child, and that they be 'instructed in reading, writing and arithmetic' for part of every working day. It also made the giving of 'at least an hour's teaching of Christianity' each week mandatory. Most importantly, night work was absolutely prohibited and children limited to a far more humane twelve hours' work per day. If enacted, Peel's legislation promised to transform Blincoe's existence for the better.[6]

Peel's Act was less a forward-looking piece of workplace legislation than a paternalistic throwback to the old society. Its framers were concerned as much with ensuring that children grew up loyal, chaste and obedient as that their health was properly safeguarded. Lawmakers fretted about the illegitimate children, chargeable on the parish, likely to arise from boys and girls who worked in dangerously close proximity, shedding clothes to cope with the heat of the mills. The thought of dozens of young, ill-clad children lodged together in poorly supervised houses horrified evangelicals and Malthusians alike. They also worried lest the children of the poor reach adulthood ignorant of their divinely-ordained duty of subservience. A further consideration was the danger of the unhealthy conditions producing a 'short-lived puny race'. Decrepit children and adults weren't capable of the tough physical labour upon which England's greatness depended. And with Napoleonic forces threatening invasion, the nation needed a good supply of fit men able to drive them back into the Channel. The 1802 Act was designed to be a grand corrective.[7]

The proprietors rose up in righteous fury. They heartily resented the state's interference and feared its economic consequences. They sent petitions and dire predictions to Westminster, warning that 'vicious' workhouse children, no longer respecting authority, would turn the country's mills into cess-pits of 'open rebellion'. Those few mills that went on operating, they estimated, would soon be eliminated by foreign competition. The same arguments were to be invoked each time factory reform was mooted in Parliament. And many owners did genuinely believe that the English lead in manufacturing would be lost if working conditions were improved. What they either didn't know or didn't care to admit was that few foreign mills had yet replaced the relative laxness of discipline associated with more traditional societies with the stern regularity of the new factory system. When an Englishman went to Rouen in the early 1800s and tried to impose factory discipline there, a strike broke out and troops had to be called in. At that stage at least, England's factory owners were in a position to make a good number of improvements without compromising their competitive advantage.[8]

There were, however, a few more reasonable objections to Peel's Act. Demanding that the apprentices be educated during daytime hours meant that factories might have to come to a standstill in the middle of the working day. The Reverend Sir William Henry Clark thought it nothing more than 'imbecility', laughing at the idea that masters and overlookers would be 'so zealous for the improvement of these Children, as to send them off, to read the story of Master Harry and the nest of Robbins, while their pieceings are standing still ... [and work] is retarding throughout the factory.'[9]

The owners needn't have worried. Unluckily for Blincoe and tens of thousands of other parish apprentices, Peel's 1802 Act lacked teeth. Every mill in the country was supposed to display two copies of the Act in conspicuous places, and magistrates in the company of clergymen were to pay regular visits to ensure compliance. But few magistrates put much energy into enforcing it. Many of them disliked coming between master and servant, others cared little for the fate of children whom they considered the sinful products of disgraceful acts, and the rest performed their duties in the most desultory fashion. As a result only one owner, George Wood of Nottingham, was ever prosecuted under the 1802 Act. He was admonished by the magistrate and fined a few pounds.[10]

In most counties, factory visits were extremely rare. A Manchester magistrate remarked in 1816: 'I am sure [the Act] is not at present in operation at Lancaster; nor I believe in Cheshire.' A cotton spinner said that the only magistrates who ever visited his mill in Skipton came out of 'curiosity' to see the insides of one of these noisy new additions to the landscape. He had no idea that night work was illegal, needlessly admitting that he was 'not very learned in the statute book'. We don't know if William and Francis Lambert heard about the Act, but since they were members of the politically switched-on Nottingham Corporation, one assumes that they did. There was no sign of its stipulations, however, anywhere in Lowdham Mill, and no mention of it was made by either overlookers or managers. The Act did set an important legal precedent, but to parish apprentices like Robert Blincoe it was as if nothing had happened. Except, that is, in one curious but significant respect.[11]

The *Memoir* tells us that in 1802 two female apprentices from St Pancras, Fanny and Mary Collier, somehow contrived to have a letter delivered to their mother in the parish. Both Fanny and Mary appear in the apprenticeship register, aged thirteen and eleven respectively on leaving London. They also had a younger sister, Jane, with them at the mill. The Collier girls had all refused to run away with Blincoe in early 1800, but a year or so later they reached a kind of inner limit and could no longer tolerate the extreme fatigue, poor food, unhealthy conditions, and the obvious failure of the Lamberts to live up to the promises made in 1799. A Susannah Collier, presumably the girls' mother, appears on the St Pancras parish pension list of 1801, alongside the names of 113 (and rising) other desperately poor men and women. Susannah took it on herself to travel to Lowdham Mill. Given the extravagant cost of coach travel in the early 1800s, it's probable that she walked the entire way. Having arrived, she stayed in Lowdham for two weeks, repeatedly visiting the mill incognito to see how the children were being treated. Then she returned to St Pancras and sought out the overseers and churchwardens.[12]

The parochial officials were almost certainly aware of Peel's Act. Its passage had been announced in *The Times* in April, and they must have known of the recent decisions of nearby St Clement Danes and St Anne in Westminster to cease sending parish apprentices to northern cotton mills. All this considered, they couldn't just dismiss Susannah Collier as a trouble-causer making baseless allegations. On the other hand, they feared the crippling costs of litigation in the event of dozens of parish children trying to have their indentures cancelled on the grounds of cruelty and false promises. Few magistrates would have decided in the children's favour, but the parish had no wish to pour money into the pockets of local attorneys. And so, as is commonly the case when those holding power face a dilemma, they played for time by agreeing to undertake an official inquiry.

A few weeks later, just as dinner was being ladled out at Lowdham Mill, in strode a parochial committee. Entirely unannounced, the St Pancras parish officers entered the dining room and proceeded to taste the apprentices' food, an experience not likely to have allayed their concerns. To the children, it must have seemed that after more than two years of sweated labour, salvation had finally come in the unlikely form of a handful of beadles and overseers of the poor. If Blincoe's own beliefs are any guide, the boys and girls still assumed that the parish guardians had been duped by the Lamberts as much as themselves. Now it looked as if they were to be restored to a workhouse on which they must have looked back with nostalgic regret.[13]

Over the next few days, the beadles and overseers carried out a searching examination, in the course of which they interviewed some of the children. Cowed by the prospect of beatings once the officers had left, Blincoe said that they gave little away. But even a cursory glance at their bedding, clothing, complexions and diet was enough to satisfy the committee that Susannah Collier had told the truth. Conditions at Lowdham Mill were unacceptable, even for these degraded work'us children. At some stage in the proceedings, the overseers and beadles made contact with the Lamberts, remonstrating with them about their failure to live up to expectations, demanding immediate improvements, and no doubt citing those little-regarded clauses on the children's indenture documents about treating apprentices 'with humanity and care'. They also approached the local magistracy to ensure that the Lamberts followed through with the improvements they were now promising.[14]

Speaking in their own defence, the Lamberts might have argued that the evils pointed out by the St Pancras delegation were the inevitable consequences of cruel market conditions. Many proprietors argued that they had to allow the overlookers to use the strap and the boot because competition in the cotton-spinning market was so intense. As Robert Owen admitted, 'seven out of ten of those who embarked their capital in manufacture, in a few years became bankrupt, or compromised with their creditors.' Nor had it helped that the costs of feeding 100 or so apprentices had spiralled out of control soon after Blincoe's party arrived. The summer of 1800 had brought a fearful drought which destroyed potatoes and other root crops. The harvesting of grain began early, but rainstorms then set in with such strength and persistency that work had to be abandoned and the crops left to rot in the fields. Severe shortages and high bread prices were the result. All over the country, horses were slaughtered for meat or left to starve, cottagers killed their pigs, and many were reduced to eating turnips and nettles. In the capital, crowds of 'poor women, without cloaks or bonnets, some with scarcely cloaths to cover them', gathered to demand cheaper bread. In Nottingham, a desperate scramble for flour ensued. Mobs railed against millers, grain barges were plundered, and knots of hungry women hurled stones at the premises of bakers. They then joined their menfolk in ambushing a detachment of yeomanry carrying a cartload of grain. Several cotton mills were also attacked on the grounds that they had caused the hardship which left most of the population too poor to buy the essentials of life. Lowdham Mill was spared, but sustaining their apprentices in 1799 and 1800 cost the Lambert brothers more than they had anticipated.[15]

None of this, however, excuses the treatment of the mill apprentices at Lowdham. There were scores of other cotton-spinning mills in the area, and not all of them maltreated their workers. Some were run with the same spirit of feudal benevolence as those of Arkwright, Strutt, Greg and Owen. And during the subsistence crisis of 1800, Messrs Davison and Hawksley, local worsted-spinners, had supplies of grain ground so that flour could be sold to their workers and the townspeople of Nottingham 'considerably below the price they had given for it'. All were subject to the same external pressures, but few stooped to inflicting on their apprentices the revolting and inadequate diet served to the Lowdham children. Nor does Blincoe's account contain any suggestion that things improved after the 'farmer's classic' of a harvest in 1801. In any case, the Lamberts might well have fared better in these difficult times had their apprentices not been rendered clumsy by poor food, anxiety and fatigue.[16]

To their credit, even if their arms had been twisted, in 1802 the Lamberts did try to redeem themselves. In the weeks following the departure of the beadles and overseers, Lowdham Mill underwent a remarkable transformation. This brought it into approximate line with Peel's Act, even if the mill still fell far short of the kindlier regimes of many other capitalists. A brand new 'prentice house was erected near to the mill, far more spacious and better ventilated than its squalid predecessor. Stern instructions were given to the mill cooks to provide better cuts of meat and to serve porridge and soup in tin cans, one for each child. The apprentices' hours of work were lessened. And, to the children's palpable relief, the brutal governor was discharged. Even if the Lamberts did then hire a new 'prentice governor, Robert Woodward, who eventually turned out to be a man of unsurpassed viciousness, in 1802 life had dramatically improved for the St Pancras apprentices.[17]

Unfortunately, as seems so typical of Blincoe's early life, fate then withdrew even these most modest of blessings. Less than a year after the parochial committee's visit, Lowdham Mill closed down. As the Lamberts perhaps came to reflect, they had branched into cotton-spinning at a singularly ill-favoured time. Throughout Blincoe's period of employment there, England was at war with France. A conflict fought across Europe, the West Indies, India and North Africa, on the high seas, and, less brutally, in the royal courts of Europe, inevitably led to steep rises in taxes. The actions of enemy privateers also reduced imports of raw cotton, and English manufacturers had great difficulty in exporting finished goods with so many of Europe's ports closed to the British merchant fleet. These hardships were felt with especial keenness by the Lamberts because within a few years they saw their Arkwright water-driven machinery rendered obsolete. By the

1780s, the more far-sighted investors were abandoning water power in favour of Boulton and Watt steam engines. As long as he had a big enough stockpile of coal, the owner of a steam engine was largely immune to the effects of dry weather. In times of drought, in contrast, a water mill had to stop, and during floods it could be overwhelmed. Steam engines made production even and predictable and this, in turn, made buyers more confident of getting their yarn on time. And reliability always attracts a financial premium.[18]

The first steam-powered cotton mill was the Robinsons' at Papplewick in the Leen valley, just a few miles from Lowdham. The Robinsons' main motivation seems to have been the huge charges made by the fifth Lord Byron (father of the poet) for their use of the Leen's water to drive their machines. But being first bought them only a temporary advantage. By the early 1800s, their edge had been lost to Manchester, where hundreds of belching chimneys soon testified to its unrivalled status as the epicentre of the cotton-spinning industry. Small rural concerns, until recently in the vanguard of the industrial revolution, were left struggling to compete. Many survived, but only those with energetic and resourceful management. Now, being in close proximity to good supplies of coal and large pools of free labour mattered most, not having access to a fast-flowing stream. This was the Lamberts' death knell. They lacked the capital to switch to steam, and by the time they had corrected the earlier abuses, creditors were at their heels.[19]

While the mill was being dismantled and sold off, the Lamberts set about cancelling the indentures between themselves and their poor apprentices. By all accounts, they wrote to the overseers and churchwardens in St Pancras offering to return them. If the latter replied, it was only to say that they wouldn't accept them back. After all, the children now had settlements in the parish of Lowdham. No sane overseer would needlessly take back 30 embittered young people, especially in a situation in which the parish debts had continued to mount every year since the children's departure. By 1802 the shortfall had risen by another 50 guineas a year. And the population of the workhouse, swollen from the disasters of the 1799 and 1800 harvest failures, now approached 600. The grime, stench and overcrowding had reached levels known only in the dwellings of the lowest of social castes.[20]

The Lamberts could have simply loaded the children back onto carts and sent them to St Pancras, but hardly a magistrate in the land would have decided in their favour. They would have been shipped back within the week as Lowdham's responsibility. This left them with few options. The children could just be abandoned, like Mary Richards, to the begrudging care of the Lowdham parishioners. But this would incur the odium of many respectable people, and might hurt the Lamberts' other business interests. So, with more hope than confidence, they instructed any children with relations in St Pancras parish to write to them. Blincoe recalled that a few, presumably those whose parents were now better off, 'found redeemers'. The 'great bulk', however, were 'left to their fate'.[21]

As a foundling, the eleven-year-old Blincoe had no one to write to. Seldom could he have felt more completely and horribly bereft. But for such children the Lamberts had another idea. In the winter of 1803, a visit was made by one Ellis Needham. He was the proprietor of Litton Mill near Tideswell, in Derbyshire's Peak District. The event had presumably been arranged by Robert Woodward, the new 'prentice governor, for his brother acted as manager at Litton Mill. Needham carefully scrutinised the children, won their confidence by dispensing a few small coins, and then contracted with the Lamberts for their indentures to be signed over to him. Within days they were en route to Litton.[22]

Things could have been worse, but only just. When Lancashire's Backbarrow Mill briefly closed down in about 1811, the parish apprentices were herded onto a cart, taken to the sands on the Lancaster road and dumped there. The full story came out before a parliamentary inquiry of 1816, at which the retired overlooker, John Moss, described the horrendous conditions of the children in the mill. Then William Travers, an overlooker sent down by the managers explicitly to refute Moss's evidence, swore an oath. Under gentle pressure from the questioners, Travers admitted that the children had been turned away, that they had been left to beg for food, and that they had been taken back only when 'the gentlemen of Lancaster' had reproached the managers for inhumanity and, one presumes, for having burdened them with the cost of feeding so many hungry mouths.[23]

At the time, Blincoe and his comrades perhaps felt fortunate to have a new master, and one at least capable of some liberality. But over the next decade, under Ellis Needham's authority, Blincoe would frequently pine for the comparatively gentle regime at Lowdham Mill. His 'former condition', he told Brown, then 'seemed comfortable'.[24]

PART 3
Litton Mill

The men who did establish themselves were raised by their own efforts ... uneducated, of coarse habits, sensual in their enjoyments, partaking of the rude revelry of their dependents, overwhelmed by success.

Peter Gaskell (1832)

Take us back to lea and wild wood,
Back to nature and to Thee!
To the child restore his childhood –
To the man his dignity!

Ernest Jones, 'The Factory Town' (1855)

'Father, I'm up, but weary,
I scarce can reach the door,
And long the way and dreary, –
O carry me once more!
To help us we've no mother;
And you have no employ;
They killed my little brother, –
Like him I'll work and die!'

Michael Sadler, 'The Factory Girl's Last Day' (1832)

11

Enter Ellis Needham

In November 1803, carts pulled up outside the 'prentice house to take the children north to Derbyshire. With few regrets at leaving Lowdham, they climbed aboard. This time, as they were repeatedly hurled from seat to hard floor as the cart's unsprung wheels bumped over ruts, stones and other debris, they had no comforting thoughts of fine clothes, pocket money or riding horses to buoy their spirits. Ellis had made a favourable impression on the apprentices in Lowdham; a few pennies will go a long way with children unused to kindness. But there was no pretence of him turning them into ladies and gentlemen.[1]

After a hard day on inferior roads, at dusk they reached Cromford in the neighbouring county of Derbyshire. Here the recently deceased Sir Richard Arkwright had begun his ascent to national fame as the leading manufacturer of cotton yarn. And here, with what his critic John Byng called 'prudence and cunning', he had provided his 'principal Workmen' with 'Twenty-seven fine Milch Cows ... for the Service of their respective Families'. At Arkwright's expense there had also been built the Greyhound Inn, complete with pediment and clock and rooms for travellers, a brand-new market place, several rows of decent houses, and a corn mill. The same enlightened ethos was maintained by those by whom Arkwright was succeeded. And although the workers in Cromford were paid only slightly more than those in nearby mills, the owners had few problems with labour turnover. A few years later, David Peter Davies, author of a *History of Derbyshire*, gave Cromford a glowing testimonial: 'industry and neatness are combined,' he enthused, 'to give an air of comfort and animation to the whole of the surrounding district.' Reflecting on the mill workers, Davies spoke of an array of 'happy human faces'. He may have overstated the satisfaction of the workers, but during these hard times the Arkwright family's Cromford mills provided humane employment for hundreds of poor men, women and children.[2]

It was in the shadow of Arkwright's multi-storeyed mills that the Lowdham children bedded down for the night, the girls in lodging houses and the boys lying on straw in barns and stables, presumably struggling to keep warm on a cold winter night. Perhaps Blincoe made the mistake of imagining, as he drifted off to sleep, that munificence was a characteristic of all Derbyshire's mill proprietors.[3]

The next day the children walked as far as Matlock Bar, where Arkwright had founded more water-powered mills alongside the choppy waters of the River Derwent. As they walked north adjacent to the river, they saw on the left the elaborate façade of Arkwright's country pile, Willersley Castle, and a little further up, on their right, the spartan but no less imposing red-brick monolith of Masson Mill, immortalised by Joseph Wright of Derby's painting of its windows brightly illuminated in the depth of night. Even John Byng conceded that with their lights blazing through much of the night, Arkwright's mills provided a spectacle 'most luminously beautiful'. At Matlock toll-bar the children were instructed to climb back onto the carts. And then, still following the course of the Derwent, they began their long but gentle ascent into the grey hills of the Peak District.[4]

With pathos typically overdone, John Brown spoke of this area's 'savage' scenery casting a gloom over the young travellers. William Bray, author of *Sketch of a Tour into Derbyshire and Yorkshire*, likewise spoke of a countryside 'bleak, open and bare of trees'. And another tourist, James Pilkington, added to this perception of wild primitiveness by declaring the inhabitants to have 'rude manners' and be 'greatly wanting in … good qualities'. Those unaccustomed to windswept escarpments, and sheer cliffs, bluffs and crags, often did find the Peak District harsh and unwelcoming, especially in winter. But the valleys offered plenty of respite, thickly wooded and formed by rushing streams, white with spume. Litton Mill stood in just such a valley, called Miller's Dale, on a bank of the River Wye. For lovers of solitude, angling, botany, or nature in its sublime and unspoiled state, such a scene was hard to better. But for a bedraggled, care-worn party of children who had never seen anything so untamed, it might well have been frightening.[5]

A traveller in the 1840s, William Adam, wrote that the Wye 'pursued its way between solid walls of limestone, lofty, precipitous, and frequently overhanging.' The river had gouged out deep gorges, and Adam warned ramblers to watch their step on the goat tracks they would have to follow, to avoid 'toppling into the deep and dark stream far beneath'. Exploring the waterway in 1841, Adam sought shelter in a bluff of cliffs during a terrifying lightning storm. Crouching to make the most of the limited cover, through the driving rain he saw Litton Mill. It lay at the bottom of a steep-sided valley, surrounded by woods and angled fields. Brown wrote of it as perfectly fitted for 'foul crimes' of 'insatiate avarice'. As thunder reverberated all around, Adam might well have agreed, but in the daylight he saw only a spot of profound natural beauty. Not even the impact of humans had marred its loveliness; Adam enthused over the 'torrent of the sparkling Wye rushing over the weir'. Brown, it needs to be remembered, was in the propaganda business. And Adam wasn't alone in speaking favourably of this area. Another wrote that Monsal Dale, on the Wye a few miles from Litton, was 'much admired for its romantic scenery and picturesque beauty'. Litton itself was a quaint hamlet. And Tideswell, the heart of the parish, 'perched in a shallow fold of the bleak uplands' three miles to the west of Litton Mill, had plenty of 'low, mean houses' but it boasted one of the finest churches in the county.[6]

John Brown's description was, however, correct in one important respect. The mill had been built, as he put it, 'in a sequestered glen'. The dense woods and stocky hills, among which it lay, muffled any noise that managed to rise above the crashing of the river. The nearest habitation, the hamlet of Litton, could be reached only by a steep path called the Slack, up the hill immediately to the north. Few noises carried that far, and local people seldom made the taxing journey down into the valley. As a result, there were few more secluded spots in the county. If he so desired, a sadistic mill owner could there indulge every barbarous whim.[7]

The carts carrying Blincoe and his fellow apprentices drew up near Litton Mill after nightfall. In the cold and the gloom they jumped down and were led straight through a small gate just off the track leading to the mill. This took them across a wooden bridge, under which the river rushed by, and into the 'prentice house in the parish of

Taddington. Once inside, their eyes adjusting to the dim lighting provided by candles, the children scrutinised everything for indications as to the character of the owner and his overlookers. They soon had their answer. As at Lowdham Mill in August 1799, the appearance of the old hands, who rushed in to collect their supper soon after the Lowdham children had sat down, provided a sorry premonition. Blincoe recalled them to have been bereft of shoes, hats and stockings, terribly pale, downcast and dishevelled. The quality of the Litton Mill cuisine quickly silenced any outstanding doubts.[8]

Thick oatcakes cooked on iron griddles comprised their first meal. Oatcakes were a popular food among Derbyshire's poor. But Blincoe tells us that these had been prepared long before, and many had gone mouldy. The children were also given bowls of water-porridge, wholly lacking in milk and incapable of providing proper nutrition. On other days they were to be given meal-balls in the shape of dumplings, and rice pudding baked in giant bags, 'the rice being very bad and full of large maggots'. Blincoe's description is confirmed both by a magistrate's report and by an account written by another Litton apprentice, 'Orphan John' of London's Bethnal Green workhouse. John was despatched to Litton Mill by parish overseers in 1811. Thirty-eight years later he briefly described his sufferings under Ellis Needham in an exposé in the *Ashton Chronicle*. Though they must have known each other for a short time, Orphan John had apparently never come across Blincoe's *Memoir*. But his five-page account tallies in all important respects with it. He too spoke of his revulsion on the first day at Litton, having tasted the oatcakes, 'as sour as vinegar'. Neither he nor Blincoe could stomach them until severe hunger had conquered their natural distaste. On Blincoe's first night, as had happened at Lowdham Mill, the less particular old timers greedily polished off their leftovers.[9]

Blincoe does not say if Ellis was there to inspect the new children upon their arrival, or if he delivered a lecture on the duty of obedience and subordination in the approved style. But they surely met him the next day. Unlike the Lamberts, Ellis took an active role in running the mill, selling the yarn it produced and disciplining its apprentices. As they grew up, his sons too assumed roles of importance in the valley. Even Mrs Needham visited often. She would attend supper there, reading to the children from the Book of Common Prayer. As she did so, one of the governors would march up and down between the tables, ready to cuff any child who had the effrontery to speak or doze off. One imagines that when Ellis Needham renewed his acquaintance with the apprentices, he wasn't nearly as ingratiating as he had been on his trip to Lowdham. Ellis could doubtless be charming and affable, but this was a dimension of a complex character of which the apprentices would see very little.[10]

John Brown provides us with a striking portrait or, more accurately, a caricature of Ellis Needham. Keen to portray mill owners in the worst possible light, in the *Memoir* he force-fitted Blincoe's new master to the template of the self-made industrialist. He characterised Ellis as a greedy arriviste driven to make profits at any cost to those around and under him. Making free use of available clichés, Brown said that Ellis had risen from 'an abject state of poverty' to great wealth. He had then coarsely displayed his riches at every opportunity, 'his house, lawns, equipage, and style of living completely eclipsing the neighbouring gentry'. But at heart, Brown went on, Ellis was 'sordidly mean and parsimonious' and motivated by a desire 'to cover and conceal his mean descent'. It was comprehensively done, and bound to please both working-class readers who could loathe the vicious apostate and the respectable classes who were sure to relish despising an upstart.[11]

In reality, Ellis Needham was anything but low-born. The Needhams were an old Derbyshire family who had been wealthy foresters in the region during the Middle Ages. Centuries later, their fortunes had revived. Ellis's grandfather, Robert Needham of Perryfoot in Peak Forest, had been a 'substantial yeoman', and three of his four sons – Elias, Samuel and John – had the ability and drive to rise above his status, living in sufficiently affluent style to be allowed to write 'Gent.' after their names. This meant they were recognised as having the status of gentlemen, a matter of enormous pride and satisfaction at a time when the primary social distinction was between 'gentlemen' and the rest. Both Elias and Samuel became substantial farmers, and the latter increased his wealth by acting as agent for several local lead mines. John married well, acquired a number of estates around Bakewell, Tideswell and Chapel-en-le-Frith, and made enough money to buy the Old Hall in the hamlet of Wormhill and an adjacent swathe of land called Hargate Wall, a fitting seat for a gentleman. There, in 1760, their first son, Ellis, was born.[12]

For his first twelve years, Ellis Needham lived a life almost the opposite of Robert Blincoe's. Supported by wealthy parents, he was given the upbringing appropriate to a country gentleman's son who lived in one of the finest homes in the locality. John Needham's fortunes continued to prosper for several years. But this idyll came to an end in 1772 when both John and his own father, Robert of Perryfoot, died in quick succession. John had been a maker of money rather than a holder of great wealth. His widow, Hannah, was therefore faced with bringing up four sons and a daughter while maintaining a genteel home on a fast-declining income. It has been plausibly suggested that the stringent economies required might help to explain the meanness of her eldest son. Either way, the Needham boys were raised to understand that they would have to acquire trades commensurate with their abilities and social circumstances as soon as possible. Hannah's second son, Robert, died in 1788, aged just 26. By then, her other sons, Samuel and John, had joined their uncle Samuel as farmers in Matlock. Ellis Needham, however, had grander ideas. The 1780s were bringing in exciting new prospects, and he sensed a moment to be seized.[13]

The Peak District had a long tradition of spinning and weaving. In hundreds of hamlets and villages, wives spun and husbands wove. For centuries the spinning, as elsewhere, had been done on single wheels. In the 1770s, a few local craftsmen had then fashioned spinning jennies. In 1809, several villages were recorded by John Farey as having 'spinning mills', often no more than lean-to sheds housing one or a few jennies. But Derbyshire was ripe for the establishment of larger, water-powered mills. The damp air kept the cotton moist and reduced breaks, there were hundreds of frothy white streams to power the wheels, and its proximity to Liverpool meant that raw cotton picked by slaves in the American south could be cheaply and easily transported to the mills.[14]

By the 1780s, the innovations of Wyatt, Highs, Arkwright, Cromp-ton and others meant that numerous small capitalists could set up and try their hand at emulating the success of the Cromford, Belper and

New Lanark mills. It also helped that, after a long legal battle, Arkwright had managed to have quashed a law that imposed stiff duties on the sale and manufacture of cottons, originally introduced to protect the wool industry from imports of fine Bengali cottons. It was Arkwright's astonishing wealth that inspired Ellis Needham. Only a few miles away, he perhaps reflected, an inventive barber had made a spectacular fortune out of spinning cotton. And Arkwright made no attempt to hide his wealth. His coachmen were said to be 'dressed in the richest Liveries ever seen', and he travelled in a coach pulled by immaculate grey horses. Arkwright allegedly boasted that he had enough money to 'pay the national debt'. Moreover, his son seemed to be repeating his father's success in nearby Bakewell. Ellis, like William and Francis Lambert, let himself believe that he too could become supremely rich. After all, two of his cousins, sons of uncle Samuel, already had a small spinning mill in a field in Castleton.[15]

The timing seemed ideal. Arkwright had recently lost the patent for his spinning machine, and so the way was open to capitalise cheaply on his ingenuity. Ellis, therefore, started prospecting for suitable locations. At roughly the same time, Arkwright too was exploring this stretch of the River Wye, and by about 1783 he had a mill, called Cressbrook, operating a mile downstream of Litton. Cressbrook Mill was put under the management of one William Newton. The son of a joiner, Newton bore the grand sobriquet 'The Minstrel of the Peak', courtesy of Anna Seward, a local admirer, essayist and poetess. In an essay for the *Gentleman's Magazine*, Seward had celebrated him as 'a prodigy of self-taught genius', a rustic jewel who had secretly educated himself in the libraries of wealthy employers and attained great skill as a poet. But Newton couldn't live on praise alone, and so he accepted the 'mechanical drudgery' of running Cressbrook Mill. In 1785 the mill burned to the ground after a lighted candle fell among some waste cotton. Newton would return twenty years later, but in 1787 the mill was rebuilt and then managed by Messrs Baker and Bossley.[16]

Ellis didn't look far to find a suitable location, quickly settling on a section of the river about two miles from the Old Hall in Wormhill. A chronic lack of capital, however, held him back. Ellis sold farm lands to raise funds, and it's likely that he borrowed money from his uncle

Samuel to get things started. Then, in 1782, he obtained a lease from Lord Scarsdale for a strip of land alongside the Wye. In partnership with a relative, Thomas Frith, he had Litton Mill built there, installing cotton-spinning machinery 'on the best Construction comprising above 900 Spindles, with Carding machines.' In addition to a substantial investment, Frith was responsible for receiving cartloads of raw cotton from merchants in the nearby town of Chapel-en-le-Frith, having it prepared for the mill, and then sending the clean bales on to Litton. Ellis's faults aside, it probably wasn't an easy relationship. Thomas Frith's wife, Emerentiana, seems to have craved an upmarket lifestyle to suit her ostentatious name. Resenting anybody who stood in the way of her achieving it, she gained a reputation for extreme miserliness. On one occasion she provoked the cotton-pickers into striking by trying to lower their wages. Little else is known of the partners' early relations with their workers.[17]

The mill's first years were a struggle. The valley selected, while very convenient for Ellis's home in Wormhill, was unsuitable in every other way. Instead of using the surging force of the River Wye, he relied on a stream which cascaded down the steep hillside into the river. This water source was much too unreliable and difficult to harness. It was only the first of many blunders. A solution to this one, though, was soon found. Ellis approached the owner of some fields on the south side of the mill, in the neighbouring parish of Taddington, and negotiated a lease on a small plot just across the river from the mill. He then constructed a weir and flooded the land, allowing a large pool of water to build up behind his wheel. It tells us much about Ellis Needham's moral calibre that, having agreed to pay the landowner £1, one shilling and one penny per year for the use of this land, over the course of 27 years he hardly ever bothered to do so.[18]

The new weir kept the waterwheel turning, but the more fundamental problems of the mill's remoteness from decent roads and supplies of labour remained acute. Whereas Arkwright in Cromford could hire the wives of local lead-miners, and Strutt in Belper the hard-up spouses and children of impoverished nail-makers, Ellis Needham had only a tiny labour pool. It comprised mostly hand-loom weavers and stockingers in the villages of Litton and nearby Tideswell. Few of them had any intention of bowing to the mill's discipline. After four years, Ellis and Frith decided to sell up. In August 1786, they put advertisements in the *Derby Mercury*, the *Manchester Mercury* and the *Nottingham Journal* offering the mill for sale. But in the event, no buyer could be found.[19]

Then Ellis glimpsed a possible way out of trouble. Adult labourers were expensive, hard to find and difficult to retain. But parish apprentices suffered from none of these defects. So, just like William and Francis Lambert at about the same time, he wrote to parish officials in London. His first shipment of children may have come from St Andrew's parish, and they were installed in a 'prentice house built alongside the mill. Before long, however, Ellis realised that he had made another serious mistake. He had fallen heavily in the esteem of the inhabitants of Tideswell parish, in which he lived and Litton was located. They knew that cotton mills frequently went bust, disgorging poor children onto the parish. And even those mills that thrived had what the surveyor John Farey called the 'inherent evil' of turning out journeymen who were unable to find work because they had only ever been trained to do children's jobs. They too became a burden on the poor rates, and in turn lowered the rents that landlords in the area could charge.[20]

Ellis Needham was not a man of principles. But concern for one's social standing can act as a substitute for a fully-fledged conscience. Seeking to restore his good name, he now bought a second parcel of land in Taddington. There he built another 'prentice house, to which most of the parish children were then moved. It was a cynical but effective wheeze which meant that any of his apprentices who, whether through injury, age or incapacity, were no longer employable would be chargeable to the rate-payers of Taddington rather than those of Tideswell. When John Farey visited the neighbourhood in about 1809, he was told by a Taddington landowner, seething with rage, that Ellis had already divested himself of so many paupers 'as to threaten an almost entire absorption of the Rental of the Lordship!' Complaints were lodged about 'the extraordinary burthen brought upon' the poor Taddington rate-payers. But Ellis Needham stood his ground. Malevolent looks from Taddington's locals could be endured by someone whose business was now picking up and who had become a valued member of Wormhill's local community and Anglican congregation. There are, however, hints that Ellis Needham had alienated the affections of those far closer to home.[21]

In early 1788 Hannah Needham, Ellis's mother, had her will drawn up. In it she made not a single reference to her eldest son. An array of meadows – the Knowles, the Two Cliff, the Winnots Headpiece and the Goodwin Green – plus barns, her family residence in Wormhill adjacent to the Old Hall, and all its 'furniture, plate, linen, china … and personal Effects', were divided among her sons Samuel and John. Ellis received nothing. Four years later, Hannah added a codicil which allowed Ellis to inherit, but only in the extremely unlikely event that her other sons died 'without issue of their Body or Bodies lawfully begotten', or not having sold the lands themselves. Her handwriting, once neat and firm, was scratchy and unsteady by January 1792. Two weeks after writing the codicil, Hannah was dead.[22]

It's not clear why she neglected her eldest son. The fact that Ellis lived in the Old Hall purchased by his father implies that he had less need for a lavish inheritance than his younger siblings. After all, in the local Jurors' Books he had been described as a 'gentleman' since 1784. But there's more than a hint that Ellis had somehow forfeited his mother's love. Perhaps she disapproved of his choice of marital partner, Sarah Beard, whom Ellis wed in January 1787. That she was pregnant at the time of the ceremony indicates that he might have been forced to marry someone below his mother's expectations.[23]

By extraordinary good fortune, we do know some details of Ellis Needham's private life in these years and the kind of people he was drawn to. Three miles from Wormhill, in the village of Tideswell, Parson Thomas Brown served as curate. He kept a diary in which, almost every evening, he wrote four or five lines in clipped prose on how he had spent the day. As a clergyman, Brown was untouched by evangelical excess, moral earnestness or, some would say, religion. Clubbable, fond of the inn and his 'ale after dinner', Brown mixed comfortably with landowners and manufacturers. He also had a taste for the cards, at which, by his own account, he usually won. Fortunately so, because he couldn't afford to lose. Tideswell's modest living meant that Brown's every shilling counted. The vicar, the Reverend Richard Shuttleworth, had vacated the parish having run up heavy debts. His absence, however, wasn't unusual in this permissive age of clerical absenteeism and pluralism. In Tideswell, as in countless other parishes, the vicar received the income for the living and then paid a portion of it to a curate to carry out the necessary duties. Once Shuttleworth had taken his cut, not much was left for the curate.[24]

But Parson Brown had every reason to be grateful, for he had acquired the Tideswell curacy without having attended university. And the curate's duties were hardly taxing. By working co-operatively with colleagues in nearby Eyam and Buxton, he had to write only about a third of the sermons he gave. Even so, Parson Brown needed to supplement his stipend. He did this in ways that would have appalled any of his Victorian successors. Brown made additional money by measuring land, gauging quantities of hay, lettering sign-boards affixed to houses and carts, giving sermons for club feasts, and farming land that he rented near Wormhill. He also served as master at the local Wormhill school, offering the children a rounded education which included learning how to manure his fields.[25]

12. An anonymous sketch of Parson Brown, Tideswell's eccentric vicar and Ellis Needham's friend.

A keen farmer, Brown seems to have worn his cassock, knee-breeches and silk stockings only on the Sabbath. By the standards of the time, Brown wasn't wholly negligent, and he was probably pious in his own modest and inconsistent way. But a cleric who might have been plucked straight out of a Henry Fielding novel tended to make enemies among the more serious and devout members of the congregation. Many would have preferred an incumbent more like the evangelical Reverend William Bagshawe, late of Wormhill chapel, who had preached violently 'on the vanity of human pursuits and human pleasures', and who deemed boys playing football on the Sabbath 'proof of the degeneracy of human nature'. The highly shockable Reverend Bagshawe would have had an apoplexy over Parson Brown's behaviour. It's indicative of Brown's relaxed attitude to both morality and parish duties that in the 1830s an investigation of local charities showed that he had misappropriated over £1,300 from Bishop Pursglove's endowment. Nor did it bring much credit on him (or the parish for that matter) that he made a very tidy profit every year operating as the local money-lender.[26]

This was the kind of man in whose company Ellis unwound. He evidently felt none of the moral outrage at Parson Brown's business activities expressed by several other leading parishioners. And when, in the 1790s, not for the first or last time, opposition to Brown came to a head, Ellis stood firmly by him. The occasion was the Reverend Shuttleworth's death, after which Brown, with unseemly haste, petitioned the bishop with a request to succeed to the Tideswell living. Brown's enemies united to block him, and it was only through the good offices of Ellis Needham, a few other local men, and Brown's distinguished brother-in-law, a professor of astronomy and geometry at Cambridge University, that he was inducted as both vicar of Tideswell and master of its Grammar School in 1796. Indebted and grateful to Ellis, for many years to come he 'drank tea at Hargate Wall with Mr Needham', or he went down to see him in Miller's Dale. Ellis clearly liked Parson Brown, probably admiring his cunning and ambition. It also suited him that the local vicar was unlikely to make trouble speaking up for God's children down at Litton Mill.[27]

At this stage, however, there's no evidence that the mill operatives were being harshly treated. The only reference we have to them is the

1 July 1789 entry in Parson Brown's diary: 'Samuel Needham at Litton Mill to-day. The Masters were treating the workpeople.' Perhaps Ellis's magnanimity is to be explained by the mill having finally broken into profit. More likely, however, the treating had everything to do with the influence of his wealthy uncle Samuel, still bankrolling his nephew's endeavour. But Litton Mill was coming more and more under Ellis's control. Thomas Frith quit the partnership in 1799, and two years later Samuel died. All the time, Ellis was selling inherited lands to increase his stake, seeing the mill as his ticket to future prosperity. Parson Brown records that he had been prepared to fork out an enormous £1,500 to buy Frith's share of the mill. In 1805, Ellis made his eldest son, John, a partner.[28]

By then, his very status as a respected local gentleman rested on the mill's profitability. He had sunk everything into it, and he needed to make it pay. In 1794, in preparation for increasing his output of cotton yarn, Ellis built his second and larger 'prentice house across the river in Taddington. Then he carted in a few dozen more apprentices. When Blincoe's convoy arrived in November 1803 from Lowdham, this is where they were lodged.

12

Reign of terror

On their first morning, the children awoke in the large stone 'prentice house, the boys in one chamber and the girls in another. The beds were arranged in tiers as at Lowdham, but here they slept three to each. Orphan John reckoned there were about 100 apprentices in 1811. Blincoe's earlier estimates, ranging from 160 to 200, are clearly inaccurate since official inspectors, in 1807 and then in 1811, both gave figures of around 80. Whatever the exact number, the apprentices were tightly squeezed in and denied any kind of privacy.[1]

Here the bell sounded before five o'clock in the morning. Immediately on hearing it, the apprentices rushed down a staircase, crossed the bridge connecting the Taddington and Tideswell sides of the River Wye, and entered the mill. The experience was in no way novel for them. The sickly smell of hot grease, the sonorous din of water in the wheelhouse, the motion of rollers, shafts, frames and flywheels, and the air thickly suspended with flue, were all just as they had been at Lowdham. And, once again, Blincoe was assigned the job of roving winder.

The children were not fed before they entered the mill. They took up their assigned positions, bellies empty and aching, with three, four or even five hours' hard work ahead of them before the bell announcing breakfast. Iron cans, seldom washed, were then deposited beside their machines. They contained a watery oaten porridge which was occasionally augmented with a few boiled onions. One or two oatcakes completed the meal. Whenever the machinery permitted, the hungry apprentices scraped off the flue and took hasty mouthfuls.[2]

They worked on until half past twelve or one o'clock. Forty minutes were set aside for lunch, though most of this was spent cleaning machines. Orphan John told of how, this task completed, the children would rush to a pantry door in the mill, across which a bar was firmly fixed. Behind it stood 'an old man with a stick' who guarded and dispensed the provisions. Oatcakes were amassed in two piles, one buttered, the other treacled. There were also cans of either buttermilk or skim-milk. Each child was asked: 'Which 'll'ta have, butter or treacle, sweet or sour?' Having made their selection, they gulped down their milk and raced back to their machines, eating oatcakes as they went. Blincoe's account differs from Orphan John's in that he claims that buttermilk was provided only 'very scantily'. Perhaps, in their attempts to blacken Ellis Needham's reputation, either Brown or Blincoe was guilty of exaggeration. But this seems unlikely, for a magistrate visiting the mill in 1811 said absolutely nothing of buttermilk or skim-milk. And given that the Needhams tried to show the mill in its best possible light when paying host to local worthies, the fact that this detail went unmentioned strongly suggests that milk wasn't routinely supplied until after Orphan John's later arrival.[3]

Robert Blincoe and Orphan John do agree on the fact that there was no sitting down to eat. Only at nine or ten o'clock at night, after more than sixteen hours of work, and with less than half an hour to rest, did the wheel finally come to a stand. The absence of milk in the mill diet, combined with near-constant standing during the day and the awkward motions required to operate the machines, took a heavy toll on Blincoe. At the age of fifteen, as he entered puberty and needed proper nutrition to build up healthy bones, his legs began to bow. Reflecting on scores of similar cases in 1836, the physician Peter Gaskell was to write that at this age the long bones of the legs are 'soft, yielding [and] bend under pressure' and are 'easily made to assume curvatures and alterations'. Continuous standing and monotonous movements ensured that for the remainder of his life Blincoe would walk with difficulty on buckled legs.[4]

Hardly a textile mill in the country required children to work such long shifts without giving them an opportunity to rest. And on some days, Blincoe recorded, the overseers forbade the children from collecting their food, an order often sweetened with the promise, seldom fulfilled, of their receiving an extra halfpenny in wages. Then they would work for upwards of seventeen consecutive hours without any respite at all. But even by the end of their first day, the children knew that life at Litton would be at least as bad as it had been at Lowdham before the parish officers had made their unexpected visit. And by Friday of this first week, they had a good idea that it was to be much worse. This was the one day a week when the apprentices were allowed to wash, and they had to use the river to do it. Instead of soap, they were each given a handful of oatmeal. Blincoe was appalled to see some of the children so pained with hunger that they ate the oatmeal. They then washed themselves as best they could with handfuls of sand and clay clawed up from the river bed. Older girls took on the unenviable job of combing the hair of the younger apprentices, waging a vain battle against head lice. According to Blincoe, particularly stubborn infestations were treated using the barbaric method of applying pitch caps to the head, which were left to dry and then torn off, bringing away pitch, lice, hair and layers of skin. What most alarmed the newcomers, however, were the bruises and weals they saw all over the bodies of the existing apprentices.[5]

Saturdays were the worst. Then, the children worked until eleven o'clock or midnight; eighteen or more hours of physical labour without a break and on the meanest of diets. During periods of drought, when the wheel turned too sluggishly to drive the shafts, the apprentices would enjoy a brief hiatus. But they made up for it once rains fell and the river was in surge. Then the wheel turned all day and all night. Overworked and malnourished, the children, Blincoe said, 'often dropped down at the frames', undone by weariness. Only on Sundays did they rest.[6]

Yet rather than being allowed to play on the Sabbath, the apprentices were corralled into a room in which a school-teacher instructed them in the rudiments of grammar. They were also introduced to carefully selected passages of scripture. Unlikely to have been one of them was Matthew 18:6: 'Whosoever shall offend one of these little ones which believe in me, it were better that a millstone were hanged about his neck, and that he were drowned in the depth of the sea.' These young boys and girls, their limbs aching and barely able to stay awake, derived little benefit from their schooling. And once lessons were over, they were herded back to the mill and ordered to clean the machinery. Making children work on the Lord's day would have shocked some of the parish's respectable inhabitants. But with Ellis

Needham as his patron and protector, Parson Brown wasn't in a position to complain, even if he did happen to disapprove. Perhaps he squared his conscience by taking false comfort in the fact that as the apprentices were all housed in Taddington they weren't his direct responsibility.[7]

The one real blessing on Sunday was the taste of meat. Even then, it was barely more than a flavour. Ellis bought in only the cheapest bacon, which was dumped alongside turnips or potatoes into a vast cauldron of boiling water. It speaks of his reliability as an observer that Blincoe admitted that the potatoes were washed. But that the vegetables were free from grit and dirt, and to some extent peeled, owed much less to compassion than to Ellis Needham's mechanical ingenuity. When John Farey visited the mill he was charmed by a contraption set up by the weir, comprising a hollow cone which could be rotated by hand. When vegetables were thrown into it they were continually dashed against its rough surface, striking off skin and detritus. A few of these vegetables were tossed into the cauldron and boiled to produce a broth which was poured into the apprentices' 'dirty wooden bowls'. Then a mush of soggy vegetables and bacon slices was divided among the children. Some of the broth was always kept back, however. It reappeared later, bulked out by water and oatmeal, as a less-than-appetising supper or breakfast.[8]

As a roving winder, Blincoe had struggled to keep up at Lowdham, but here at Litton Mill the slivers were passed through the rollers at an even greater speed. Over and over again he fell behind. The children's chaperone on the journey had been Robert Woodward, their governor at Lowdham. Now an overlooker at the mill, he noticed Blincoe's difficulties and struck the boy to the ground with a heavy, open-handed blow. The brutality of Robert and his brother William was to be one of the constant features of the next decade of Blincoe's existence. Seldom was there a let-up.

Blincoe couldn't say how often he was beaten; he simply remarked that for ten years his body was 'never free from contusions, and from wounds inflicted by the cruel master whom he served, by his sons, or his brutal and ferocious and merciless overlookers.' Brown doesn't give us much in the way of a narrative for Blincoe's stay at Litton. Instead he provides a detailed and horrifying litany of the sadistic cruelties practised. There must have been days when even Robert Woodward left the boy alone, but the abuse was constant enough to make Blincoe's life all but intolerable. In these years he began rueing the day on which he had been taken to Dr Woodville's smallpox hospital to be inoculated. Blincoe almost certainly became prey to depression.

This is hardly surprising. The *Memoir* describes how Robert Woodward would kick him into the air, floor him with slaps and punches, or thrash him with sticks and rope-ends. The overlookers, Brown heard, exulted in these barbaric displays of their arbitrary power. They gathered round, laughingly tormenting Blincoe and the other victims. Both Blincoe and Orphan John spoke of many different sadistic practices. If they were too slow, clumsy, or even just happened to be there, the apprentices were flogged with belts, the metal buckles cutting into flesh; they had heavy metal rollers hurled at their heads, occasionally cracking against skulls and causing bleeding, bruising and severe swelling; they were lifted up by the ears and hurled to the ground, having been shaken violently; they were forced to eat dirty pieces of candle and tobacco spittle, and to open their mouths for the overlookers to spit into; they had sharp nails dug into their ear lobes; they were tricked into eating tar, thinking they had been given treacle; and they even had their teeth filed so that, guffawed Robert Woodward, they might 'eat [their] Sunday dinner the better'. A favourite trick was to hang weights from children's shoulders and then insist that they work encumbered for the rest of the day. Another involved screwing hand-vices, weighing a pound apiece, to the children's ears. Such cruelty left permanent scars. In 1833 Blincoe revealed to one of His Majesty's Commissioners the heavy lines of scarring behind each ear where finger nails and small vices had punctured and gripped. John Brown too noted these mutilations.[9]

Blincoe identified Robert Woodward as the most savage of his tormentors, but two others, Merrick and Charnock, were willing sidekicks. Not unlike medieval torturers, the three appear to have taken pride in their malicious ingenuity. Litton Mill had spinning machines rather like the mules devised by Samuel Crompton in 1779, and Woodward devised several techniques of abuse involving them. Blincoe repeatedly had his arms strapped to the cross-bar running over the mules, so that his legs dangled down into the path of the carriage as it was first drawn away from the wall and soon after pushed back by the spinner. Each time the frame moved outwards and then returned, Blincoe had to raise his legs. If he didn't, he would receive severe bruises or broken bones from the heavy carriage and its row of fast-turning spindles. But his abusers ensured that harm was always done by beating him around the shins.[10]

At other times, Blincoe was sent beneath the mule to clear away waste cotton. To avoid serious injury from the carriage returning after a draw, this was a job to be done little by little, the child removing some on each cycle and then rapidly getting out of the way. On one occasion, Blincoe was told to clear all the cotton waste in a single draw. With the alternative a severe drubbing from Woodward and his associates, he swung under as soon as the carriage moved outwards and frantically pushed the cotton before him, hoping to exit the other side before the returning carriage trapped him inside. He wasn't quick enough. His head became jammed between the carriage and the headpiece, tearing skin and rupturing blood vessels. Unrepentant, Woodward thrashed him and bid him return to work.[11]

The mechanism of the mule suggested to Robert Woodward another vicious diversion. Blincoe was made to stand on a cylinder, about three feet high, in front of the machine. His hands were tied behind his back. As the carriage came out, it knocked the can over and Blincoe went sprawling across the floor. The pleasure for the over-lookers was to see their victim strive with all his might to avoid falling onto the spindles, since doing so would probably 'have lamed him for life'. Another sadistic sport practised in Miller's Dale involved tying the children's hands and one leg behind their backs and then forcing them to hop in the vicinity of the spinning machines. If apprentices didn't move with sufficient 'activity', the 'overlooker would strike a blow with his clenched fist, or cut his head open by flinging rollers.' At other times, Woodward and his acolytes would fetch heavy sticks from the woods around the mill and then force the boys to carry one another upon their backs while they chased after them, delivering savage blows to their heads and backs.[12]

Before long, the *Memoir* tells us, Blincoe had been so brutalised that there 'was not … a free spot on which to inflict a blow! His ears

13. Auguste Hervieu's depiction of the interior of a cotton factory for Frances Trollope's 1839 novel *Michael Armstrong*. It shows dreadfully malnourished child scavengers, unkempt and overworked female piecers, and several brutal overseers.

were swollen and excoriated, his head, in the most deplorable state imaginable.' Even his tormentors recoiled when Blincoe was stripped naked for another thrashing to find that 'many of the bruises on his body had suppurated.' So tender were his wounds, Blincoe recollected, that 'he was forced to sleep on his face, if sleep he could obtain, in so wretched a condition.' And yet, as he took pains to point out in his *Memoir* and elsewhere, others were treated far worse than he. A young man called James Nottingham, nicknamed 'Blackey' because of his dark eyes, hair and complexion, was beaten so often and so severely that he declined into a state of melancholy oblivion. Incontinent 'of stools and urine', unable to work, and incapable of defending himself, Nottingham was routinely plundered for his rations. Over and over again he was hurled into the pool behind the weir, to the delight of Woodward and his fellows. He was then made to sit in the open as water was pumped over him, and 'some stout fellow was employed to sluice the poor wretch with pails of water, flung with all possible fury into his face.' Nottingham took to creeping 'into holes and corners' so as 'to avoid his tormentors'. More than a decade later, John Brown claimed to have found him working in a factory at Blackburn. Although he was prone to exaggeration, Brown's account sounds authentic. Nottingham, he said, was perfectly tranquil and his knees free from deformities. But he claimed to have amnesia from his Litton days, having 'nearly lost [his] senses'. Another victim of abuse, a local girl called Phebe Rag, is said to have been clamped in heavy leg-irons to restrain her from running away. In a fit of desperation, she flung herself into the pool from the bridge leading to the 'prentice house. Close to death, she was hauled out. Worried that others might emulate her, Ellis sent her back to her parents in nearby Cromford.[13]

The *Memoir* tells us that several of the Litton overlookers had been parish apprentices themselves. For John Brown, this fact displayed 'human nature in its worst state'. Having been cuffed, punched and kicked in their time, they served up the same rough treatment to others. They perhaps felt that to withhold their own blows would have involved an implicit recognition on their part that the Litton apprentices were somehow better or more deserving than they had been in their own day. Never happy within themselves, seeing children in a state of abject fear and suffering also brought them, the abused, the satisfaction of knowing that there were others far worse off than themselves. And when apprentices trembled before them it gave them at least an illusion of power and importance. Thus the cycle of cruelty turns through the generations. The callousness of the original abuser is perpetuated.[14]

In 1833, Blincoe was asked whether or not the masters participated in the ill-treatment of apprentices. A frequently posed question, it was informed by the common belief, endorsed by Andrew Ure, that any physical violence was meted out by vicious overlookers who did so without the knowledge of the mill managers and proprietors. Sometimes this was the case. As we have seen, Robert Peel never flogged apprentices at Radcliffe Mill, and he probably didn't reflect enough on what happened in his mills to wonder if others did. But in 1833 Blincoe, speaking of Robert Woodward's sadistic practices, answered unequivocally: 'The masters have often seen them ... and have been assistants in them.'[15]

Orphan John's story is in full agreement. Blincoe considered Ellis to be as cruel as any of the overlookers. And while his own barbarity was bad enough, having indulged it, he gave the overlookers licence to do as they pleased. Orphan John told of how Ellis would punch and kick, then walk away, before suddenly wheeling round to deliver further blows. He would do this over and over again until exhausted or pacified. Blincoe had particular contempt for John Needham, Ellis's eldest son and business partner. John, a mere teenager when the St Pancras children arrived at Litton, strictly followed the 'example of his father'. Only one thing did Blincoe have to say in his favour – John once exercised discretion and decided against beating him. He had sent Robert Woodward to a nearby coppice, called the Twitchell, to fetch a decent stick, and then 'laughingly' made Blincoe strip. Finding him to be already covered in bruises and suppurating welts, as was so often the case, John had enough residual decency to abstain from giving the boy another 'flanking'.[16]

To avoid charges of lewdness, Blincoe's *Memoir* said little of John Needham's treatment of young girls, though it referred darkly to him making 'those unhappy creatures ... at once the victims of his ferocity and lust'. By the time Orphan John arrived, two other Needham sons, Charles and Frank, were in their teens. For years, he said, 'they too lorded it over the children at the mill', thrashing them with hazel sticks and lifting up the petticoats of the girls 'out of bravado' to flog them as well. Nor was Mrs Needham innocent of what happened down in Miller's Dale. It didn't seem to perturb her that apprentices aged seven, eight and nine were apparently struck as she read from the Book of Common Prayer.[17]

It has occasionally been suggested by historians that the kinds of cruelty meted out to Blincoe and the other Litton Mill apprentices rarely exceeded the routine violence used to reform wayward children in the free schools attended by many thousands of poor boys and girls. This is nonsense. Masters at these schools were told to punish repeat offenders by confining them in closets, suspending them in baskets, washing them in public, or making them wear fool's caps. These were rituals of corrective humiliation, not potentially lethal exercises in cruelty.[18]

Of course, in practice most of these poor man's schools meted out far severer discipline. As master of Wormhill school, on one occasion Parson Brown was severely chastised by a parent for thrashing a boy too hard. In his diary he once recorded without comment that he had given his maid a 'good drubbing' for stealing butter and raspberry wine. Brown's reliance on corporal punishment is also indicated by a diary entry of 1790: 'Will Allsop brought me some birch to school this morning and I made 4 rods.' Members of the lower orders in Georgian England were often beaten harder and more often because they were assumed to have a higher tolerance for pain. When Dr Monro, the physician of London's Bethlehem Hospital, was challenged about the wretched state of the lunatics in his care, he replied that only 'pauper lunatics' were put in 'chains and fetters' since 'a Gentleman would not like it'. The author of *The Chimney-Sweeper's Friend* felt the need to remind his readers that 'plebeian flesh is as sensible of pain as that which is noble'. Flogging a parish orphan simply didn't trouble the conscience as much as beating the child of a social equal. Most people also recognised that work'us children could be difficult to handle. Ill-treated or not, they were often surly, spiteful and disobedient. At nearby Cressbrook Mill, two boys were whipped for plucking roses from a bush outside the master's house. Asked why, they couldn't explain. In their defence, Wordsworth might have said that they had been inspired by an instinctive love for natural beauty; more likely, however, it was a compulsive act of angry rebellion that was bound to be punished or their master lose face. Confronted by unruliness, most apprentice masters reached for the birch with little or no reflection. In this respect, Ellis Needham was not alone. Since parish apprentices were a long way down the social hierarchy, they tended to have only the lightest hold on the sympathy of their betters.[19]

Yet very few people behaved with the callousness of the master and overlookers at Litton Mill. Parson Brown struck his pupils, but also played marbles and cards with them when not in the mood for the *Colloquies* of Corderius or Oliver Goldsmith's *History of England*. The only treat offered by the Needhams, after those rare celebrations recorded in the 1790s, was half a pint of beer on Christmas Eve. Arkwright, Owen, Greg and Strutt had shown that there were many ways of securing compliance among parish apprentices. At Litton Mill, the owners and overlookers had only one: naked force.[20]

One or two scholars have also questioned whether the enormities Blincoe described ever took place. The magistrates who were soon to arrive at the mill, and who wrote up highly unfavourable reports, provide some corroboration. So does the testimony of Orphan John, and that of another apprentice, John Joseph Betts, who wrote to back up Blincoe's account after its first publication in a Radical newspaper. But we also have more tangible evidence. The dreadful scarring on Blincoe's ears is powerful confirmation of his story. An overlooker capable of screwing hand-vices to a small boy's ears is more than capable of making him sweep cotton waste in one draw and suspending him above a dangerous machine. There's no cause to doubt that Robert Woodward had gratuitous malice in abundance; and there's good reason to think that Ellis Needham had a violent temper. In 1816 Anthony Gregory, Litton's headborough (essentially a local constable), brought a suit against Ellis and his son Samuel Needham for having assaulted him while in the execution of his duty. Ellis and Samuel entered a plea of not guilty, but ignored repeated orders to appear before the magistrates. Presumably bullied into appearing by their sureties, who faced losing £20 each, they came before the Epiphany Sessions of 1817, where both father and son changed their pleas to guilty. Perhaps, after two decades of thrashing young boys and girls at his mill, Ellis found that violence had become a habitual response to his being obstructed or crossed.[21]

The death toll at Litton Mill lends further support to Blincoe's tale of woe. The *Memoir* claims that at one time 'forty boys' were 'sick at once', so that for a while the mill had to be closed. Blincoe also spoke of apprentices dying in their scores and Ellis Needham having to bury them in the churchyard at Taddington to avoid raising criticism among the more humane residents of his own parish of Tideswell. The burial registers of Tideswell, Litton, Wormhill and Taddington do not support the allegation of waves of child fatalities. Even so, the wretched diet and long hours explain why in fewer than thirty years, from 1783 to 1810, 27 apprentices died at Litton Mill, whereas only six perished at nearby Cressbrook cotton mill. There was a severe smallpox outbreak in the region in 1803, but this leaves unexplained the disparity in mortality rates between Litton and Cressbrook. At a fairly well-conducted spinning factory like Thomas Ashton's in Hyde, just across the county border in Lancashire, the annual mortality rate was roughly one in 200. Needham presided over a yearly death rate well over double this figure; and even this is to understate the death rate as not all those who died were recorded as apprentices in the parish registers. And Blincoe spoke entirely truthfully of Needham's cunning in dividing the burials among several churchyards. Not even a bastard orphan could be denied a proper Christian burial, so five were interred in Tideswell, one in Ellis's own hamlet of Wormhill, and the majority, 21 in total, on the other side of the river in Taddington. Ellis was hiding the evidence as best he could.[22]

Despite these deaths, Ellis refused to allow children to return to the 'prentice house unless totally unresponsive to the whip and fist. Then he would occasionally send for a physician. In line with contemporary medical wisdom, which saw epidemic disease as the result of foul air, asphyxiating gases, and effluvia arising from filth and vermin, the doctor would then burn pitch and tobacco in the 'prentice house and sprinkle vinegar on the floor. The sick were also treated to tea sweetened with treacle, wheaten bread and small portions of mutton and boiled beef. Blincoe recalled a physician visiting the mill and remarking, as he repeated many years later, that all the poorly children needed was 'kitchen physic and more rest'. Ellis Needham's brutality, and the regime of neglect at Litton Mill, is all the more surprising given that he stood to lose out considerably from his apprentices dying. Fatalities created the need for more to be shipped in and trained. More to the point, masters received a second instalment of the parish's fee once an apprentice reached 21. Intelligent self-interest, however, wasn't Ellis's strong suit. He had a knack for mistaking plain inhumanity for commercial adroitness.[23]

There are occasional glimpses in Blincoe's *Memoir* and Orphan John's recollections of how the apprentices bore their appalling sufferings. Long years of cruelty magnified different aspects of human nature. At times they exulted in the victimisation of their peers, relieved that the fury of masters and overlookers was directed elsewhere. On occasion they would steal food from one another. Brutality could make boys and girls callous, leaving them coldly insensitive to the pain of others. Blincoe told of one boy, Thomas Linsey, having decided on a Sunday night to save some of his dinner for the early morning. He took a sliver of bacon, pressed it between two pieces of oatcake and took it to bed, placing it under his head (the children did not have pillows). At three or four in the morning, some of the apprentices realised that Thomas had died in his sleep. Without hesitation, they began ransacking his cold body for the bacon sandwich they had seen prepared with jealous hunger. The boy's pockets were frantically turned out, and the tin from which he ate his porridge and soup upturned, long before his demise was reported. Malnutrition had left the mill children with little comprehension of the usual niceties surrounding the deaths of comrades and friends.[24]

Blincoe tells us that he was driven by his groaning belly even to go rummaging in the mill's dunghill for discarded cabbage leaves and potato or turnip parings. His preferred ruse, however, was to steal from Ellis Needham's pigs, kept in a sty close to where he worked. Whenever he could, Blincoe crept to the sty, 'plunged his hand into the loop holes' in the fence, reached into their trough, and drew out the doughy oatmeal balls made for them. Brown wrote:

> The food thus obtained from a pig's trough, and perhaps, defiled by their filthy chops, was exultingly conveyed to the privy or the

duck-hole, and there devoured with a much keener appetite than it would have been by the pigs.

Blincoe wasn't alone in this risky undertaking. In fact, so many children stole the pigs' food that, although mistakenly (as Brown put it) 'esteemed the most stupid of animals', the pigs let out a chorus of squeals and immediately took their oat balls and dropped them in the mud each time they saw a child approach. This would bring the swineherd rushing over to investigate the commotion, whip in hand. When Brown remarked that depriving the pigs of food was irrational, given that their flesh formed a part of the apprentices' diet, Blincoe replied that this good pork and bacon was sold in nearby Buxton, while the meat dropped into their gruel was 'the very worst and cheapest of Irish-fed bacon'.[25]

But survival required a careful balance between comradeship and pure self-interest. Those who could afford small treats with the pennies occasionally disbursed for working through dinner shared their wheaten cakes and gave bites of pickled herring to trusted friends. The owner would hold the delicious food up to the mouth of his or her fortunate comrade, allowing only a tiny fraction to protrude from a tightly-clenched fist. Similarly, children too sick to eat gave their food to another in the fairly confident expectation of a favour to be returned. Presumably, the body of the boy who died in his sleep was plundered and treated with disrespect because he was now in no position to reciprocate.[26]

So hard did hunger bite that on Sundays the children used what little spare time they had to forage for more food in neighbouring fields and meadows. Somewhat unwisely, a Taddington farmer called Mr Megginson elected to grow turnips not far from the 'prentice house. The boys and girls descended on them whenever they could. A reasonable man, Megginson offered to plant them a half-acre patch if they would steal no more, but he had the goodwill to restrain from beating the malefactors; the skinny, ragged appearance of the children spoke of anything but greed. If they managed to find a turnip, the children would race into a nearby lane and feast upon it. According to the *Memoir*, the more desperate stole turnips from the field and then threw them into the privy to keep them out of sight. Later they were retrieved, washed in the river, and consumed. Others, including Blincoe himself, climbed into the woods that stretched up the valley sides in search of what they called 'bread and cheese' – hips, hip-leaves, clover and anything else remotely edible.[27]

There were also occasional victories to be savoured. Blincoe told of how, after maybe a year at Litton Mill, he was assigned to take a cop of spun yarn to the counting house. There he met another apprentice, Isaac Moss. At once, both sets of eyes fell upon a hefty treacle can, recently carried down into the valley from Tideswell by the mill's hard-worked jackass. The temptation was irresistible. Blincoe had no spoon, so Moss lent him one that he was keeping safe for another child. They proceeded to scoop great dollops of it into their hungry mouths, Moss constrained by a jaw swollen from the blows of William Woodward, the mill manager. Only minutes into their frantic ladling, Woodward suddenly 'stole upon them'. Having received several kicks and punches, Blincoe promptly fled, his chin and shirt front sticky with guilt. He was later dragged back to the counting house, where he received one of Woodward's 'flat-handed slaps, fetching fire from his eyes, and presently another, another and another' until he was begging for mercy. But the manager had a better idea than further violence. He commanded Moss and Blincoe to finish the entire can, saying: 'Damn your bloods, you rascals, if you don't lap up the whole can … I'll murder you on the spot.' Hardly able to believe his good fortune, and needing no encouragement, Blincoe set to. Before long he had nearly emptied a several-pound can of treacle. Horrified that his attempt to sicken the children had backfired, and humiliated by the other overlookers' mirth, William Woodward had the two malefactors handcuffed together. When Blincoe, his wrists slender through years of malnutrition, managed to extricate himself, Woodward ordered that he spend the night – in the depth of winter – on the hard, cold floor of the 'prentice house.[28]

Some adults at Litton did have a capacity for kindness. Every mill required at least one blacksmith and mechanic, and these men were often of a higher calibre than the journeymen spinners. Theirs was a respectable calling, requiring a true apprenticeship rather than the crude economic exploitation of the parish system. As they could not easily be replaced, especially in remote valleys like Miller's Dale, even masters like Ellis Needham had to treat their skilled workers with some respect. At Litton, a local man named William Palfrey was responsible for the maintenance of the carding, spinning and stretching machines and, less agreeably, for riveting errant children into leg-irons. It was Palfrey who bought the children wheaten cakes and herrings from Tideswell with the small change they earned by working through dinner. Palfrey deplored the brutality practised against the parish apprentices and did what he could to shame the overlookers into desisting. At his bench upstairs, he would bang hard against the floor, shouting: 'For shame! for shame! Are you murdering the children?' Blincoe claims that Palfrey warned Ellis he would leave if the thrashings continued. Not a complete fool, Ellis seems for a time to have reined in the overlookers. But after seven o'clock in the evening, when Palfrey went back to his cottage in Litton village, normal service was resumed. It was a common ruse among the children to tell the overlookers that 'Palfrey and the joiner are going to work all night.' Sometimes it bought them a brief let-up.[29]

Even so, life at Litton Mill was terribly harsh, and for some it was short. After five years working there, Blincoe's body was showing signs of poor nutrition and excess demands placed on immature bones and muscles. He was of unusually short stature, his knees turned sharply inwards, and scars like seams ran across his head, face and ears. The healthy workhouse boy, tall for his age, had grown into a crooked young man. And yet, despite near-continuous beating and belittling, Blincoe held on to a clear sense that this treatment was wrong, and that any decent person who lived outside of Miller's Dale would unhesitatingly agree.

13

An inspector calls

For many centuries the English shires had been subdivided into units called Hundreds, encompassing several parishes, each with its own court presided over by local Justices of the Peace. These courts dealt with a range of judicial and civil business. Peel's Act had added to their responsibilities by mandating that at every midsummer sessions, a JP and clergyman should be appointed visitors of textile mills and should report a year later as to which were or were not conforming to the specifications of the 1802 Act. But the Palace of Westminster could seem very remote from the moorland, valleys, forests and isolated settlements making up the High Peak Hundred in which Litton lay. Four years elapsed before the High Peak justices felt inclined to act on Peel's legislation. These were four years in which Blincoe and the other St Pancras cast-offs were transferred from a much-improved Lowdham Mill to the horrors of Ellis Needham's Litton.

Like most humanitarian legislation of the age, Peel's Act was routinely ignored. Some JPs, even clergymen, had money invested in mills. Most were on friendly terms with at least one mill owner, and few liked interfering in the relationships between masters and men. More prosaically, riding from one mill to another, up and down rough tracks, was hardly a congenial way of spending time. Hence, few magistrates appreciated being made into mill inquisitors. Some were, however, more faithful to the duties of office than others. In the Derbyshire Hundred of Wirksworth, Philip Gell and John Chaloner, and in the Scarsdale Hundred, Josiah Jebb and Edward Otter, all visited local mills every two or three years. Perhaps having been shown up by this punctiliousness, in 1806 the High Peak JPs at long last summoned up the resolve to do Parliament's bidding. It's unlikely that the two men selected to tour the mills, Dr Joseph Denman and the Reverend James Grundy, relished the prospect. That Grundy's signature didn't appear on the final report suggests that he may have pleaded parish commitments and shirked the duty altogether.[1]

Joseph Denman was living proof that the upper classes of the old society constituted an open elite, its approaches never entirely closed to those who combined drive, pushiness, ability and good fortune. A skilled doctor with a charming bedside manner could go far, since a word of praise from one wealthy patient could open up the bed-chambers of many more. Dr Denman was one such case. The son of a Bakewell surgeon-apothecary, he had trained as a physician and taken over his father's practice, but he spent much of his time in the resort town of Buxton, four miles west of Tideswell. The Romans had valued Buxton's warm springs, as had Mary Queen of Scots. In the late 1700s, however, Buxton was becoming one of Europe's most fashionable spa towns. Grand hotels and a 'very splendid' crescent of stylish town-houses spoke of the new wealth brought in by holidaying aristocrats and successful merchants, tradesmen and manufacturers. Joseph Denman was well placed to share in the profits. With unrestrained enthusiasm, in a 1793 book on the topic, *Observations on the Effects of Buxton Water*, he extolled the virtues of spring water for purifying the body, cleansing the arterial system, and eliminating even the most obdurate of maladies. Denman deemed it especially effective in treating 'inflammation of the bowels', a common problem among an upper class that consumed plenty of red meat and relatively few vegetables. But he added a strict warning about the risk of overdosing: 'Its active properties are such, that young persons in the highest health seldom drink it with impunity.' Unwilling to settle for second best, Dr Denman dedicated the second edition of his book to the richest personage in the county, the Duke of Devonshire. By then, he had no reason to fear a refusal from this all-powerful magnate. Denman was already an insider. Well-heeled, highly sought-after, and spending much of his time in the company of the local gentry, he had met one Elizabeth Finney, whose family owned the extensive old hall in the village of Stoney Middleton. They married and the hall eventually passed into his family's hands.[2]

So it was a wealthy and upwardly mobile medical man who, on 1 August 1807, filed a report with the High Peak justices having spent several days touring the region's mills. By now, Blincoe was fifteen years old. He had been working as a roving winder at Litton Mill for four long years. All this time there had been no let-up in the cruelties inflicted by the Woodwards and the Needhams. Blincoe's *Memoir* gives no details about visits by magistrates – it merely comments that they happened and that they had no effect. But records of their reports do survive, and Blincoe would have been heartened by their findings.[3]

The mills at nearby Bakewell and Calver received Dr Denman's complete approbation. So did Cressbrook's cotton mill. Cressbrook Mill was still owned by Richard Arkwright, but it was now under the management of Edmund Baker and Barker Bossley. Denman thought the floors of this mill could have done with a good wash, but the apprentices' rooms were 'clean, not crowded, and apparently well conducted'. Nothing, however, was said as to whether the mill worked at night, whether the children received lessons in reading and writing, or whether the hours worked were excessive. It's quite possible that Denman was hazy on the exact stipulations of Peel's Act. Questioned by a parliamentary committee in 1816, a Manchester barrister and stipendiary magistrate, David Evans, admitted that he had been vaguely aware of an Act to do with factories but had never had the curiosity to look at its provisions. Few JPs troubled to keep up to date with recent rulings, and most of them applied their judicial authority in the manner least prejudicial to their own interests. In Henry Fielding's *Tom Jones*, Squire Western felt that swearing was a moral disgrace, except when he did it. Most magistrates had a similarly partisan approach to implementing criminal law. For all this, there was evidently nothing that appalled Denman about Baker and Bossley's regime at Cressbrook Mill.[4]

The perambulating doctor did have a few negative comments on the state of one of the factories and weaving shops in the village of Eyam. Messrs Daintry and Co. were chastised for selecting a building much too small for its purposes. As a believer in the key role of the environment in maintaining health, Denman expressed alarm at the close and cramped conditions in which their weavers laboured. He did, however, exonerate the masters of blame, attributing the choice of workplace to the poor judgement of the 'truly respectable' owners.[5]

Litton Mill was a very different matter. Magistrates gave proprietors ample warning before turning up at their mills. Blincoe noted, and there's every reason to believe him, that their coming was preceded by frenetic but careful preparations. 'The worst of the cripples were put out the way', the rooms swept, and the children left in no doubt as to the likely repercussions if they spoke out. This last precaution wasn't usually necessary. Parish apprentices were over-awed by these fine-clothed gentlemen with their elegant mounts, powdered wigs and fancy stockings. And, in a state of complete ignorance about the 1802 Act, few imagined that visiting JPs were there to scrutinise their own treatment. Most JPs did nothing to enlighten them. In fact, Blincoe remarked that visiting inspectors were given a cursory show round the more salubrious parts of the mill and then escorted up to Hargate Wall to dine at Ellis's 'luxurious table'. The gossips at the mill were full of bitter talk of the sumptuous feasts and lavish entertainments laid on for local worthies at Worm-hill's Old Hall.[6]

Whether or not Dr Denman was easily swayed by fine hospitality, he probably had no desire to find fault. This would, after all, entail taking the side of parish orphans, poor bastards among them, against one of their social betters. Bringing legal action in such circumstances was virtually unthinkable. Masters simply did not expect the law to be used against themselves. In their eyes, the chief purpose of parliamentary legislation was to protect their property. Accordingly, when the colliery-owning aristocrat James Lowther, first Earl of Lonsdale, lost a legal action taken against him over a case of subsidence in 1791, he was so outraged that he decided to shut down all of his coal mines, throwing thousands out of work. It took a petition signed by 2,560 people and a guarantee of complete indemnity in future cases before he would allow the workers back. There are a myriad similar examples. One notorious case involved the noble Brandling family. In 1814 John Hodgson, vicar of Jarrow, lost 92 members of his congregation in a single mining accident. The standard procedure was for the matter to be instantly hushed up, and it took enormous determination and courage on the part of Hodgson and the judge Sir John Bayley to make the disaster known to the public; 'braving the displeasure of the affluent Brandlings' who owned the mine, Hodgson published an account of what happened. Few clergymen or magistrates played this fast-and-loose with their reputations. Ellis Needham commanded far less authority than the Brandlings or James Lowther, but by the time of Dr Denman's visit, he was a respected member of the local community. Already a churchwarden in Wormhill, from 1806 to 1812 he also served Tideswell in the same capacity. And in 1802 and 1803 he even acted as steward for the Tideswell assemblies, hosting and organising evening dances and soirees for the 'better sorts'.[7]

Moreover, Ellis was no mere barber-upstart or artisan-made-good who could be bossed around by a local JP. He was a born gentleman. Even if he did own a cotton mill, everyone knew that Ellis's true *métier* was the soil. Having visited Wormhill in about 1809 on his tour of Derbyshire, John Farey had openly praised him as being one of the county's most 'distinguished agricultural improvers', and he used Ellis to refute the suggestion that manufacturers made 'bad Farmers'. Ellis had power, influence and immunity from all but the most conscientious of JPs. And Dr Denman was no Sir John Bayley.[8]

Despite all this, when Denman visited Litton Mill in 1807, he sent to the High Peak Sessions a report that did very little credit to its much-respected proprietor. 'Two Rooms in this Mill were clean, and all the Working Rooms whitewashed, and in all there was a free ventilation', was how the report began. But the magistrate went on to list the variety of ways in which Ellis was in breach of Peel's Act:

> The Privies not well conducted. There are about Eighty Apprentices, many of them I believe from the Foundling Hospital, who are kept in a Lodging House at no great Distance from the Mill. These Apprentices work successively in the Night, though this is expressly prohibited by the Act. It is by no means certain to what Hours they are confined. They are not instructed during the working Hours. There is no Copy of the Act of Parliament in any Part of the Mill.

Dr Denman was particularly displeased with the size of the apprentice house where, he said, the 'Rooms appeared crowded'. 'Upon the whole', he wrote in conclusion, 'from the Dimensions of the Building it appears almost impossible to contain so many Persons consistently with Health and any thing approaching Comfort.'[9]

This was a stern indictment, and it contrasts sharply with the reports on other cotton mills that Denman inspected, and those examined by his brother JPs in other Derbyshire Hundreds. Denman's seat of Stoney Middleton was replete with the small and often damp cottages of lead miners, so the good doctor wasn't new to scenes of deprivation. Even so, the 'prentice house at Litton Mill roused his indignation. And Denman's report amply confirms the spirit of the *Memoir*. No time was set aside during the day for learning; the mill operated long hours; and none of the apprentices knew of Peel's Act. Ellis Needham's mill came out of the year's inspections as by far the worst in Derbyshire.[10]

For the parish apprentices working for Baker and Bossley a short walk downstream, conditions were immeasurably better. The masters had taken on about 60 boys and girls and housed them in small cottages on site. The children were given time to play in nearby fields, and every Sunday they were led to Tideswell Church. There is only one recorded case of ill-treatment under their management, and this hardly reflects badly on their regime. In 1800 a young boy, William Williamson, was beaten by a mill overlooker and then fled to his mother in Staffordshire. In the intervening weeks he somehow became crippled. After the boy was sent back to Cressbrook Mill, Bossley assured him that he 'would be a good master, if he would be a good boy.' But the boy was severely debilitated and his mother asked for him to be sent home to her. Bossley obliged, giving him three shillings for his return fare and then the weekly sum of one shilling and sixpence for 64 weeks until he could no longer afford the expense.[11]

In dozens of mills in Derbyshire and elsewhere, parish apprentices were maltreated. But very few were worse off than those in Litton Mill, and there's ample evidence to show that the vast majority were considerably better treated. There are stories of cruelty during William Newton's second stint at Cressbrook, but it's significant that when Blincoe was at Litton, Cressbrook's masters took a personal interest in the fortunes of a lame child in a spirit of generosity entirely alien to Ellis Needham.[12]

14

Middleton of Leam Hall

Dr Denman's report was filed away and forgotten. It was abundantly clear that Ellis Needham had contravened nearly every stipulation of Peel's 1802 Act, but he was protected from prosecution by his birth and local contacts. There's no indication that JPs or clergymen made official inspections of the spinning mills for four years after Denman's tour. There's clear evidence, however, that Ellis Needham's position became more secure than ever. Apparently unharmed by Denman's revelations, in 1808 he was appointed steward for the Buxton assemblies. A mark of the high regard in which he was held by the local gentry, his role was to act as host for the balls held every Wednesday and Friday throughout the holiday season. These dances were ostensibly public affairs, though in the interests of averting social embarrassments, measures were adopted to keep out tradesmen. The entry fee of six shillings a night kept all but the most successful *arrivistes* away. But part of Ellis Needham's role was to preserve the elitist character of the Buxton assemblies. One suspects that he carried out his duties with considerable relish.[1]

As Ellis performed his duties of entertainment and exclusion in 1808, Anna Seward, patroness of William Newton, wrote characteristically acerbic letters to her friends, complaining that Buxton that year was less 'adorned by the graces of polished life' than in previous seasons. Seward was piqued because, being of relatively humble origins, only Lady Shaftesbury of the aristocratic set bothered to speak to her. In one letter, the gossipy Miss Seward told of an incident in which the Marquis of Hartington, son of the fabulously wealthy Duke of Devonshire, arrived in Buxton from the family estate of Chatsworth. The Marquis proceeded to behave with such 'cold-blooded insolence' towards his social inferiors that 'an old Gentleman of the Company' told him 'with stentor-lungs that he was a <u>Puppy</u>.' In the ensuing 'ferment', recorded Miss Seward, most of the guests had sufficient respect for caste to side with the obnoxious young Marquis.[2]

One imagines that, had Ellis been there, he would have done the same. The steward of the assemblies required a keen understanding of the importance of rank. Deeply proud of his own status as a gentleman, Ellis knew how to combine affability with deference when addressing his social betters. How different a figure he must have cut before the dukes, earls and baronets of Buxton society than before the Litton Mill apprentices. But these two worlds overlapped in one important sense. In Buxton, Ellis was regularly socialising with the magistrates who were duty-bound to inspect his mill and, if necessary, press charges in line with Peel's Act. They weren't about to prosecute and humiliate the man who had arranged so many fine suppers and dances. Blincoe and his fellow apprentices were now wholly beyond the protection of the law.

But Ellis's taste for polished society and his craving for local influence were causing him to neglect his business affairs. His eldest son, John, was by now running Litton Mill on a day-to-day basis. He was no less adept with the birch than his father. Yet very careful management was needed if the mill were to survive, and John had virtually no acumen at all. Baker and Bossley's Cressbrook Mill went bust in 1809, unable to compete with the larger, steam-driven firms of Lancashire to the north. Litton too was struggling, and international events were making life ever harder. After the Peace of Amiens with Napoleonic France in 1802 there had been a surge in imports and exports, but it hadn't lasted long. With the resumption of hostilities, Emperor Napoleon abandoned his plans of invading the British Isles and undertook to starve his most implacable foe into submission. These were difficult days for mill owners, deprived of markets and raw material. After 1808, having subdued Prussia at the Battle of Jena in 1806, 'Boney' gained control of many of the hundreds of ports dotted along Europe's northern coast. He then ordered that British merchant ships docked there be seized, and all others refused admittance. A year later, following their crushing defeat at Friedland, the Russians too joined the blockade. Coming on top of escalating income taxes and poor rates, Napoleon's vast Continental System of economic warfare now began to hurt the British badly. Frozen out of the European markets on which they depended, manufacturers reeled from a precipitous decline in orders. Many of the weaker went to the wall. The Chancellor of the Exchequer, Spencer Perceval, then made matters a great deal worse by introducing the 'Orders in Council' which placed any European port refusing to trade with Britain under a state of blockade. This soured relations with America, helped bring the two nations to war, and dramatically reduced the amount of raw cotton available to England's spinning mills.[3]

Between organising balls, hosting soirees and keeping the peace among the upper and middle orders, Ellis Needham did what he could to shore up the ailing family finances. Parson Brown had made a comfortable profit lending money to Tideswell parishioners who didn't stand a chance against sensible bankers. Brown's shrewdness had lowered the risks, and he had done very nicely. Seeing his mounting wealth, Ellis elected to do the same. But, far less astute than the wily vicar, he quickly ran into difficulties. Ellis loaned money to Mollie Baker, landlady of Litton's Red Lion Inn, and in 1810 she defaulted, leaving him £50 out of pocket. Unperturbed, he also gave John Baker about £30. Ellis then took the outrageous gamble of lending one Joseph Lingard nearly £2,000. If Lingard didn't pay up on the promised date, Ellis would be in deep trouble.[4]

By now, in 1810, Blincoe was eighteen years old, a less-than-strapping young man with another three years of his apprenticeship still left to run. His body already showed the price he had paid for the magistrates' lack of concern. His knees were irretrievably bowed inwards, his growth stunted, and his face bore the careworn expression of someone much older. It was at this juncture that the High Peak justices finally decided it was time for a second round of mill inspections. Marmaduke Middleton, magistrate, sheriff of the county, keen gardener and dabbler in poetry, was selected for the task. Between midsummer of 1810 and late spring 1811, he undertook a tour of mills in Glossop, New Mills, Mellor, Cressbrook and Litton. On 18 April he filed his report with the High Peak Sessions.[5]

A contemporary antiquarian observed that a 'distal line' of 'lineal descendants of the old Middletons' lived in Sheffield 'in the humblest of life possible', showing that, as some like Dr Denman ascended the social chain, others sank towards its lower reaches. But Marmaduke Middleton had an assured place in the foremost ranks of High Peak society. The resident of Leam Hall, outside Eyam and about five miles from Litton, by all accounts he was a good-natured squire, fondly described by a local chronicler as 'an old English gentleman, who was alike distinguished for understanding, sound sense, and literary taste.'[6]

That Marmaduke had nothing in principle against mill owners is clear from the fact that in 1822 he dedicated his *Poetical Sketches of a Tour in the West of England* to female descendants of Jedediah Strutt, the wealthy textile manufacturer of Belper, Derbyshire. Nor did he have an instinctual contempt for the lower orders. His poetry occasionally reveals an ability, by no means common among the magistracy, of seeing the world from the bottom up. Walking the Cornish coast, he was inspired to include the following stanza in his *Poetical Sketches*:

> Think of the dangers miners undergo,
> For scanty pittance toiling far below, –
> Debarr'd the blessings of a single ray
> To chear their spirits from the orb of day.[7]

It's not great poetry, but it shows plenty of the 'understanding' that impressed Eyam's historian.

Before arriving at Litton Mill, Middleton visited the mills of Glossop and New Mills. None of these had parish apprentices, but he could and did issue instructions for some prompt whitewashing and the opening up of more windows to improve ventilation. Of Samuel Oldknow's mill in Mellor, which did employ workhouse children, he was effusive in his praise. 'Any Commendation of mine', he wrote, 'must fall short of Mr Oldknow's very meritorious Conduct towards the Apprentices under his Care, whose Comfort in every respect seems to be his Study; they were all looking very well, and extremely clean.' This was high praise indeed. Perhaps Middleton was friends with Oldknow, though his opinion was echoed in the reports of many other contemporaries.[8]

With Cressbrook Mill, reopened after its bankruptcy and once more operating under William Newton's management, Middleton was also impressed. 'They go into the Mill at Six o'Clock in the Morning', he noted, 'and come out again at Eight o'Clock in the Evening.' This was a long day, but Middleton added: 'they have an Hour for Dinner, are very comfortable, and live well. Their Diet consists of Milk, or Milk Porridge for Breakfast and Supper, and they have Fresh Meat every Day at Dinner; they looked well, and appeared perfectly satisfied with their Situation.' It's hard to say how reliable an assessment Marmaduke Middleton could make when the masters were eager to impress and the apprentices too timid and deferential to complain. But the ease with which abuses could be – and usually were – papered over by canny proprietors makes his scathing report on Litton Mill all the more telling.[9]

Middleton, like Dr Denman, found the Taddington apprentice house to be clean, but on his arrival something extremely unusual, perhaps even unprecedented, occurred. Two of the apprentices approached him and issued a 'Complaint of being worked too hard, and of not having sufficient Support.' Things must really have been desperate for these children to risk the bloody wrath of master and overlookers, for them to put aside their lowly rank and take their complaints to the squire of Leam Hall. The *Memoir* says nothing of this event, presumably because Blincoe considered magistrates indifferent to the plight of apprentices or powerless to ease their condition. Middleton, however, was no hard-nosed patriarch. Evidently taken aback, he took action:

> I thought it right to examine some of the Apprentices under Oath as to the Facts they complained of, and the Substance of their Deposition is as follows, viz. That they go into the Mill about Ten Minutes before Six o'Clock in the Morning, and stay there 'till from Ten to Fifteen Minutes after Nine in the Evening, excepting the Time allowed for Dinner, which is from Half to Three Quarters of an Hour; that they have Water Porridge for Breakfast and Supper, and generally Oatcake and Treacle, or Oatcake and poor Broth, for Dinner; that they are instructed in Writing and Reading on Sundays.

It was a bald commentary which in no way captured the anxious, rapid and intense speech of the boys and girls he questioned. One can only assume that, Middleton having publicly announced his intention of examining some of the apprentices, they realised that they had to moderate their complaints. If they didn't, their treatment at the mill would get a whole lot worse before, if ever, getting any better.[10]

But the picture of Litton Mill that Middleton's report presents is very much as Blincoe and Orphan John told it: long hours and utterly inadequate food. Porridge was standard fare in mills across the country, but without milk it made a wholly insufficient breakfast and supper. Blincoe's heavy scarring, the corroborative testimony of other apprentices, and the burial entries in local parish registers tell us what Middleton missed: that Litton Mill was a brutal as well as an unhealthy place to serve an apprenticeship.

Disturbed by what he had seen and heard, Middleton confronted John Needham. It must have been a strange experience for a young man whose word was law in this remote spot of Miller's Dale to have to act the penitent. Faced with a man who couldn't easily be brow-beaten and, if sufficiently annoyed, might just unleash the power of the law, John made excuses. He said that the children were working long hours because the waterwheel had been broken for 'a Month in the Winter'. They were, it seemed, making up for lost time. Most water-powered mills did work long hours after stoppages caused by breakages or droughts; Blincoe referred to the latter himself. But these children were worked the gruelling shifts that Middleton heard about for most of the year, not just when production had fallen behind schedule. John Needham was lying.[11]

Father and son must have been rattled when they read Middleton's report. Here was someone whose opinion in local affairs mattered. Put alongside his descriptions of Cressbrook and Mellor, and bearing in mind that the ruling elites were habituated to seeing the poorer classes in wretched conditions, Middleton's condemnation demon-strates that the Litton Mill apprentices were in a bad state indeed. The Needhams, however, took little action. Perhaps it was in the after-math of this visit that Ellis installed a dairy at the mill, to provide the milk which Orphan John mentioned. But as both Orphan John and another apprentice later commented, over the following years the children's diets would only deteriorate further.[12]

Yet the nastiness of life at Litton Mill reflected more than the brutal natures of owners and overlookers. The Needhams were failing to make much money from spinning cotton, and so they tried to maximise their profits by cutting costs. Blincoe says that they spun only coarse yarn, requiring less processing; but the major savings took the form of reduced rations for the apprentices and obscenely long hours. Despite these economies, due to Ellis Needham's pitiful lack of business sense, his lending schemes were about to plunge the family into ever-greater debt. In 1811, John Baker's bankruptcy cost him over £30. But it was Joseph Lingard going under in the same year, still owing £1,700, that crippled the Needhams. In May of this year, Ellis rushed to his Tideswell attorneys, Shaw and Cheek, to secure a mortgage to keep his creditors at bay. They stumped up £700 and with this he paid off debts to his Buxton bankers, Messrs Goodwin. As the Needhams' woes worsened, the mill children inevitably bore the brunt.[13]

By then, copies of Denman's and Middleton's reports had been despatched to the Home Office in London. They probably weren't read on arrival, but in Westminster calls were mounting once again for the interests of parish apprentices to be safeguarded by humane legislation. In 1811, Wilbraham Bootle, MP, introduced a Bill which would outlaw the apprenticing of children to any master more than 40 miles from their parish. To his surprise, the leading mill owners didn't react with quite the fury expected of them. They dragged their feet and shook their heads, but they didn't form a united front to stymie Bootle's suggestion that the state interfere in the provision of labour to mills and mines. This wasn't because the collective conscience of mill owners had been stirred into responsiveness by discoveries like Middleton's. Many of them were more than happy to allow Bootle's Bill to pass, for the simple reason that they no longer needed parish apprentices to keep their mills going.[14]

The economy had moved on since 1799 when Blincoe and the other St Pancras children were ushered onto a wagon bound for the north. Since then, many of those who had earlier seen these boys and girls as cheap, pliable labour had realised that apprentices with mothers and fathers who disciplined and cared for them usually turned out to be better workers. Much more importantly, there were now so many 'free' children on the job market that there was far less need to take on the added responsibility of housing child labourers. Many were the children of hand-loom weavers. By now, this skilled trade was in a miserable state. In 1795, when mills glutted the market with yarn, there had been plenty of work for the weavers. Those who had worked hard had brought in a handsome wage in the region of 39 shillings a week. But the boom time was now at an end, never to return. Wages had been driven down to subsistence levels by too many entering the trade. And by 1810 they were hurting badly on just fifteen shillings a week. In due course, even Andrew Ure, no friend of the working classes, would recoil at the wretchedness of the life endured by the hand-loom weavers and their families: 'Ill-fed, ill-lodged, and ill-clothed, with care-worn and anxious countenances,' Ure wrote with rare sympathy, 'they constitute a peculiar class of misery.'[15] In 1809, desperate weavers petitioned Parliament for a minimum wage and the upholding of Tudor apprenticeship statutes. In a bitterly ironic stroke, the government seized the opportunity to sweep away all regulations relating to apprenticeship. Now anyone at all, with weeks rather than years of training, could become a journeyman weaver. The market had been deregulated. Comprehensively defeated, and their trade more glutted than ever before, many surrendered themselves to the factory regime. One way of staving off the inevitable was first to offer up their children, in the early hours of the morning, to the nearby textile mills.

But there was another reason for the decline in popularity of parish apprentices. Steam-powered mills were now in the ascendant. And since these weren't reliant on fast-flowing streams, they could be built in large towns like Manchester, Leeds, Sheffield and Bolton, places with ready sources of indigenous child and adult labour.

All these factors combined to lessen the hostility of mill proprietors to Bootle's attempt to regulate the use of indentured workhouse children.[16]

Perhaps unsurprisingly, Bootle's fiercest critics were the London parishes which still had large surfeits of children to be got rid of in any way they could. Sir Robert Peel also demurred, remarking that it was the 'happiest possible thing' to separate these children from their 'miserable and deprived parents' and save them from being 'educated to picking pockets'. Battered by the London parishes and a few dogmatic political economists, Bootle eventually traded his Bill for a committee of inquiry, convened in May 1815 and comprising Sir Samuel Romilly, clear-thinking law reformer, Leonard Horner, social reformer and geologist, and Samuel Whitbread, the son of a wealthy brewer and a leading Whig politician with some sympathy for the plight of the lower orders.[17]

The committee met, received depositions and ruminated for four long years. During the course of its deliberations, it found that a quarter of parish apprentices had simply disappeared, that fewer than a twelfth of them remained in the same trade having completed their apprenticeships, that one in twenty were dead or permanently crippled, and that nearly as many had had no choice but to enlist in the army or navy at the age of 21. The system of apprenticeship at a distance had blighted thousands of young lives. Notwithstanding Peel's Act and the visits of two magistrates, Robert Blincoe was among this sorry number.[18]

15

Wild, inarticulate souls?

Blincoe didn't know for certain that his masters were breaking the law. Not even Middleton had apprised them of Peel's 1802 Act, and the Needhams never did comply with the law's insistence that they display copies in their mill. Even so, Blincoe's innate sense of justice told him that what they were doing could not be right. In 1812, emboldened by age (he was nearly twenty years old), he made a pact with three other Litton employees, William Haley and John Emery, fellow apprentices, and Thomas Gully, an overlooker. They agreed to stop working until their hours were shortened. To the Needhams their resolution was rank mutiny.[1]

It was also criminal. In 1799, after a petition from the London master millwrights, a Parliamentary Select Committee had recommended legislation 'to prevent Unlawful Combinations of workmen employed in the Millwright Business.' The measure was modest in scope, toughening up common law, and it applied to one trade only. The Bill looked set to pass both Houses without any fuss. Then William Wilberforce, evangelical and champion abolitionist, elected to intervene. He suggested a Bill to prohibit all union organisations in all trades. Trades unions, more commonly known as 'combinations', had existed in one form or another for centuries. Their twin aims were to limit competition and resist attempts to drive down wages; and, as Sidney and Beatrice Webb pointed out, 'Strikes are as old as history itself.' Prime Minister William Pitt, agreeing that combinations 'cause very serious mischief' and fearful of any militancy among the lower orders, seized on Wilberforce's proposal. The Combination Act of 1799 allowed magistrates to commit members of trades unions to 'gaol for ... any time not exceeding 3 calendar months; or otherwise be committed to some House of Correction ... for any time not exceeding 2 calendar months.'[2]

This Act reflected a worrying new trend in social relations, an atmosphere of mounting distrust between masters and men. Economists spoke of there being an identity of interests among capitalists and wage-earners. In abstract terms that was arguably true, but in practice there was often little sign of it. The ties of deference and duty that had held rural society together rarely applied to the textile mill. Owners trying to succeed in competitive markets, with everything gambled on success, drove workers hard and disparaged those who asked for more money or shorter hours. And many were those who, as John Brown falsely said of Needham, felt ashamed of their humble roots and so treated employees with an exaggerated disdain. In their turn, the operatives, with smaller personal stakes in the firms they sweated for, were generally unwilling to make the sacrifices their bosses expected; they wanted as much for as little as they could give. Both sides reciprocated distrust. This was exacerbated by the tendency of prosperous mill owners, aping the squirearchy, to spend their money ostentatiously, buying country estates, sometimes tactlessly located in full view of the mills. When wages were cut or hands laid off, fine houses and neatly laid-out gardens became the focus for bitter discontent. But for the capitalists, it seemed only right and fair that those who risked all to set up mills, and who thereby created jobs for poor families, should be allowed to luxuriate in the profits if they ever accrued. And they fumed at the apparent inability of the workers to understand that higher wages and better conditions cut profits and imperilled their jobs. Mutual antagonism was usually the result. Thus the physician and health reformer James Kay-Shuttleworth openly worried that the 'separation' of the classes 'has succeeded to suspicion, and many causes have tended to widen the gulph over which the golden chain of charity too seldom extends.' At Litton Mill, however, the situation was unusually bad. The workers despised their masters and the Needhams had only contempt for them.[3]

Had the Needhams recognised earlier that it paid to win the loyalty of workers, and that well-fed children could work harder and made fewer mistakes, they might actually have made a success of the mill. In 1811, with creditors baying, they were in no position to make concessions. The involvement of Thomas Gully, one of the overlookers, in the Litton Mill strike indicates that grievances were no longer confined to the abused children. Ellis and John had only one option – the strike would have to be crushed. And so when William Wood-ward learned of the four-man rebellion and sent a letter up to Ellis at Hargate Wall, he promptly sent back orders that all four were to be turned out of their lodgings for the night. Blincoe managed to persuade a friendly overlooker to provide him with shelter, but no food. The other three shivered in the woods.[4]

The next morning, nine o'clock on a Monday, Ellis met them at the counting house. As Blincoe approached, the boss removed his jacket and waistcoat and proceeded to thrash him with his walking stick, shouting: 'I'll run you out, you damned rascal.' Faced with an incipient strike which might easily have closed his works down, it's not surprising that Ellis was prepared to break his stick upon one of the malefactors' backs. By now, however, Blincoe's blood was up.[5]

Having calmed his nerves, Blincoe returned to work to the sounds of Haley and then Emery catching 'their share' of Ellis Needham's fury. It's interesting that John Brown says nothing of the treatment of the fourth conspirator, Thomas Gully. He was not, however, an indentured apprentice and therefore couldn't be beaten with impunity. Moreover, it was an overlooker called Gully whom Orphan John recalled striking an apprentice so hard that he fell against the machinery and had the 'flesh and muscles of his right arm torn off'. This wasn't the kind of man one assaulted without careful reflection.[6]

By noon, Blincoe hadn't eaten for an entire day. But having devoured his meagre share of oatcakes, he did something extra-ordinary. Reminiscent of his attempted escape from Lowdham in 1799, he turned and fled the scene, running at full pelt out of the mill gates and up the Slack towards Litton village. Blincoe had it all planned out. He was too wise now to think that he would receive any succour from St Pancras parish, even if he did manage to walk hundreds of miles to the south. His destination this time was Stanton-Hall, the fine residence of Henry Bache Thornhill, a county magistrate of long standing.[7]

For a young man who had hardly ventured outside the mill walls for a decade, this was an undertaking of the boldest kind. His journey would take him eleven miles from Litton on roads he had travelled only once before, back in 1803, and to a destination he knew virtually nothing about. Driven on by righteous anger, he ran 'at full speed' until the mill was far behind him. What's particularly remarkable is that this work'us boy had the audacity to go above the head of his master to appeal to higher authorities. It's not surprising that he knew that magistrates had the power to right wrongs; he may also have heard that Thornhill was an unusually go-ahead magistrate. But it was still an audacious step for a young man, totally oblivious of Peel's 1802 Act, to seek his assistance.[8]

It took a powerful personality to rebound from years of hunger and mistreatment to undertake such a mission. Perhaps Blincoe's fierce sense of indignation and his refusal to submit to the Needhams' arbitrary rule arose from a belief that he was no mere pauper's child, that he was the son of an educated clergyman who would not have felt out of place in the parlour of a gentleman's mansion. A child fathered by a cleric had a right to expect redress. It's one of the fascinating twists of the relationship between *Oliver Twist* and Blincoe's *Memoir* that while Oliver had no idea until much later that he sprang from respectable parentage, Blincoe's probably mistaken conviction about his own father may have given him the courage and assertiveness to take on his oppressors.

After about five miles at a fast trot, Blincoe arrived in Bakewell. A handsome town nestling among 'wood-clad hills', it was best known for its bi-monthly cattle markets. There were also two large cotton mills, plus lead and zinc mines nearby, and a stone quarry. Local politics were in the tight grip of the Duke of Devonshire. Once a year, at Michaelmas, he was driven in state to the town from the family seat of Chatsworth. There he would hold court and appoint the parish officials. But Blincoe took in little of his surroundings. Running now at full tilt, terrified of being identified as a runaway apprentice, he kept his head down and made for the house of one of the Lowdham overlookers who he had heard now lived in Bakewell. Johnny Wild was astonished to see young Parson, 'terror in his looks and reeking with perspiration', appear at his door. Years earlier, presumably alienated by the long hours and harsh discipline of the mill, Wild had turned to weaving stockings. Although fighting for survival in a declining trade, he and his wife at least had the resources to provide their visitor with a bowl of bread and milk. They also lent him a hat, and then directed him on his way towards the Thornhill seat of Stanton-Hall. [9]

The final stretch took Blincoe alongside the River Wye until he came to one of its tributaries, the River Bradford. He then veered south towards the village of Stanton in Peak, perched on the side of a steep hill. Having run along its winding road and passed by a string of ancient gritstone dwellings, Blincoe arrived at the gates of the hall. He had then to walk a further mile-and-three-quarters through an extensive deer park before arriving at the hall itself. The local author David Peter Davies described this as a most 'elegant mansion'. For Blincoe, seeing the grandeur of a squire's seat for the first time must have been discomfiting. But, his back still stinging from Needham's walking stick, and having already travelled eleven miles in little more than rags, his courage held up. He boldly knocked.[10]

A manservant came to the door. 'What do you want?' he said, one assumes with some disgust at the sight of the malodorous, knock-kneed young man who had presumed to call at dinner time and at the front door. The *Memoir* tells us that Blincoe responded with the words: 'I am an apprentice at Litton Mill, master has beaten me cruelly, do look at my shirt.' 'Never mind, never mind', the servant replied, 'you cannot see Mr Thornhill today; he is at dinner; there will be a bench of justices tomorrow, about eleven in the morning at the Sign of the Bull's Head, facing the Church at Eyam, you must go there.' Perhaps the servant thought this would close the matter. If so, he under-estimated the resources of the tired, crooked and ill-dressed fellow standing before him.[11]

Blincoe knew that Eyam was fewer than three miles from Litton Mill, and so he resolved to go there the following day. For now, though, he left Squire Thornhill to an uninterrupted dinner and made his weary way back to the mill. Passing through Bakewell he returned the borrowed hat, though he had now exhausted the Wilds' fund of generosity and had to trudge the final seven miles back without any refreshments. He arrived at Litton Mill at 10.30 at night, sore and disappointed. Almost immediately, William Woodward seized him and demanded to know where he had been, in 'a tone, about as gentle as that of a baited-bear, and an aspect much more savage.' Blincoe explained that he had gone to see 'Mr Thornelly [*sic*]'. No doubt disconcerted by the young man's bravery and the mention of external powers, Woodward let him be, simply declaring: 'I'll Thornelly you tomorrow.' By now Blincoe was so ravenously hungry that even a 'mess of water-porridge' tasted wondrously delicious. Having gulped down his meal, Blincoe went straight to bed, sleeping on his front due to the tenderness of his striped and bloodied back. Next day, a Tuesday, Blincoe rose with the other apprentices and started work at his mule. But before eight o'clock in the morning, when William Woodward could impound him, he had made off for Eyam and the magistrates' bench.[12]

16

At the Bull's Head Inn

The reputation of the place boded well for a triumph of good over evil. Famous throughout the district as the 'plague village', Eyam's name is forever associated with heroic self-sacrifice. In August 1665 bubonic plague broke out when a tailor opened a package of cloth sent from London. Within days the infection had killed several villagers. The typical response to epidemic disease was, in the words of one physician, 'fly from it!' But everyone knew that this spread the malady further afield. So the rector persuaded his flock to do something altruistic. They agreed that no one would leave the village. This meant that they had to be provisioned from outside, so people from neighbouring settlements left food and drink on the village boundary; though even at the risk of cross-infection they exacted payment, insisting that the Eyam villagers first soak their money in holes filled with vinegar. Fulfilling his duties of Christian stewardship, the Earl of Devonshire donated food and medicine for free. After fourteen months and 260 deaths, the plague finally died down.[1]

For most people, Eyam was only about an hour's walk from Litton, though Blincoe's buckled legs would have made it take far longer and feel much harder. But for all the hardships of getting there, the village he entered on that day in 1812 was highly picturesque, surrounded by tree plantations and lying in the shadow of precipitous cliffs. Most of the buildings fringed a single main street, and the Bull's Head Inn was roughly half-way along. Blincoe recalled that he made the trek to Eyam on a warm day in late summer as the 'hay was about'. And, despite his anxieties, Blincoe felt 'delighted by the sweet air and romantic scenery'. Certainly, it would have made a welcome change from the noise, fumes and suffocating flue of a cotton-spinning mill. Finding himself, presumably by the church's clock, to be an hour and a half early, he entered the churchyard directly opposite the inn, perhaps lying in the ample shade provided by its much-admired sycamores. Here several rows of ivy-covered gravestones kept alive the memory of the plague years.[2]

Magistrates, like overseers of the poor and churchwardens, conducted much of their routine business in public houses, the tedium of shire affairs being somewhat relieved by the aromas of ale and pipe-smoke. First to arrive there was Tideswell's attorney, William Cheek. He was to act as officiating clerk. Blincoe knew that Cheek lived in a mansion called Whetstone Hall outside Tideswell, and that he had long been attorney to the Needham family. Entering the Bull's Head himself, Blincoe walked up to Cheek and proceeded to list a long series of grievances against his masters and to call for whatever legal protection could be offered.[3]

Blincoe hadn't washed properly since the previous Friday, and he had walked many miles within the last 24 hours in the summer's heat. His odour was the first thing that Cheek noticed. 'Well, well, I can hear you, you need not come so near; stand back', Cheek implored, according to Brown's plausible rendition. Out of smelling range, Blincoe continued detailing the woes of the apprentices: the rank food, long hours, frequent beatings, and John Needham's improprieties. Blincoe was the most credible of plaintiffs. His obvious desperation, malformed legs, and nervous looks all spoke of real and continued hardship.[4]

Yet Cheek probably didn't look upon him as an innocent behind whom should swing the full might of impartial justice. Blincoe's chances of receiving a fair hearing at the Bull's Head were contingent on far larger historical forces and sets of deeply entrenched social attitudes. Peel's 1802 Act had been passed to assist those such as Robert Blincoe, but when a member of the upper classes looked at a young man like him they usually saw only a lowly work'us orphan, maltreated but still a delinquent insolently unwilling to accept his master's will. Such apprentices, if encouraged by sympathy or legal representation, set dangerous precedents of insubordination. The excessive whipping of pauper children was to be regretted, but unless their crime was conspicuously wicked, members of the elites were tacitly given immunity from prosecution. Of course there was a major disparity here between the rhetoric and the practice of the law. Praising the English constitution in comparison to the French, in 1792 Prime Minister William Pitt had proudly declaimed: 'it was the boast of the law of England that it afforded equal security and protection to the high and the low, the rich and the poor.' The reality was somewhat different. As Henry Brougham, the brilliant Whig reformer, told the House of Commons, in legal settings it was common to hear such remarks as: 'He is a monstrous good magistrate: no man commits so many persons.' But rarely were these men or women being sentenced to death, hard labour or transportation their social equals. To apply the law evenly was to invite accusations of class treachery, and it contravened the received view that the poor were degraded because of divine injunction and that rough treatment was a salutary means of reminding them of their place in the social hierarchy. It was to be expected that sometimes a master would go too far in his discipline and punishments, but this was surely better than excessive liberality, especially in the boiling wake of the French Revolution.[5]

Indeed, the Terror of 1792, an orgy of internecine violence resulting in the deaths of as many as 40,000 French aristocrats, clergymen and other royalists, had convinced many of England's elites that an iron fist was absolutely required in order to prevent the masses from falling prey to the 'wicked and delusive principles instilled into their minds' by working-class demagogues. In the atmosphere of conservative reaction that settled in for more than three decades after the guillotining of Louis XVI, deference assumed precedence over justice.[6]

For those who had been too young in 1792 to tremble at the murderous ferocity unleashed by the Terror, the previous year-and-a-half had provided another sobering lesson in the willingness of the long-suffering labouring orders to rise up against the propertied classes. In early 1811, letters had begun to circulate in Nottingham from a fictitious General Ned Ludd and an Army of Redressers. Soon after, nocturnal raids left hundreds of textile machines shattered by clubs and staves. Over the following months, the violence spread into Yorkshire, Lancashire, Leicestershire and, most seriously for Blincoe's chances of eliciting the sympathy of the magistrates in Eyam, Derbyshire as well.

The grievances of the machine-breakers aren't hard to identify.

Wheat prices were soaring once more, diminishing the forbearance of thousands of labourers who were seeing their livelihoods destroyed by new methods and machines. In Nottinghamshire, unskilled machine operatives were turning out cheap, low-quality 'cut-ups' which undersold the fine hosiery made on Lee's stocking frame. Skilled Yorkshire wool-finishers were being rendered obsolete by a new shearing frame. And in both Lancashire and Derbyshire, desperately poor weavers, sickened at the failure of the state to guarantee them a living wage, were now being driven to starvation by, as they saw it, the gradual introduction of the power-loom. Gone were the days when they could afford silver tea services and mahogany clocks or ostentatiously display £5 notes in their hatbands. Now, their leaders being egged on by Home Office informers, a series of Luddite outrages were directed against spinning and weaving mills. In April 1812, West Houghton mill in Lancashire was burned. Shortly after, two Luddites were shot dead trying to wreck a mill at Huddersfield in Yorkshire. Encouraged in the belief that 'revolutionary measures of the most dangerous description' were afoot, the Home Secretary hit back. Several Luddites were hanged in accordance with a freshly-minted law.[7]

The poet Lord Byron, speaking in defence of the frame-breakers in the House of Lords, reminded peers that Luddism had 'arisen from circumstances of the most unparalleled distress'. But the government was immovable, giving no quarter to those who damaged property and failed to heed the reigning orthodoxy that no state should interfere 'with the freedom of trade'. And the year 1811, reflected the Tory administration, was no time for half-measures. Large swathes of the English countryside were being convulsed by agrarian riots, while the British army was fully occupied in fighting the French in the Iberian peninsula, and the Americans south of the Canadian border, around Chesapeake Bay and in the Gulf of Mexico. In these circumstances, a large uprising of discontented labourers could threaten the state itself. In reality, the Luddites were fighting over knife-and-fork issues. They had little interest in talk of revolution or democracy. But the High Peak justices didn't necessarily see it this way. When they heard of depredations against manufacturers, like so many of their class and education, they caught a strong and unsettling whiff of revolution.[8]

In such a climate, Blincoe needed very persuasive grounds for complaint to move the magistrates' bench in the Bull's Head. Even the fact that the Litton apprentices were made to work on the Sabbath was unlikely to either surprise or appal. Evangelical lords, ministers and preachers wrung their hands when the Duke of York travelled to Newmarket races on a Sunday (he was forgiven when he explained that he had carried a Bible and Prayer Book in his carriage). But few cared that, right across the country, mill bosses were making their workers labour for several hours every Sunday. They didn't mind because to the propertied classes this was time devoted to proper subordination. They disapproved only when Sundays were spent in carefree enjoyment, known as 'dissipation', and relaxation, for which they read 'idleness'. Hence the attempts to prevent workers and servants going to London's Theatre Royal on Sunday evenings, and the persecution of the large numbers (mostly Irish) who played the game of hurley in Tothill Fields on the Lord's day. Gatherings of working men anywhere but in churches or workplaces were felt to teeter worryingly on the verge of sedition.[9]

As Blincoe unburdened himself to Mr Cheek, the attorney took brief notes. By the time he had finished, the magistrates had all arrived. There's some evidence to suggest that Cheek was being more co-operative with Blincoe than was usually his style with members of the lower orders. For years, the Needhams had gone to the firm of Shaw and Cheek to borrow money. But in October 1812, Ellis and his eldest son John went elsewhere to raise funds. Shaw and Cheek were not short of reserves, so something had presumably happened to estrange them. If there had been a falling out, it might be that Cheek had a score to settle with the Needhams and saw in Blincoe a useful instrument. Either way, Cheek had the courtesy to read Blincoe's deposition to the assembled magistrates. They then allowed him to be sworn in. The first to speak was Marmaduke Middleton, whom Blincoe surely remembered from the previous year's mill inspection. 'Where is Mr Needham?' he asked. 'He's gone today to Manchester market', was the reply. Another of the magistrates, shocked at the boy's presumption if not at the unpleasant fragrance rising from his clothes, nonchalantly said: 'Go straight to the mill, to your work.' Blincoe choked: 'Oh! Sir, he'll leather me.' He had risked much in coming to Eyam, and couldn't afford to leave empty-handed. One of the magistrates then reassured him: 'Oh, no! he durst na' – he durst na'.' The idea then occurred to someone, probably Middleton, that a letter be written to John Needham reminding him of the contents of the law. Middleton then concluded the proceedings with the generous remark: 'If he leathers you, come to me.'[10]

Blincoe told John Brown that he had carried the magistrates' letter to Litton Mill as if it were a 'talisman'. Retracing his steps through Litton village and down the Slack into Miller's Dale, he was puffed up with the anticipation of victory and a new sense of invincibility. To a mere work'us boy, the compassionate response of a magistrate who stood in relation to Ellis Needham as the latter did to Blincoe himself must have felt like a divine intercession. It was indeed remarkable that he hadn't simply been sent on his way with a stern admonition to remember his place and to thank God it wasn't lowlier still. But it was presumably because Middleton knew what he said was true, and also because at least some of the magistrates disliked manufacturers, that Blincoe's mutinous complaints were taken seriously. With Middleton's heartening words in his ears, he strode manfully up to William Woodward, told him that he had come straight from the magistrates' bench in Eyam and handed him a folded piece of parchment, saying: 'Here's a letter for Mr John Needham.' The effect of this revelation on Woodward's countenance was gratifying. No hand was raised in violent reproof. Higher authorities had been invoked, and William Woodward was out of his depth. His business done, Blincoe went to bed in fond anticipation that his hardships at Litton Mill were now at an end.[11]

Early the following morning, John Needham returned from Manchester market, where he had gone to sell the mill's yarn and buy up bales of raw cotton. As soon as he reached the mill from Wormhill, William Woodward handed him the magistrates' letter. The seal broken and the contents digested in shocked disgust, he called for Blincoe. Leaving his mule, Blincoe obeyed the summons. 'Take off your shirt, you damned rascal!' were John Needham's first words.

Worse was to follow. As the profanities poured forth, the horse-whip fell over and over again. Blincoe pleaded for mercy, promising complete obedience for the future. Still the blows rained down.[12]

The Needhams weren't ill-bred entrepreneurs, indifferent to their reputation among the High Peak gentry. Theirs was an old, proud family and, declining fortunes or not, they cared what people said about them. This lowly bastard had compromised the family's name. So John Needham's horse-whip lashed Blincoe's back until he was striped with bruises and weals. Finally, his fury expended, John instructed Blincoe to put his shirt back on and return to work. As Blincoe crossed over to the mill, Needham roared with passionate animosity: 'You'll go again, will you?'[13]

17

Seeking redress

In agony, Blincoe limped back to his spinning machine, 'scarcely able to stand, and covered with additional bruises from head to foot.' Escaping again wasn't going to be easy. In response to his truancy, security measures at the mill were tightened up. Roll-calls were taken at every dinner time in the 'prentice house, and the mill gates locked when the journeymen had left for the night. Blincoe was in any case too sore to travel any distance. It took four days for him to recover sufficiently from the blows he had received to put into action a new plan.[1]

Blincoe knew that unless he managed to pull the wrath of the magistrates upon John and Ellis's heads, then he would go on suffering grievously for going to Stanton-Hall and Eyam. He could be certain that further retribution was to come. So, on Sunday night, he stealthily followed the journeymen as they approached the gates on their way home. Crouching low, he then rushed out unseen by the warder. Within minutes the roll-call was under way and Blincoe's absence was noted. The 'door warder', however, adamantly insisted that he hadn't escaped through the main gate. A general search then began of the mill and its grounds. This was just as Blincoe had hoped, and he now had time to make good his escape. Having climbed the Slack, he arrived in Litton village and called at the house of Joseph Robinson, the mill's humane joiner.[2]

Robinson spared him some supper, allowed him to sleep in the same bed as his sons, and in the morning furnished him with bread and meat. Having promised never to reveal the identity of his benefactor, Blincoe then set off for Leam Hall. It was raining, and Blincoe recalled in his *Memoir* how he had struggled through the wet with neither hat nor coat. The walk took him through Eyam, past the Bull's

Head, and then directly north alongside the fast-flowing River Derwent. After walking for about seven miles, Blincoe saw high up to the left of the river, through the groves of trees that lined the banks, the outline of Leam Hall. An elegant bay window looked down towards the valley, and a venerable spread of ivy covered much of the hall's exterior. With trepidation and tired limbs, Blincoe approached its pillared entrance.[3]

By the time he arrived there, the rain was beating down. Knocking at the door, Blincoe was admitted by a manservant and ordered to wait. It wasn't yet time for squires to arise. Some minutes later, Marmaduke Middleton finally appeared. Blincoe deferentially approached, 'crawling like a spaniel dog', and said (his lines no doubt rehearsed much of the way there): 'Sir, I have come again, Mr Needham has been beating me worse than ever, as soon as he read your letter over.' If it happened as Blincoe later told the story, it was artfully done. For all of his fawning deference, he had left Middleton with the unpleasant feeling that his own explicit instructions had been casually ignored by a mere manufacturer. Blincoe's insubordination now seemed far less brazen. The Needhams were the ones requiring a stern reminder of their place.[4]

Noticing the boy's wretched state, Middleton told him to 'go into the kitchen and rest'. He then added: '[You] should not have come here first; you should have gone to Mr Cheek of Whetstone Hall, and he would have given you a summons.' Confused by the magistrate's talk of protocol, Blincoe realised that this was likely to turn into a fool's errand. And he had gambled much on success. 'Eh, Sir', he began, emboldened by desperation, 'he will do nought for me – he is so thick with my master – they are often drinking together.' 'Pshaw, pshaw', responded Middleton, 'he's like to listen to you, he must.' But, a man of the world, Middleton took the precaution of writing a letter to the attorney. Blincoe gratefully seized the parchment, gorged himself on bread and cheese from the magistrate's extensive larder, and then set off on a twelve-mile hike, through the now driving rain, to Whetstone Hall.

Having arrived there, cold, drenched and hungry, Blincoe was surprised to see a familiar face. Sally Oldfield's husband had been governor of the 'prentice house at Litton. He was now dead, and his widow worked for Shaw and Cheek as a housekeeper. 'Eh, Parson! What do you want here?' she said suspiciously. 'I have a letter from Mr Middleton to Mr Cheek', was his reply. Catching on quickly, Sally recoiled: 'Are you going against your master?' Blincoe told her of the savage ill-treatment he and others had endured, none of which could have surprised her. Sally was impassive. All that mattered was that this paltry work'us apprentice was committing a sin for which there could never be any justification, Hanway and Peel notwithstanding: 'Eh!' Sally exclaimed, 'Thou should'st not go against thy master.' Further debate was futile. But not entirely cold-hearted, she plied him with bread, cheese and beer from her employers' larder, repeating her inviolable rule: 'Parson, thou mun never go against they master.' She then bid him wait.[5]

Several hours later, Blincoe still sat in the kitchen of Whetstone Hall, waiting. No one spoke to him and no mention was made of the letter he had brought from Marmaduke Middleton. In all likelihood, Cheek was in Tideswell where he did most of his business. But having been betrayed, as Blincoe now realised, by the St Pancras parish officers, and then by both the Lamberts and the Needhams, he was quick to feel the victim of a ruse. Doubting that the magistrate was serious or that Cheek would ever renege on his own client, he left the kitchen, let himself out, and walked the four or so miles back to the mill.

Back at Litton, Blincoe played an intelligent hand. His mission had been a disaster, and John Needham's fury promised to be lethal in its intensity. But he went straight up to William Woodward, told him that he had been to see the magistrate and the attorney, and said that he would agree not to take formal legal action if Woodward guaranteed that he would receive no further beatings. 'On these conditions', Woodward apparently said, 'I will, if I can.' And between then and the end of his period of apprenticeship in 1813, Blincoe said that he was spared the rod. Other children were thrashed with impunity, but his courage won him a reprieve. A young man who had traversed much of the High Peak in search of redress was deserving of respect. And the overlookers no doubt realised that if legal action were taken for the ill-treatment of apprentices, the iron fist of the law would fall heaviest on themselves and not the owners.[6]

The Needhams were in a different kind of trouble. Around about the time that Blincoe made his appeal to the justices in Eyam, Ellis Needham and his two eldest sons, John and Ellis, went into Buxton and arranged to borrow £628 from Messrs Goodwin, town bankers. They then behaved with astonishing stupidity. Having paid back the first half of the loan shortly after, they fell out with George Goodwin and refused to pay any more. The predictable result was that they lost the £319 they had paid and incurred the penalty of £1,258. In desperation, Ellis Needham secretly mortgaged the Old Hall for £10,000 to a Mr Fogg. He had just a few years to pay his debts, otherwise he would have to give up the family estate.[7]

Blincoe had no idea about the woeful financial state of his employer. But sometime in the summer of 1813, now aged 21 and therefore at the end of his period of apprenticeship, he at last received his indenture papers. Leaving the counting house, he held in his hand the thin sheaf of parchment, signed by two St Pancras magistrates, which had condemned him to fourteen years of miserable servitude. His feelings must have been mixed. Deciphering the handwriting on the document, Blincoe discovered that his official name was 'Robert Blincoe'. Seeing his surname for the first time, he perhaps felt at long last a concrete link with his antecedents. No longer need he feel so completely cut adrift, so severed from the past and so entirely alone. Like Dickens' Noah Claypole, he too now had the satisfaction of being able to trace his genealogy back to his parents. But while Blincoe's indentures had answered a burning question, the answer he received could only have intensified his already deep sense of loss. For Blincoe still had no definite idea whether any of his family still lived, or why he had been abandoned at the workhouse back in 1796.[8]

Coming to the end of his period of apprenticeship did mean that Blincoe could start earning a wage. He had no fondness for Litton Mill, but this was as near to a home as he had, and he knew that he couldn't leave without some savings to tide him over until he found work. So he stayed for a further year after his 21st birthday. His wage was four shillings and sixpence per week, well below a living wage anywhere else, and beneath the dignity of most journeymen spinners. Blincoe, however, knew no better. When he received his first pay he felt 'incalculably rich', splurging it on a feast of wheaten cakes and pickled herrings.[9]

As a journeyman spinner, Blincoe was also now free from the threat of physical abuse. Many of his fellow parish apprentices, as seems to have been the case with William Woodward, at this juncture graduated into abusers themselves. We have two indications that Blincoe resisted this fate. In 1833 he told an official investigator into factory conditions that he had taken on a poor cripple unable to get work anywhere else. This was the action of no ordinary employer, bent only on making a fast return. Moreover, in 1828 a letter appeared in a newspaper called *The Lion* written by a man, John Joseph Betts, claiming to have worked at Litton Mill alongside Blincoe. In fact, Betts said that he had worked under Blincoe when the latter had become a spinner 'without receiving any harsh treatment from him'. He went on:

> – nay, so far was Blincoe from ill-treating the apprentices employed under him, that he would frequently give part of his allowance of food to those under his care out of mere commiseration, and conceal all insignificant omissions without a word of reproach.

John Joseph Betts was the secretary of a cotton-spinners' union in the nearby town of Ashton, his ire against his earlier abusers channelled into a campaign against the mill-owning class at large. It's highly unlikely that he lied about having been apprenticed to Ellis Needham – he had too many enemies who would eagerly seize on any evidence of dishonesty – and it most certainly wasn't his style to conceal episodes of ill-treatment in cotton mills. So it would seem that Blincoe bucked convention and matured into a humane and generous young man.[10]

After a few months, however, Blincoe sickened of Litton Mill. His initial euphoria at receiving a wage was checked by the recurrent failure of the Needhams to pay him his dues. Each month on pay day, he was simply told to be patient. And while rumours perhaps did penetrate the glen as to the Needhams' mounting debts, these would have brought him small comfort, for Ellis and John were staving off their creditors with money deducted from their workers' wages. When finally Blincoe was due six months' salary and received a meagre 30 shillings, he decided that he would be better off almost anywhere else. And so, on 15 May 1814, memorable as the day of Tideswell's May Fair, Robert Blincoe left Litton Mill. He had a new name, a new status as a journeyman spinner, and several coins jangled in his pockets. But he wasn't the strapping 22-year-old he would have been if apprenticed into a gentler, domestic trade. Blincoe's health and youth had been wrecked by the imperative of first the Lamberts and then the Needhams to make cotton-spinning pay.[11]

Blincoe walked out of the mill yard, passed its gates, and wove his way up the Slack for the very last time. While he had no idea where he would spend the night, he left Litton with a strong sense of purpose. He headed north to the village of Chapel-en-le-Frith, determined to seek guidance from one of its most famous residents, Old Beckkà, the 'celebrated fortune teller'. Blincoe knew her by reputation. William Woodward had often gone to see her when things had gone missing at the mill to learn the name of the culprit; considering her fame, many a purloiner must have admitted his or her guilt as soon as her name was invoked. Blincoe sought her out to ease the painful anxiety of not knowing where he was to go, and perhaps also to find out something about his parents.[12]

He found her in a small dwelling, with an appearance perfectly suited to her vocation. She was, Brown wrote, a 'haggard, black, horrid-looking creature, very old, with a long beard, and dressed like a person who lived in ages past.' Blincoe timidly approached, handing her the shilling piece she charged for each consultation. It was equivalent to more a day's work at Litton Mill, but Old Beckkà was said to have made so much money from her oracular gifts that she owned a fine house and lands. Given the potency of superstition in Derbyshire at the time, this may have been true. John Farey deemed the High Peak region to be deplorably addicted to 'humbug'. He cited the belief that hazel-sticks held in the hand could be used to detect veins of lead ore; that colts castrated under certain signs of the Zodiac would die; and that fairy elves lived in the caves behind Lumsdale waterfall. Only the common people of Wales and Scotland are more 'prone to superstition and credulity', he concluded with a xenophobic flourish. Blincoe didn't for a moment doubt Old Beckkà's Delphic powers. Awed by her fame and terrified of her sorcery, he sat down before her. She passed him a cup of tea, instructed him to 'shake it well', then took it back, poured out the water leaving only the leaves, and proceeded to tell his fortune. She began, the *Memoir* tells us: 'You came from the outside of London, did you not?' Blincoe's awe deepened. 'You came down in a wagon, and have been at a place surrounded with high rocks and great waters, and you have been used worse than a stumbling stone?'[13]

Of course, these were not Old Beckkà's exact words. They were recalled by Blincoe nearly a decade after the event; but there's no cause to doubt that the scene unfolded in all essentials as the *Memoir* described. Within moments, Blincoe was transfixed. In a long life of clever deceit, Old Beckkà had probably never had an easier brief. Here was a young boy, entirely on his own, in a strange county, whose clothes reeked of oil and were probably still decorated with cotton fluff. Working in a cotton mill in the High Peak inevitably meant that he toiled near water, and the fact that he was just a few miles from Litton, Cressbrook and Calver mills strongly suggested that there were cliffs nearby. Working out that he was originally from London was easy too. The majority of parish apprentices were from the city's workhouses, and even the slightest imperfection in his Derbyshire accent made certain that he was one of the hundreds of local children brought up in wagons.

Pressing home her advantage, Old Beckkà now told Blincoe something that he was desperate to believe true. 'Your troubles are at an end', she said, 'you shall rise above them and those who have cast you down so low. You shall see their downfall, and your head shall be higher than theirs. Poor lad! Terrible have been thy sufferings. Thou shall get up in the world; you'll go to another place, where there'll be a big water, and so go thy way in peace.' It was a consummate performance, and even if what she said was plainly counterfeit to the more seasoned mind, it was all in a good cause. For Blincoe left Old Beckkà's hovel in the highest of spirits, his dread of the future temporarily lifted in the confident expectation of a better life to come. Unfortunately, Beckkà had been hazy on the specifics. As he marched to the edge of Chapel-en-le-Frith, Blincoe arrived at a large crossroads and had no idea which way to go. Flipping a coin in the air, he resolved to walk in whichever direction it rolled. And so, on the afternoon of 14 May 1814, he headed north again.[14]

18

A belated political education

For ten long years, sequestered in remote Miller's Dale, Blincoe had been isolated from the political currents of the world. It had been in the interests of the Needhams to seal off their apprentices lest they hear of Peel's 1802 Act or Romilly's parliamentary inquiry. They may also have feared that their operatives would read of cotton-spinners' strikes or hear radical talk of manhood suffrage. Worse still, they might encounter Tom Paine's scandalously seditious writings. In prose rippling with rhetorical power, Paine's 1792 *The Rights of Man* told the lower orders to sweep away tyranny in all its forms. Not only harsh manufacturers were left trembling in its wake; most of Paine's ire was directed against the combined forces of the established Church and monarchical state. It's almost certain that word of the Luddite outrages also reached Blincoe's ears. News of Admiral Nelson's victories at the Nile and Trafalgar surely infiltrated the glen too, but very little else besides.[1]

Over the next few months, Blincoe found work in villages and towns with access to newspapers of all stripes: Whig, Tory and Radical. He now underwent a belated political education. Perhaps the most striking change from the days when Jacob Leroux had galvanised the respectable citizenry of St Pancras against seditious elements was that criticism of the government was no longer immediately associated with anti-patriotic Jacobinism. In the 1790s, xenophobic and distrustful of new ideas, most Englishmen had turned on the Radicals in their midst. Hundreds of makeshift effigies of Tom Paine were burnt, and the Tory *Manchester Mercury* implored its readers to 'crush those insidious vipers who would poison the minds of the people.' Needing little encouragement, 'Church and King' mobs had smashed the windows and torched the houses of well-known supporters of the French Revolution. The democrat chemist Joseph Priestley saw years of work and a fortune in scientific equipment incinerated by a Birmingham loyalist mob. But by the 1810s, 'Church and King' mobs were hard to muster, and while Tom Paine was beloved of only a small minority, few were the inns that now posted signs on their doors reading 'No Jacobins admitted here'.[2]

After more than a decade of a war which was short on victories but vast in its expense, critics of the Tory administration multiplied. Following the 1808 'Orders in Council', Spencer Perceval's misguided retaliatory measure designed to stifle French trade, larger manufacturers joined the chorus of opposition. As raw cotton supplies plummeted, distress in manufacturing towns and villages escalated. Thirty-two cotton mills were said to have stood idle in Manchester in 1812, and embittered merchants and manufacturers compiled huge petitions demanding repeal. When Perceval, by then Prime Minister, was assassinated in late 1812, at least one wealthy industrialist felt that divine justice had been served. 'It is indeed disgusting', he admitted, but 'the finger of a benevolent Providence is visible in this horrible event.'[3]

For the present, the capitalist classes said little about constitutional reform. Such talk surfaced periodically in Westminster, though aristocratic Whigs were now blowing cool on the matter. They had once seen the idea of giving the vote to the middling orders as an effective means of limiting the power of the King and his Tory ministers. But the Terror of 1792 had impelled most of them to beat a retreat into a safer conformity. Outside Parliament, patriotism, fear, and a habitude to quiet suffering induced a state of relative social harmony. There were occasional riots, Luddism gave the manufacturers an unpleasant scare, and a series of industrial strikes disturbed the social equipoise. But between 1797 and 1815, despite crippling levels of income tax and repeated martial setbacks, Radicalism failed to thrive. That it continued to worry Lord Sidmouth, the arch-Tory Home Secretary, had much to do with the energy of four men. After leaving Litton Mill, Blincoe heard their names often: Sir Francis Burdett, Major John Cartwright, William Cobbett, and Henry Hunt.

Burdett was born into an old gentry family with its lands in Warwickshire and ambitions in Westminster. As an MP after 1796, he became a vehement Tory-baiter, attacking Pitt for going to war with France, for raising taxes to fund the war, and for repressing those who disliked Pitt's hawkish policies. Political Radicals of the day demanded an extension of the voting franchise to embrace the middle and, sometimes, the lower classes, but like many of them, Burdett saw extending the franchise as a means of restoring an Anglo-Saxon Arcadia. While his radicalism pulsed harder than that of any Whig, he had little taste for full manhood suffrage, advocating a rate-payer franchise, annual parliaments, and equal electoral districts. Burdett was 'dangerous' but he was also a 'large-acred man', and after a youthful flirtation with revolutionary politics, his gentlemanly origins steered him away from Jacobin extremism. Yet Burdett was radical nonetheless and in 1810 troops stormed his London house and escorted him to the Tower after he had attacked the government's running of the war. Riots erupted, troops and rioters clashed in the streets, and with his martyrdom, Burdett's fame crescendoed.[4]

Burdett's preferred allies in the struggle to return the constitution to the pristine state enshrined, he said, in Magna Carta were often land-owning gentlemen rather like himself. Burdett spoke for the 'people', but he lacked easy familiarity with them. Major John Cartwright's radicalism was also alloyed with patrician sensibilities. Hailing from a family of landowners, Cartwright began his career as a talented naval officer. During the American war, he concluded that English political life had been corrupted and that only parliamentary reform could regenerate it. Initially partial to the idea of manhood suffrage, his radicalism had weakened by the 1790s. But no one spent as much time as Cartwright in carriage or on horseback promoting the Radical cause. Although over 70, he spent 1812 and 1813 as a 'political missionary', touring the country collecting signatures for petitions demanding a tax-paying franchise and annual parliaments. His 1813 tour alone amassed 130,000 signatures. The Hampden Clubs that he pioneered, named after the gutsy opponent of Stuart tyranny, spread the gospel of reform across the north of England.[5]

But the written words of William Cobbett rose above the rest. A supreme journalist and master rhetorician, his prose was direct, muscular and refreshingly vernacular, and he had the true-born Englishman's distaste for what he called 'feelosofers'. According to the Lancashire Radical Samuel Bamford, by late 1816 Cobbett's *Political Register* was selling between 40,000 and 50,000 copies a week, and being 'read on nearly every cottage hearth in the manufacturing districts of South Lancashire, in those of Leicester, Derby and Nottingham.' Long before then, Cobbett was the toast of poor weavers, stockingers, colliers, and thousands more. With his 'ruddy countenance' and dress of 'blue coat, yellow swansdown waistcoat' and 'top boots', Cobbett was the image 'of a respectable English farmer', and as a younger man, he had had the bluff Tory politics to match. In fact, he had started his *Political Register* in 1802 as a pro-government rag. But when Pitt's government offered him a hefty bribe in return for continued loyalty, both he and it underwent a remarkable metamorphosis. Cobbett started to read his nemesis Tom Paine seriously, and came to believe that what his old enemy had had to say about government corruption, vote-buying and sinecures was shockingly close to the truth.[6]

Now Cobbett turned his enormous talent on those he had once defended. He called it 'The Thing', a system of 'corruption and financial plunder' which serviced thousands of political placemen, stock-jobbers, political peculators, government contractors, pensioners, sycophants, and financial speculators who, Cobbett said, kept the war with France going to fill their own pockets and reaped huge profits from the taxes paid by those who could least afford to do so. Politically scurrilous, but commanding the moral high-ground, the *Political Register* was always there to expose government corruption and excess. In 1809 Cobbett was arrested and tried for sedition before a packed court-room and a judge who obviously loathed him. The next two years he spent in Newgate prison. But Cobbett was a gentleman and, although a convicted criminal, he was treated with dignity. Living in relative ease in rooms let by the gaoler, he went on issuing the *Political Register*. On his release, 600 fellow Radicals threw a dinner for him, and church bells were rung in towns and villages as he made his way to his Hampshire farm. More than ever he was a thorn in the Tory's side.[7]

While he enthused his poor readers with blistering attacks on government corruption, Cobbett in the early 1810s was no advocate of manhood suffrage. He wrote disapprovingly of giving the vote to 'menial servants, vagrants, pickpockets and scamps of all sorts'. In essence, he was a romantic conservative. He had a visceral hatred for state sleaze and the political timeservers into whose pockets so much of the nation's taxes poured. But here his radicalism ended. Cobbett had no interest in helping to fashion a working-class ideology. For the lower orders he had in mind an improbable return to a gentler age in which free labourers had land to farm and cattle to tend. 'I wish to see the poor men of England', he wrote, 'what the poor men of England were when I was born.' Cobbett hadn't adjusted to the factory age. Despite this, in years to come he would hold forth against the capitalist exploiters of children.[8]

If Cobbett's true medium was the written word, Henry Hunt's was the mass platform. Hunt too had all the credentials of a well-heeled farmer. An unreflecting Tory in his youth, he threw himself into the life of the country gentleman. Hunt's farming innovations had restored his family fortunes, but his showiness and social aspirations alienated the gentry in his native county of Wiltshire, and with extraordinary viciousness they turned against him. Hunt was invited to shoot pheasants on their land and then sued for trespass. For this he was sent down for six months, though his accuser was left seething that in court the defendant had been 'passed off as a gentleman'. Further slights from Wiltshire's snobbish squirearchy finally drove Hunt into the arms of Burdett and Cobbett. But his final falling out with the squires was the result of him falling into the arms of a friend's wife, Mrs Vince, in 1802. Hunt left his wife for her, and she abandoned her husband. Cobbett deplored such behaviour, not least because it tarnished the image of radicalism. 'Beware of him! He rides the country with a whore', he later regretted writing (particularly when sharing a prison cell with Hunt in 1810). Hunt, though, made up for his private life by cutting a dash on the podium. Six foot tall, powerfully built, with a proud bearing and resonant voice, no other mob orator could match him. By 1813, Hunt had emerged as a leading advocate of full manhood suffrage.[9]

In his own way, each of these Radical leaders was vain, opinionated, self-righteous and arrogant. Burdett and Hunt were notoriously proud of their gentlemanly origins, and they all thrived on popular adulation, finding it ample compensation for the indignities of persecution and arrest. A blend of courage and hard-headedness drove Burdett, Cobbett, Hunt and Cartwright to keep the Radical movement alive during the long years of war and repression. But they shared the Radical platform with local leaders, men with far greater kinship with the poor, often weavers, spinners and colliers themselves. A few were Spenceans, followers of the deceased Yorkshire schoolmaster Thomas Spence, who extolled the abolition of property and violent revolution. Most low-born Radicals advocated the more modest but still seditious and headily ambitious principle of manhood suffrage. And they set examples for their brethren to follow, striving to make themselves 'worthy' of the vote by espousing and practising prudence, temperance and literacy. These were serious men who had dragged themselves up from privation to small-time respectability.[10]

But local Radical leaders weren't gentlemen. And so, if they were convicted of sedition or blasphemy there would be no courteous treatment, no gaoler's lodgings, no pen and parchment, no sumptuous feasts on their release. Their campaigns were also frustratingly stop-start, since popular radicalism ebbed with oscillating wages, bread prices, and the peaks and troughs of maritime trade.[11]

Even so, in twenty years radicalism had grown in popularity and intensity. The days of tugged forelocks, respectful bows and reflex deference were numbered. Tory squires still spoke reverentially of 'the duties of property and station', but the inward-looking village in which such attitudes thrived was no longer typical of the nation. Large numbers of working people now saw themselves as members of a distinct social class, its identity derived from a feeling that they were locked into a perpetual struggle against capitalist masters. Not all thought this way, and class antagonism relied on hunger and fear for its sustenance, but the mind-set of the labouring orders was undergoing change. A worried member of the upper classes wrote in these years: 'The cord had been snapped by the revolt of the labouring classes from their natural protectors and best friends.'[12]

In part due to the efforts of Burdett, Cartwright, Hunt and Cobbett, by the 1810s it was no longer possible for the ruling elites to crush radicalism out of hand. The treatment of child workers may not have been at the forefront of the Radical's mind in 1814, but when, two decades later, Michael Sadler, Richard Oastler and George Stringer

Bull addressed the assembled masses in Manchester, the political elbow room they enjoyed had been secured for them by this earlier generation of political outsiders. Talk of democracy remained wild, even visions of limited constitutional reform seemed beyond the pale of practical politics, but the common man and woman were on their way up. The political currents washing across the towns and villages to which Blincoe was bound in 1814 were to create conditions in which he could tell a much wider world of how he had been abused at Litton Mill.

19

Pastures new

Late on Blincoe's first day of walking from Litton, everything he owned slung over his shoulder, he arrived in New Mills. In most directions from Chapel-en-le-Frith he would have found cotton or silk mills, but he must have thought this small town particularly promising. The terrain perfectly suited water-powered spinning. The River Goyt, which flows through the town, had cut a deep gorge into which a series of fast-flowing tributaries poured. These were initially harnessed to process wool, but in 1785 a cotton mill had been built to exploit the turbulent waters of the River Sett. By the time Blincoe arrived, there were at least five cotton-spinning mills. At each of these he applied for work, but without success.[1]

Blincoe, now aged 22, faced the awful prospect of joblessness. This wasn't unusual for former parish apprentices. As Samuel Romilly's parliamentary committee was discovering, when work'us children completed their apprenticeships they were very often cast aside without scruple, adding to the burgeoning ranks of young men and women trained for nothing but drudgery at child's wages. Theodore Price, a Warwickshire magistrate, reported one such case. By chance, he had come across a young woman lying in a ditch by the roadside with an injured leg. She explained to him that she had been laid off from her mill because her fingers were 'now too large to go between the threads'.[2]

Blincoe had, at least, spent some time as a journeyman spinner at Litton Mill, operating his own mule, and now he approached the mill owners requesting the same employment. Few could have been willing, however, to take a gamble on this unhealthy-looking stranger. As any half-decent mill proprietor knew, one spinner was not like any other. Experience and natural acuity made some of them expert judges of cotton fibres, their quality and tenacity. And it required great skill and delicacy to know at what speed to return the mule carriage. Spinners also differed in their reliability and attitudes; those with a 'love of liberty', who were quick to strike, often had to travel large distances to find work, having been blacklisted in one locality. Given all these factors, it's not surprising that one prominent owner remarked: 'We seldom if we can avoid it engage strangers.' A personal recommendation, or 'character', would sometimes do the trick, but Blincoe had had no chance of extracting one of these from the Need-hams. Hence his worrying lack of success at the New Mills factories.[3]

Blincoe walked dejectedly on, still heading in a northerly direction, further and further from Litton. He came next to Mellor. Here lay Samuel Oldknow's mill, about which Dr Denman and Marmaduke Middleton had been so emphatic in their praise. Starting with relatively little, during the 1780s Oldknow had made a fortune as a muslin manufacturer, totally dominating the English market and shipping his wares as far afield as Botany Bay. Oldknow had looked set to become as rich as the Peels and Arkwrights, but then he turned to cotton-spinning and his empire began to crumble. He fell heavily in debt to Richard Arkwright, his muslin monopoly lost its value, and his spinning works failed to thrive. It was his great good fortune that Arkwright was willing to indulge his energetic debtor, such that Oldknow died without the odium of bankruptcy, owing him an enor-mous £205,000. It was also thanks to Arkwright's forbearance that he was able to partly realise his dream of creating a 'garden city'.[4]

At Mellor, in Derbyshire, Oldknow purchased an extensive estate and built what Robert Owen described as 'a large, handsome and very imposing cotton mill'. When Blincoe approached the mill in 1814, it comprised six storeys with three staircases jutting out from the side as an architectural flourish. Owen added that the mill was 'beautifully situated', lying amid extensive lawns and alongside two large ponds excavated to drive the waterwheel. But cotton-spinning was, for Oldknow, only the beginning. Striving to create a self-contained com-munity, he built scores of houses for workers and apprentices close to the mill. He then bought farmland in which he sunk coal pits and later set up lime kilns. As a keen farmer, Oldknow also established tree plantations, carefully selecting Spanish chestnut for use as fence posts, as well as introducing merino sheep, rearing beef cattle and setting up a dairy. Oldknow's workers were even supplied with their very own smallholdings, and encouraged to keep cattle for milk and meat. To improve communications with the outside world, Oldknow finally had roads and bridges constructed, partly from his own quarries. His hope was to make Mellor self-sufficient.[5]

In this ambitious plan he ultimately failed. Oldknow nonetheless created a working environment for his operatives and apprentices rivalled by few. The work'us orphans he had sent up from London were in many respects better off under his care than they had been in their own parishes. Mellor apprentices had milk porridge and wheaten bread for breakfast and, according to reliable testimony, some form of meat every day, and tasty pies every other day. The children were also allowed to pick and eat fruit from the orchard. And even if their hours – from six in the morning until seven in the evening – were long, they compared favourably with those of any other mill. Official reports and oral traditions long kept alive by the descendants of the parish apprentices confirm that Oldknow was, for the time, an unusually humane employer, one with the air of a benevolent squire. As an elderly local recalled in 1925, 'No one ever had owt to complain of at Mellor.'[6]

Blincoe went directly to the counting house, no doubt marvelling at the scale of the mill and the fineness of its grounds. There he asked to see the under-manager, John Clayton, Oldknow's half-brother, who

14. An engraving of Mellor Mill showing one of the reservoirs that dominated its attractive site.

was in effective charge of the mill's operations. Clayton tried to establish some credentials, inspecting Blincoe's indentures and asking where he had come from. Blincoe later told of how the conversation piqued the interest of two or three men who happened to be standing nearby. One of them asked: 'Did you come from Pancras workhouse?' Blincoe responded in the affirmative, to which his questioner is said to have replied: 'Why, we are all come from thence! We brought many children the other day to this Mill.' These parish officials examined Blincoe's papers and told him: 'Some of these officers are dead.' Next they asked him how his legs came to be so terribly bent and twisted. Blincoe briefly described the poor diet, long hours and cruelties he had endured at Lowdham and Litton mills. Anxious to avoid seeming rebellious in front of Mr Clayton, he kept to himself the deep bitterness he felt about the lies their predecessors had told of roast beef, plum pudding and horse riding. The officials, the *Memoir* says, took notes on this 'victim of parochial economy' without further comment. Then they departed.[7]

If we had only John Brown's words to rely on here, this part of the story might sound too far-fetched to be believed. Blincoe happening to encounter officers from his own parish of birth sounds like the kind of coincidence, stirring but wildly implausible, in which Charles Dickens specialised. In *Oliver Twist* we're asked to accept that Mr Brownlow, the stranger whose pocket Oliver was falsely accused of picking, had known his mother; that Oliver's half-brother Monks recognised him as kin just by seeing him in the street; and that the house that Oliver was forced to burgle with Sikes was the home of his dead mother's sister. The fluke of meeting parish officers in Oldknow's mill is less dramatic, but the odds against it were extremely long. It says much for Blincoe's reliability, however, that the St Pancras parish register contains a list of nineteen children sent from the workhouse to Samuel Oldknow's mill on 21 June 1814. This was a month after Blincoe left Needham's employ, so the timing is perfect. The St Pancras children had just been delivered, in person, by the beadles and overseers. Presumably in response to growing public outrage, the parish officials were now checking to see that conditions weren't too scandalous in the mills to which they sent work'us children. Blincoe met them as they were completing the task.[8]

Perhaps sympathising with Blincoe's plight, John Clayton offered him a position at Mellor Mill starting the following morning. At once, the under-manager instructed someone to show Blincoe to his new lodgings. He must have been struck by the vast improvement in his situation when comparing his new rooms with the dreary and overcrowded Litton Mill 'prentice house. But Blincoe tells us that he didn't tarry. Rushing back into the town, he asked around to find out where the parochial officials were staying, burning with a desire to find out from them something 'as to his parentage'. He soon discovered, to his horror, that they had already departed for London.[9]

The following day, Blincoe arrived at the mill at six in the morning. He considered it no worker's paradise. The operatives and apprentices had to work hard, and the mill doors were locked during work hours to prevent them from taking impromptu breaks. But Blincoe explained to John Brown that Mellor was vastly better than Litton. This speaks extremely well of the honesty of his reflections and the relative probity of his biographer. Although both had a vested interest in blackening the image of cotton mills and the entire breed of men who ran them, Blincoe told of how the parish apprentices 'looked healthy and well', were 'well fed' with meals 'good and sufficient', and were also 'kept clean, decently dressed, and every Sunday went twice to Marple Church, with Mr Clayton, their under-master, at their head.' It's hard to imagine Ellis Needham leading the ragged, listless Litton Mill apprentices to Tideswell Church.[10]

For several months Blincoe worked, uneventfully, as a journeyman spinner in Mellor Mill. Then he found out that he was receiving three or four shillings less a week than his fellow spinners. Since he was habituated to a Spartan diet, the eleven shillings he earned was easily enough to cover his needs; he even managed to set aside three shillings a week in savings. But Blincoe's ingrained sense of justice rebelled against Clayton's parsimony, so one evening, after work, he went to the counting house and asked to see him. Blincoe said: 'Sir, if you please, will you be so good to rise my wages?' These words were anathema to any mill boss, and Clayton swung round, saying: 'Raise your wages! Why, I took you in upon *charity only*.' Now Blincoe had his answer. As John Brown pointed out, it was in fact quite typical for those injured or crippled in one mill to be paid less in others. But in describing this scene, Brown gives us a rare insight into his subject's personality. We're told that Blincoe had a 'rich vein of sarcastic humour', and so he replied, in 'somewhat ironical terms', with the words: 'I am sure it was very good of you, Sir.' Given what he had been through, such bitterness was to be expected. But sarcasm could be an effective form of subversion among the lower ranks, a way in which underdogs could mock their superiors while seeming to behave with due deference. It's easy to believe that in this manner Blincoe preserved his self-respect. Clayton merely sent him on his way with a vague, 'Well, go to your work, I'll see.'[11]

Two weeks later, Blincoe found his pay raised by two shillings a week, still less than the other spinners but a marked improvement. Then he received alarming news. Soon after his appeal for a raise, Mr Clayton hired a new man at the mill. Blincoe was thereupon sent his wages at his mule, along with an order to depart immediately. He had been sacked – 'getting the bag' in contemporary parlance. After seven months of faultless labour, he once more faced destitution. Clayton had been severe, but men had been kicked out for less. An overlooker who later gave evidence to a government commission told of how he had been 'ordered to turn them away … for very trifling offences; I have known them to be turned away out of my apartment for stopping too long at the necessary making water.' Blincoe, however, was horrified, and rushed to the counting house. Knowing it was futile to seek reinstatement, he earnestly entreated Clayton to at least provide him with 'a character'. 'O no; O no!' he is said to have replied, 'we never give characters here.' Blincoe had seriously erred in asking for more. There's no reason to think that Clayton was especially hard or intolerant. Tailoring pay to a worker's level of need was standard practice, and stamping down assertive employees was all part of the mill's disciplinary regime. Blincoe's righteous appeals were inevitably read as expressions of militant inclinations.[12]

Returning to his lodgings, Blincoe wrapped his few possessions together, tied them to a stick, slung it over his shoulder and set off once more. He had managed to save several pounds during his time at Mellor, and frugality was by now so deeply rooted in his nature that he ate only penny cakes on his walk, quenching his thirst from rivers and streams along the way. Blincoe walked about eighteen miles into the neighbouring county of Cheshire, and eventually found work at the cotton mill of a Mr Lomax in the village of Bollington, not far from the thriving silk town of Macclesfield. Lomax told Blincoe that he would have his own mule to operate within two weeks, and offered to hire him in the meantime to work in the carding room. Blincoe reluctantly agreed – as he knew from experience, working amid the dust and flue emanating from carding engines was notoriously hard on eyes, throat and lungs. Richard Arkwright, son of the inventor and entrepreneur, and not one to mince his words, said that before the later introduction of proper ventilation, 'it was the most dusty of all the rooms'; adding with greater emphasis, 'it was excessively dusty.' In this oppressive atmosphere Blincoe worked his fortnight, doing labour usually reserved for women and children, stripping cotton off cards and passing it on to the spinners.[13]

After a fortnight, Lomax failed to come up with the promised mule, perhaps never having intended to do so, and Blincoe therefore left. It was now around spring of the year 1815. Once again, as if deter-mined to leave Litton further and further behind, Blincoe walked north, eventually arriving at the town of Stalybridge. Here, in what lately had been a quiet village of no more than 150 people, mostly farmers with a sprinkling of domestic spinners and weavers, eleven large cotton mills operated by 1811. Their waterwheels and steam engines rotated more than 100,000 spindles, while new canals linked Stalybridge to the coalfields of Ashton and Dukinfield and to the markets of Manchester. The town, in short, was thriving.[14]

Blincoe soon discovered that one of his Lowdham overlookers, William Gamble, had the same role at one of Stalybridge's largest factories. Gamble secured for him a job at the mill where he himself worked, Thomas Harrison's spinning factory at Rassbottom. It had been dubbed 'The Bastille' by locals because of its formidable size and the fact that a high wall surrounded the site. In finding Blincoe a job, Gamble had a less than paternal regard. He insisted that the younger man stay with him and pay for bed and board. Blincoe's wages went straight to Gamble, and little was left after his expenses had been met. Quickly tiring of being fleeced, and probably finding an old oppressor uncongenial company, Blincoe moved out. He found his work no more tolerable. Once more confined to the carding room, he had to strip a considerable six pounds of cotton per day from the cards in order to keep his employment.[15]

Sick of the hard labour and low wages at the Bastille, after several months Blincoe gave notice, quit his job, and after a short time found work in the mill owned by one John Leech. In 1805 Leech had built the first of Stalybridge's steam-powered cotton mills, on Grosvenor Street, its fourteen-horsepower Boulton and Watt engines driving dozens of mules. A genuine pioneer, he was also the first to introduce gas lighting into his mills. But Blincoe was once again subject to the 'foul and dirty' carding room. Without a character, it seemed that no one would let him loose on a mule. So he went to Leech and asked for his wages in advance for the three days he had already worked. Then, to his boss's abject horror, Blincoe left the mill, not to return. In a small place like Stalybridge, where the owners knew one another intimately, this was an extremely risky move.[16]

It seems that Blincoe's reward was to spend some weeks unemployed in the summer of 1815. Had it lasted long, he would have been forced to return to Tideswell where he had a Poor Law settlement. Finally he did get another position, albeit in the hated carding room, at William Bayley's mill on Queen Street. As the *Memoir* explained and independent records confirm, William's father Joseph had had his arm torn off by spinning machinery a few months before, and died hours later due to shock and blood loss. Evidently, the smaller masters spent plenty of time on the mill floor. But if masters like the Bayleys took so few precautions to make their mills safe for themselves, there was no hope for their employees.[17]

Around the autumn of 1815, Robert Blincoe left Bayley's employ. He then walked the seven or eight miles from Stalybridge to Manchester. Fed up with the suffocating flue of the carding room and its meagre wages, he decided to try his luck at the centre of the English textile industry. The mighty Cottonopolis had a new recruit.

1. St Pancras Old Church in the late 1700s set amid open meadows. © Camden Local Studies and Archives Centre

2. James Gillray's 1809 cartoon of Woodville's smallpox hospital shows Edward Jenner administering cowpox with disastrous, albeit humorous, results. Gillray's caricature illustrates the scepticism which Jenner's discovery elicited. Woodville was an early convert. Private collection / Bridgeman Art Library

3. Sir Richard Arkwright, inventor and entrepreneur, whose water-frame revolutionised the spinning of cotton. © National Portrait Gallery, London

4. Samuel Crompton's mules in action. An adult spinner pushes back the mule carriage as a female piecer ties broken threads together and a young scavenger clears away waste cotton. The mules at Litton Mill would have been smaller and would have required more workers.

5. The Old Hall in the hamlet of Wormhill. From this fine residence, Ellis Needham ran the mill in the valley below. This photograph was taken around the middle years of the 19th century, but the house remained virtually unchanged from the days when the Needhams had lived there. Courtesy of Helen Mycock

6. The weir at Litton Mill as it looks today. Most of the buildings date from the late 1800s, but one can see the surging waters of the River Wye and the steep hills and woods surrounding the mill. © Julian Hill-Landolt

7. Leam Hall, seat of Marmaduke Middleton, as it looks today. The exterior of the house has hardly changed since this 'old English gentleman' received a bedraggled Robert Blincoe. © Julian Hill-Landolt

8. The Bull's Head Inn in the village of Eyam, at which Blincoe appealed to the High Peak justices. It has since been converted into residences. © Julian Hill-Landolt

9. Detail from James Gillray's cartoon 'Posting to the election, – a scene on the road to Brentford, Novr 1806' showing William Cobbett beating the drum of political reform. Few political writers troubled the government of Lord Liverpool more than Cobbett, yet in appearance he was, as Samuel Bamford put it, the 'perfect representation of what he always wished to be – an English gentleman-farmer'. © National Portrait Gallery, London

10. 'The Peterloo Massacre': a depiction of the Manchester yeoman cavalry charging the crowd gathered to hear 'Orator' Hunt, Richard Carlile and others speak on 16 April 1819 in St Peter's Field, Manchester. This terrible event took place only a few minutes' walk from the home of Mr and Mrs Blincoe. British Museum / Bridgeman Art Library

11. Lord Ashley, later the seventh Earl of Shaftesbury. Lord Ashley spearheaded the Ten Hours Bill after Michael Sadler's demise, and ensured that the issue of factory reform remained on the parliamentary agenda. © National Portrait Gallery, London

12. The only surviving photograph of Robert Blincoe. He was in his late 50s at the time of this sitting. Courtesy of Edward Blincoe

13. A photograph, unfortunately in poor condition, of Martha Blincoe (née Simpson). Courtesy of Edward Blincoe

14. Bank House on Gunco Lane in Macclesfield, the residence of Martha and George Parker. Both Martha senior and Robert senior died here. Courtesy of Julian Blincoe

15. The Reverend Robert Blincoe in his prime. Copies of this lithograph portrait of an 'able, energetic, and accomplished divine' were advertised for sale in the *Illustrated London News* in 1855. Courtesy of Edward Blincoe

16. The Reverend Robert Blincoe as an older man. His photograph exudes little of his youthful confidence. Courtesy of Edward Blincoe

17. Frances ('Fanny') Trollope, author of the controversial novel *Michael Armstrong*, much of which was based on the experiences of Robert Blincoe. © National Portrait Gallery, London

18. St Luke's Church, designed by Nicholas Hawksmoor, where the Reverend Blincoe preached for seventeen years. © London Borough of Islington

PART 4

Cottonopolis

Civil government … is in reality instituted for the defence of the rich against the poor, or of those who have some property against those who have none at all.

Adam Smith, *The Wealth of Nations* (1776)

… the chimney of the world. Rich rascals, poor rogues, drunken ragamuffins and prostitutes from the moral, soot made into paste by rain the physique, and the only view is a long chimney: what a place!

General Napier on Manchester (1839)

Surely there never was such fragile china-ware as that of which the millers of Coketown were made. … They were ruined, when they were required to send labouring children to school; they were ruined, when inspectors were appointed to look into their works; they were ruined, when such inspectors considered it doubtful whether they were quite justified in chopping people up with their machinery; they were utterly undone, when it was hinted that perhaps they need not always make quite so much smoke.

Charles Dickens, *Hard Times* (1854)

20

'Peace mad'

Nearing Manchester back in 1798, the working-class politician Samuel Bamford had been struck by 'a vast gloom darkening before us'. A few miles closer and he 'heard the rumbling of wheels, and the clang of hammers, and a hubbub of confused sounds from workshops and manufactories.' Then there had been only one cotton mill in the city, Richard Arkwright's giant near Shudehill. Looking west across the Rivers Irwell and Irk in those days, one could see 'green and undulating uplands, intersected by luxuriant meadows'. Seventeen years later, when Robert Blincoe arrived, much of it was hidden beneath cobblestones and newly-laid streets. Manchester was the shock city of the industrial age. Its population had swollen by 100,000 souls and there were now 86 steam-powered spinning factories, not to mention scores of foundries, machine manufacturers and firms specialising in precision engineering. The din of mill, warehouse, foundry and forge produced a thunderous wall of noise.[1]

Long before he reached the city's outskirts, Blincoe could see ribbons of smoke partially obscuring huge red-brick spinning mills, church steeples straining to outdo more numerous factory chimneys, and a skyline corrugated with the roofs of row after row of jammed-in workmen's houses. Approaching from Stalybridge, Blincoe walked close by Ancoats Hall, an elegant Tudor timber-framed mansion on the eastern side of the city. There were still a few fields thereabouts, but Ancoats was in the process of being transformed into a densely-packed industrial suburb. Here lay several of the larger mills, well served by canals which connected the city to the domestic source of raw cotton in Liverpool. Few of those who had been charmed by the cotton mills set among the rugged hills of the Peak District saw anything to admire in these constructions. For all the horrors that took

215

place there, Litton Mill had a charming situation. Cressbrook was more attractive still, with lilies growing in thick clumps along the river and wild mint flourishing on the surrounding banks. That sworn enemy of the urban world, Robert Southey, described Manchester's mills as being 'as large as convents without their antiquity, without their beauty, without their holiness.' Only the magnitude of the city's industrial infrastructure could impress. Thus a visiting Swiss engineer commented in 1814 with a blend of admiration and awe: 'in a single street in Manchester there are more spindles than in the whole of Switzerland.'[2]

Passing through Manchester's suburbs, Blincoe could see that every conceivable space not occupied by mills, canals and warehouses was crammed with what were called 'infill dwellings'. Manchester could boast a number of fine buildings, old and new: the opulent residences of Mosley Street and Ardwick, the medieval Grammar School alongside the River Irk, the Ionic-style Town Hall, and the Doric-style Exchange. But its countless small-fronted workers' houses, mostly one-up one-down terraces thrown up by 'jerry builders', gave the city a gloomy, squalid character. The builder's knowledge of his craft often ran dry long before completion, and houses were too often finished with a 'that'll do' shrug. The effluence of twenty or more such houses typically drained into a single, seldom-emptied cesspool. And many hundreds, mostly poor Irish immigrants, crowded into damp basement tenements, starved of light and fresh air and terribly prone to lung diseases like consumption and bronchitis. Here they were hidden from view, wrote the Irish journalist William Cooke Taylor, 'by piles of stores, mills, warehouses, and manufacturing establishments', such that they were 'less known to their wealthy neighbours … than the inhabitants of New Zealand or Kamtschatka.'[3]

Blincoe had arrived in late 1815 in a city of extremes. The warehouses which occupied much of the city, and often doubled as shops, sold some of the finest fabrics in the world. Yet poor weavers, factory piecers and domestic servants were already subsisting in the conditions that Friedrich Engels and his readers would find shocking and repulsive 30 years later. Having worked in factory villages like Samuel Oldknow's Mellor, ruled with a paternalistic regard for the conditions of the labourers, Blincoe found himself in a world in which those with a little capital were making money too fast and too easily to think about the moral and physical well-being of their workers. The gospel of laissez-faire, the new panacea of the urban middle class, here ruled supreme. And almost any amount of suffering on the part of the poor could be waved away as regrettable but necessary, with the easy reflection that economic progress, that high road to universal happiness, was achievable only if the market and its capitalists were left well alone. From pulpit and podium, the labourers were told that all were powerless before the market. Many accepted this wisdom, until the price of bread and potatoes reduced them to beggary. But plenty were never convinced. When political economists, worldly and hard-headed, told them that heaven could be made on earth if they just managed to restrain their primitive impulses to riot, strike, combine or smash mules, they just heard a variation on an old theme. The manufacturers sounded like well-fed priests, all their talk of the market differing little from the clergy's traditional reply to the aggrieved poor – 'Thus saith the Lord.'

Adam Smith's *The Wealth of Nations* was the capitalist's bible. But, like the holy book, it was more often sworn over than actually read. Manchester's commercial classes would have been surprised to read that Smith had peppered his great work with warnings about their dangerous rapacity. He wrote of the 'impertinent jealousy' and 'monopolising spirit' of a section of society 'whose interest is never exactly the same with that of the public, who have generally an interest to deceive and even to oppress the public.' He was right. While workers were banned from forming unions for mutual protection, mill proprietors routinely gathered to suborn the market and set common wages and prices. Meanwhile, their aversion to public expenditure created a city steeped in sickness, desperation and vice. It also alienated worker from master. An unadulterated spirit of commercial gain made palaces of industry but a human wasteland. As de Tocqueville said: 'Everything in the exterior appearance of the city attests the individual powers of man; nothing the directing power of society. At every turn human liberty shows its capricious creative force.' Blincoe, however, was unfazed by the stinking canals and decrepit houses. He told John Brown that he had felt only awe at this vast labyrinth of streets, factories and waterways. He went so far as to say that he thought Manchester the 'grandest place in all the world'. Perhaps he felt more secure amid the city's milling crowd. The quiet wooded valleys to which so many others wished to escape, for him represented only places in which brutality could go on unobserved and unchecked by the law.[4]

Blincoe arrived anonymous but not friendless. Somehow he knew that one James Cooper, another victim of the Needhams' brutality at Litton Mill, lived in St George's Road, near Shudehill. Cooper had been ten years old, according to the parish register of apprentices, at the time of his indenturing to the Lamberts. They had obviously forged a friendship, and Blincoe made straight for his lodgings. The *Memoir* says that Cooper received Blincoe warmly and took him in as a lodger.[5]

These were exciting days to be in a great city. A few months earlier, Emperor Napoleon's army had been narrowly defeated at the Battle of Waterloo. And as France speedily capitulated, the whole of England rejoiced. This wasn't merely an expression of patriotic fervour. It suddenly seemed that more than twenty years of ruinous taxation were at an end, that European markets would once more be opened to English manufactured goods, and that cheap raw materials could start pouring through her ports unmolested by the broadsides of French privateers. Apart from a few wiser voices, the nation anticipated peace and plenty for all. 'The country ... is peace mad', remarked the Foreign Secretary, Castlereagh. 'Many of our best friends think of nothing but reduction of taxes.'[6]

Early in 1815, however, a few months before a final peace was brokered at the Congress of Vienna, the political fissures which were to mar the post-war years began to open up. The Tory government of Lord Liverpool passed a Corn Law. It sounded innocuous, but this much-hated Act kept out all foreign corn until domestic prices had reached a near-famine level of 80 shillings per bushel. During the war, landowners and farmers had put huge areas of rough land to the plough, making money only because Napoleon's blockade artificially drove prices up. With the war about to end, there was a danger of widespread bankruptcies. The Corn Law was designed to prop up the farming sector, with the longer-term hope that Britain would become self-sufficient and so not reliant on imports from across the Channel.

In facing down the Luddites, Lord Liverpool had said that inter-ference in the market could only be pernicious; farming, it seemed, was an exception.[7]

To manufacturers and town labourers alike, the 1815 Corn Law was rank class legislation. It seemed geared only to maintaining the wealth of a greedy landed interest which controlled legislation to the detriment of the rest of the nation. In many parts of the country, owners and workers took to the streets. A large meeting in Manchester, presided over by the borough reeve Hugh Hornby Birley, condemned the Corn Law as 'short-sighted', 'unjust', and guaranteed to inflate the price of labour, thereby handing 'France, Switzerland, Germany, and the Netherlands' a commercial advantage. The state seemed out of touch. As Mancunians seethed, in London the windows of Frederick Robinson, Vice-President of the Board of Trade, were smashed, and Nicholas Vansittart, Chancellor of the Exchequer, was burned in effigy.[8]

The Wiltshire radical Henry Hunt now came into his own. At Spa Fields in London, a giant crowd gathered to hear him denounce the Corn Law as having been passed 'under the protection of a military force, in defiance of the prayers, the petitions, and the remonstrances of a great majority of the people of England.' The Whigs recoiled at the volatility stirred up by Radical demagogues like Cobbett and Hunt. But while they deprecated the kind of radical change that might career out of control, plenty of Whigs and even some Tories now favoured piecemeal reform which would lessen the injustices of the system. It was in this cautiously reformist spirit that on 19 May 1815 the committee investigating the condition of parish apprentices issued its official report. Samuel Romilly and his colleagues spoke with con-tempt for the practice of sending friendless children hundreds of miles from their families to work for uncaring factory masters. Blincoe's story, it seems, was far from unique.[9]

Within days, Wilbraham Bootle had reintroduced his 1811 Bill designed to limit apprenticeships to a 40-mile radius from the child's parish of birth. It eased through the Commons. Serious difficulties were then encountered in the House of Lords, where so much humanitarian legislation foundered on the determination of peers and bishops to bludgeon the labouring classes into a meek submission to the law as it stood. Not until the next session, the following year, did Bootle's Bill pass into law. Even then it was only a modest victory for the humanitarians, for the Act benefited just a small fraction of those it would have helped had it been passed twenty years earlier. For Blincoe, and tens of thousands of other young men and women, the damage was already done.[10]

While no doubt gratified by Wellington's victory at Waterloo, Blincoe soon realised that he hadn't arrived in Manchester at the best of times. The Corn Law hadn't yet begun to hurt, but it was about to. As hostility towards the government mounted in cities like Manchester, Lord Liverpool hoped that a good harvest would deflate the opposition. He was out of luck. In 1815 the Tambora volcano in the Dutch East Indies erupted, sending immense quantities of sulphur dioxide into the atmosphere and creating a canopy right across the northern hemisphere. For several years there were brilliant sunsets, but crops were starved of sunlight and grew stunted, if at all. As bread prices approached intolerable levels, the Corn Law stopped imports coming in. Long before corn had reached 80 shillings a bushel, 'Bread or blood' riots broke out, resulting in five executions (a Treasury solicitor deemed them to be most 'salutary'). Philanthropy alone kept tens of thousands of labouring families alive in what even Lord Liverpool felt to be a 'Stormy Winter'. Back in Blincoe's native parish, Lord Camden donated £100 to charity. Hunt lashed out: 'The noble lord's receipts for the last year amounted to £38,400', meaning that he had given to the starving 'just three farthings in the pound out of this enormous sum extracted from a distressed and impoverished people.'[11]

Then, on top of a terrible harvest came a trade depression. This was a disaster for a jobless young man like Robert Blincoe. Long before merchants broke back into European markets, a massive fall in the state's demand for ships, cannons, firearms, swords, bayonets, shot, bullets, tunics, buttons, knapsacks and the like brought hundreds of foundries, collieries, shipyards and factories to a standstill. Lord Liverpool's administration looked on without much pity. They felt that the economy had to find its own level, and that business failure was a fitting, and divinely ordained, penalty for imprudence; the postwar economic purge was in accordance with the stern theology of the political leaders. But the situation became explosive when 300,000 soldiers and sailors were unceremoniously dumped back onto an already glutted home labour market. Finding himself competing against hundreds of men just out of uniform, many of them natives of the city, Blincoe realised that arriving in Manchester at the return of peace was, to say the least, bad timing. And it was made much worse by the fact that everyone had expected peace to bring plenty. 'Alas, for the vanity of human expectations!' said the local Radical Archibald Prentice. The agonies of readjustment shocked Liverpool's administration too. 'The play is over', a government newspaper had enthused in 1815, 'we may now go to supper.' It took William Cobbett to point out the grim reality that quickly unfolded: 'No, *you cannot go to supper*', he stormed. 'You have not yet paid for the play. And, before you have paid for the play, you will find that there is no money left for the supper.'[12]

These were times of savage distress. Day after day, Blincoe must have arrived early in the morning at the offices of mill bosses, cap deferentially in hand, beseeching them to grant him work. Indeed, so widespread was the suffering that for four years it looked to many as if the nation might well be convulsed by violent revolution. Manchester, the nation's second city but still with no seat in Parliament, now emerged as a hotbed of Radicalism. It seemed more obvious than ever that the interests of trade and labour would lose out so long as the constitution remained in its present form. Cartwright's Hampden Clubs flourished; and in rented chapels and on high windswept moors in all weathers, weavers and spinners gathered to listen to Radicals holding forth on 'Equal Representation', 'Annual Parliaments', and 'Old Corruption'. Cobbett and his Radical brethren preached a heady gospel of parliamentary reform as the only antidote to state repression, corruption and aristocratic self-interest. This stress on a political remedy for the woes of the labouring orders lent the agitation coherence. It also, incidentally, reduced the level of riot and the potential for revolution.[13]

Sometime in 1815, Blincoe's prayers were answered. He beat the odds and secured a position in a spinning factory. Adam and George Murray's 'gigantic' New Mill had been built in Ancoats in 1804, alongside the Rochdale Canal. The rising cost of land in Manchester made it worthwhile building high. At eight storeys throughout its

160-foot length, the Murrays' mill dwarfed many a royal palace; and while its façade was unornamented, the Murrays went to the expense of interspersing red bricks with burnt dark-blue headers to create a chequerboard effect. In all, there were three Murray mills on the site, built to enclose a large canal basin into which barges were brought carrying raw cotton and coal. Having discharged their cargoes, these were then loaded with finished yarn for distribution to weaving mills. This seemingly never-ending cycle was orchestrated and accompanied by the rhythmic beat of the mighty Boulton and Watt engines which made the whole enterprise possible.[14]

The mills of Messrs Murray were much airier than many of the smaller water-powered concerns, but the huge engines generated roasting temperatures and an oppressive atmosphere. Thousands sweated in 80°F or higher, and the shock of walking into the cold air outside at the end of their shifts induced discomfort in all and serious illness in many. Blincoe's initial euphoria at having a position faded fast. He found working for the Murray brothers 'almost suffocating'.

15. A view of several cotton mills in the Ancoats district of Manchester. The giant mill in the foreground is Adam and George Murray's New Mill. Blincoe laboured there briefly in 1815. John Doherty was also employed by the Murrays as a spinner in 1818.

Worse still, the post-war slump meant that the mill was operating on only four-and-a-half days a week, and the wages were derisory. Unwilling to accept further privations, Blincoe took another risk and resigned. Again he was lucky. Blincoe found work at Robinson's factory on Water Street, earning a little under eleven shillings a week stripping top cards.[15]

By anyone's standards, Robert Blincoe was a fickle employee. Cotton operatives seldom had fixed contracts, but they usually agreed to work for periods of around three months. For two years now, ever since quitting Miller's Dale, Blincoe had drifted from place to place and from job to job, rootless and non-committal. It may appear at first glance that his early life had destroyed his capacity to build relationships so that he continually moved on, even when it meant giving up jobs in a period of chronic unemployment. But if Blincoe was left with indelible emotional scars, the spirit that had seen him yearn for the life of a sweep, flee from Lowdham Mill, and later take on the Needhams, remained firmly intact. A man of real ability, he had clung on to his faith in himself despite appalling privations. Now aged 23, Blincoe would not settle for second-best. And while in the short term he had to compromise to survive, all the time he was watching and waiting for an opportunity that would enable him to break through to a better life. John Brown records an incident of this time which supports this interpretation. When Blincoe was starting work for Mr Robinson, we're told that the mill's overlookers insisted that he be initiated into their company by paying a 'footing' of two shillings and then repairing with them to a public house. Unwilling to buck long custom, Blincoe did as he was bid. He told Brown with considerable regret several years later that as a result of this 'silly and mischievous' convention he became severely drunk. A hangover lasting several days cured Blincoe of any future inclination to drown his worries in strong Manchester beer. And to avoid being imposed on again, he spent several months in Robinson's carding room 'as it were alone in a crowd'. It appears that for all of his past grief, Blincoe maintained sufficient determination and hope for the future to spurn the ale-house. Before too long, this self-belief was to pay dividends.[16]

21

Bold departures

The moralising bourgeoisie said that patience, sobriety, application and prudence were all that was needed for the poor man to better himself. In reality, these qualities were seldom enough. At the very least, one also needed a large store of self-assurance. Plenty of working men, knocked back one time too many, slipped into a malignant apathy. Life's vagaries sought out and wore away at any slight nick in their emotional armour. Hence the philosopher William Godwin, a resident of Blincoe's own parish of birth, spoke of how the peasant child born with a 'quickness of observation, an ingenuousness of character, and a delicacy of tact' had usually, by the age of fourteen, been 'brutified by immediate and unintermitted labour. Their hearts are hardened and their spirits broken.' Francis Place wrote candidly of how he had fought depression as he and his wife struggled to make their way in their London garret during an economic downturn:

> I know not how to describe the sickening aversion which at times steals over the working-man and utterly disables him, for a longer or shorter period, from following his usual occupation, and compels him to indulge in idleness.[1]

Overwork and anxiety sapped the working man's ambition and imbued him with a fatalistic belief that it was best not to strive for anything above the station to which he had been born. Given his lowly origins and his long history of exploitation, abuse and neglect, Blincoe's chances of improving his lot were slim, to say the least. Work'us boys like him were doubly unfortunate. Years of sermons on the duties of their lower station dampened their aspirations, and early lives bereft of parental love but rich in discipline and disdain produced few men and women with the confidence to excel.

But in 1816 Blincoe thought he saw a way of elevating himself from the lower tiers of the labouring class. He had heard, the *Memoir* tells us, that 'many of the most proud and prosperous of the master cotton-spinners of Manchester' had started out as dealers in waste cotton. This involved selling wads of cotton fibres, discarded as unusable for better-quality work, for use in coarser fabrics or for padding and filling in coats and cushions. Blincoe saw this as his ticket out of a life of drudgery. The only difficulty was that he had virtually no capital. The few pounds he had saved from working in Mellor, Stalybridge and Manchester had been lifted from his pocket by 'some of the light-fingered gentry' when he went to see a horse-race on Kersal-Moor. So, once again, Blincoe did something bordering on the reckless. Resigning from Robinson's factory, he took a job in a mill on Bank-Top owned by a Mr Young, stoking the boilers.[2]

It was notoriously exhausting work. The roaring heat and near-constant shovelling made heavy demands on Blincoe's twisted frame. Stokers tended to work extreme hours. Several of those who later gave evidence before government inquiries spoke of working compulsory overtime, labouring all day Monday and Tuesday with hardly a break, before being released in the early hours of Wednesday morning. Blincoe shortened his journey from work to bed by electing to sleep, exposed to the elements, in the mill's coal-yard. He had a good reason for practising such extreme self-denial. Blincoe had now firmly resolved to amass sufficient capital to set up his waste cotton business, and so he decided to save on paying rent. At a wage of eleven shillings a week it would still take him some time, but Blincoe was willing to accept much immediate discomfort to improve his future prospects. From his workhouse days, Blincoe had always craved something better, and now he expected to realise it. He had an added impetus: at the age of 27 he was as physically capable as he would ever be. Another decade and he would struggle to keep up with the steam engine, carding machine or spinning mule at which he worked. Then, in company with thousands of other ageing men and women, he would be unceremoniously laid off in favour of straighter limbs and tauter muscles. If he still lacked children able to help him in his old age, he would then face a grim fight to survive on starvation wages. It was well known that once a cotton worker reached the age of 40, he was considered an 'old man' to be 'cast off like useless lumber'. Many work'us apprentices, especially those sent into overstocked trades, eventually came full circle. Blincoe was determined that he would not be one of them.[3]

Unfortunately, the *Memoir* contains only a few isolated remarks for these years, and Blincoe disappeared too far into Manchester's industrial undergrowth for other records to shed light on what he was doing. But we do know plenty about the environment in which he lived and worked in these fraught years. Throughout this period the political temperature, in Manchester and beyond, went on rising. As the trade slump continued and bread prices failed to fall, distress led to an escalation of political radicalism. In late November, the Prince Regent refused to accept a huge petition, begun by 'Orator' Hunt, demanding parliamentary reform and manhood suffrage. In response, a coterie of Spencean revolutionaries staged an attempted coup, seizing weapons and making for the Bank of England and the Tower of London. Forewarned, a large party of soldiers lay in wait. In the following months, most Radicals abandoned the use of violence. Their aims switched firmly in the direction of securing an extension of the franchise by putting moral pressure on the government. Soon after Blincoe's arrival in Manchester, a large open-air meeting had been held in support of parliamentary reform. Similar events were staged across the country. Lord Liverpool's government, reactionary and misinformed, looked anxiously on, seeking an opportunity for repression. On 28 January 1817, they were handed one. As the Prince Regent made his way in state to open Parliament, his carriage was encircled by a furious London mob. Then someone launched a well-aimed brickbat which shattered the glass. Citing the attack as evidence of a dangerous breakdown in the state's authority, in February and March 1817 Liverpool suspended Habeas Corpus and passed a Seditious Meetings Act, prohibiting gatherings of more than 50 persons not sanctioned by a magistrate. A government servant then approached Cobbett in the vain hope that he would agree to stop writing in return for a sizeable bribe. Predictably, Cobbett refused and, realising that he was in danger of arrest, fled to America.[4]

In March 1817, hundreds of hungry men from Manchester sought to evade the government's repressive legislation. They split into gangs of ten and set off for London to present petitions asking for the working man to be given the vote. Their action earned the sobriquet 'the Blanketeers' March' because the men took little with them besides rough blankets to sleep under. Several days short of London, the march was halted by well-armed troops and the Blanketeers' leaders were gaoled. A few Radicals now became desperate. One petition after another had been rejected, and MPs had shown complete indifference to the sorry plight of the poor. The idea of a general uprising now gained support in the towns of the north and the Midlands. On 8 June a few hundred men mustered on the moors outside Huddersfield in Yorkshire. They fled at the approach of mounted yeomanry; but the Pentrich rebellion, on the following day, went much further. About 300 labourers, including large contingents of stockingers and iron-workers, set off from the foothills of the Peak District to seize Nottingham Castle and declare a provisional government. It turned into a fiasco when the 15th Hussars put the rebels to flight. The only blood shed on the day was that of a farm servant mistakenly shot by the rebels. Following brief trials, a number of them were executed.[5]

Blincoe knew of these dramatic events – they galvanised local opinion and filled copious newspaper columns – but in 1817 his chief concern was securing his own future. To this end, he left Young's factory. He later said that the master there, a Mr Ramsbottom, had behaved towards him with 'more humanity ... than he had been accustomed to experience', but 'disturbed by some petty artifices of the manager ... and an attempt being made to lower his wages', he decided to quit. After many months of hard labour, sleeping in close proximity to the mill's power plant, Blincoe had a fair amount of capital saved. But leaving his employment was still a huge gamble. He chanced everything on succeeding as a dealer in waste cottons, but he had much to learn about the business. And for the first few months his hard-earned savings diminished rapidly as little money came in. These were anxious days.[6]

It wasn't a good time to be starting up a cotton business. Between 1816 and early 1818 an export slump led owners to cut the wages of their adult spinners by around a quarter. This spate of wage reductions had probably spurred Blincoe on to leave his job. Others decided on a more risky strategy. Although the 1799 Combinations Act had made any form of collective activity illegal, some workers were still prepared to use the strike weapon. Spinners' unions had been formed in Manchester and Stockport in 1792 to limit the numbers of apprentices and safeguard wages. Unions persisted, under different names, despite Wilberforce's Act. In the early 1800s spinners had forced wage concessions several times. Then, in 1810, they had unleashed a rolling strike across Lancashire, with specific areas striking in rotation as their working comrades provided funds for the out-of-work. This time they over-estimated their powers. The masters hit back with a county-wide lock-out. Starved into submission, after four months the spinners returned to work at reduced rates. In mid-1818 they tried again. Several thousand spinners from Manchester, Wigan and Stockport struck, relying on 'weekly stipends' drawn from reserves paid over many months into a central kitty to support themselves. Pickets were sent to working mills to make it hard for the 'knobsticks', or strike-breakers, to get inside. This time an Irish-born spinner called John Doherty – who would later play a significant role in Blincoe's life – was in the fore of the planning. When, on 26 August, a local proprietor called Birley opened his mill, Doherty joined the 200 who gathered outside obstructing the men who, out of need, fear or principle, refused to join the strike. John Doherty, conspicuous due to his energetic picketing, was arrested and dragged inside. The crowd, determined to rescue him, stormed the mill. Soldiers were summoned and, behind a phalanx of bayonets, they marched Doherty off to the New Bailey Prison just outside Manchester. There the enraged mob hurled stones until a magistrate read the Riot Act.[7]

Shortly after, the strike collapsed. Union funds had been exhausted, a situation reached rather earlier than expected after the treasurer absconded with about £160. In the clamp-down that followed, some of the strike leaders were pressured into signing a written declaration denouncing combinations. Others were blacklisted and denied work; more than a decade later the 'leader of the pickets', one Daniel Brough, was still on such a list and barely subsisting as a rag-and-bone man. John Doherty fared badly too. When his case came before the Lancaster Quarter Sessions in late 1818, he was sentenced to two years' imprisonment with hard labour in Lancaster Castle gaol. It was a harsh sentence explicitly designed to serve as a warning to other disaffected cotton operatives. The textile masters of Manchester, Wigan and Stockport were overjoyed.[8]

Blincoe doubtless sympathised with the strikers, but he was his own boss now and he had to persevere. Despite the declining profits of the cotton industry, he spent the year building up his personal acumen, business contacts and practical knowledge. At last, in early 1818, Blincoe began to turn in a profit. The *Memoir* tells us:

> being pretty well initiated into the mysteries of trade, and having acquired a competent knowledge of raw and waste cottons, he commenced his second year, in much better style, and at the end of that year, he had not only regained his lost capital, but added £5 to it.

For Blincoe, the year 1818 ended on a positive note. He spent Christmas the proud renter of warehouse space and in his own lodgings. In two years he had come a long way.[9]

Blincoe's success in setting up his own business was remarkable. It had taken rare courage and tenacity, personal qualities not usually well supplied to the bruised victim of the parish apprenticeship system. Blincoe had the stomach and the will to succeed where the vast majority of his brethren failed dismally. The source of his drive is not easy to identify. Perhaps it did arise from a mother's love briefly but liberally bestowed in the years before he was dumped at the workhouse. Or maybe it came from a belief in his own gentility, an irrepressible feeling, strengthened by Old Beckkà's bogus prophecy, that a parson's son deserved better.

In 1819 Blincoe became what he had perhaps never dreamed of being, an eligible bachelor. In 1822, speaking to John Brown, he had no difficulty in recalling the day on which his single status became a subject of amusement to those who knew him. It was Sunday 27 June 1819, and Blincoe was at the christening of a neighbour's child in a local inn. A butcher acquaintance turned his wit on both Blincoe and a middle-aged spinster called Martha Simpson. Why don't you two wed, he joked, 'and then we'll have a good wedding, as well as a christening, today.' Blincoe leaned across to Martha and said: 'Well, if

Martha will have me, I'll take her and marry her tomorrow.' Martha issued a demure affirmative. Blincoe was taken aback. Recovering himself, his mind racing with uncertainty, he proposed to her again. She gave him her word. 'I'll not run from mine, if you don't', was Blincoe's cautious but sincere reply. Now the company at large sensed some fun to be had. A crowd gathered round where Blincoe and Martha were seated. The butcher, no doubt delighted at the effectiveness of his jibing, bet a leg of mutton that they would back out. Several more immediately chipped in bets as well. Blincoe didn't recall anyone taking a chance on them going through with the plan.

Blincoe's resolve strengthened rapidly. 'Well', he announced, 'that I may not be disappointed, I'll even go to see for a licence tonight.' Things were turning serious, and so two of those who had laid bets left with him. By now Blincoe was an unmarried man of about 26. For an eligible man it was late in life to be still unhitched. Perhaps unsurprisingly, there are hints in the *Memoir* that, although respected and liked, Blincoe found it hard to trust. For a man spurned by family, deceived by parish officers, and cruelly treated by mill masters and overlookers, an instinctual wariness was only to be expected. And as he trotted towards the nearest vicarage to obtain a marriage licence, self-doubt got the better of him. Fearing a hoax on Martha's part, and suspecting that the rest of the party was having fun at his expense, Blincoe retraced his steps, just as he had done in 1812 having sat for hours in lawyer Cheek's kitchen. Back at the inn, he told Martha that he couldn't procure a licence without her presence. She agreed to accompany him, but Blincoe still wasn't reassured. So he said, not altogether truthfully: 'I have not money enough in my pocket, will you Martha, lend me a couple of pounds?' Without hesitation, she passed him the silver. Not even thinking to seal the bargain with a kiss, he then led her to the home of the 'not *very reverend Joshua Brookes*'.[10]

It was fitting that in the nation's foremost industrial city, Joshua Brookes should have brought the principle of mass production into the Church. By the time of his death in November 1821, Brookes had baptised, married and buried more people than any Anglican clergyman since records began. He achieved this singular feat by adopting the unorthodox practice of obliging parishioners to baptise their children and get married in mass ceremonies or 'shoals'. Naturally, it required stern authority to marshal so many lovers, mothers, infants, aunts, grandmothers, nurses, relations and friends; but this didn't present a problem to Brookes. The son of a crippled shoemaker nicknamed 'Pontius Pilate' due to his evil temper, Joshua had inherited his father's gift for terrifying people into adherence to his will. The local novelist Linnaeus Banks, one of many writers to note the Reverend's eccentricities, told of him bellowing at mothers clutching their newborns as he worked to fit dozens of them between the Cathedral's altar rails: 'You come here! You kneel there! Yon woman's not paid! … make room, will you?' He would even explode in wrath mid-psalm, to yell out: 'Give that screaming baby the breast!'; and services were routinely interrupted by Brookes hurling coarse rebukes at inattentive boys. His coarseness inevitably repelled some of the more respectable parishioners, many of whom disapproved of his rich language and improprieties, the shabby clothes he wore on all days but Sunday, and his unconventional three-cornered beaver hat.[11]

Yet Brookes was a fine Bible scholar, a poor boy whose talents had been rewarded with donations and scholarships allowing him to graduate MA from Brasenose College at Oxford University. His love of learning was evinced by a fine library, even if the distinctly unrefined jottings in his books' margins weren't to everyone's taste. And while Brookes had little of either tact or human understanding, Linnaeus Banks insisted that within this 'rough, crusted, unpolished black-diamond' lay a 'true heart beating under the angular external crystals.'[12]

It was in Manchester Cathedral, before Joshua Brookes, and most likely alongside several other couples, that Robert Blincoe and Martha Simpson stood on the morning of 28 June 1819. They had taken a coach to the church from near Blincoe's lodgings in Bank-Top, having won several shillings and a leg of mutton for the wedding feast. The match seems to have met with the approval of Martha's family, as one Abraham Simpson acted as a witness. For reasons which are no longer known, Blincoe signed the register 'Robert Blinkhome'. Possibly this was an affectation adopted for business purposes and later dropped. Martha signed with an 'X'. Her illiteracy was anything but unusual for the times: in the 1780s, it's been calculated, fewer than two-thirds of grooms and a sixth of brides could sign their own names, and these figures improved little until the mid-19th century. Not that this mattered to the newlyweds. From the manner of their engagement one suspects that both had long wished for tender intimacy and companionship, and the impression Blincoe gave John Brown was that they found it. 'They have lived', the *Memoir* reads:

> with as great a share of conjugal tranquillity as falls to the lot of many, who are deemed happy couples, and he has ever since kept upon the advance in worldly prosperity.

By the close of 1820, Martha had given birth to the first of three children, a daughter, christened Ruth.[13]

As the Blincoes settled into marriage, the wider world became ever more torrid. Following the disastrous failures of both the Pentrich rising and the Blanketeers' march, working-class hopes now coalesced around the issue of parliamentary reform. Early in 1819, 'Orator' Hunt thrilled a crowd 10,000-strong in St Peter's Field in the heart of Manchester. The same evening he was thrown out of the city's Theatre Royal by a group of soldiers and some roughs led by the Earl of Uxbridge. When another meeting was arranged a week later, hundreds of working men gathered outside 'to protect Mr Hunt if requisite'. His popularity went on rising as the trade recession continued to deepen. Through 1819, Manchester was once more in the grip of severe unemployment and the sufferings it unleashed. So when Hunt and his comrades decided on a massive show of support for parliamentary reform in St Peter's Field on 16 August, the city's authorities grew alarmed. 'We cannot have a doubt that some alarming insurrection is in contemplation', wrote several magistrates to Viscount Sidmouth, the Home Secretary. Rumours of hundreds of desperate men drilling with pikes on moors in the far north intensified anxieties. Lord Liverpool's cabinet for once took a more level-headed view, stressing the 'inexpediency of attempting forcibly to prevent the meeting'.[14]

In preparation for the 16 August pro-reform gathering, the organisers called on a new star in the Radical firmament, Richard Carlile, to join them on the podium. The son of a Devon man who had tried his hand at cobbling, teaching and soldiering, and then finally given himself up to drink, Carlile had spent his early years as a tin-worker. Moving to London in 1813, he was rapidly exposed to the political radicalism of the artisan class. There he started writing for and publishing Radical journals, for which he was arrested and held awaiting trial for four months in 1817. In the following years, he emerged as the true successor to Tom Paine, publishing his views on the evils of monarchy, aristocracy and the established Church in widely-read pamphlets. Carlile spoke of abstract rights, not re-establishing long-lost Anglo-Saxon liberties. But he was no socialist. Instead, Carlile believed that everybody had a responsibility to improve themselves through reading, labour and sobriety. Nothing could be achieved, however, until the people were first freed from the forces of oppression. A true Paineite, Carlile felt that the Church was just as much an instrument of tyranny as the state itself, and he defamed priests as 'black slugs' who plundered the poor. A clever writer and vigorous campaigner, he was also one of the few leading Radicals who actually knew what it was like to labour long hours for a miserable wage. Those organising the St Peter's Field event knew Carlile would help pull in a mighty crowd.[15]

On 16 August thousands of people poured into the streets of Manchester, heading for St Peter's Field, less than half a mile from the newlyweds' home. The leaders had taken every precaution to maintain the gathering's legality. On the morning of the event, Hunt even offered himself up for arrest. While this offer was refused, the magistracy felt anything but reassured. Few local justices could distinguish the different stripes of Radicalism. According to most of them, the Radical was by definition 'a libellous, seditious, factious, levelling, revolutionary, republican, democratical, atheistical villain.' But by the afternoon of the big day, between 30,000 and 200,000 people had congregated in St Peter's Field to hear them speak. Estimates as to the size of the crowd vary according to the axe the observer had to grind. The lowest figure, however, which came from a hostile and short-sighted magistrate, should almost certainly be discounted. *The Times* guessed at around 100,000. The city's yeoman cavalry, made up mostly of middle-class tradesmen and shopkeepers, was also there in force – some, it was said, having taken strong drink. These apart, observers like the *Times* reporter were struck by the orderliness of the gathering and the number of women and children present, many of them in their Sunday best. It was among the largest assemblies of people in English history, and it's hard not to believe that Mr and Mrs Blincoe were somewhere among the vast crowd that roared at the arrival of Hunt's barouche as several amateur bands gave their renderings of 'See the Conquering Hero'.[16]

It should have been Orator Hunt's finest hour, a huge peaceful gathering of working men and women that sent a clear message about their fitness to exercise the right to vote. But scarcely twenty minutes into the proceedings, a shout was heard from the yeoman cavalry. 'They shouted again', recorded Samuel Bamford, 'waving their sabres over their heads; and then, slackening rein and striking spur into their steeds, they dashed forward, and began cutting the people.' They had been ordered to seize the tricolour flags flying on the barouche. But they went about their work with bloodthirsty relish, swinging their sabres wildly as they charged into the densely-packed crowd, their horses' hooves trampling, crushing and gouging men, women, children. Within a few minutes, the 15th Regiment of Hussars arrived, and they too rushed the crowd. With greater presence of mind than the angry and in many cases intoxicated amateurs, they restrained their comrades. Still, after half an hour of hacking and slashing, eleven lay dead, including two women, and 400 were wounded. One man had had his nose sliced clean from his face.[17]

Liverpool's government rallied behind the headstrong magistrates and the Manchester yeomanry who had followed their lead. A third of the casualties were declared to have been 'self-inflicted' because they had been caused by stampeding horses rather than by the sabre. And the military was praised for its 'prompt, decisive and efficient measures for the preservation of the public tranquillity.' Subsequent investigation also revealed that one of the dead women was a 'bad sort' who had been heard to criticise a curate. Hunt was arrested and subjected to eleven days of solitary confinement. On his release, large crowds gathered wherever he went, as many as 80,000 in Manchester alone, many of them wearing replicas of his trademark white hat bearing the motto 'Hunt and Liberty'. More than twice this number greeted his return to London. And in September, about 30,000 men demonstrated on moorland in Yorkshire, holding aloft a banner draped in black crepe. By then, the events of 16 August had been dubbed 'Peterloo' in ironic reference to the Battle of Waterloo. The fact that John Lees, who had died after three weeks of severe pain from a sabre blow, had fought under Wellington at Waterloo, gave the name added resonance. For months after, the Radicals sought to bring the Manchester magistrates to justice. Predictably, they failed. And when Burdett wrote that they were 'bloody Neroes', he found himself in the dock for seditious libel.[18]

Hunt was eventually convicted of being a person 'of a wicked and turbulent disposition' who had 'conspired ... to create a disturbance of the peace ... in a formidable and menacing manner, with sticks, clubs and other offensive weapons.' He was sentenced to two-and-a-half years in Ilchester gaol. This time he would suffer great privations and come close to losing his mind. And while he languished behind thick walls of stone, and as the other Radicals worked fruitlessly for legal redress, the government passed the Six Acts which, among other things, restricted public gatherings and imposed a stiff stamp duty on cheap Radical publications. These Acts have often been seen as conspicuously repressive. In fact, they just tightened earlier legislation and led to relatively few convictions. Lord Liverpool's ministry gave little ground to the Radicals, and it treated the victims of misrule with contempt, but this was no reign of terror.[19]

Cobbett returned to England from America in November 1819, carrying the bones of Tom Paine to be buried in his native soil. But as trade improved and bread prices at last began to fall, the Radical movement now started to lose its momentum. The government received a scare in February 1820 following the uncovering of the Cato Street Conspiracy, in which a group of Spenceans attempted to blow up the entire Cabinet as it sat down to dinner in Grosvenor Square in London. A government spy, perhaps acting as agent provocateur, kept Sidmouth informed throughout, and the ringleaders were caught, found guilty of high treason, hanged and decapitated. In the months following, the Radical cause was hijacked as supporters were diverted by a mere cause célèbre. Princess Caroline, estranged wife of the future George IV, secured widespread popular support in her vain attempt to assume the title of Queen. Working-class discontent was mis-spent as thousands rallied to the cause of a woman exceeded in arrogance, indulgence and irresponsibility only by her detested husband.[20]

In gaol, in hiding, and with public enthusiasm temporarily diverted, the Radical leaders experienced a rare period of quiet. A series of decent harvests and an economic upturn then reduced the willingness of the labouring classes to risk imprisonment by attending open-air meetings. As William Cobbett remarked, 'I defy you to agitate a man on a full stomach', a basic truth known to every successful revolutionary. While unemployed or overworked and underpaid workers might feel fervently about manhood suffrage, they were impelled to demonstrate and riot by hunger more than moral righteousness. The weaver William Radcliffe felt that 'in no instance did these disturbances proceed from sedition or dissatisfaction with the government.' Although this overstates the case – ideas do count for something – he was correct to see 'the deepest distress' as the spur for everything from the resurgence of Luddism to the vastness of the crowds that gathered to hear Hunt and Carlile speak. Once the harshness of life briefly abated, the political aspirations of the labouring classes were put on hold. In Manchester, new mills, rows of back-to-backs, and municipal buildings were erected. Thousands of hand-loom weavers worked long hours in candle-lit garrets, cotton-spinners took advantage of a boom in trade, and capitalists made and lost money. Lord Liverpool's administration had weathered the storm. After years of strife, property was safe, the monarchy secure, and the Tory government relaxed.[21]

Blincoe too, now 26 years old, had found calmer waters. He had come out of the slump with his waste cotton business intact and was making enough money to support his wife and daughter. For the next three years he did nothing that made an impression on the historical record, nor anything that he deemed worth relating to his later biographer. This long period of anonymity came to an end, however, when he made a strange new acquaintance. In January or February 1822 a Lancashire journalist called John Brown entered Blincoe's life. Brown's presence was strange, intense and, though fleeting, ultimately extremely positive. But it wasn't accidental – Brown had a clear purpose in mind and he wanted Blincoe's assistance. The background to their meeting takes us back in time, and to the Palace of Westminster in far-off London.

22

Factory children on the agenda

Since Peel's 1802 Act there had been a series of attempts to reduce the hours that boys and girls worked in textile mills. In 1814 a Manchester spinner called John Lawton had established a 'short time' committee to agitate for a reduction in hours for factory children. He received money from a local merchant called Nathaniel Gould, who spent about £20,000 on the campaign and left a further £5,000 in his will. These were large sums of money, but the campaign won few converts and aroused little interest. Then in 1815 Robert Owen made a public appeal on behalf of overworked factory children. Sir Robert Peel was initially sceptical. He had excluded 'free' children from the 1802 Act and was reluctant to interfere in the market. Owen made him change his mind.[1]

The new steam-powered mills, Owen pointed out, were far hotter than their water-driven predecessors. Children of seven years of age were being forced to scavenge for waste cotton and piece broken ends for thirteen or more hours a day in temperatures as high as 85°F. A convert to the cause, in June 1815 Peel introduced a Bill to prevent the employment of children under ten in factories, and to lower the hours of older children to twelve-and-a-half per day, with only ten-and-a-half of these spent in 'laborious employment'. Peel also planned to have paid inspectors enforce his Act. Meeting fierce resistance from mill owners, he changed tack and dropped the Bill in favour of a Select Committee inquiry the following year. And so, between April and June 1816, 43 witnesses – physicians, surgeons, magistrates, proprietors, and advocates of the factory child's cause – were subject to detailed questioning and cross-examination.[2]

Predictably, the owners of silk, cotton and woollen mills nearly all testified to the effect that their child employees were fit, healthy, mentally acute, and more than able to tolerate long hours and suffocating heat. Few of them denied that work hours ranged from thirteen to fifteen a day with no more than an hour given for refreshments, but some went so far as to say that mill labour invigorated the young constitution. The factory child's morals were also said to be better than those of children apprenticed to weavers or nailers. The kinds of excess to which Robert Blincoe and so many others had been subjected were brushed aside as the crimes of a more primitive age.[3]

A few physicians stood resolutely behind the mill bosses. Dr Charles Pennington insisted that the child apprentices employed by James Robinson and Son, who owned mills in Papplewick, Nottinghamshire, were 'healthy and strong'. Given that he was also the Robinson family's personal physician, Pennington's reliability is open to doubt. In fact, the majority of physicians and surgeons who testified declared factories to be thoroughly unsuitable places for the young. Such luminaries as Dr Anthony Carlisle and Dr Gilbert Blane, the latter of whom had played a key role in introducing lime juice into the British seaman's diet, all agreed that the heat and long hours to which young bodies were exposed could do them only harm. Even Kinder Wood, an Oldham surgeon anxious lest he upset his factory-owning father-in-law, stated that cotton mills were 'very detrimental' to any child's heath.[4]

Blincoe appreciated far better than the physicians and proprietors who appeared before Peel's Committee what conditions were like for children in cotton mills. By now he had worked in nine, spread over four counties. And although he had been exposed to wildly varying treatment, he knew that the savage abuse of parish apprentices still went on, that long working days bent soft young bones, and that unfenced machinery ripped off fingers, tore skin and broke limbs. His own twisted body and striated ears provided vivid testimony to the absurdities of the evidence given by mill owners and their pet physicians. Blincoe may have seen healthy apprentices working in Oldknow's Mellor Mill; but as the writer Peter Gaskell noted, only a tiny minority of mills were run by men 'of enlarged benevolence and active philanthropy'. Such places, Gaskell said, 'are rather beautiful examples of what may be done, than illustrations of what is done.' Blincoe would have agreed heartily. And, from long experience, he understood that even in the best-conducted mill extreme demands were made on children's bodies. The entire mill regime, Blincoe recognised, was geared to the physical capabilities of adult spinners. Since adults could and would labour for long hours, the children who were needed to scavenge and piece had to be there as well. So if adults felt the tyranny of the machine – 'You must go with the speed of your engine', lamented one – the children were also subject to the gruelling demands of keeping pace with fully matured men. As Joseph Brotherton, MP for Salford, put it: 'The system is such, that the weak and the strong, the young and the old, must work together at the same time.' With these ugly facts Blincoe was well acquainted. Unfortunately, however, no one with influence seems to have thought of summoning Blincoe or anyone like him to give evidence to the Committee.[5]

Not calling up any actual factory labourers weakened Peel's case, as did his failure to question more than a handful of physicians who had even set foot in a factory. Doctors like Carlisle and Blane came not from smoky industrial cities but from the bedchambers of the capital's social elites. They knew much more about the gouty diatheses of well-fed aristocrats than the combined effects of excess labour and poor rations. Furthermore, while Peel's 1816 Committee tried to present the matter as a simplistic clash between greed and morality, the situation was actually more complicated. Westminster humanitarians and metropolitan medicos were not always attuned to the conflicting interests of those they claimed to be defending. As many a master pointed out, some poor families, especially those of hand-loom weavers, couldn't survive without the two or three shillings every week brought in by their younger children. Many boys and girls worked in mills to compensate for the deaths of parents from accidents or sickness. Nearly a fifth of children in Georgian England lost a parent by the age of fifteen, and since this was usually the father and main bread-winner, sending the child out to work could be the only alternative to penury or a degrading reliance on parish funds. But few of the richer sorts, including some of those on Peel's Committee, understood the true scale of privation among the lower orders; hence the physician Anthony Carlisle was asked if he thought that parents who let their children toil in mills had 'a want of feeling and tenderness'.

To many poor families, mill work was a lifeline. And, as several owners insisted, children were also vital to the smooth running of the mill. If young piecers and scavengers worked fewer hours, then adult spinners would have to quit early too. This would arguably lead to a decline in wages all round. A Manchester magistrate later told Home Secretary Sidmouth that if Peel's Bill were passed, there would be another cotton-spinners' strike in Lancashire on account of the indirect reduction in their wages. Nor did the mill owners always exaggerate the risks of going out of business. Of the 90 cotton factories in Manchester in 1815, only 36 were still operating in 1825. More than two-thirds had gone bust. It was survival of the fittest in an unforgiving environment, made worse by over-production, trade slumps, European conflict, revolutions, stock crashes and defective banks.[6]

But while these were plausible arguments, the opponents of Peel and Owen pushed them too far. Those poor parents who sent children to scavenge and piece derived no long-term benefit from their young children ruining their constitutions and physiques. In any case, the successes of Owen, Greg, Strutt and Oldknow demonstrated that humane management could be both affordable and economical. Moreover, as the advocates of factory reform asserted, mills in places like Manchester tended to go under not because they couldn't fulfil orders on time but because they over-produced and then weren't able to sell their stock. Since it was the continual cycle of boom and bust that tended to cripple them, squeezing as much work out of operatives in the shortest possible time wasn't always good business. After all, crates of unsold yarn had to be stored, and the men, women and children who had produced it still had to be paid even if money wasn't coming in. If legislation had forced mills to work shorter hours all year round, not just when a slump occurred, then the problem of over-production might actually have lessened. But, however logical, such talk was rank heresy in an age of ascendant political economy.[7]

Still, the pressure exerted by the mill owners did force Peel to moderate his Bill. Fearing that Britain's commercial superiority would be compromised by his legislation, he agreed to allow an extra hour of work for children, meaning a thirteen-hour working day inclusive of breaks. He also decided that the minimum age for work in mills should be nine, not ten. This, Peel surmised, would 'not place our foreign trade in any unfavourable situation'. Despite these concessions, many of the factory workers now swung behind Peel's Bill. In early 1817, eager to maintain the momentum, groups of Lancashire spinners adopted a petition to support him. Sir James Graham, MP and political economist, scolded the signatories as 'idle, discontented, discarded, and good for nothing'. They were discontented to be sure, but far from idle. 'Short time' men collected funds from working spinners and despatched to the capital John Hollis, a spinner obliged to retire due to ill-health, to deliver their petitions. A working cotton-spinner, John Doherty, made a generous donation of sixpence. He was soon to enter Robert Blincoe's life.[8]

In February 1818, Sir Robert Peel introduced his modified Bill. George Philips, MP, denounced it as disastrous to English trade, and painted so elegiac an image of factory labour that Sir Robert's son, also Robert, joked that the state should set mills up as health resorts. In spite of the carping of Philips and Graham, the Bill passed the lower House. Then in the Lords it fell before Lord Lauderdale, a staunch political economist. Lauderdale prided himself on being able to laugh reformers off the stage, though his humour was notoriously laboured. The Whig statesman, playwright and far subtler wit Richard Brinsley Sheridan once said after hearing a droll story: 'Don't tell that to Lauderdale, for a joke in his mouth is no laughing matter.' Amusing or not, Lauderdale managed to persuade his fellow lords that another inquiry was needed. This one was to be carefully stage-managed to satisfy the mill proprietors.[9]

The Lords Committee heard hours of testimony from physicians and surgeons who had been invited to visit mills and had been escorted around them by their owners. The evidence of Henry Hardie, a Mancunian physician, was standard fare. He had carried out an inquiry into the health of children in seven local mills, and was questioned on it by Lord Kenyon. Hardie flatly denied that factory children were more often stunted, deformed or sick than other youngsters, or that inhaled cotton flue could be unhealthy. And he parried the suggestion that carding for fourteen hours was potentially bad for the lungs, saying – contrary to the long experience of the carders – that the 'daily Expectoration throws off the cotton'. Hardie

16. Sir Robert Peel, a wealthy mill owner who was created a baronet, entered the House of Commons and managed to pass the 1802 Health and Morals of Apprentices Act and the 1819 Factory Act. His son, also Robert, was to become a Tory Prime Minister.

was then asked: 'Who determined as to the seven which were to be visited out of the forty-seven factories?' His answer was enlightening: 'The proprietors.' Other witnesses went to extraordinary lengths to thwart Peel's plans. Manchester's Dr Holme refused to accept that even 23 hours of labour would inevitably induce ill-health. Lauder-dale felt vindicated by this testimony. But he evidently didn't peruse too closely the reports written by JPs who had visited cotton mills in compliance with Peel's 1802 Act, and which were included in the Committee's write-up. Those of Marmaduke Middleton and Dr Joseph Denman were among them.[10]

The new year brought fresh resolution to the factory campaigners. It also brought new advocates. Lord Liverpool sided with them, and so did the Bishop of Chester, who had made the effort over the Christmas recess to inspect the cotton mills in his locality; he quickly saw that Lauderdale's medical experts had been deceived. With Lord Liverpool and the Bishop on side, in February a third parliamentary inquiry convened. This time the physicians and surgeons didn't hesitate to indict factories as deleterious to the child's mind and body. For the first time, a number of workers also made the journey down to London to testify. One of them, John Farebrother, told of a master called Luke Taylor who waited for the child workers not far from the mill 'with a horsewhip under his coat', with which he lashed those who arrived any time after five o'clock in the morning. Farebrother also detailed how, as an overlooker, he had been instructed to whip children if they failed to meet a target or if their attention flagged. He and other operatives who gave evidence found work hard to come by on their return to Lancashire, but their testimony hit home. Despite the efforts of the masters to discredit them, in July 1819 an Act passed prohibiting the employment of children under nine in cotton mills, and restricting the hours of actual work for those under sixteen to twelve hours per day.[11]

The Bill's backers had been gratified to receive support from a number of master manufacturers. As many as seventeen proprietors had signed a petition for reduced hours that had been sent to Peel by Stockport spinners. Despite what later chroniclers said, plenty of mill owners were troubled by the treatment of children, the hours they had to endure, the heat of the factories, and the foul air of the carding room. But fear of being undercut by less high-minded competitors held them back from making changes. Some of those mill owners who cheered Robert Peel on were also men who cared about metropolitan opinion and wished to enjoy their wealth without ignominy. Many humanitarians felt the same way. They wanted to be proud of their nation's rise to economic greatness, without having to reflect guiltily on its cost in children's bones, minds and morals. Having visited Birmingham in 1815, Robert Southey wrote: 'Think not that I am insensible to the wonders of the place ... but watch-chains, necklaces, and bracelets, buttons, buckles, and snuff-boxes, are dearly purchased at the expense of health and morals.' The abuse of children was a moral crime that had to be washed away.[12]

Yet, many were the workers, humanitarians and ex-apprentices who felt that Peel's 1819 Act didn't go far enough. They rightly complained that there were no real provisions for the Act to be enforced, since Peel's idea of paid inspectors had come to nothing. John Brown was one of those left unhappy by the new legislation. Sometime in the early 1820s he had fallen in with William Smith, later editor of the *Bolton Chronicle*, then the city's leading agitator for shorter hours for factory children. Brown had suggested to him the founding of a new journal to advance the campaign. He had then set out to find good copy.[13]

23

A strange acquaintance

Somehow, John Brown heard of Robert Blincoe's plight at Lowdham and Litton mills. We don't know how the story travelled from Manchester to Bolton. It's probable, however, that Blincoe was less than chary in telling of his past suffering. Whether out of catharsis, anger or loquaciousness, he had told enough people for word to reach Brown's ears. Once the two men had spoken, sometime in spring 1822, Brown realised that he had in Blincoe the ideal advocate for the 'short time' cause. Brown later wrote in the *Memoir* that his new acquaintance wasn't noisily bitter or cynical about his past treatment. Rather, his speech was 'temperate' and his 'statements, cautious and consistent'. Blincoe also had the perfect appearance for Brown's political purposes, his twisted legs and small stature, his scarred head, deep-set eyes and 'worn, melancholy countenance' all serving to authenticate his claims of vicious maltreatment.[1]

There were plenty of other parish apprentices in Manchester, not to mention in Bolton, Leeds, Stockport and Macclesfield, who could have told stories of abandonment and abuse. But in one sense Robert Blincoe's biography was unusually powerful. With extraordinary temerity, he had repeatedly gone above his master's head, seeking redress from higher and better authorities. Far from resigning himself to the wanton brutality of the Needhams and their overlookers, he had risked savage retribution to change the way he was treated. Blincoe had known nothing of Peel's 1802 Act. He didn't need to, for he possessed the strength of character and intrinsic sense of right to realise that his treatment at Litton Mill was morally wrong. Where many parish apprentices simply ran away, he had the guts and self-respect to approach the squirearchy of a strange county to demand justice. The acute moral sensibilities Blincoe displayed were all the more impressive because, in the minds of many in Georgian and then Victorian England, work'us boys very rarely possessed them.

For all the humanity of *Oliver Twist*, even Charles Dickens seems to have shared this preconception. The theme of noble ancestry underpinned the entire plot of the novel. For it was Oliver's decent parentage that made it believable both for Dickens and his readers that a low-down work'us boy could have resisted the blandishments of Fagin's clan of pickpockets and prostitutes. Illegitimate or not, Oliver's character was 'uncorrupted and incorruptible' because – unlike Sikes, Nancy and the Artful Dodger – his veins coursed with the blood of respectable forebears. Thus Oliver was, as one reviewer put it, 'a pattern of modern excellence, guileless himself, and measuring others by his own innocence; delicate and high-minded, affectionate, noble, brave, generous, with the manners of a son of a most distinguished gentleman.' Pearls may be found in dunghills, *Oliver Twist* implied, but only if gentlefolk accidentally drop them there. In fact, even this concession went much too far for some of Dickens' contemporaries. One of the most influential reviews of the novel appeared in the Tory journal, the *Quarterly Review*. For its critic, not even Oliver's heredity made his later goodness credible. 'Workhouse boys are not born with original virtue', he pronounced, 'nor was any one except Daniel exposed to wild beasts without being eaten up.' The mere suggestion that boys growing up in workhouses could become decent citizens was, he went on, likely to 'degrade the national mind'.[2]

As Brown realised, Blincoe's life was the most eloquent rebuttal to this callous verdict. Sober, industrious, and firm in his morality, he was the beau idéal of the self-improving working-class male. He bore his sufferings apparently without spite, and sublimated the wrongs done to him into a desire to rescue other children from the same kind of exploitation. Bar a few forgivable lapses, including filching from Litton Mill's pigs and Taddington farmers, this parish apprentice really did have 'the manners of a son of a most distinguished gentleman'.[3]

Brown included in the *Memoir* the rumour of Blincoe's 'priestly descent', but he didn't discuss it with any conviction. The story probably meant much to Blincoe himself, but for Brown, a working-class agitator, it was useful only insofar as it illustrated the selfish ineptitude of the upper classes. Brown had more interest in showing that even a boy hailing from the lowest social strata could grow into a good man, that being low-born didn't preclude one from having high moral principles. And all the evidence we have suggests that Brown didn't need to distort or invent in order to make Blincoe's story a counterpoint to the image of factory workers as degraded, bestial and too thick-skinned to have tender feelings. Brown quickly saw that Robert Blincoe was a fighter, a small-time hero, a man whose story could enthuse factory drudges with the thought of bettering their situation irrespective of the raw power of bosses and overlookers. And in the same way that Blincoe had cowed William Woodward by invoking the venerable authority of the squirearchy, the short time movement hoped to secure from Parliament the power to face down the millocracy.

So Brown persuaded Blincoe to relate his life story, and from it he assembled a remarkable biography and a work of memorable propaganda. He enjoined his subject never to allow his sense of past wrongs to lead him to 'transgress the limits of truth'. And aside from the exaggerations to be expected in a man looking back to his childhood, there's every reason to think that Blincoe took Brown's injunction to heart. Brown himself, though, felt free to put his subject's life to political use. Hence, although the story he told is mostly reliable, from Blincoe's later testimony to a government inquiry we can tell that it has little of the simplicity of feeling and expression with which it left his lips.[4]

John Brown's overdone pathos mostly effaced the more direct and down-to-earth manner of Blincoe's own speech. He wrote in angry earnest, with a passionate verbosity which could hardly be more different from the droll sarcasm of Charles Dickens. But if Blincoe's personality is often stifled by Brown's writing, we learn much about the author from the fervour of his prose. And even if little is known of Brown's life history, a fair amount can also be gleaned from his various publications.

Brown seems to have been a native of Bolton in Lancashire. His knowledge of Greek and Latin, apparent in one of his books, also suggests a proper education. But in January 1806 he was living far from his birthplace, in Great Yarmouth, evidently with contacts in the Royal Navy. In this year he wrote a book entitled *The Mysteries of*

Neutralization, a literary onslaught directed at supposedly neutral states, in particular Prussia, which were helping the French to contravene Chancellor Perceval's Orders in Council. They were doing so, Brown said, by supplying French ships for a price with 'fabricated papers' signed by legitimate authorities which falsely claimed that the vessels were neither French nor carrying French goods. The Prussians, Brown also asserted, permitted the enemy to fly the Prussian flag from their main masts. In consequence, thousands of French vessels every year sailed through the British naval cordon, undermining one of 'the main pillars' of England's martial strategy.[5]

The Mysteries of Neutralization went beyond patriotic ardour, condemning the 'foulest perjuries' of Prussian magistrates, bankers, traders and owners with fanatical invective. In short, the book was not written by a mentally stable individual. Many years later, Manchester's Reverend Charles Gillespie remarked that Brown had suffered from 'melancholy', and that this 'augmented' the pathos of his writing style. Gillespie was surely correct. But if Brown's was a melancholic temperament, he was also prone to episodes of mania during which he became convinced that he was being persecuted. All but his first book began with a preface explaining his need to flee from vile oppressors; his second work, for example, *The Northern Courts*, lavished praise on the Swedes for their 'hospitality and every social virtue' and thanked them for providing him with 'a secure and most agreeable asylum'. In 1807 a sense of persecution drove Brown to leave English waters. There are strong hints that he had previously spent time in Germany; now he sailed to the north.[6]

In Scandinavia, Brown travelled widely. When he finally came to publish an account of his travels, he claimed to have associated 'with persons of … great rank and consequence'. We are told of his having political debates with the urbane nobleman 'Edlercrantz' and 'Chevalier Geyer'. In Brown's recollections of these discussions, we see a young man avidly reading William Cobbett, and speaking to his hosts of the desirability of an English government with 'annual parliaments and the right of election commensurate with direct taxation.' This is consistent with another of his claims. Brown asserts that a political faction set on deposing the Swedish King Gustav IV, if he didn't accept constitutional reform, selected him as an emissary to sail for home and seek support from the British government. Brown tells us that, having accepted the brief from Sweden's 'reform party', he wrote to the British Prime Minister, Spencer Perceval. They were already somewhat acquainted, we're told, following Brown's revelations in *Mysteries of Neutralization*. Perceval apparently agreed to meet Brown, and they discussed the possibility of English involvement in Swedish affairs. In the event, Perceval did nothing. Gustav IV was arrested and soon after sent into exile.[7]

It's hard to know whether or not to believe Brown's astonishing narrative. That he travelled in Sweden is pretty certain. But his sally into international politics is less easy to substantiate. His story does have an air of believability, however, not least because to have invented it would imply a degree of mania hard to square with his later achievements. Moreover, it would seem that when not weighed down by fits of melancholia, Brown's manic personality gave him a beguiling charm. His energy and earnestness could be arresting and flattering; Brown at his best could doubtless have charmed himself into a royal court. Yet, we have no record at all of his whereabouts from 1808 to 1818. We do not know if he spent these years living off inherited wealth, pursuing a trade in humble obscurity, or working for the government in a covert capacity. It might well be that he was mentally incapacitated for the whole period. But after *The Northern Courts* finally appeared in print in 1818, Brown was busy once more, churning out popular histories, mostly comprising chapter-long quotations from other authors. Always in these books there were injured parties for Brown to defend against the grossest of calumnies and other authors to accuse of bungling unfairness.

Brown's 1821 *Anecdotes and Characters of the House of Brunswick* is typical of his emotionally unchecked style. King George I, said Brown, was wicked and profligate; Lord Bute, once George III's chief counsellor, a 'pestiferous influence'; the Princess Dowager a wronged party; and Horace Walpole a cynical misanthrope. This work is particularly interesting because Brown's political views were more boldly expressed. Brown eulogised the retired King George III for his unpretentiousness, but his political radicalism was on unabashed display. He looked back wistfully, like Cobbett, to earlier decades when 'pale-cheeked poverty and squalid want were unknown'. 'All that we have gained, in power, dominion, and glory', he concluded, 'we have more than lost in morals, happiness and freedom.' Brown was a Radical of a romantic stripe, peering back in time to a 'golden era' of rustic calm and social harmony. But, again like Cobbett, there was nothing quaint in his invective. He made not-so-subtle comparisons between the ruling monarch of the day, George IV, and a 'coarse, vindictive, gross and sensual' George I, who had falsely accused his wife of adultery. Always partial to the injured and weaker party, he sympathised with the late Queen Caroline, and deplored the conduct of her husband George IV.[8]

None of Brown's books sold well, and it's not at all clear how he survived or funded his trips abroad. But while residing again in Great Yarmouth in late 1821 or early 1822, he had a go at satisfying the popular appetite for the picaresque with his *Historical Gallery of Criminal Portraitures, Foreign and Domestic*. Again, sales were poor. Brown then returned, perhaps fleeing once more from imaginary persecutors, to his native Lancashire and the fast-growing industrial town of Bolton. It was at this juncture, in the early spring of 1822, that he met Robert Blincoe. The short hours campaign was highly seductive to a man like Brown. There were weak and innocent victims with whom he could identify, and powerful foes whom he could attack with righteous and cathartic zeal. Focusing on a single individual also suited his emotional *métier*. Throughout the *Memoir*, Brown writes as one who has projected his own fear and agony onto another. He felt too close to the victim to write in the measured prose of a campaigning novelist or a cool analytic philosopher. Writing about Blincoe and his oppressors, Brown battled with his own inner demons.

The two men must have spent many hours together over the following months, Brown taking rapid notes and Blincoe dredging up long-repressed memories, keen that his story be told. In November 1822, Brown announced in the pages of the *Manchester Gazette* the planned birth of a newspaper to be called the *Manchester Examiner*. Its aim would be to expose the horrors of the factory system. The advertisement added that an early edition would contain the startling revelations of one Robert Blincoe. Brown's newspaper, however, never materialised. And soon after the *Gazette*'s announcement, the meetings between himself and Blincoe ceased. After less than a year, as Brown confessed in the final manuscript, he 'was seized with a serious illness'. We're not told what form it took, but the rest of the passage shows that it was his old problem:

> Such atrocious conduct was pursued towards me, as would have fully justified a prosecution for conspiracy. Animated by the most opposite views, the worst of miscreants united to vilify and oppress me; the one wanting to get my papers, in order, by destroying them, to prevent the enormities of the cotton masters being exposed; and another traducing my character, and menacing my life, under an impression that I had basely sold the declarations ... received from oppressed workpeople to their masters.

Brown also said that Blincoe was 'led away' by some of these persecutors. Feeling himself besieged from all sides, Brown was once more plunged into mental agonies.[9]

His anxieties were not necessarily baseless. Some cotton masters could be vindictive if their interests were threatened, and Brown had, after all, alerted them to his intentions in the *Manchester Gazette*. Furthermore, all working-class movements were targets for the infiltration of government spies, and Brown's snooping may well have raised suspicions among the supporters of factory reform. If he told them of his private audience with Spencer Perceval, this would only have exacerbated their distrust. Yet if Brown did meet with malicious opposition, it worked on a mind quickly unhinged. And given that he had suffered similar breakdowns in the past, always accompanied by paranoid delusions, it's probable that his accusers were entirely imaginary.

For yet another year we have no idea what John Brown was doing or how he was managing to support himself. Then, in late 1823, he recovered sufficiently to begin writing again. On 18 and 19 March 1824, he renewed his contact with Robert Blincoe and asked him to read a draft of the *Memoir*. Blincoe, we're told, confirmed its accuracy and added several more details; Brown took notes, and then the two parted company. It's not clear if they met again, but Blincoe would hear nothing of the *Memoir* for four years. In Brown's possession it simply gathered dust. Why Brown now failed to publish is far from clear. Perhaps even Radical publishers turned him away. Interest in factory reform was at a relatively low ebb, with hardly a murmur on the subject in Parliament between 1819 and 1825. Trade was good, and jobs as plentiful as they ever got, and so it wasn't easy to stir working men and women into concerted action. Perhaps, in this relatively tranquil political environment, it was felt that a book about servitude in factories wasn't likely to capture the public mood.[10]

24

Fall of the
House of Needham

We don't know if Brown or Blincoe first heard the news of the Needham family's fall from grace and gentility. But with a rich sense of poetic justice, Brown wrote towards the end of the *Memoir*:

> He has lived to see his tyrannical master brought to adverse fortune, to a state of comparative indigence, and, on his family, the visitation of calamities, so awful, that it looked as if the avenging power of retributive justice had laid its iron hand on him and them.[1]

This is typical of Brown's prose, heavy-handed and melodramatic. But it was accurate in its essentials. The Needhams had indeed fallen on very hard times. They had been cutting costs in any way possible for years before Blincoe's departure, and after he left, conditions at the mill had gone on deteriorating. John Joseph Betts told of how the apprentices' privations became so bad by 1814 that they were reduced to subsisting 'principally upon Woodland sustenance'. The financial woes of the Needhams had deepened. They were heading for bankruptcy.[2]

Blincoe would have heard only fragments of the full story, but following the insolvency of Joseph Lingard and the spinning mill's failure to pay, on 31 January 1815 a warrant for bankruptcy was served on Ellis and John Needham. Since they were unable to redeem Hargate Wall or the Old Hall, they both passed to Mr Fogg, and the Needhams suffered the indignity of having to pack up their belongings and vacate their treasured family home. Now the mill wheel came to an abrupt stop and, as the Derbyshire county deeds record, it 'was left for a considerable time empty or unworked'. The Needhams' grand hopes of the 1780s, when it seemed that anyone with capital and a little sense could turn cotton into gold, had come to nothing. But having to depart the elegant hall bought by John Needham senior must have been the most devastating blow.[3]

As churchwarden and steward of assemblies, Ellis Needham had acquired considerable local influence and respectability. For several years he maintained his position, but at the cost of ever-growing debts. In early 1815 he could no longer hide his financial ineptitude. Nor, as a bankrupt, could he expect to remain a churchwarden in either Wormhill or Tideswell. Bankrupts, like bastards, carried a heavy burden of stigma. Neighbours and associates were quick to assume that they had brought it on themselves by greed or cupidity. Thus in George Eliot's *The Mill on the Floss*, the bankrupted Mr Tulliver is accused of having been 'wicked and wasteful'. In the Needhams' case, the accusation would at least have been just. And having lost nearly everything to his family's creditors aside from a few small parcels of land, Ellis would thenceforth have to forgo adding 'Esquire' to his name. It was plain old Ellis Needham from now on.[4]

John Brown may have felt that justice had been served, but when a mill ceased operating, its owners were rarely the hardest hit. Parish apprentices, permanently debarred from their places of birth by the Act of Settlement, were nearly always the worst off. Those at Litton Mill, many of whom had worked there for more than a decade, were simply abandoned by Ellis Needham and his sons when the mill closed in 1815. The county deeds tell us that they were 'left destitute of support other than from the Township [of Taddington] to the number of eighty and upwards.' For both the children and the parishioners, this was an unmitigated disaster. The mill's closure brought 'very considerable expense' onto the luckless inhabitants of Taddington. They had benefited in no way from Litton Mill when it was up and running, and now had to take care of Needham's rejects. Taddington comprised only 89 families in 1811, each of which was now effectively responsible for feeding and clothing another child. Gradually the apprentice children were farmed out, probably without much discretion, to any masters who would have them.[5]

At least one group of children, including Orphan John, fled starving from the mill before it closed down. They arrived back in

London, but were promptly returned by the London overseers and sent to work for William Newton at the re-opened Cressbrook Mill. By some accounts, Newton's was a less benign regime than that of Baker and Bossley. But ten of Needham's apprentice children, 'too debilitated' to work after years of excess labour, experienced the cruellest fate. They lived on parish hand-outs and were all dead by 1818.[6]

But the Needhams hadn't yet finished with Litton Mill. In March 1815, Ellis's fourth son, Robert, set the waterwheel in motion once again. It would seem that Ellis and John had legally transferred the concern to Robert so as to prevent it falling into the hands of creditors. Robert now faced the same problem of labour shortage as his father had in the 1790s. Before going out of business, Ellis had promised the Duke of Devonshire's agent, a Mr Knowlton, that he would take on no more apprentices who might end up as a burden on the Taddington locals. Soon after, Knowlton left the county for a short while. Seizing the opportunity, Robert sneakily contacted London's Saffron Hill and Hatton Gardens overseers of the poor, who gladly despatched cartloads of children to Litton Mill. When Knowlton and the rate-payers of Taddington heard of this, they were furious. To make matters worse, one of Robert Needham's new apprentices, Sarah Heeley, was crippled and quite incapable of work. Robert demanded that the Saffron Hill parish take her back, but they refused.[7]

Robert Needham died in 1816, a deeply unpopular man. At this juncture, Derbyshire's magistrates stepped in and had Sarah Heeley transported back to London as 'a fraud upon the Township'. It was a foolish piece of brinkmanship, for it was clear that she now had a settlement in Taddington. It didn't take the London magistracy long to recognise this fact, and so Sarah Heeley was loaded back onto a cart and sent north, in abject distress at the thought that she was to end up in a parish far from whatever family she had, and among people who, too poor to be generous or sympathetic, resented her daily presence. The Taddington parishioners could at least rest content, however, that she was assigned a new settlement in Tideswell parish. She was dumped from the cart in Litton village, soon following into the grave four more of the Litton Mill apprentices, all in their early- to mid-teens, who were buried by Parson Brown in Tideswell's grave-yard between March and May of 1817. Over the course of more than twenty years, the Needhams had inflicted terrible misery on hundreds of young boys and girls. Finally, after a lengthy series of complaints, Lord Scarsdale cancelled the Needhams' lease on the land in Miller's Dale where Litton Mill stood.[8]

Ellis Needham had another go at the cotton trade before wisely giving up. What he did thereafter is not known, though his wife Sarah seems to have kept them going by setting up a 'ladies' boarding school' in the town where they lived out the remainder of their lives, Chapel-en-le-Frith, about seven miles of moorland distant from Wormhill. John Needham became a pattern-maker in Manchester. And Ellis junior seems to have worked in Castleton's fluor-spar museum, showing visitors the stunning crystalline rocks discovered by lead miners in the area. So far as we can tell, none of the Needham children ended up begging to the parish, but not one of Ellis and Sarah's sons had a gentlemanly occupation. To those born into a class of rural gentlemen, this decline in status was fast and humiliating. Ellis senior died in 1830, leaving behind at least ten children. He was able to bequeath them nothing. His estate was valued at under £100, and what remained went to his widow. Nor, in his Letters of Administration, was Ellis described as a 'gentleman'. His bankruptcy and poverty disqualified him from inclusion in the ranks of respectable society. After years of child-bearing and worry, in 1830 Sarah Needham left the running of the boarding school to her daughter. She died not long after.[9]

Litton Mill eventually did re-open, and Miller's Dale resounded again with the sound of the waterwheel and the din of machines. Under far more efficient and humane management than the Needhams ever provided, it went on producing textiles for another century-and-a-half. This would seem to imply that, had Ellis Needham and his sons encouraged and nurtured rather than bullied and whipped their parish apprentices, they could have made a real success of Litton Mill.

This is only, of course, one part of the story. Remote, water-powered mills like Litton were ill-matched to compete against the multi-storey, steam-driven giants of Manchester and elsewhere in

Lancashire. All cotton-spinning mills in the region – Cressbrook, Calver, Cromford and Matlock – lurched from crisis to crisis in these years. As Napoleon's Continental System of economic warfare against Britain took hold, and as imports of raw cotton plummeted following the declaration of war against America, many capitalists were ruined. Less efficient concerns, like those in the High Peak, were often the most exposed and the first to go under. Even so, many of the older mills in the area did weather the storm of the Napoleonic blockade, the war with America, and the rise of Lancashire's cotton industry. The spinning mills of Matlock, Cromford, Belper, Bakewell, even Cressbrook, would turn profits for many decades more. And Litton Mill would make money for a succession of owners for over a century. The structural problems that hastened the Needhams' ruin did not doom it to inevitable closure. Had their apprentices been less tired, better nourished and more gently governed, they would surely have produced yarn of a higher and more consistent quality which found readier buyers.[10]

Indeed, even to some contemporaries it was obvious that exhausted operatives made mistakes, got injured, and made yarn that snapped too readily. But, impelled by a contempt for the lower orders and the assumption that only coercion kept them from idleness, many bosses created a workforce unable to work effectively through fear, weariness and melancholy. Not all, however, saw it this way. For Lord Lauderdale, the House of Lords' arch-exponent of doctrinaire political economy, capitalists were always the best judges of what was in their own interest. 'The employer', he explained, 'was the person most likely to be acquainted with the different degrees of strength possessed by his workmen, and most likely to avoid overworking with a view to his own advantage.' Selfishness alone was enough to safeguard the interests of the labouring classes. But Lauderdale's fondness for cosy abstractions obscured the fact that many employers, like the Needhams, were utterly incompetent judges of their own interests. While the cruder sorts of mill proprietor beat, tortured and deprived, the more successful extracted more labour from their employees while raising the whip hand only in exceptional circumstances. Owen, Arkwright, Greg, and the Strutts of Belper in Derbyshire, demonstrated that one could be kind and still thrive in the cotton business.

The brutal factory discipline that Lauderdale and other political economists accepted as a necessarily evil, pardonable because it contributed to national prosperity, in some cases played into the hands of the more humane of foreign competitors. The closure of Litton Mill should stand as a classic demonstration of the grotesqueness of Lauderdale's economic philosophy. At the very least, it can be said that the wretched state of the apprentices and the depleted morale of the adult workers rendered the closure of the mill certain, not just probable, in the age of steam-powered cotton factories.[11]

With the bankruptcies of Ellis and John Needham, as John Brown observed, by 1815 one part of Old Beckkà's prophecy had been fulfilled. Blincoe's oppressors had been brought down low. But the fortune-teller of Chapel-en-le-Frith had also promised future prosperity to her avid young customer. Reflecting on this, Brown concluded the first draft of the *Memoir* with the optimistic suggestion that the 'old sybil's' predictions would be realised in the fullness of time:

> It is in the compass of probability that, he may, in the meridian of his life, be carried as high, by the wheel of fortune, as in the days of his infancy and youth, he was cast low.[12]

Brown was evidently impressed by his subject's industry, application and determination to better himself. But success in business was a slippery commodity, as Blincoe was shortly to discover to his cost.

25

Up in flames

The year had started too well. When Brown was completing his manuscript in March 1824, Blincoe's business affairs were thriving. Success now bred over-confidence and ill-luck. Blincoe was doing so well that he decided to try something more ambitious than dealing in waste cotton. He gave up his cotton-waste business in Bank-Top and moved to a house in Edge Place in the neighbouring town of Salford, already inseparable from Manchester's insatiable urban sprawl. He then bought 'some machinery for spinning of cotton', almost certainly a version of Crompton's mule, and 'took part of a mill of one Mr Ormrod, near St Paul's Church, Tib-Street' in the Piccadilly area of Manchester.[1]

It was a standard arrangement in early industrial Cottonopolis. A few years before, as many as two-thirds of spinning firms had been renting or sharing space in larger factories. Since spinning mules were relatively cheap, ambitious working men who had put aside a little capital could buy one or a few and set up in rented factory rooms. Blincoe followed suit, agreeing to pay the owners of the steam engine for the use of power. But while many had gone before him, he was taking a risk. As the number of Manchester's spindles soared into the millions, the market for cotton yarn became keenly competitive. An official inquiry of January 1823 observed that 'profits are reduced on all staple articles, [so] great attention and skill, as well as quick returns, are requisite to obtain even a small remuneration for capital and risk.' In short, it was tough going for the small manufacturer. Profit margins were slimmer than ever.[2]

Despite the gamble he had taken, after six weeks of preparation when the last spindle was fitted in place and the rollers primed, Blincoe must have stepped back to observe his machines with some satisfaction. The work'us boy had risen to the heady heights of cotton manufacturer. Then disaster struck. On his very first day of cotton spinning, a fire broke out in an adjoining room of Ormrod's mill. Within minutes his mule was engulfed in flames and destroyed. Out in the street, watching the clouds of smoke billow out from his floor, Blincoe could only rue his failure to take out insurance. In all likelihood it had been a necessary risk. But fires in cotton mills, caused by illicit smoking, gas lighting or steam engines exploding, were by no means uncommon. The *Manchester Guardian* recorded several others in the same year as the fire at Ormrod's, though these were all fatal conflagrations. Smaller blazes like the one which affected Blincoe usually went unrecorded, presumably because they weren't out of the ordinary. Recognising the risks, wealthier capitalists invested in fireproof factories. Blincoe couldn't afford to take such precautions.[3]

Soon after the fire, he spoke to John Brown for the last time. The *Memoir* recorded Blincoe's melancholic declaration that he would 'have nothing to do with the spinning business again – what with the troubles endured when apprenticed to it, and the heavy loss sustained by fire.' He was, wrote Brown, 'completely sick of the business altogether'. Blincoe was no longer in a position to rejoice at the Needham family's downfall.[4]

John Brown now moved on, deciding next to write a history of Greater and Little Bolton. Seventeen instalments of this work, a crazy assemblage of history and geology, were published between 1824 and the end of 1825. With his trademark intensity, Brown upbraided earlier scholars for their 'exuberant imagination', 'wild surges' and 'imbecility'. And throughout there are again strong hints of a persecution complex. Only two issues into his history, Brown collapsed again. Having recovered after a few months, he penned an emotional explanation for the back cover, thanking those who had stood by him 'through every storm raised by detraction' and despite the 'many artifices devised and applied to impede his course'. It was a tragically familiar refrain.[5]

Seven instalments short of the promised 24, Brown suddenly threw his history project aside. In researching the issue which dealt with the dawn of the factory age, he had gone to see Samuel Crompton, inventor of the spinning mule, by then an old man residing in a Tudor mansion at Hall-in-the-Wood. Falling into conversation with Crompton, Brown soon realised that here he had found a new cause, one perfectly suited to his emotional idiom: the defence of a wounded man who had apparently been wronged by the most powerful vested interests.

Crompton's mule was one of the most important innovations of the early industrial age. Designed and built entirely by himself in 1778–9, it was a huge success. But Crompton hadn't taken out a patent, relying instead on other cotton-spinners willingly giving up a share of the profits they made from the machine. In comparison with the money that his invention generated for others, Crompton received a pittance. Eventually he appealed to Sir Robert Peel for a parliamentary grant, and a committee agreed in 1812 to give him £5,000. Crompton was appalled at this stinginess, and in 1825 he unburdened himself to Brown, who promptly ditched his history of Bolton to take up the cudgels on Crompton's behalf. Inspired by the successes of Edward Jenner and the inventor of the spinning jenny, Edmund Cartwright, in getting large parliamentary pay-outs, Brown made Crompton's cause his own.[6]

Gilbert French, one of Crompton's early biographers, alleged that Brown had a 'pecuniary interest' in securing a second parliamentary grant for Crompton. But Brown was not animated by a love of lucre. At bottom he was driven by a need to ground his own sense of martyrdom, normalising his persecution complex by making the enemies of others his own. Won over by Brown's vicarious sense of outrage, Crompton gave him documents from which to prepare a memorial to the Lords of the Treasury. In Bolton-le-Moors, on 29 May 1825, Brown finalised his plea for Parliament to consider granting Crompton 'a reward commensurate with high deserts'. It was vintage Brown: passionate, sincere and overdone. But to reassure his old allies in the factory reform movement, Brown insisted in his memorial that Crompton had no share in producing the 'evils of the factory system'.[7]

In late 1825 or early 1826 John Brown borrowed money from an acquaintance in Manchester, leaving some of his personal papers, including notes relating to Robert Blincoe, as surety. Then he went to the capital to fight Crompton's cause. As Brown disappeared into the hubbub of the metropolis, Blincoe too vanished once more from view. For the next three years he left hardly any discernible trace of his activities. All we know is that on 2 June 1826 he and Martha had a second child whom they christened Robert. The next we hear of the Blincoes is less than happy.[8]

PART 5

Rising from the Ashes

*If the English creditor has not taken his knife with Shylock
… he has wielded a scarcely less formidable machinery of
bolts and bars. Engines of infliction he had in plenty,
degradation and confinement for all, and starvation
besides for the truly insolvent debtor.*

The Times (1844)

*Every man for himself, and God for all of us, as the
elephant said as he danced amongst the chickens.*

Henry Scott Holland (1889)

*… the proofs of long and cruel toil were most remarkable
… A friend of mine collected a vast number together for
me; the sight was most piteous, the deformities incredible,
like a mass of crooked alphabets.*

Lord Ashley (1844)

*Had the producers of wealth been the makers of laws,
would they have left those who made the country rich to
perish by starvation?*

John Doherty (1831)

26

Back behind walls

Sometime in the mid-1820s, Blincoe's years of hard work and self-reliance were wiped clean away. In heavy debt and unable to pay his creditors, he was served with a legal writ and loaded onto a cart once again, this time bound for the indignity of an extended stay in Lancaster Castle debtors' gaol. We don't know exactly when this occurred. Blincoe's whereabouts from late 1825 to early 1828 are an almost complete mystery. All we can say is that for some of this period he languished in gaol. In the autumn of 1827, when the Radical publisher and Peterloo veteran Richard Carlile tried to make contact, he was informed that Blincoe was or had been in debtors' prison. That Carlile failed to find him suggests that he was still confined at the mercy of his creditors. Either way, he had left to fend for herself a wife with a young daughter and a son already born or soon to be delivered. Tragic at any time, Blincoe's insolvency had occurred at the cruellest of moments.[1]

The fire of 1824 in Ormrod's mill almost certainly had something to do with Blincoe's financial ruin. He would have spent in the region of £30 for his spinning mule – at roughly half a spinner's annual wage, this was no mean sum. If he borrowed money to buy it, his creditor may then have brought him down. More likely, however, he was forced to borrow to survive in the months following the fire as he tried to get back into business. Even the smallest advance of credit could lead to ruin. The novelist Anthony Trollope told of how a loan of £12 from a tailor 'found its way into the hands of a money-lender'. He proceeded to borrow £4 from this man, and the two debts 'grew monstrously under repeated renewals' until he 'paid ultimately something over £200'. This was such a 'common story', Trollope added, 'as to be hardly worth telling.'[2]

It's also possible that Blincoe was hit by the sudden banking crisis of late 1825. After years of irresponsible lending, scores of banks folded. Their customers lost all their savings, leaving many thousands ruined. In that fraught winter, it even seemed that the Bank of England would crash. A brief but severe slump in trade then multiplied the pain. If Blincoe reeled from the banking crisis and trade depressions of 1825 and 1826, many hand-loom weavers had been reduced to near-starvation. One of them, William Thom, kept a diary. On one freezing day over Christmas 1825, he recorded in heart-rending detail:

> The only food in the house is a handful of oatmeal – our fuel is exhausted. My wife and I were conversing in sunken whispers about making an attempt to cook the oatmeal when the youngest child woke up beyond his mother's powers to hush it again to sleep. He fell into whimpering and finally broke out in a steady scream, rendering it impossible to keep the rest asleep. Face after face sprang up, each saying 'Mother! Mother! please give us something.'[3]

The weavers, as usual, had it worst. But thousands of financially-exposed manufacturers, like Blincoe, suffered alongside them. The advent of the machine age made many a fortune, but it introduced a chronic instability into the businesses of tradesmen, merchants and producers. As such, when Blincoe arrived at the debtors' gaol in 1826 or 1827, there were already between 300 and 400 resident insolvents, many of them victims of the boom–bust oscillations of the early industrial economy. Only 30 years earlier, before Arkwright made his fortune, Crompton invented his mule, and Boulton and Watt steam engines appeared, just 30 debtors had been incarcerated in Lancaster Castle gaol.[4]

Blincoe was now in the grip of the Byzantine 19th-century law of debt. Convoluted in its origins and often absurd in its execution, it was designed to prevent those scoundrels who, 'craftily obtaining into their hands great substance of other men's goods, do suddenly flee to parts unknown, or keep their houses, not minding to pay or to restore to any of their creditors their debts and duties.' Laws had been passed over the centuries to allow creditors to recover losses from their debtors. But it was also recognised that if businessmen were allowed to claim the status of the bankrupt when their fortunes disappeared, it would act as an incentive for them to own up to their plight rather than dragging more and more people down with them. This all sounded simple enough, but the difficulty came in ensuring that being lenient to the more deserving cases didn't act as an incentive to roguery. So it was mandated that tradesmen only – those engaged in buying and selling for their livelihood – could be declared bankrupts. Anyone else, it was felt, must have incurred their debts through avarice, incompetence or selfishness; the fault was theirs and they deserved no protection from the law. Non-tradesmen who fell into debt became 'insolvent debtors'. They didn't automatically forfeit their property, but they were subject to imprisonment in the most squalid conditions. Poor debtors rotted in the Fleet gaol in London or any of hundreds of equally low-down dives scattered across the counties. Thousands succumbed to typhus fever, the classic malady of want and overcrowding. And they rarely met with clemency in court.[5]

On a word and a small fee from a creditor, debtors like Blincoe were introduced to gaol, or a 'sponging house'. There they would be incarcerated and charged extortionate rates for victuals. Up until this stage, they had been charged with nothing – their arrest was merely a precaution lest they decamp without feeling their creditors' wrath. Blincoe presumably spent a while in a sponging house in Manchester. He would then have been escorted from the cells to appear before a court. In Blincoe's case, his creditors refused to extend mercy and the court obviously decided that he wasn't a tradesman. Unable to gain the protection afforded to the bankrupt, he was therefore despatched to debtors' gaol.[6]

Regaining his freedom was no easy matter. The law was contrived to deter fraudsters from running up debts without a thought for the poor tradesmen they defrauded. And to prevent such persons wriggling free, before an Act of 1808 insolvent debtors could be kept in gaol even after they had agreed to pay off their debts. Some of the more spiteful or aggrieved creditors preferred to leave their debtors mouldering in rat-infested cells rather than allow them to gain their freedom so they could start repaying their debts. Vengeance was very much the creditor's. The 1808 Act was a definite improvement. It guaranteed the release from gaol of anyone in debt of less than £20 after a single year. A Court for Relief of Insolvent Debtors was established in 1813, geared to reducing the burden on debtors' prisons by identifying those worthy enough to be released. These two Acts probably shortened Blincoe's stay in gaol. But even after 1813, many were the insolvent debtors who – like Dickens' William Dorrit – spent decades behind bars, sliding ever further into debt, and remaining there so as to evade their remaining creditors.[7]

Limiting the right to be declared bankrupt to tradesmen hurt nearly all non-tradesmen who slipped into the red, with the exception of the law-making classes themselves. The aristocracy did rather nicely out of the arrangement. No one was going to arrest a duke or an earl as an insolvent debtor, but since they weren't tradesmen their creditors couldn't take their family estates when they gambled themselves into financial embarrassment. No matter how much an earl borrowed, defaulted and overspent, his property was safe. And the legal definition of 'tradesman' was carefully tailored to the nobility's self-interest, simply ignoring the fact that most of them routinely engaged either directly or through servants in buying and selling land, mines or cattle. The Earl of Camden rightly observed that if anyone who ever bought and sold 'was liable to be a bankrupt, many of the first persons in the kingdom might be liable to be so.' Royals were even more insulated: Parliament in 1811 agreed to pay off £190,000 in debts incurred by the Prince of Wales. It was politely suggested that in future he squander less on frivolous entertaining and horse-racing, advice that 'Prinny', selfish, arrogant and profligate, couldn't accept. The losers in this system were those with the benefit neither of bankruptcy nor of aristocracy. It was into this company that Robert Blincoe fell.[8]

Having taken his leave of his young family and left his business career in ruins, he was escorted on the 70-mile journey to Lancaster. After a couple of days on the road, Blincoe passed under the castle's gatehouse. He was then deposited in the courtyard outside the debtors' wing and assigned to his quarters.

To Lancaster Castle gaol the Manchester Radical and trades unionist John Doherty had been brought in chains in 1819 to serve his two-year sentence with hard labour. He spent mind-numbing hours on the prison's treadmill, his footsteps powering looms and water-pumps. Blincoe's period of incarceration overlapped with that of about 70 poor weavers from east Lancashire who were awaiting trial, transportation or execution for their alleged parts in a resurgence of Luddism in the county in 1826. A few months after William Thom's moving diary entry, gangs of starving weavers had set off to mills all over east Lancashire, smashing the new power-looms which they blamed for their worsening plight. At Accrington, the 1st King's Dragoon Guards wilted on seeing their emaciated faces and, having issued a warning, gave the poor men and women their sandwiches. Elsewhere the soldiers made arrests, at least one weaver commenting that he would welcome gaol, since there he would at least 'get a skilly [a thin broth or soup] three times a day'. But in Ramsbottom the 60th Rifle Corps killed five men, one of them wholly innocent of frame-breaking and shot in cold blood. In these desperate months, Manchester's factories had also become targets. A stave-wielding mob marched through the city setting fire to mills containing power-looms. A panicked government, one eye always trained on Manchester's volatile labouring class, filled the city's barracks to overflowing with reinforcements. Barges arrived crammed with detachments of the Royal Horse, the 10th Royal Hussars, the 2nd Battalion Coldstream Guards and the 1st Battalion Third Guards. And as fear took hold of Lord Liverpool's Tory government, the 27-man Rocket Troop arrived too, its seven-pound cannon and twelve-pounder rockets ready to be loosed into the midst of the revolutionary proletariat.[9]

Despite the fact that the weavers had been impelled to frame-breaking by years of intolerable suffering, Justice Park in the Shire Hall at Lancaster Castle took no pity on the men and women who stood before him. Several were hanged on the gallows just opposite the castle's church. And Blincoe almost certainly saw some of those destined for Botany Bay as they left the gaol. They were chained in groups to the tops of stagecoaches to maximise their shame; at the inns they passed on the way to London's docks, they were refused use of the lavatories and had to make do with deserted barns and rough ground.[10]

Fortunately for Blincoe, the experience of debtors was very different to that of felons. His category of prisoner had its own wing looking onto the courtyard, and considerable freedom of movement. An inspector in 1847 noted that the debtors' section 'resembled a somewhat noisy tavern or tea garden'. And a small book of engravings by 'E. Slack, a briefless barrister' from the 1830s suggests that there was a similar atmosphere in Blincoe's day. This insolvent barrister drew five different living quarters, all sleeping four or more men and having names like 'The Snug', 'The Pigeons', 'Smugglers' and 'The Chancery'. The inmates are shown smoking pipes, playing cards, drinking ale, and playing the fiddle. The rooms are large, stone-flagged and relatively clean, if sparsely and cheaply furnished. But the debtors were assigned to different quarters depending on what they could afford. The gaol played host to a wide range of social ranks. When the artist Benjamin Haydon was hurled into King's Bench debtors' prison in London in 1823 he found himself among 'baronets, and bankers, authors and merchants, painters and poets, dandies of

THE QUAKERS
1st Class Day Room for Debtors.
LANCASTER CASTLE

17. An engraving by E. Slack, a 'briefless barrister', of a communal dining room in Lancaster Castle's debtors' wing. Blincoe would almost certainly have taken his meals in this room. Courtesy of Lancaster City Museums

rank in silk and velvet and dandies of no rank in rags and tatters, idiotism and insanity, poverty and affliction, all mingled ... with a spiked wall twenty feet high above their heads.' As in King's Bench, at Lancaster Castle there were a number of comfortable rooms for those with money to spare. Those with cash-flow problems but still enjoying an income could also hire servants, purchase newspapers and buy whatever provisions they needed from a market set up in the courtyard below. Blincoe was mostly denied such luxuries. Lacking investments and annuities, he must have felt that despite years of dogged hard work and discomfort, he had been plunged right back into the parish workhouse.[11]

Blincoe had fought for his independence, and gained it. He had started from close to the bottom of the social hierarchy and, through his own personal virtues, risen up towards social respectability. His had been a wonderful success story, and now it had come to nothing. Depressingly, the regimes of gaol and workhouse did have much in common. As a poor debtor, Blincoe had to work for his keep. Long hours of cleaning and odd jobs brought in three ounces of bread and four ounces of oatmeal per day, and one ounce of salt and ten pounds of potatoes each week. Meat, cheese and beer had to be purchased from whatever funds were left.[12]

In one sense, however, debtors' gaol was a levelling experience. Be they rich or poor, insolvent debtors invariably found their stay to be deeply damaging to their reputations. Slack's etchings of inmates show a few with the nonchalant expressions of practised crooks and those pleased to be free from their creditors. But most look sombre and forlorn, with distant expressions, down-turned mouths, closed eyes, corrugated brows, and pursed lips. Nearly all bear the physiognomies of the depressed. From one of them, a George Bradley, a bundle of desperate letters survives. In each of these, Bradley begged his remaining friends and acquaintances to intercede on his behalf to procure his liberty, calling in favours to end his disgrace. Robert Blincoe's insolvency meant that he too suffered a drop in his hard-won social esteem.[13]

The stigma settled on Martha and her children as well. How they survived during these months isn't known. Robert Blincoe the younger wrote many years later that he had spent some time in Liverpool, and it's quite possible that the family uprooted and moved there to be within a shorter ride of Lancaster Castle. Maybe the Simpsons had relations there who could provide them with shelter and provisions. But upon Robert's release, the Blincoes were living once more in Manchester, and it was there that serendipity, so often Blincoe's nemesis, now chose to look on him kindly.[14]

27

Local hero

In July 1827 the Devonian Radical Richard Carlile travelled to the north of England. His plan was to tour the northern cities giving speeches in which he would rehearse his choice blend of Paineite sedition and personal theology. The sworn enemy of bishops, Carlile was set on creating a network of 'atheist chapels'. But he had also been alerted to conditions in textile mills. A major role in his education on the sins of the factory system had been played by a sheaf of hand-written pages that had fallen into his possession. For three long years, John Brown's manuscript had lain somewhere, silently yellowing. Now, its 100 or so pages were in the hands of Carlile, someone who had the power to bring Blincoe's story to a wide audience. When he arrived in Manchester in the summer of 1827, one of his objectives was to establish the veracity of Blincoe's story. But it was already too late to question its author.[1]

Regrettably for Brown, the *Memoir* had been completed at a time when the movement for factory reform had fallen to a low ebb. William Smith of the *Bolton Chronicle* had moved on to subjects more likely to revive the radicalism of the labouring classes. And around the end of 1825, still without a buyer for his manuscript, Brown had departed Bolton to campaign in London on behalf of the inventor Samuel Crompton. His trip was to fall far short of his glorious expectations. He had left the north of England bearing a memorial containing the signatures of most of the 'influential inhabitants of Bolton'. But as Crompton's first biographer wrote, Brown was 'evidently more sanguine in his hopes than judicious in his plans for realizing them.' He drew up a petition in early 1826 which was to be presented to Parliament. Then he suddenly gave up, failed to present the petition, and hinted darkly in a letter to Crompton of 22 April 1826 that Sir Robert Peel had foiled his efforts. 'Now, without throwing a greater load of griefs upon your mind [than it] may be able to bear', Brown wrote, 'I tell you my firm belief to be, that your primitive enemy has undermined you in every department of the executive government.'[2]

It's likely that Peel did frustrate Brown's efforts, but the black dogs of depression and paranoia seem to have set in once more. He signed off with his usual pathos: 'Adieu, my friend. Not always may the oppressor prosper!' There's also a tone of finality in this farewell. Brown may have known already that he was soon to take his own life. This he did sometime over the next few months. A biographical note penned around 1904 contains an incomplete list of his publications followed by a bald summary of his last days: 'Brown's life in the metropolis was in all ways a failure, and in despair he committed suicide in his London lodgings.' A contributor to Manchester's *Notes and Queries* magazine in 1888, who signed off 'Fred Leary', provided a similar account. Presumably alone, his hopes and ambitions dashed, and subject to delusional fears of persecution, Brown had reached an inner limit of endurance.[3]

Before his tragic suicide, it would seem that Brown had sought a publisher for Blincoe's *Memoir*. As perhaps the best-known of London's Radical publishers, with a shop and printing press on Fleet Street, Carlile would have been the obvious man for him to approach. Having been caught up in the 'Peterloo massacre', Carlile had already acquired a national following. But his popularity redoubled in October 1819 when he was handed a sentence of six years for publishing Tom Paine's *The Age of Reason* and issuing a seditious account of Peterloo. At his trial, Carlile then pulled off the coup of reading *The Age of Reason* from cover to cover, his defence being that only then could the jury decide whether it was blasphemous. Carlile knew that verbatim trial transcripts could be published, so by reading Paine's great work in court he was giving Radical publishers carte blanche to print it for popular circulation. It was a master-stroke, but the powers-that-be retaliated – Carlile spent much of his six years in solitary confinement. He was, though, allowed books, newspapers, quills and parchment, and with the help of his sister and wife, his radical journal *The Republican* went on appearing on the shelves of working-class vendors. Thousands of pounds were collected around the country by free-thinkers and republicans to pay his debts and expenses.[4]

*Richard Carlile
on his liberation after
six years of imprisonment
in
Dorchester Gaol.
Nov.ʳ 18 - 1825*

London Printed & Published by R. Carlisle, 135. Fleet S.ᵗ

18. Richard Carlile, the Radical atheist and Paineite who first published Blincoe's *Memoir* in his journal *The Lion* in 1828. © National Portrait Gallery, London

In November 1825, not long before Brown arrived in London, Richard Carlile won his freedom. It's highly likely that Brown appeared at his Fleet Street shop with Blincoe's story in hand. If so, perhaps Carlile considered publishing it right away. Times were, after all, once again propitious. With the onset of yet another trade depression, as bellies groaned and working-class radicalism intensified, calls for factory reform were renewed. In September 1824 William Cobbett, after a visit to a cotton mill, raged in his *Political Register*: 'Can any man, with a heart in his body, and a tongue in his head, refrain from cursing a system that produces such slavery and such cruelty?' In the next few months, Lancashire operatives were galvanised into action once again. Early in 1825, two of their representatives, Thomas Foster and David McWilliams, travelled to London to press for a further reduction in the length of the child's working day. After six years of silence, the question of factory reform now returned to the Parliamentary agenda.[5]

On 6 May, John Cam Hobhouse, MP, moved for leave to introduce a Bill which would reduce children's hours to eleven per day. The amended version of the Bill demanded that children be worked no more than 69 hours per week, with a nine-hour limit on Saturday. Hobhouse was a Radical of a moderate stripe. A close friend of Lord Byron's, and best man at his wedding, he also befriended Sir Francis Burdett. In 1819 he published a pamphlet which wondered rhetorically 'What prevents people from walking down to the House [of Commons], and pulling out the members by the ears, locking up their doors, and flinging the keys into the Thames?' For this he spent several months in Newgate prison. A year later he was elected as MP for the Radical Westminster constituency. Hobhouse then took up where Peel left off. He pointed out that, despite widespread contraventions of the law, the 1819 Act had led to only two convictions; this made Peel's second Act twice as effective as his first, but still absurdly easy to evade. In May 1825, Burdett rose to his feet and spoke in favour of Hobhouse's Bill, deploring the overworking of 'children in the cotton manufactories'. 'Why,' he rhetorically asked, 'has any man a horse that he could think of putting to such toil? It is shocking to humanity!' With such able advocacy, Hobhouse's Act became law on 22 June 1825.[6]

Mildly gratified, Lancashire's short time campaigners tried to persuade mill owners to adhere to the new Act. McWilliams issued an impassioned appeal 'To the Cotton Masters of Manchester and its Neighbourhood', imploring them to observe the new regulations 'as men, as Christians, as fathers'. In late 1825, Brown then helped to set up a 'committee of respectable persons' to prosecute masters who failed to comply. They had little in the way of success, and this was Brown's final contribution to the movement for factory reform.[7]

Such activism at least ensured that when Richard Carlile visited the north two years later, he took time out from lecturing and debating to visit one of Manchester's hundreds of cotton factories. In his published account he explained that not even the 'ogling of some of the pretty faces' in the reeling room could assuage his horror at the conditions inside. He was shocked at the 'masculine, quarrelsome, and fighting appearance' of women engaged in batting the raw cotton to free it from dirt and husks, at the terrible 'dust and cotton-fuz' of the carding room, at all the prematurely old women who had exhausted their 'animal functions' in hard labour, and he concluded, displaying the endemic racism of his age, by remarking that as a result of factory conditions, Lancashire was producing 'a very diminutive and degenerate race of people', a race of sub-humans 'below, in wretched appearance, any that have been known to live within the temperate zone.' Constant toil, Carlile complained, drives men and women to the degradation of the ale-house. Their children, he continued, are ill-clad, haggard and 'uniformly exhibit bad health', with 'inflamed eyelids' and 'weak eyes'. Carlile considered it preferable that the factories close down, no matter how much they added to the nation's wealth. Unfortunately, he added, 'the aristocracy which forms the legislature of this country flourishes upon the vices and miseries of the working people.' All that the worker could do – and here Carlile broke into his familiar refrain of self-improvement – was 'be the reformer of his own condition'.[8]

Before returning to his Fleet Street bookshop, Richard Carlile also visited some of Manchester's Radicals to see if they knew anything of Blincoe's whereabouts. He was told that he was probably still in gaol, but Carlile did manage to get hold of the papers that Brown had left behind in 1825 in return for a loan. It seems that these were to have provided the basis for a series of notes 'in illustration of [Blincoe's] strong personal assertions'. Carlile later indicated that these convinced him that the *Memoir* contained truthful testimony. Up until now, Carlile had had little understanding of the factory system, but he returned to London with a burning conviction that here was another crime perpetrated by the 'haves' against the 'have-nots', which it was his duty to bring to public attention.[9]

Carlile arrived back in the capital in September 1827. In early January 1828 he started a Radical newspaper called *The Lion*. It contained standard Carlile fare: blistering attacks on established religion and the corruption of the aristocratic elites. But he now turned on his new breed of exploiters, 'the extensive manufacturers [who] profit by human misery and become callous toward it; both from habit and interest.' It had become painfully clear that Hobhouse's 1825 Act was proving ineffectual. Carlile wanted to provoke working men and law-makers out of their apathy, and so on 25 January he included the first of five weekly instalments of Blincoe's *Memoir* in the pages of *The Lion*. Brown's manuscript was printed without addition or subtraction, along with a three-page preface in which Carlile paid generous homage to its author's overriding humanity. Carlile's words, honest and astute, suggest a fairly intimate knowledge of Brown's character:

> The Author of this Memoir is now dead; he fell ... by his own hand. He united, with a strong feeling for the injuries and sufferings of others, a high sense of injury when it bore on himself, whether real or imaginary; and a despondency when his prospects were not good. Hence his suicide. Had he not possessed a fine fellow-feeling with the child of misfortune, he had never taken such pains to compile the Memoir of Robert Blincoe.[10]

This passage makes a fitting epitaph to a man whose deep sense of personal misery impelled him not only to suicide but also to an empathy of such rare keenness that he was able to do something truly timeless. He wrote the biography of a young man hailing from a class whose sufferings were below the notice of the vast majority of those with the freedom and the education to write. Melancholy and often tormented by false fears, he was drawn irresistibly to those in pain like himself, be they long-dead princesses, underrated inventors, or low-down parish bastards. Questions of class or station mattered little to Brown. Oppression was the common denominator in all of his works.[11]

In his preface, Carlile took up one of the short time campaign's favourite refrains: the willingness of the ruling classes to tolerate the savage abuse of factory children while pouring scorn on the continued use of African slaves in the plantations of America. Carlile estimated that the condition of the 'Negro slaves' was 'not half so bad, as that of the white infant-slaves, who had to assist in the spinning' of the cotton that black slaves had farmed. Of William Wilberforce, the revered abolitionist and architect of the 1799 Combination Act, Carlile remarked: 'The religion and black humanity of Mr Wilberforce seem to have been entirely of a foreign nature.' And he concluded with an admonition for the working classes to strive to avoid public houses, 'intoxicating nurseries, for vice, idleness and misery', and to take up the fight on behalf of factory children, since reform would 'never be sought fairly out, by those who have no interest in seeking it.'[12]

As with those popular novels relished by the middle classes, working men and women now read of Blincoe's tale of woe in successive parts, awaiting each new instalment with a combination of excitement and morbid curiosity. Over the course of five weeks, until the last episode on 22 February 1828, hundreds of textile workers, skilled artisans, trades unionists, Radical politicians, and politicised weavers, stockingers and miners now read of Blincoe's progress from St Pancras workhouse through the misery of apprenticeship, up to his incarceration in Lancaster's debtors' gaol. Since so much of the populace of England was illiterate in the 1820s, several times as many would have heard his story read out loud in clubs and pubs, or simply picked up the salient details in general conversation. In Radical households, inns and chapels, and from the small workshops of the capital to the factories of Manchester and the giant wharfs of Liverpool, Blincoe's life story was told and retold, and the Lamberts and Needhams excoriated as men of the darkest hue. Blincoe was anonymous no more. Sixty years later, a local man recalled the *Memoir*'s publication and spoke of how its subject had become known affectionately as 'Bobby'.[13]

It's hard to say just how famous Blincoe became in early 1828. Carlile's star had waned somewhat by the time *The Lion* appeared. Unorthodox theological speculations and a book advocating birth control had alienated many of Carlile's respectable readers among the lower classes. *The Lion* sold nowhere near as many as *The Republican* in its heyday. Even so, it had a circulation of at least 1,000, and powerful stories of bourgeois brutality spread far in times of want and rising unemployment. In Manchester itself, where many workers knew Blincoe personally, his past had become common knowledge. And such was the attention it attracted that Carlile quickly issued a pamphlet detailing his entire story. Regrettably, not a single copy seems to have survived.[14]

Local fame caught Blincoe unawares. Upon learning of the *Memoir*'s publication, he felt instantly aggrieved. After all, no one had had the courtesy to ask him before publishing it. He then found that Carlile's introductory remarks referred openly to the appalling embarrassment of his recent insolvency. Perhaps worse, his story, narrated to Brown for printing in a factory reform newspaper, had actually been published in the seditious rag of a notorious atheist and Paineite; a man like Blincoe who craved a share of middle-class respectability could do without such an association. So it was in high dudgeon that Blincoe sought out one of the publisher's friends in Manchester to remonstrate. In *The Lion* on 28 March, Carlile printed a letter bearing on Blincoe's complaints:

> Blincoe called on me last week, to ask why you had published an account of his life without his permission, and seemed, at first, inclined to be angry about it. I heard all he had to say, and began a defence of you. Before we parted, he became good-humoured, and acquiesced in the propriety of it being published. I then presented him with a copy in your name, which he promised to read, and to call upon me again with his opinion of the work.

It was explained to Blincoe that, as Carlile had said in his preface, he had tried but failed to track him down when in Manchester. Carlile's friend must also have spoken of the critical importance of works like the *Memoir* for re-animating the short time movement. Mollified by these arguments, Blincoe left in better spirits. On the next day, *The Lion* tells us, he returned, pointing out several small but sloppy errors in the text. He also confirmed the *Memoir*'s general accuracy, adding that 'the enormities practised in Litton Mill were much greater than those related in the memoir.' Then Blincoe furnished a more vivid proof:

> He shewd me various scars on his head and face, which had been inflicted upon him, and the backs of his ears were covered with seams, which had been caused, as he told me, by the pincers and hand-vices, which his merciless task-masters applied to his ears to punish him, for real or supposed offences.

Finally, Blincoe stressed, as he had to John Brown, that 'he was not so ill-treated as many others.'[15]

Robert Blincoe must have been relieved to hear his testimony about Litton Mill corroborated in *The Lion* of 24 February by John Joseph Betts, the Ashton-under-Lyne trades unionist. Betts, a fierce but clubbable Radical, told of how in 1806 or 1807 he had been sold as a parish apprentice from St James, Clerkenwell, in London, to a Nottinghamshire mill owner called Mr J. Oxley, then to another in Sheffield, and finally to 'Ellice Needham'. Perhaps most importantly, Betts remarked on Blincoe's conspicuous decency as an overlooker. And he rounded off his letter with a striking anecdote set about two years earlier:

> Happening to call at a friend's house one day, he asked if I knew Robert Blincoe. I replied in the affirmative. Because, added he, I saw a prospectus of his biography some time past; and related the same to W. Woodward, who was on a visit here, and who immediately said, 'HE'LL GIVE IT MA', and became very dejected during the remainder of the visit.

No one could have been more surprised than William Woodward to hear that the agony inflicted in a secluded High Peak dell had made it to the printed page – except, that is, the Needhams.[16]

It's not possible to establish if Ellis and his sons learned of the *Memoir*'s publication. But we do know that *The Lion* penetrated the towns and villages of the High Peak Hundred. An anonymous correspondent, who said that he had known 'the then master of the

Mill, some of his sons, the magistrates, and their clerk, and most of the principal characters named in the memoir', wrote to Carlile to substantiate Blincoe's story from inquiries he had made himself. This writer had been led to look into the conditions at Litton Mill, having on 'his first reading' been 'much inclined to think the statements it contained were greatly exaggerated.' His reason was that he had lived his entire life within 'fifty miles of the place' but didn't recollect 'ever before having heard of the cruel treatment.' The testimonies he collected, presumably from surviving apprentices working in and around Taddington and Tideswell, amply confirmed what Blincoe had said. But like Orphan John, whose account would appear seventeen years later, this writer added that 'the girls were frequently prostituted to the carnal lusts of the young masters, who did not (as occasion required) scruple to make use of the most base means of screening their own infamy.' Clearly well informed, *The Lion*'s correspondent confirmed that 'Old Needham is a pauper' and that 'his wife teaches a few little children the A.B.C.'. He was also of the opinion, credible but less easily verified, that 'the sons are vagabonds'. That neither William nor Robert Woodward still worked at Litton Mill is strongly indicated by his closing remarks:

> The Litton Mill, we understand, is now at work; but, from the generally healthy and decent appearance of the children employed, there is little doubt, that the present master has some humanity about him.[17]

The publication of Blincoe's *Memoir* in *The Lion* prompted another victim of the parish overseer's parsimony to write in to tell his tragic story. Samuel Davy had been sent from the parish of St George's, on the south side of the Thames, at the age of seven to a mill in Preston, Lancashire. The cruelty he experienced at a succession of mills, Davy said, 'though not quite so bad as that described by Blincoe, approached near to it.' He told of one boy beaten to death, of being pinioned by chains, and of having been forced to stand naked in the winter cold. Eventually he sickened of his treatment and fled back to London, 'though followed by men on horseback and on foot.' For ten years, Davy claimed, he and his brother then worked in the parish of their birth, but the parish officers refused to tell them the fate of their mother. It eventually transpired that the 'supposed loss of her children, so preyed upon [her] mind, that, with other troubles it brought on insanity, and she died in a state of madness.'[18]

In early 1828, the publication of an orphan boy's memoir kick-started the campaign for factory reform. Once he had been a power-less victim; now Blincoe and his story had become the collective property of all those who wished to shorten the working day of children in mills. And at this crucial moment, one man of exceptional boldness and drive rose to the fore of the campaign. Since 1818, when he had been arrested and imprisoned for breaking the Combination Act, John Doherty's activism had steadily increased. Albeit briefly, he had managed to bring several different trades together in an over-arching union organisation; he had taken a lead part in the successful overthrow of Wilberforce's Combination Act in 1825; and having proved himself a skilled planner of strikes, in 1823 he became Secretary of the Manchester cotton-spinners' union. With this role he juggled his leadership of the short hours movement. We get a sense of his character from the description of Tom Trollope, brother of novelist Anthony Trollope, who met him in 1837. Despite being 'very small', Doherty made a strong impression on Tom, who later recalled:

> an Irishman, a Roman Catholic, and a furious Radical, but a *very* clever man. … He came and dined with us at our hotel, but it was, I remember, with much difficulty that we persuaded him to do so, and when at table his excitement was so great and continuous that he could eat next to nothing.[19]

Irishness was a liability for any trades unionist in the 1800s, when a self-interested aversion to Irish labourers united English-born work-ers. But John Doherty managed to convince union members that his loyalty lay with his adoptive land. No less impressively, he succeeded in drawing some of Manchester's mill proprietors into the campaign for shorter hours. Before long, he would perceive in Robert Blincoe another potent ally. And in company with Doherty, Blincoe would soon play his part in bringing about factory reform.[20]

28

The altar, the throne
and the cottage

The years following the *Memoir*'s publication were good ones for the Blincoes, now a family of five following the birth of a second daughter, called Martha. Moving to 19 Turner Street in Manchester, they set up a small grocer's shop. Robert, 36 in the year the *Memoir* appeared in print, resumed his earlier career as a waste cotton dealer. He supplemented his income by manufacturing sheet wadding, and for this purpose rented power and a room in a nearby Stockport mill. By 1832 their eldest daughter, Ruth, had completed school and worked with her mother in the shop. Their son Robert still went to school every day, as did young Martha. After the shame and distress of their bankruptcy, the Blincoes were now the epitome of small-time respectability.[1]

We owe these glimpses of Blincoe's progress to the fact that the *Memoir* brought him into the sphere of politics. Those who suffer hardships aren't always anxious that others be spared, but Blincoe was to become a devoted advocate for the short time cause. And he owed his entrée into the movement and his privileged place in the history of factory reform to the friendship he developed with John Doherty. On 14 April 1832, Manchester's trades union leader printed an extract from Blincoe's *Memoir* in his Radical newspaper, the *Poor Man's Advocate*. Later the same year he published the whole *Memoir* in pamphlet form. Blincoe's story then came to the attention of politicians, journalists, scholars, tens of thousands of working men and women, even the country's most popular female novelist. But this is jumping ahead. That the *Memoir* appeared again on Radical bookstands was due to the earnest campaigning of a series of short time leaders. Among the most important of these was Doherty himself.[2]

Born in Ireland in 1798, at the age of eighteen Doherty fled to

England along with many thousands of his brethren. The government at Westminster carped at the influx of poor working men and women, but the origins of the mass migration lay in its own abolition of the protective tariffs that had once sheltered Irish textile firms from competitors across the thin strip of sea separating the two lands. Fleeing an industry in decline back home, Doherty found himself in a country suspicious of strangers and hostile to the Irish. He couldn't afford to be overly scrupulous, and so it seems that he forged a character reference and used it to get a job in a Manchester cotton mill. In 1818, when the spinners' strike began, he was working in the New Mill, where Blincoe had briefly laboured, owned by George Murray. From 1828, as secretary of the spinners' union, he drew a wage for promoting the interests of its many members. In this capacity, foreshadowed by his sixpence donation to the cause way back in 1816, he set up the Society for the Protection of Children Employed in Cotton Factories.[3]

While Doherty made a dogged adversary, he could also make common cause. He saw that several of Manchester's cotton lords were happy to have Hobhouse's 1825 Act implemented. They were reluctant to abide by it, however, until mills in 'remote parts of the country' changed their practices too, rather than trying to undercut their law-abiding competitors. Doherty also realised that most magistrates were too supine or hostile to enforce the Act, and so winning the acquiescence of some powerful masters was necessary for securing convictions. To this end, in 1828 he began a newspaper called the *Conciliator*. It started well enough. With the help of several other union leaders, breaches of the 1825 Act were discovered and informations filed at local magistrates' courts. To avoid bringing their positions into disrepute, magistrates had to convict the more persistently gratuitous offenders. Thus a J.J. Parker was penalised £20 for working child piecers and scavengers at night, and John Latham received a £10 fine for employing an under-age boy after the magistrate rejected his assertion that the child's age was unascertainable since 'any spinner, knows that many children in factories did not grow so tall as others.'[4]

But Doherty's greatest coup was to face down the Wigan masters. In January 1829 he had asked them to desist from working illegal hours. The mayor had also been approached; though since he too was a cotton lord, he predictably refused to help. Doherty next held a public meeting, which was sparsely attended because several spinners had already been fired simply for having spoken to the Manchester men. So Doherty wrote to the Home Secretary, Robert Peel. The son of Robert Peel the mill owner and factory reformer, this Robert was to become a Tory Prime Minister. Ardently wedded to the logic of political economy and conscientiously opposed to interfering with trade, Peel nevertheless saw that the Wigan masters were breaking the law. He therefore acted on Doherty's complaints. Two months later, Wigan's mayor received a stern rebuke from the Home Office warning that if the masters didn't comply with the law, the mayor's power would be repealed. The masters quickly fell into line.[5]

These were, however, isolated successes. Over and over again, witnesses who had been threatened, bullied or bribed by mill owners and overlookers failed to turn up at the magistrates' courts, refused to give evidence, or withdrew their earlier affidavits. By April 1830, only 24 convictions had been secured out of 187 cases brought. Doherty had tried hard to win the support of the owners, but only a minority had joined with him. He could hardly expect them to rally to his cause, however, when he was simultaneously the fiery secretary of the Manchester cotton spinners' union, a role that made him in the minds of most proprietors an 'impudent and conceited ape', as the Tory *Stockport Advertiser* colourfully described him. Indeed, most Lancashire masters saw Doherty's espousal of the 1825 Act as no more than a cover for his trades union activities. And even those proprietors who had risked upsetting their peers by backing him withdrew with the onset of a spinners' strike in April 1829 led by Doherty himself. Its cause was a trade depression combined with a long-term decline in the profitability of spinning cotton, to which masters had responded by trying to reduce the operatives' wages. Lancashire's spinners had struck over the same issue in 1826. Then they had been starved into submission. Now, with John Doherty calling the tune, they tried again. Doherty publicly asserted that a spinner should have an income of £111 a year. This was a fair sum in 1829, double what most were already earning, but a very modest amount when, he said, a bishop received £20,000 per annum just 'for reading, or it may be writing, an hour's discourse once a week.'[6]

Keen to win middle-class sympathy, Doherty warned the strikers against violent pickets and vitriol-throwing. He also set up a room in the city where workmen could go to read improving books. But the unanimity of the masters gradually wore away at the resolve of the strikers. Deprived of pay and, in many cases, parish aid, the men were hungry, desperate and increasingly hard to restrain. Within six months, strike-breakers were being kicked, punched and soaked in vitriol. Soon after, the strikers returned desultorily to work and the spinners went back at the new, lower rates, their determination sapped by hunger.[7]

The movement for factory reform fizzled out too. The one real success of Doherty's committee was to persuade Manchester masters to work their children no more than twelve hours. But hundreds of spinning mills in Wigan, Stockport, Bolton, and numerous small, outlying towns and villages, went on working their young piecers and scavengers long hours and often deep into the night. One of the Manchester short time men recalled that by 1830 they were 'disheartened and almost broken for want of support'. Yet, just as the movement ran into the ground in Lancashire, in the neighbouring county of Yorkshire the treatment of children in factories was about to become the sensation of the season. A new combatant of great oratorical skill was to bring the campaign back to life.[8]

A full-blooded Tory, Richard Oastler devoted much of his later life to driving forward the campaign to ease the plight of factory workers. It may sound paradoxical, but there was no real contradiction. For Oastler, the money-grubbing behaviour of *nouveau riche* capitalists represented the greatest threat of all to the traditional social order of deference and hierarchy which he, and all other sincere Tories, were set on upholding. Oastler, just like Southey, saw capitalism as the true enemy of the old order because it seemed to be destroying the organic ties that had always held society together. Everything for him had gone downhill since the days when, as Oastler's friend and ally Michael Sadler put it, 'every cottager had a cow and every cottager's wife had a spinning wheel.'[9]

Tories like Sadler and Oastler identified with a vanishing world of self-contained villages presided over by kindly squires commanding the spontaneous loyalty of the labouring poor. The touchstone of

19. Richard Oastler, the 'Tory Radical' who reignited the short time cause in 1830. He believed that the upper classes had a duty of Christian stewardship over the labouring orders. © National Portrait Gallery, London

their political philosophy was summed up in Oastler's sayings: 'My station and its duties'; and 'the altar, the throne and the cottage.' Here was a valorisation of order, duty, obligation and deference, and it drew far more on emotion and tradition than on reason or reflection. As a philosophy it led Oastler to feel that his personal loyalties, and the true interests of his caste, lay in alliance with the poor, not the rich. Together, he reckoned, they could humble the growing might of the manufacturer. And by sticking up for the humblest, the romantic

Tories hoped to shore up the place of the nobility and squirearchy in English society.[10]

In September 1830, Oastler took a short break from his role as steward for the squire of Fixby Hall in Yorkshire and visited a friend, the Bradford worsted manufacturer John Wood. For years, talk of child labour in factories had found its way into newspapers, political oratory and private discussion. But for all of Peel's and Hobhouse's efforts, it remained on the margins of political consciousness. Oastler had not even the vaguest idea that there was a battle to be fought, and on the eve of his departure from John Wood's house he was staggered when his host, clutching a Bible, suddenly burst forth with the words: 'I have been reading this Book and in every page I have read my own condemnation.' Wood proceeded to unburden himself, entreating Oastler to help him in easing the plight of the factory children. Five years before, Wood had attempted to persuade other factory owners in Bradford to reduce their hours to ten per day. They had flatly refused. But Wood's account of the terrible lives of factory boys and girls triggered Oastler's social conscience, dormant now for many years. Wood's emotional appeal inflamed an existing aversion to the cut-throat capitalism which was eroding the antique ties of deference and dependence.[11]

On his return to Fixby Hall, Oastler wrote the first of a series of famous letters to the *Leeds Mercury*, in which – just like John Brown and William Cobbett – he argued that the 'Negro slave' enjoyed better treatment and conditions than the English-born factory child. Only a rank hypocrite, Oastler stormed, could defend the black slave and yet ignore the white slaves in their midst. Warming to this theme, he wrote in his first open letter:

> The very streets which receive the droppings of an 'Anti-Slavery Society' are every morning wet by the tears of innocent victims at the accursed shrine of avarice, who are compelled (not by the cart-whip of the negro slave-driver) but by the dread of the equally appalling thong or strap of the over-looker, to hasten, half-dressed, but not half-fed, to those magazines of British infantile slavery – the worsted mills in the town and neighbourhood of Bradford!!!

The *Leeds Mercury* was published by Oastler's friend Edward Baines, an advocate of political economy whose main audience was the industrial middle class. The letter wasn't exactly to Baines's taste, so he undertook to make inquiries himself. Finding that Oastler had identified a 'real' evil, he printed the letter.[12]

Yorkshire's mill workers were ready to listen. A severe depression hung over the north, with many families slowly starving on a diet of potatoes and gruel. It made little difference that Oastler's pity had been reserved for the young. His letter was printed as a broadsheet, glued to walls and doors all around Leeds, and he was toasted at large Radical meetings as the true friend of all 'white slaves, both male and female, young and old.' In the pages of the *Leeds Mercury* for several weeks Oastler was reproved and congratulated by turns. His eloquence, combined with the fact that he was a gentleman, not a demagogue, had caused mill owners acute embarrassment. Within weeks, 40 Bradford owners were asking for legislation to protect children from overwork.[13]

But as Oastler's campaign gathered momentum, an issue of far greater political import rose alongside it. With bread prices curving upwards again, and export markets in a state of precipitous decline, the movement for parliamentary reform revived with fresh conviction. The Whig leader Earl Grey described 'a state of general distress such as never before pressed upon any country.' These were the perfect conditions for William Cobbett's rippling prose. Indicting the government in classic style as 'tax eaters' and 'drones' who consumed the honey 'collected by the industrious bees', he channelled popular discontent into the fight for manhood suffrage. And, on the benches of the House of Commons, to which he had been elected in 1830 by the mass electorate of Preston, Orator Hunt also kept the issue squarely before his fellow MPs.[14]

Most unsettling for Tory opponents of reform was the fact that the middle classes, inspired by newspaper editors like Edward Baines, were adding their voices to the reformist cause. Many Whigs had coveted the idea of constitutional reform for decades. Now they too came into the open, advocating a Reform Bill as a necessary means of recognising the talents and national importance of the middle classes. Against this tumultuous political backdrop, food riots exploded in rural counties and Luddism sputtered back into life in the north.

Hobhouse then introduced a new Bill calling for a reduction in the hours that children could work, which applied to all textile factories. The masters savaged this latest Bill because it proposed outlawing night work, and even the pliant Bradford owners now reneged on their earlier commitment to factory reform. Oastler rattled off letters in support, but Hobhouse's Act, when it finally passed into law in late 1831, was a shadow of its former self. It didn't even apply to woollen or worsted mills, and there was no machinery for imposing it. Incensed, many Yorkshire operatives formed Short Time Committees to maintain pressure on the government by holding rallies and collecting signatures.[15]

But the question of factory reform was soon pushed to the periphery by the Reform Bill. Introduced by the Whig peer Lord John Russell in March 1831, it proposed getting rid of seats from 'pocket boroughs' (constituencies effectively in the gift of local landowners and often comprising just a few dozen electors) and then reassigning them among the new industrial towns. The vote would also be extended to anyone living in a house worth more than £10 a year in rent. The Whigs' Bill passed the Commons by just a single vote, and Earl Grey persuaded the King to call new elections. The Whigs were returned stronger than before, but then the House of Lords kicked out the Bill. Almost immediately, large parts of the nation were convulsed by rioting. Barricades were erected in Bristol's streets, Derby's town hall was stormed, and Nottingham Castle, where Blincoe had walked three decades earlier, was incinerated.

Throughout these embittered, fractious and chaotic months, when shopkeepers rioted alongside cobblers and tailors, Oastler had said nothing in public about the Reform Bill. It was a judicious decision, for he found the very idea of constitutional reform to be repugnant, a barbaric slight against an already perfect constitution. John Doherty at first felt that the Yorkshire spinners were being hoodwinked into an alliance by a Tory clique led by Oastler, bent on distracting them from the cause for parliamentary reform. The *Mercury* sensed the fragility of the partnership and accused the Tories of 'contemptible trickery' in winning over local workers. But at dozens of short time meetings held in Yorkshire during 1831, the Tory blue and the Radical white flags were still unfurled and fluttered side by side.[16]

Until now, Oastler was known as a fiery wordsmith, not as a natural speaker. But on 10 December 1831 at a large meeting in Leeds he found his true calling. After hearing charges laid by Edward Baines and his son, also Edward, he rose to answer them. 'Whatever the size of our trade', he stormed, 'if it depends upon making infants work more than adults and upon supporting the most horrid system of slavery in the world, I would say: *sink your commerce, and rise Humanity, Benevolence and Christianity.*' At the end of his speech he was lavished with cheers and applause. The elder Baines shakily accepted that 'quite a new light has been thrown upon my mind by Mr Oastler's speech', and then seconded the motion to express gratitude to Oastler for his oration. The younger Baines, an avid political economist, made no such concessions. But on this night, the short hours movement acquired a star orator able to kindle mass support from the soap-box with the same virtuosity as Orator Hunt himself. The short time leadership also now had an objective on which to focus its zeal. During the Leeds meeting, Oastler announced that Michael Sadler, MP, was on the verge of introducing another Bill, where Hobhouse's had failed, limiting factory labour to ten hours a day for all under eighteen years old. The real novelty of Sadler's Bill was that it proposed harsh penalties for transgressors: a fine of £20 for a first offence, £40 for a second, and up to a year's imprisonment for a third. The masters could also be charged with manslaughter if workers died having fallen upon unfenced machinery. The operatives delighted in the Bill's sheer effrontery.[17]

Across the border in Lancashire, the spinners' societies rallied to Sadler's cause. Doherty began his paper, the *Poor Man's Advocate*, to admonish individual mill owners, from the master who gave £20 to relieve cholera victims but then deducted it from his workers' wages, to the one who had cold water drip into the mill privies to discourage long stays and who blankly refused to put a door on the female lavatories. Utterly uncompromising in its tone, few Manchester booksellers risked stocking it. But it went on selling, and in early 1832 Doherty opened up his own bookshop and printers at 37 Withy Grove in Manchester, from where he sold pamphlets on politics and improving texts on the importance of sobriety, education and self-betterment, alongside money-spinning works of popular romance and fiction. Customers could also go there to read books and journals for one penny a day. Doherty and his wife served behind the counter.[18]

Throughout late 1831, Oastler captivated huge crowds with his withering attacks on individual factory owners and the advocates of political economy. He made no secret of his Tory paternalism, vilifying a factory system which, he said, had 'destroyed that feeling of reverence and affection amongst workmen towards their employers which I remember existed when I was young.' On Boxing Day 1832, the Reverend George Stringer Bull stepped onto the platform of the short time movement and gave a bravura performance which sealed his place among the Ten Hours leadership. A few weeks later, on the eve of the reading of Sadler's Ten Hours Bill, a rally in Leeds attracted 12,000 supporters.[19]

Chronically insecure, Sadler wasn't an ideal parliamentary advocate. But on 16 March 1832 he spoke movingly during his Bill's second reading. Deploring the power of the factory masters, he held aloft examples of thongs used to punish young children. 'Our ancestors could not have supposed it possible', *Hansard* records, 'that a generation of Englishmen could exist ... that would task lisping infancy, of a few summers old regardless alike of its smiles or tears ... until, in the dewy morn of existence, the bud of youth faded, and fell ere it was folded.' It was emotive fare, if somewhat overdone. And one imagines that the scene would have appealed to Charles Dickens, by now working as a parliamentary reporter for his uncle's newspaper, the *Mirror of Parliament*, and observing at least some of these debates from his seat in the visitors' gallery.[20]

Sadler's camp was being distinctly romantic about childhood before the factory age. The history of the thong, after all, went back much further than the first cotton-spinning mill. But such historical details didn't overly concern the assembled MPs. The clean logic of political economy dominated the debate. Henry Thomas Hope forcefully countered Sadler, rehearsing the owner's and economist's trustiest arguments:

> It is obvious, that if you limit the hours of labour, you will, to nearly the same extent, reduce the profits of the capital on which the labour is employed. [So] the manufacturers must either raise

the price of the manufactured article or diminish the wages of their workmen. If they raise the price of the article the foreigner gains an advantage. I am informed that the foreign cotton-manufacturers, and particularly the Americans, tread closely upon the heels of our manufacturers.[21]

Hope and his allies parried the Ten Hours Bill into Select Committee stage. *The Times* fumed: 'Why a select committee should be required to ascertain whether or not it be right and proper to confine infants of seven, eight, nine, or ten years of age more than 12 hours a day, at unremitting labour, in the atmosphere of a factory, is beyond our imagination.' The short time men were also incensed. Oastler exploded: '*I hate Whigs with a most perfect hatred* ... They are the great supporters of the Factory system – which is fast destroying the *Landed interest* and the *Labouring classes*.' Middle-class ideology, embraced by lords and commoners, had scotched any chance of speedy reform.[22]

It was now more important than ever that the Short Time Committees maintain pressure on Parliament from outside. And to this end, on 21 April 1832, two days after the opening of the Select Committee's investigations, Doherty published a brief extract from John Brown's *Memoir* in the *Poor Man's Advocate*, describing how Mary Richards had been pulverised by a fast-moving shaft in Lowdham Mill.[23]

By far the most memorable event of the week, however, was the 'Pilgrimage of York', when several thousand Yorkshire men and women converged on the ancient city of York for a giant rally in support of the Ten Hours Bill. Many had walked 120 miles over moors and rough tracks, clothed in little more than rags, resting in barns along the way and feeding on whatever scraps they had been able to bring along. In the early afternoon, large numbers congregated in Castle Yard to hear Richard Oastler speak. He didn't disappoint. Nor did Mr Samuel Smith, a Leeds surgeon who spoke of how the awkward postures and excessive standing of factory work caused children's 'ligaments to give way' so that they grew up 'knock-knee'd'. Smith's pièce de résistance was to hold aloft a drawing of 'a poor girl from Bradford' who had been subjected to horrendously long hours and whose 'lower extremities' were hopelessly buckled. Having signed Oastler's petition after a long day of speeches, cheering and standing, the hordes of workers departed, exhausted, hungry but jubilant, back to their homes. Three days later, the Whig peer Lord Morpeth, owner of sumptuous Castle Howard in Yorkshire, rose to his feet in the House of Lords holding one end of the petition started on 24 April. Stretching 800 yards, it contained 138,000 signatures and marks. No easy convert to a Radical cause, he told his fellow peers that reform had become imperative.[24]

Having read Blincoe's *Memoir* and heard of Mr Smith's performance in York, Doherty now grasped the power of highlighting individual lives. He saw that endless statistics and abstract arguments lacked the emotive force of a single, tragic human story. And so, as John Brown had done back in 1822, he set about tracing specimens of men and women left disfigured by working from a young age in what he called 'the accursed factory system'. At the same time, he made contact with one William Knight Keeling, a skilled Manchester portrait-painter and drawing-master. Destined for a highly successful career, Keeling had already provided illustrations for Sir Walter Scott's novel *The Betrothed*. In April 1832 he agreed to provide woodcuts of the crooked limbs, missing fingers, and stunted bodies of Doherty's factory victims. Over the next month, Doherty published five short biographies, four accompanied by Keeling's portraits.[25]

Courtesy of Oastler, the 'poor girl from Bradford' spoken of by Samuel Smith appeared first, alongside a man whose legs had failed to grow to a proper length due to his being overworked as a boy. A fortnight later, Doherty told the story of John Mears, horribly beaten and overworked, left with knees that folded inwards and lower legs that splayed out. Mears, he said, was now in desperate poverty having spent his youth increasing 'the riches of the country and the fortunes of the few'. Henry Wooley appeared the week after, crippled by long hours standing when his bones were too soft and his muscles too weak to tolerate the strain. Wooley could work no more than could an old man. Blincoe appeared second in the series, a brief summary of his life appearing beside a particularly striking Keeling woodcut, its crudeness and simplicity adding authenticity to his story.[26]

29

Sins of the masters

In preparing his series of biographies of men and women crippled by the factory system, Doherty met Robert Blincoe. As he had to John Brown, Blincoe told the story of his clerical paternity. Had he felt real shame at the implication of his own bastardy, he would surely have said nothing on the matter to either man. But, still deriving emotional comfort from it, he ensured that the workhouse rumour appeared in the sketch of his life printed in the *Poor Man's Advocate*. Doherty, who had his reasons for despising clergymen, seized on it avidly, adding whimsically: 'Oh! these parsons.' In his short account, Doherty also described several of Robert Woodward's ingenious forms of torture, and spoke of the scarring he had seen on Blincoe's head and ears. The woodcut, however, spoke more vividly of his terrible deprivation.[1]

Keeling's portrait shows Blincoe standing face-on. Next to him is a crooked bollard, giving the viewer a clear idea of his shortness of stature. The bollard's acute angle, making it seem as if it had grown crooked out of the ground, also symbolised and emphasised Blincoe's twisted gait. His legs were now, and probably had been since puberty, collapsed inwards at the knee; below, they were splayed out, and his thighs had been driven close together. Walking, as Blincoe later confirmed, wasn't easy. His face also bore deep furrows, excavated by years of want and anxiety. His eye sockets were deep and dark, and he wore his hair long, perhaps to conceal the scarring on his ears.

What Blincoe felt as Keeling sketched him is hard to imagine. However flattering it was to have his story told, he knew that he was to be paraded as an example of human wretchedness. Yet Blincoe's portrait differed strikingly from those of Wooley and Mears. For along with abundant evidence of cruel ill-use and under-nourishment was

A

MEMOIR

OF

ROBERT BLINCOE,

𝔄𝔫 𝔒𝔯𝔭𝔥𝔞𝔫 𝔅𝔬𝔶;

SENT FROM THE WORKHOUSE OF ST. PANCRAS, LONDON,
AT SEVEN YEARS OF AGE,

TO ENDURE THE

Horrors of a Cotton-Mill,

THROUGH HIS INFANCY AND YOUTH,

WITH A MINUTE DETAIL OF HIS SUFFERINGS,

BEING

THE FIRST MEMOIR OF THE KIND PUBLISHED.

BY JOHN BROWN.

MANCHESTER:

PRINTED FOR AND PUBLISHED BY J. DOHERTY, 37, WITHY-GROVE.

1832.

20. Frontispiece of Blincoe's *Memoir*. The woodcut of Blincoe clearly shows the effects of overwork and malnutrition.

the absolute bourgeois respectability of his dress: a sober combination of trousers, knee-length frock coat and top hat. His situation had noticeably improved. He could stand before the artist with a sense of genuine accomplishment.

The trade directories and Doherty's brief account tell the same story. With a growing family, a grocer's shop, and two textile businesses, he was doing well for himself. We know virtually nothing of his family life, how easy or otherwise it was for an emotionally-starved boy to give and receive affection as a grown man. But speaking in May 1833, Blincoe expressed a strong sense of responsibility towards his children. All three enjoyed full-time education, and he didn't just rely on the nearest dame school, dubious institutions in which children learned, if at all, from rote memorisation of the Bible, the Book of Common Prayer, and introductions to English grammar. Instead, they had to walk two miles to school, a good indication that they were attending a superior establishment.

In late April 1832, John Doherty issued the *Memoir of Robert Blincoe* in pamphlet form, bearing Keeling's woodcut on its title page. 'It is now a standard work, to which future ages may refer', Doherty wrote in its preface, prematurely if prophetically, and with heavy sarcasm, 'as to a specimen of the Christian character of some of the people of England, at the commencement of the nineteenth century.' Copies were distributed widely. One would come into the possession of the novelist Frances Trollope; another may have found its way into the hands of Charles Dickens. Over 70 years later, a number of Mancunians could still remember its publication. And as a matter of course, Victorian accounts of the short hours movement were to include excerpts from the *Memoir*. Contemporaries appreciated that whatever the quality of the prose, here was something of real importance, for Blincoe and Brown had provided an account, well-verified and minutely-detailed, of the most sadistic brutality, practised by a pioneer of the cotton-spinning industry. Never before had the sins of the masters been documented with such precision or with such obvious authenticity. And Blincoe's story also made a good yarn. Generations of factory workers and their supporters were to exult in the eventual humbling first of the Lamberts and then of Ellis Needham and his clan.[2]

In the coming months, Blincoe's name tripped off the tongues of hundreds of Lancashire's short time campaigners. As Sadler's Bill hung in the balance, Doherty had cleverly turned Brown's stirring tale of hardship and abuse into brilliant propaganda. He knew very well that while plenty of modern factories were fearful places to work in, few were run with quite the savage disregard for the child's welfare as Litton Mill. Even Needham's old concern was now under relatively humane management. But Doherty also realised that Ellis Needham and his rapacious sons conformed to all the crude stereotypes of the mill proprietor which middle-class humanitarians needed to buy into if Sadler's Bill was to pass into law. Doherty had to paint for them as black a picture of mill life as possible. In this respect, the *Memoir* had it all. Blincoe might have reflected that he was being used by the textile operatives as he had earlier been exploited by parochial officials and factory masters. But this time it was different. He sympathised with the cause and happily acquiesced.

By the time the *Memoir* appeared, Sadler's Select Committee had been sitting for nearly two weeks. It would conclude its business in early August. Members and witnesses were drawn from both sides of the debate, though most, like Sadler himself as well as John Cam Hobhouse and George Strickland, were sympathetic to the workers' cause. (Strickland was a Yorkshire squire with a well-known aversion to nouveau riche industrialists.) They ensured that plenty of evidence of the horrors of factory labour came to light. Their witnesses, many of them reflecting on the same period when Blincoe laboured in Miller's Dale, spoke of fifteen- or sixteen-hour working days, with all but an hour of this time spent on their feet. James Kirk explained how he had been forced to work 24-hour stretches three times a week, heaving bulky pieces of wet cloth, until his knees buckled and he had been forced to retire. David Bywater was too tired at the end of his shifts to walk home, so he slept among the baulks in the mill. He stood up before the committee to show them his buckled knees and twisted thighs. Elizabeth Bentley told of how she had begun work pulling heavy baskets in a flax mill when she was just six, so that her shoulders were now deformed and no one would employ her. If she flagged at her duties, Elizabeth was whipped by the overlooker. Too damaged to work any longer, and with both parents dead, in June 1832 she was living in the Hunslet 'poorhouse'. Her prospects of happiness were effectively nil. The panel concluded by asking her to reflect on the 'hardship and cruelty' of her life. It was the first open question she had been asked. Her response was recorded thus: 'The Witness was too much affected to answer.'[3]

The commissioners were told of the damage wrought on young bodies by 'throstle' spinning machinery, requiring child piecers to bend continually on their right knees while swinging their left shoulders upwards. Many were left permanently disabled, their muscles unequally developed and their legs bent. Numbers of witnesses also bore incomplete fingers, ripped off at the knuckles by moving machinery when fatigue made them clumsy. William Swithenbank's son had his right arm dragged into a machine: 'it tore it all to bits; it tore the veins from the arteries, and tore the muscles of the arm out; it was all torn.' There would have been no compensation. Lung complaints were also common. Those who had worked in carding rooms, where they had inhaled large quantities of dust, flue or hair, fought for breath and suffered from asthma and other chest complaints; William Cooper remembered often being 'stuffed' from the flue.[4]

There were several lurid accounts of physical abuse. Billy rollers, whips, leather straps and fists figured prominently. Overlookers were frequently implicated, but so were factory masters. Alexander Dean spoke of a Scottish mill in which he served as overlooker. A young girl tried to escape, but was caught and sent to gaol at Dundee for seven months. On her release she returned to the mill, where one day screams were heard. Dean rushed to see what was going on. He found the master grabbing 'the hair of her head, and ... kicking her on her face till the blood was running down.' Dean was dismissed for helping her to escape; the girl, he said, later became a prostitute. James Paterson also discovered his factory's boss savagely kicking a girl. When he arrived, she was 'bleeding at both nose and mouth'. Paterson later asked her what had been the cause of the master's behaviour. She replied, the witness told Sadler's committee, that 'he wanted familiarities with her'.[5]

The spinner Thomas Bennett described the lives of his own children in moving and harrowing detail. They cried from exhaustion, he said, when woken in the mornings, they struggled through the working day, and were beaten by Bennett himself in the last hour to keep them from flagging. He then carried the youngest child home at night, asleep in his arms; having arrived back, the rest of his offspring were typically too tired to eat and quickly fell asleep, their hands still moving rhythmically as if tying together broken threads. Samuel Downe experienced the same kind of sadistic treatment meted out to the Litton Mill children. He was flogged while tied to a pillar, and then had a knot of rope forced into his mouth and the ends tied around his head. When an overlooker in a Dundee mill was fined by a justice for ill-treating a young girl, the master reimbursed him and fired the victim and two of her friends. Those overlookers questioned explained that they beat children in order to make enough money on piece rates to satisfy the masters and to pay their bills. They had to keep the children awake by blows, because if they didn't there were plenty of less scrupulous spinners in dire need of work who would gladly accept their situations. As the overlooker Joshua Drake – himself no stranger to beating or being beaten – remarked to Michael Sadler in April, if a child failed to perform his or her role, 'the overlookers came into disgrace'.[6]

A few weeks into the committee's proceedings, Sadler decided to invite no more operatives as witnesses. William Osburn, the Leeds Poor Law officer and Sunday school superintendent, named six in his district alone who had been fired for assisting the commission. David Bywater said that he had already been fired, and that the job of his brother was in jeopardy too.

Nor was this the only evidence of chicanery on the part of the masters. The Select Committee heard of how Holland Hoole, a Salford mill owner and for long Doherty's nemesis, had obliged his workers to sign a document without telling them its contents. Only later did it transpire that it was a petition, supposedly signed freely by the operatives, condemning any attempt to reduce hours. It was also revealed that there were more names on the list than workers in the factory.[7]

But the short time men hadn't gone about their business with complete objectivity. The witnesses had been carefully selected and primed by the Yorkshire and Lancashire Short Time Committees, and many had been posed outrageously leading questions. The greatest shortcoming of Sadler's inquiry, however, was that it relied on the testimony of very few children. It was a deliberate strategy on the part of the short time men, for they knew that since Blincoe's day conditions in many factories had improved, at least with respect to ventilation, dirt and the intensity of labour. In a premeditated move, Sadler called virtually no one from Manchester. As everyone familiar with the mill districts knew, even if the city was dirty, overcrowded and malodorous, its factories were vastly more wholesome than those in far-flung valleys and hills.[8]

This isn't, however, to say that the complaints that Sadler's team heard were false or irrelevant. Beatings went on, and children were still working extremely arduous hours; indeed, in many parts of the north, mill life was entering its most gruelling phase. The physicians and surgeons called to give evidence were unanimous in declaring the long hours of factory labour to be detrimental to health. The children, said Dr William Lutener, a practitioner from Montgomeryshire, 'are not those rosy healthy children that our agricultural children are; they are thin and sallow looking ... It is impossible that human nature can support this labour.' Data on the heights of rural versus urban children lend support to their analyses. Dr Lutener had had 'frequently to amputate the hands and fingers of children' who, when sleepy towards the end of a shift, let their hands drop into rollers, frames, carriages and carding engines. The Leeds general practitioner and student of occupational health, Charles Turner Thackrah, likewise remarked that factory children lacked 'that degree of health, that muscular power, and that buoyancy of spirits which we find in children not confined and congregated in mills.' James Blundell proudly quoted a phrase he had coined years before: 'I look upon factory towns as nurseries of feeble bodies and fretful minds.' Blincoe was a case in point.[9]

But while the Lancashire Short Time Committee was well aware of Blincoe's story, he didn't appear as a witness in front of Michael Sadler's committee. Before long, however, he would be so well known to the antagonists in the factory debate that he would be called to give evidence as a matter of course.

30

Emissary for John Doherty

Doherty's *Poor Man's Advocate* pulled no punches. Each Saturday he raged against millocracy and nobility, hurling verbal vitriol on the powers-that-be and those who made fortunes at the expense of the bodies and minds of the working classes. Every issue contained a short feature on factories said to have broken the 1825 Act in the previous seven days, entitled 'MIDNIGHT ROBBERS'. Several of the mill owners spotlighted were also magistrates. Dragging the names of wealthy industrialists and powerful personages through the mud left Doherty susceptible to costly accusations of libel. But it was a clergy-man, not a mill owner, who came closest to bringing him down.[1]

In March 1832, Doherty printed a story in the *Advocate* claiming that the Reverend Martin Gilpin of Stockport was in cahoots with local surgeons and had helped them procure fresh bodies for anatom-ical investigations. The rumour had been circulating for some months after a grave robbery had taken place in this rector's churchyard, but it was given substance by the fact that a couple of years earlier Gilpin's brother-in-law, himself a medical man, had been found to have the body of an Irishman taken from another Stockport graveyard in his possession. The Reverend Gilpin had already sued a local gossip for libel over the matter. He had won the case, and in all likelihood was wholly innocent of the charges. Doherty, however, had been assured by a colleague, Thomas Worsley, that Gilpin was guilty, and in an article entitled 'Clerical Resurrectionism' he used the case to indict the ruling classes for the indignities they inflicted on the poor. A few weeks later, Gilpin appeared with his attorney at Doherty's Withy Street shop and demanded a full public retraction. Doherty refused and libel proceedings were initiated.[2]

While Blincoe's *Memoir* became a talking point in clubs, inns and chapels, the Tory press lambasted Doherty for his attacks on the Reverend Gilpin. Seizing eagerly on any attempt to blacken the reputation of this Radical trades unionist, they dubbed him 'a vile miscreant' and the *Advocate* 'a weekly vehicle of sedition and slander.' On 8 May 1832, Doherty had to solicit a donation from Worsley allowing him to travel to the court of King's Bench in London to hear the libel charge lodged by Gilpin. Just a fortnight later he had to return to the capital, where he complained that having to defend himself in London meant incurring excessive legal costs. Gilpin's counsel responded tartly that if a man was poor 'he should take care not to write atrocious libels.' Apparently the judges agreed, and the case was marked down for a later jury trial in London. Unfazed and still convinced of Gilpin's guilt, on 9 June Doherty published a scurrilous poem which included the stanza:

Jesus and G–lp–n, so 'tis said,
Both in their turn have rais'd the dead;
One gave them back to light and life,
The other to the surgeon's knife.

In a fit of whimsy, he placed beneath the poem the absurd comment: 'Copied from a Magazine, supposed to have been written by a Welshman, one thousand and seven hundred years ago.' Less than a fortnight later, unable to afford the coach fare to London to enter his plea, Doherty was arrested for his failure to appear. On 28 June, he found himself back in Lancaster Castle gaol. Without money to pay for bail, it looked as if he would remain there for many months. So an earnest appeal for funds was launched in the pages of the *Advocate*, with arrangements being made for money to be left at the Spread Eagle public house in Stockport. When the publican of the Spread Eagle was warned that his licence would be revoked if he received money for Doherty, the venue was switched to the shop of the Radical Manchester bookseller Abel Heywood. Over the next few months, the *Advocate*'s appeal raised nearly £90, with donations from sympathetic mill owners like John Fielden, hundreds of cotton-spinners, various unions, the musician and composer Paganini, and numerous anonymous donors who left a few pennies or even shillings under such pseudonyms as 'An enemy to Tyranny', 'A Cobbettite', 'A Lover of Truth', and 'An Enemy of Dealers in "cold Meat"'. Robert Blincoe was among these subscribers. His contribution of two shillings was noticeably high for an individual donation, equal to over a day's take-home pay for a cotton-spinner. Nor did he mask his identity; he was proud of what he was doing. Doherty had clearly made a very good impression on him.[3]

Blincoe had every reason to come to Doherty's aid. Naturally he felt indebted to the man who had brought his sufferings and modest triumphs to a wide readership. Richard Carlile's *Lion* had had a limited circulation in the north, but the contents of the *Poor Man's Advocate* were disseminated rapidly throughout the industrial districts. There was, however, another reason why the *Gilpin vs Doherty* suit won many thousands of working men, including Blincoe, to Doherty's side: they believed implicitly in the guilt of a man accused of a crime that filled many among the working classes with rage and revulsion.

It was only four years since the conviction and execution of Burke and Hare in Edinburgh. And while they had circumvented the grave-robbing stage by murdering the men and women whose corpses they sold, their crimes had sparked huge demonstrations against both 'resurrection men' and the surgeons and physicians who paid them to plunder. All sections of society attached great importance to the bodies of the deceased. Secularising science had not yet demystified the corpse, and working-class burial rituals were many, complex and integral to their cultural life. Hence anatomists and the surgeons they trained were widely despised for their callous disregard for the after-lives of those whose bodies they bought, dissected and, sometimes, preserved in alcohol. The discovery of disturbed soil in churchyards frequently sparked rioting among the lower orders. In 1828, for instance, two Scottish medical students apprehended trying to dig up a fresh corpse begged to be kept in gaol to avoid a huge crowd waiting outside, baying for their blood, many with axes in hand. Four years later, a dog unearthed the decomposed remains of a human in the grounds of the Aberdeen anatomy school. A mob comprising as many as 20,000 incensed locals torched the building and then prevented the fire engine from reaching the blaze. In Manchester itself there had been a 'great ferment' in early 1824 when two resurrection men, caught with six 'recently disinterred' bodies, including one of a six-year-old girl, were prosecuted for theft alone.[4]

But in the early 1800s the number of stolen corpses mounted rapidly as doctors became ever more fascinated by the internal workings of the sick body. Historically, physicians had rarely conducted post mortems; they had handled their rich patients very gingerly, and because they knew little about the physiology of illness they had tended to confuse mere symptoms, like a runny nose, fast pulse, fever and vomiting, with the disease process itself. In post-Revolutionary France, however, the new state officials had demanded that medical academies produce doctors who combined the bookish learning of the physician with the surgeon's practical knowledge of anatomy. As medicine's gaze shifted, academies everywhere had to procure more bodies. The corpses of the condemned were never going to be enough. So, in mid-1832, the British Parliament debated a Bill which would allow registered anatomists to appropriate the bodies of those who died in workhouses and public hospitals and who weren't promptly collected by their relations. To many Radicals, like Doherty and presumably Blincoe as well, this was as grotesque a piece of class legislation as the 1815 Corn Law, since in the early 1800s the filth, overcrowding and terrible rates of infection meant that only the very poor ever resorted to public hospitals. At a stroke, hard-up men, women and children would be denied the basic dignity of a Christian burial.[5]

The hard-headed utilitarians who pressed for the Act, and secured it on 1 August 1832, knew full well that it would never apply to the better sorts. But they didn't appreciate how much importance the poorer classes attached to a decent funeral. In fact, it was one of the few things on which impoverished families refused to economise; as Mrs Pemper Reeves observed some years later, the death of a poor child often 'carries with it pauperisation of the father of the child', because he would spend his family's last shillings on a respectable sending-off. The Anatomy Act meant treating the bodies of the deceased poor as if they were animal carcasses destined for the butcher's hook. Blincoe, once the denizen of a workhouse himself, must have shared the widespread feeling of disgust at an Act which would hurt only those of his own station and below. In 1832, the Reverend Gilpin became a target for the rage of virtually an entire social class.[6]

Blincoe's loyalty to Doherty and his cause ran deep. The money left at Heywood's shop between June and October just about covered Doherty's legal costs. But in order to gain temporary liberty he needed to find people willing to pay two sureties of £40 each. It was a sizeable fee, equivalent to what many a working man earned in a year. And, unfortunately for Doherty, he was flat broke. It was now that Blincoe stepped in. He raised the money and handed it over to the court officials. The fact that Blincoe had ready access to £40 tells us that by 1832 his businesses were thriving. Even after paying for power and space at the Stockport mill, and for the education of his two youngest children, he evidently still had plenty of cash to spare. Blincoe remained a small manufacturer, but his work'us origins were now a long way behind him. With exceptional fortitude he had recovered from the disasters of the mid-1820s.[7]

Within a week, partly due to Blincoe's good offices, Doherty had his freedom. But it was only a brief interlude. For months, Doherty's wife Laura had experienced extreme anxiety as her husband's fate remained uncertain. As her condition deteriorated, Doherty realised that he needed to draw the affair to a close. He couldn't bring himself to make a public retraction, and so he went to see Gilpin's attorney, and then Gilpin himself, imploring him to drop his suit on the grounds that he had been misled by Thomas Worsley (which he now admitted) and that the Reverend had already had 'pretty ample vengeance'. Gilpin flatly refused and Doherty returned disconsolately to his Withy Street address. There, a few days later, Laura contracted cholera.[8]

Doherty was well versed in cholera's symptoms. The *Poor Man's Advocate* had charted its arrival in Manchester on 7 May 1832, and in several issues he had cited the divergent opinions of a fractious medical community, some of whom said it was contagious and some of whom insisted that it arose from an unhappy combination of airborne poisons and climatic conditions. As a result, Doherty knew the signs to look for, and when Laura fell violently ill, unable to stand or speak, Doherty diagnosed cholera. A local physician agreed. Convinced that the 'imagination possesses great power in bringing on this disorder' and in determining its outcome, the physician decided to tell Laura that Gilpin had dropped the case against her husband. But later the same day, Doherty received a summons to appear for trial at the court of King's Bench. It seemed that he would have to leave his gravely sick wife and young children behind as he was hurled into a metropolitan gaol. Seldom had Doherty been or felt so desperate.[9]

In a last-ditch attempt to avoid his client having to leave Manchester, Doherty's physician signed a certificate confirming that Laura had cholera, and he wrote a letter begging in the name of humanity for Gilpin to request a postponement of the trial. Doherty even offered to double his bail payment. The letter and certificate were entrusted to a man who had obviously become a close friend and confidant: Robert Blincoe. On Tuesday 20 November, Blincoe left Withy Street for Stockport. He went first to see Mr Wright, Gilpin's attorney, who had the civility to commend the proposal, but explained that he didn't have the power to accede to Doherty's wishes without the permission of his client. Since the latter was out of town, Blincoe returned on the Friday. He then went straight to the vicarage and 'waited upon Mr Gilpin'. It was a very different Blincoe from the one who had knocked on the door of Henry Bache Thornhill's stately residence and then sat nervously in the kitchen of Marmaduke Middleton's mansion in 1812. He was now older and wiser, respectably dressed, with money in the bank and the master of his own affairs; but above all he was filled with the confidence of someone who found himself an important player in a national campaign supported by tens of thousands and led by Westminster politicians, squires, dukes and earls.[10]

It's possible that Blincoe's mind turned to his alleged clerical parentage as he waited in Gilpin's parlour. But his mission left the Reverend unmoved. When Gilpin eventually appeared and read the certificate and the note, he simply announced: 'The law must take its course.' It wasn't the most Christian of acts, and Doherty left for London on the Sunday terrified that he would never see his wife again. Gilpin, though, had cause to be implacably angry. Not only had he been falsely accused but, as Doherty himself said, in his neighbourhood the rumour was very tenacious. If he was to have any hope of restoring his good name, Gilpin had to utterly discredit his accusers. And he was in no mood to wait.

Determined to clear his name and to close what had been a painful episode of his life, Gilpin insisted on a quick resolution. He behaved ungenerously towards Doherty, but the fiery trades unionist failed to see how grievously he had hurt Gilpin by his libels. Finally, however, at the court of King's Bench, Doherty was sentenced to one month in gaol and placed under bail for five years 'not to publish another libel'. Hobbled by the judgement, he wrote one more piece for the *Advocate* and then desisted. The one positive development for Doherty was that Laura made a full recovery.[11]

As Doherty had been fighting his personal battle, bigger campaigns were afoot. Sadler's Bill was stalling as the Whigs' Reform Bill over-shadowed, trivialised and then swept aside all other parliamentary business. In May 1832, when the Lords voted down another Reform Bill, a political crisis ensued. Bishops and Tory peers were spat at, verbally abused, and pelted with rotten fruit in the street. The new King, William IV, was hissed as his carriage passed through London. And for nine days, the nation found itself leaderless as the hopelessly divided Tories tried to cobble together an administration, failed, and left the field open for the Whigs. Fear of violent revolution mounted, and a rash of public disturbances unsettled the complacency of lords and bishops. Alarmed by the rising heat outside, in the new parlia-mentary session the Lords finally capitulated. The 'Great Reform Bill' received royal assent in June 1832. Anyone living in a property with a rental value over £10 was now entitled to vote in parliamentary elections. The electorate instantly doubled.[12]

Cobbett, Hunt and Carlile, however, were left angered and aggrieved. They complained bitterly – and accurately – that the 1832 Bill fell a long way short of granting full manhood suffrage. Indeed, in the short run at least, it was amply to fulfil Earl Grey's hope that, by carrying through a measured reform of the constitution, property owners would go on ruling without fear of revolution, middle- and working-class alliances would be smashed, and the idea of democracy would wither on the branch. The mighty ranks of the middle classes were now hitched firmly to the constitution, and they had no further use for their working-class allies of the previous months' demonstrations, marches and petitions. As if to rub in this fact, the passing of the Great Reform Bill was followed by an adjournment of Parliament which scuppered the Ten Hours Bill. Oastler feared the worst. A greatly enlarged electorate would now decide the complexion of Parliament, but the gains went to the middle classes and many of their representatives would be hooked on the principles of political economy. They could be expected to fight doggedly against factory reform. Oastler fumed that the Act 'had given the poor into the hands of the highest and middle classes and shut out entirely the great mass, the wealth-producing class', adding: 'the people do not live in ten-pound houses.' A sense of having been deserted by the middle class as soon as it had gained the vote did much to sour class relations in the ensuing decades.[13]

Orator Hunt eagerly fomented the growing resentment felt by the working classes. Returned again as MP for Preston in the 1832 elections, on 18 August he arrived in Manchester to be met by a devoted crowd several hundred strong. His supporters put on a display, explicitly designed to unnerve the propertied class, of 'a score or two flambeaux, and some few pistols … torches and tar barrels blazing away.' He spoke once more on St Peter's Fields, deploring the fact that the Whig Reform Bill had done nothing for the 'seven millions' of working men denied the vote. Hunt said little on the subject of factory reform, but the fate of Sadler's Bill now galvanised opinion in Manchester. In August, hope of the Ten Hours Bill passing later in the year remained alive.[14]

The decision was taken in early August that the first instalment of the Select Committee's evidence be published without delay, although it wouldn't appear in print for five months. In the meantime, the short time men stepped up their activities. On 25 August 1832, the huge demonstration took place at Camp Field in Manchester at which Oastler, John Wood of Bradford, Michael Sadler, the Reverend Bull and several others spoke to a vast crowd of adults and children waving flags, banners and branches. The route to be taken, from Ardwick Green's Shakespeare Inn all the way to Camp Field, had been announced in the morning in Doherty's *Poor Man's Advocate*. So, on the appointed day, London Road, Piccadilly, Mosley and Great Bridgewater streets were all lined with jubilant crowds. Where the speakers' open-topped cart and its entourage turned off Piccadilly to head south down Mosley Street, they passed only 200 yards from Mr and Mrs Blincoe's house on Turner Street. But Blincoe knew of the event well in advance. Over the previous days, presumably at Doherty's instigation, hundreds of Keeling's woodcuts had been printed on paper and fabric to be raised on banners. On the day itself, the crowd bristled with likenesses of Blincoe, Wooley, Mears and other victims of factory abuse.[15]

It was an extraordinary thing for a work'us orphan like Blincoe to see hundreds of images of himself swaying in the air above the surging crowd in one of the most important and spectacular events of the entire short hours campaign. The banners were ironic plays on those used in martial or royal processions, but the day was a celebration of the authority of the labouring classes, and Blincoe was an integral part of it. And despite the reservations he had expressed in early 1828, one imagines that his past sufferings seemed less futile, less stigmatising and less hard to reflect on, now that they were the collective property of a city, a class, and a cause of which he ardently approved.

Three years later, the giant Manchester rally still rankled with that most zealous of the mill owner's friends, Andrew Ure. 'They collected about 4,000 of the youngest', Ure decried, 'mustered them in tawdry array, and paraded them through the streets … brandishing straps and bludgeons as emblems of their masters' tyranny, but really the instruments of their own wickedness.' Doherty and Blincoe would have taken heart from knowing how much the spectacle still irritated a man so keen to whitewash the behaviour of the millocracy.[16]

While Mancunians cursed Blincoe's abusers, Oastler tried a new tack, drawing on what remained of the moral authority of the hero of Waterloo after his dismal political career. The Duke of Wellington met with him several times, and Oastler published florid descriptions of what passed between them. The new industrialists, Oastler stormed, revealing why he had warmed so strongly to the short time cause, 'were pushing the old country gentlemen out of their estates, making the people believe that the Aristocracy and Clergy were the only tyrants.' 'I assured him', Oastler went on, 'that the only way the aristocracy and clergy could regain the affections of the people and save themselves from ruin was ... to rescue the working classes from the thraldom and delusion in which the money and steam powers held them.' Here were Oastler's true colours. Rural gentlemen, the squirearchy to which he was so sentimentally attached, needed the workers to confound the ambitions of the rising bourgeoisie.[17]

Following the passing of the Reform Bill, Oastler felt this imperative more vehemently than ever. The power of the industrialists had been amplified; and for many Tories, backing Sadler's Ten Hours Bill was now an act of retaliation for June 1832. The friends of the mill bosses weren't fooled. Among others, Andrew Ure detected 'in the late Parliamentary crusade against the factories' a new version of that 'ancient feeling of contempt entertained by the country gentlemen towards the burghers.' Such writers pointed out that while Sadler and Oastler fretted about the plight of the factory child, on landed estates and down hundreds of mines, adults and children were working appalling hours, in wretched and dangerous conditions, taking home a fraction of the pay of textile operatives.[18]

Deeply sensitive about these charges, Michael Sadler did his best to scotch the claim that Tory paternalists were motivated by a hatred of industrialists more than they were by a love for the working man. At the dinner following the Camp Field speeches on 25 August 1832, Sadler rose to speak before a merry gathering of short time men and one *Manchester Guardian* journalist. He denied that he represented only the 'agricultural interests' or that he had ever concealed 'the suffering and degradation of the agricultural labourers'. Even before entering Parliament, Sadler said, he had felt deeply for the 'poor, depressed, impotent and degraded' factory children, and had been drawn to their plight as the most disgraceful example of how the 'lust of gold' caused masters to act like savages. It was no doubt sincerely felt. Sadler probably had no real idea of how punishing and precarious existence could be for England's poor rural workers. One contemporary said that their miseries were 'rarely witnessed by casual spectators except during fine weather', with the result that squires and lords often assumed their lives to be all snug cottages, crackling fires, green meadows, wholesome food, deference and simple piety. They failed to see the 'shattered hovels' that many rural families had to live in, or the 'children perishing from sheer hunger in the mud hovel, or in the ditch by the wayside.'[19]

And in order to keep the nation warm and the fires of foundries and forges alight, tens of thousands toiled in coal, tin and copper mines in conditions far worse than those of all but the most sadistically-run cotton mills. Not for another decade, however, did the humanitarian lobby turn its attention to this crueller industry. The worst tyrants in the early 1800s weren't always the low-born mill owners, though they were the easiest for both operatives and landowners to despise; it was the lordly owners of mines, like the Earls of Lonsdale, who were to quash any attempt to regulate the hours worked by colliery children with imperious disdain.[20]

Despite all of this, factory children in the 1830s were a legitimate object of humanitarian pity. These youngsters worked for twelve or more hours, were subject to routine verbal and physical abuse, and had been forced by poverty into a trade which took on many more boys and girls than it could possibly hire as adults. Sadler and Oastler had a blind spot when it came to the suffering inflicted by lords and squires, but the poor targets of their reformist zeal were undeniably deserving.

There's no evidence that Robert Blincoe ever met Oastler or Sadler, and given that Doherty was in King's Bench Prison on 25 August, it might be that Blincoe wasn't invited to the dinner following the Camp Field event. One suspects, however, that any meeting between them would not have been a great success. Doherty was for Blincoe much more congenial company. He had been a spinner himself, he knew what it was to experience real hunger, and he also carried with him a distrust of the 'better sorts' which Blincoe by now must have shared. Doherty evidently reciprocated Blincoe's comradely regard, and on his release from prison he would continue to make sure that the *Memoir* remained on the conscience of England's industrialist class.

31

Enter Lord Ashley

When Parliament returned to business in August 1832 the Ten Hours Bill quickly foundered. Sadler had planned for his Select Committee to begin by hearing from the operatives, overlookers and physicians, and then to allow the masters to have their say. But Parliament was prorogued in October and dissolved in December for fresh elections. Not surprisingly, given his Tory credentials, Sadler's seat was among the 'rotten boroughs' abolished by the Great Reform Bill. Turning down easier briefs, he decided to stand for Leeds against Thomas Babington Macaulay. It was a highly-charged contest, pitting a clever and cocksure champion of political economy against a diffident and pious old-world Tory. 'Orator' Hunt came to Sadler's aid, albeit with some uneasiness on both sides; but his attempts to organise mass demonstrations of local labourers were foiled when magistrates ordered that masters keep their workers locked in their factories. On election day, the newly enfranchised middle classes wasted no time in reneging on their working-class allies. After a series of rowdy and ill-tempered meetings, Sadler was beaten by 388 votes. With Macaulay's ascendancy, the ethos of rugged individualism prevailed.[1]

Sadler retired from the Ten Hours movement. He tried to get back into Parliament in 1834, but failed; and he died, probably of heart disease, at his home in Belfast in July 1835. 'Sadler is a loss', Robert Southey wrote after the Leeds election; 'he might not be popular in the house, or in London society, but his speeches did much good in the country, and he is a singularly able, right-minded, and religious man.' Sadler had hoped that the landed aristocracy would be able to rule the nation with moral rectitude and impartiality. It was pure romance. Peers weren't usually interested in humanitarian causes. Even those who didn't own coal mines or have money staked in the textile industry tended to be converts to political economy and ill-disposed to any attempt to challenge the power of masters over men. There were, however, exceptions, and it was another Tory, also pious and sentimental, who took over where Sadler left off. He was Lord Ashley, later the seventh Earl of Shaftesbury.

Like Oastler in 1830, Lord Ashley had heard virtually nothing about the short hours movement until a close friend enlightened him. In Ashley's case, the friend wasn't a humane mill owner but Robert Southey, poet, writer and archetypal Tory romantic. The Reform Bill's passage had sickened Southey. It heralded, for him, the demise of the world of paternalistic squires, and the erection in its place of a class society in which coarse industrialists bullied sullen workers into resentful compliance. Southey predicted that it would end in blood-shed. 'Governments that found [security] upon manufactures, sleep upon gunpowder', he warned. He had long deplored the despoliation of the rural landscape and of ancient social bonds wrought by textile mills. But in 1832 he, like many other Tories, grasped the uplifting fact that by pressing for the Ten Hours Bill he could take some, if modest, revenge against the middle-class industrialists who had helped desecrate the timeless English constitution. It was typical of Southey that he told Lord Ashley never to enter a cotton mill himself; for him it wasn't necessary to know what they were like before attacking them.[2]

Southey's descriptions alone horrified Lord Ashley. Always quick to identify with those in pain, he spent his life working to relieve the distress of the poor and downtrodden: factory children, chimney sweeps, child mine-workers, the insane, and animals subjected to vivisection. His extreme emotional sensitivity arose from an affection-starved youth, his father terrifying his sons into silence whenever in his company and his mother wishing them out of the way so that she could organise her glittering balls and soirees in peace. Bullied or ignored at home and then at school, by the time he left Oxford, Ashley was convinced of his own worthlessness. At the same time he chastised himself for falling short of the high aspirations he had set himself of becoming a wise and 'zealous' government minister.[3]

Ashley's aptitude for self-criticism pushed him towards evangelical religion. He took easily to the evangelicals' emphasis on the need to atone for one's inherent wickedness, and he gladly responded to their call for the worthy to go out and do good works among the weak. But Ashley's humanitarianism also drew upon the Toryism that Southey helped to imbue. Behind all of his endeavours there was the same aversion to the utilitarian and materialist sensibilities of the new middle classes, and an unswerving commitment to the values of the Tory paternalist. Lord Ashley was a class warrior of a gentle but determined kind.[4]

As Doherty, Oastler, Bull and their allies discussed who should now succeed Sadler, news reached them that the Whig peer Lord Morpeth was about to introduce an Eleven Hour factory Bill. This was a careful compromise between Morpeth's belief in the moral necessity for legislative interference to protect children and a concern lest reform hinder the profitability of the woollen mills in his native county of Yorkshire. Determined to scuttle Morpeth's plan, Parson Bull left the north for London to anoint a new sponsor prepared to submit the original Ten Hours Bill. Ashley later recalled that, when approached, he felt sheer 'terror at the proposition'. But having been 'disgusted' by the excerpts from Sadler's report printed in *The Times* in February 1833, he nervously agreed, declaring: 'I know not how a cotton mill can be otherwise than an abomination to God and man.' For all his reservations, this was a crusade tailor-made for Ashley. In satisfying his evangelical yearning to bring succour to the needy, he could strike a blow against the urban world he so detested. It was the right cause for a man who delighted in the Bible's Book of Ruth because he found there 'A beautiful picture of agricultural life, a happy peasantry, and a good landlord.'[5]

Sadler's report inspired a widespread condemnation of mill owners. One daily newspaper argued that Germany should prohibit imports from Britain on the same basis that anti-slave traders abstained from American sugar. Seizing the initiative, the Short Time Committees despatched dozens of petitions, and on 23 February 1833 Sadler, Oastler and Robert Owen took part in a giant meeting in London in praise of the Ten Hours Bill. Sadler spoke movingly of the iniquity of the modern ethos of 'letting-things-alone'. In the event, Lord Morpeth tabled his more conciliatory Bill first. Morpeth and Ashley had been close childhood friends, though they could hardly have been more different in terms of temperament and personality. Ashley had little of Morpeth's suavity (Oastler loathed 'sleek and oily Morpeth'), and by now they didn't have much left in common. However, on the grounds that Ashley had been the first to enter Parliament, Morpeth graciously stepped aside when his old friend moved to reintroduce the Ten Hours Bill.[6]

Among the petitions reaching the Whig administration in March 1833 was one from a large group of northern mill owners. A few days later, a motion was introduced for a new inquiry to be formed to hear their point of view. Ashley put up a determined fight, but by a single vote the motion passed. Once more the Ten Hours Bill had been derailed. Speaking in Manchester, Oastler was driven to incendiary language: 'If the mill owners will drive me to use the word, let them – at their own bidding and not at mine – let them dread *the dagger and the torch* … I have ceased to reason.' Yet the mill owners had at least some justification.

Doherty, Ashley and Oastler spoke of the Bill as a simple matter of justice versus greed. This was an over-simplification, for while the short time men focused only on children working in mills, they knew that the effect of shortening their hours would almost certainly be a reduction in the hours worked by adults too. Factories across the country would have to close several hours earlier. But lessening the hours worked promised to diminish the capitalist's already slender profit margins, so the masters feared that a Ten Hours Bill would erode their competitive edge in foreign markets and cause them to close down. Thereby, they pointed out, hundreds of jobs would be eliminated at one stroke. As the *Manchester Guardian* warned in 1832, reflecting on foreign rivals: 'It is time … for John Bull to look sharp.' Nor did it improve the industrialist's temper that Tories like Oastler actually wanted them to go bust, naively believing that their demise would then bring back 'domestic manufacture, which would be the greatest blessing that could be introduced into Old England.'[7]

Some advocates of the Ten Hours Bill also overlooked the risk – obvious to many in the debates leading up to the 1819 and 1825 Factory Acts – that shortening hours would plunge the incomes of some poor families below subsistence levels. Before Sadler's committee, a Richard Wilson explained that he used to help his father carry a crippled brother to the mill every day to do what work he could, since his parents were just too poor to 'maintain us except we went to the mills'. Richard Carlile implied in the preface to Blincoe's *Memoir* that 'infant children' were sent to labour in mills only so that parents could 'live in idleness and all sorts of vice'. This was hopelessly naive. Plenty needed the money and had to turn a blind eye to the effects of mill work on their children's health and future prospects. Conversely, many an adult male mule-spinner relished the long hours he could work on piece rates which, in good times, brought in a decent wage; the Ten Hours Bill threatened the financial well-being of those with the stamina and ambition to labour for fifteen hours at a stretch. Moreover, adult operatives who supported factory reform were often motivated by the less-than-heroic desire to reduce competition for jobs by limiting the number of youngsters entering the trade. Male operatives fought hard to keep mule-spinning a job exclusive to themselves and beyond the reach of women and children. Others, like William Swithenbank, questioned by Sadler in 1832, heartily approved of the Bill, since 'stopping the labour of children would effectually stop the labour of the grown-up people.' To plenty of adult mill operatives, the child's welfare was of secondary concern.[8]

Even so, the massive parades in York on 24 April and Manchester on 25 August 1832 demonstrated that a large proportion of adult spinners and their wives welcomed the Ten Hours Bill with genuine zeal. They were content to forsake higher wages to be able to spend more time with their families and to give their offspring greater opportunities for leisure and, above all else, a decent education. And many a spinner could afford to do so, since an adult mule operator earned roughly three times as much as a weaver or stockinger. Admittedly, they were often responsible for hiring and paying their own piecers and scavengers out of this sum, but despite this, the spinner did better than most of those who worked with their hands. A sizeable proportion felt that they could bear a slight drop in income so as to improve their children's chances of escaping sweated labour in an increasingly overstocked trade. And few parents relished seeing their offspring return late at night from the mill, hollow-cheeked, narrow-shouldered and too exhausted to eat. If they could bear the loss of a shilling or so a week, then a majority of labouring families backed the Ten Hours Bill with real enthusiasm. Their children would then be able to work without sacrificing their futures.[9]

According to Doherty and Sadler, however, shorter hours wouldn't equate to less pay. The mill owners insisted that any cut in the time that operatives worked would cause a decline in their profits, which would translate into wage cuts. They called this a cast-iron law; but the short time men turned this logic on its head. They said that by forcing the mills to close early, demand for textiles would exceed supply, leading to price increases which would in turn allow for higher wages. In other words, mill operatives would get more for doing less. The main problem with this argument was that uncompetitive mills would be squeezed out of foreign markets, and so all would lose out. But it wasn't clear how close European and American mills were on the heels of their British counterparts. In any case, Doherty and his allies had a reply to the foreign competition argument. As in 1816, they claimed that reducing the hours worked by each mill would help stamp out the evil of over-production and so rein in the boom–bust cycle that brought so many capitalists down. This was still a good argument. The free market was fair but wasteful. Masters hungering for short-term profits lost everything when boom turned to bust. A system of modest regulation, which involved limiting the number of hours which each could work, might well have saved mills from going under.[10]

In short, neither masters nor men had a monopoly on plausible economic arguments. It was clear that there would be losers and gainers either way. Most working parents, however, calculated that a reduction in their children's hours, even if it meant a fall in household income, was a price worth paying. Lord Ashley's Ten Hours Act would lessen the risks of their bodies being twisted by overwork and mangled by machinery. And for all but the poorest families – those in which only the children could get work – it would allow them to send their offspring to school. For most parents of child workers, the setting up of a new parliamentary committee dominated by the testimony of mill owners didn't bode well. But it was to give Robert Blincoe the chance to tell his story to those with the power to make it count.

32

Blincoe's voice is heard

The cumbrously-named Commission for Inquiring into the Employment of Children in Factories convened in April 1833. Twelve commissioners, split into four teams each comprising two civil servants and a physician, were quickly despatched to the nation's centres of industry. This time, leading Benthamites, not Tory paternalists, packed the Central Board which stayed in London to collate their results. These men were drawn from middle-class professions like law and medicine, with a highly practical taste for any reform likely to promote the greater good. Ardent followers of the utilitarian philosopher Jeremy Bentham, tradition had no charm for them. Everything had to be judged according to its contribution to the nation's wealth and happiness. Things were beautiful, admirable, helpful and sensible only insofar as they promoted the greatest happiness of the greatest number.

Three of those on the Central Board – Edwin Chadwick, Thomas Tooke and Thomas Southwood Smith – were simultaneously hard at work finding out why there were so many paupers claiming parish relief, and what should be done about it. Chadwick was a trained lawyer, Tooke an economist, and Southwood Smith a physician at London's fever hospital who had recently had the honour of dissecting the body of his intellectual guru, Bentham. Like many utilitarians, those on the factory commission deluded themselves into the belief that they were approaching big issues with complete disinterest. But right from the start, as everyone knew, they were disciples of political economy, a philosophy that suited the way they saw the world. In order to find easy solutions, most Benthamites allowed themselves to see only simple problems. And so the anarchic complexity of real social issues resolved itself into crisp and neat formulae. In caricature form, crude but with an essence of truth, these were the Gradgrinds of central government, clever but simple-minded.

Doherty's and Oastler's Short Time Committees knew that the Royal Commission was stacked with their foes. Some commissioners didn't even bother to hide their antipathy. One of them, Edward C. Tufnell, wrote scathingly of the Lancashire Ten Hours campaigners, with only modest attention to the truth: 'Doherty … originally came to Manchester with a forged character, and was subsequently imprisoned for two years for a gross assault on a woman; the second is a keeper of a small tavern in the purlieus of the town; the third is an atheist.' If the commissioners were to back any kind of factory reform, they had to be convinced that children were not free agents in the market and that therefore it was acceptable to protect them. From the outset, however, they were opposed to any suggestion of reducing adult working hours.[1]

The Short Time Committees, furious at the decision to hold yet another inquiry, blankly refused to co-operate. Doherty dubbed the new inquiry 'the millowners' commission', and Lord Ashley declined an offer to attend the Board. A dedicated opponent of aristocratic rule, Chadwick was not Ashley's idea of congenial company. Nevertheless, the short time men made their annoyance felt. On 4 May 1833 the commissioners Tufnell, J.W. Cowell and Bisset Hawkins arrived in Manchester, bound for the York Hotel. Their brief was to question mill owners, workers, and anyone else who might shed light on the moral and physical status of factory children. They were also charged with checking the veracity of the stories told to Sadler's committee, and all of this in less than six weeks.[2]

A pamphlet addressed to the three Lancashire commissioners asked menacingly: 'Have you all made your Wills?' It set the tone for their reception. Before they had even arrived at the hotel, Tufnell, Cowell and Hawkins were met by a procession of over 2,000 factory children and handed a lurid memorial on the 'Evils of the Factory System'. The Yorkshire campaigners trumped this spectacle. In Leeds, 3,000 filthy children marched past the hotel where the commissioner John Drinkwater stayed. Shortly after, in Huddersfield, effigies of the commissioners were torched. The Scottish divine Thomas Chalmers said they were so realistic that the spectacle 'was fitted to prepare the actors for burning the originals instead of the copies'. In both counties, the commissioners were shadowed everywhere by observers sent by the Short Time Committees.[3]

Over the next five weeks, the commissioners, with their shadows, toured the factory districts of the entire nation. They administered oaths and then asked questions; inspected factory floors, windows and privies; noted the distance between floor and ceiling, the quality of drainage, the temperature of the work rooms, the amount of 'effluvia' in the air; and observed the complexions and cleanliness of thousands of factory children. Being tailed by hostile workers while bearing so much responsibility did nothing for their morale. Behind the scenes, Cowell and Tufnell rowed furiously. After a few weeks, they couldn't stand to be in one another's company. Finally, Tufnell packed his trunk and left the York Hotel. Probably deliberately, he didn't loiter long enough to pay his bill.[4]

This behaviour fits with what we can tell of Tufnell's personality from the report he sent to Chadwick and the Central Board. With conspicuous dislike, he accused the advocates of the Ten Hours Bill of 'calumny and falsehood'. Nearly all the beatings, Tufnell insisted, were perpetrated by the adult workers themselves, the very men who then claimed that their only aim in supporting the Ten Hours Bill was to protect the poor children. Feelings of humanity on the part of adult operatives, he fumed, 'have not the smallest weight in inducing them to uphold the Ten Hours Bill.' It was a patently exaggerated verdict, even if it did accurately account for the opinions of a minority of workers.[5]

Dr Bisset Hawkins wisely kept apart from Tufnell's ugly little feud with Cowell. The son of a distinguished London surgeon, Hawkins had already accomplished much. Only in his mid-30s, he was a fellow of the Royal College of Physicians, and in 1833 was serving as Professor of Materia Medica at King's College in London. Unlike Tufnell and Chadwick, Hawkins didn't have an innate aversion to state interference. On the contrary, he would soon write a book arguing that Prussian centralisation had many merits. Nor was he easily daunted by the difficulties of improving intolerable situations. In his 1829 work *The Elements of Medical Statistics*, Hawkins had proudly backed 'human art' over the awesome power of disease. In Manchester in 1833 he saw that the latter had the edge. 'I have never been in any town in Great Britain nor in Europe', Hawkins later wrote, 'in which degeneracy of form and colour from the national standard has been so obvious.' From the York Hotel, Hawkins sent out dozens of questionnaires to local doctors asking for their views on the health and morals of the factory children. He also questioned several workers.[6]

One of them was Robert Blincoe. Twenty years before, Derbyshire's magistrates would hardly listen to him. Now, on 18 May 1833, he had the undivided attention of an urbane and well-connected physician sent on behalf of Parliament, the highest authority in the land. Since Doherty and the other short time men were refusing to co-operate, it's fair to assume that it was the publication of his *Memoir* that drew Blincoe to the commissioner's attention. As Hawkins spoke to operatives, masters and philanthropists, Blincoe's name must have cropped up often; he was, after all, a poster boy for the short time cause. How Doherty responded to his ally agreeing to tarry with the enemy isn't known, but Blincoe had never been a 'yes-man', and he certainly wasn't a mere mascot. His was a story that could only assist the Ten Hours Bill, and he was determined to tell it.

It's unlikely that Blincoe had previously set foot in Manchester's opulent York Hotel. It wasn't the kind of place where a 'small manufacturer', as Hawkins aptly called him, would go to take tea. But Blincoe probably wasn't fazed. He had, after all, spoken to magistrates and knocked on their mansion doors when a filthy, malodorous apprentice; he was now well dressed and justifiably proud of what he had achieved. Hawkins asked Blincoe to swear an oath on the Bible. They then proceeded with the question–answer format of government inquiries. In his report, compiled two weeks later when comfortably ensconced back in his fashionable Golden Square address in London, Hawkins transcribed Blincoe's testimony. In the Royal Commission's Second Report, his true voice, unmediated, appeared in print for the first and only time.[7]

Blincoe told Hawkins that he had begun work in cotton factories aged eight, having been abandoned at St Pancras workhouse. Hawkins asked: 'Do you know the name of your parents with certainty?'

The doctor was aware of the practice of inventing names for work'us orphans. Blincoe admitted that he didn't know his real name for sure, but that his indentures stated it to be 'Robert Blincoe'. Hawkins next asked: 'Do you work at a cotton mill?' Blincoe replied, with more than a hint of pride: 'Now I have a work of my own. I rent power from a mill in Stockport, and have a room to myself; my business is a sheet wadding manufacturer.' Explaining why he had stopped working in cotton mills, he added: 'I got tired of it, the system is so bad; and I had saved a few pounds. I got deformed there; my knees began to bend in when I was fifteen; you see how they are.' At this point he boldly stood up, showed Hawkins his buckled legs, and added: 'There are many, many worse than me in Manchester.' Even so, he elaborated, merely walking could be taxing – a 'very little makes me sweat'; 'I have not the strength of those who are straight.'

Next he was asked about sickness and injuries in mills. Growing in self-assurance, Blincoe's answers now lengthened out. He described in some detail how he and many others had been ''prenticed out from St Pancras parish' and had succumbed to a series of severe maladies for which the astute doctor from Litton had recommended 'kitchen physic and … more rest'. Blincoe told the tragic story of Mary Richards, still a cripple, who had been 'lapped up by a shaft underneath the drawing frame' long ago at Lowdham Mill. He spoke of a boy badly injured at Litton Mill; and he said that 'there is plenty about Stockport that is going about now with one arm', who couldn't get proper work as a result, and so were reduced to going 'about with jackasses and such like' selling scrap. Blincoe also told Hawkins of how the master of the Stalybridge mill at which he had worked had been fatally injured by one of his own spinning machines. From the testimony he gave, it's clear that such memories as Mary Richards being thrashed about the mill floor were still painfully fresh in Blincoe's mind. But he could easily cite more recent accidents. 'On the 6th of March last', Blincoe recounted:

> a man [was] killed by machinery at Stockport; he was smashed, and he died in four or five hours; I saw him while the accident took place; he was joking with me just before; it was in my own room. I employ a poor sore cripple under me, who could not

easily get work any where else; a young man came good-naturedly from another room to help my cripple, and he was accidentally drawn up by the strap, and was killed.

This fleeting reference to the fact that he had hired a 'poor sore cripple' is illuminating. Not many small manufacturers would gamble their profits on employing a crippled workman; few allowed their sympathies to come in the way of the imperative to maximise returns. Moreover, it was to be expected that the parish apprentices of Lowdham and Miller's Dale would turn abuser themselves. Not so Robert Blincoe. The blows delivered by Needham and the Woodwards had had the opposite effect. Blincoe empathised with those who had suffered like him, and he did what he could to assist those in a worse state than himself. It was for this reason that he acquiesced in Doherty's publication of his *Memoir*, and why he came to be sitting in the York Hotel on 18 May.

Hawkins next posed some more searching questions: 'Have you any children?' and 'Do you send them to factories?' Blincoe replied that he would rather have his three children 'transported' than send them to work in the textile industry:

> In the first place, they are standing upon one leg, lifting up on one knee, a great part of the day, keeping the ends up from the spindle; I consider that that employment makes many cripples; then there is the heat and the dust: then there are so many different forms of cruelty used upon them, then they are so liable to have their fingers catched and to suffer other accidents from the machinery; then the hours is so long, that I have seen them tumble down asleep among the straps and machinery, and so get cruelly hurt; then I would not have a child of mine there because there is not good morals; there is such a lot of them together that they learn mischief.

One can detect in Blincoe's speech a gentle Lancashire lilt and the grammatical idioms of the north. The tones of St Pancras had entirely vanished. With a little editing, however, Blincoe's reply to Dr Hawkins might have been drawn from a manifesto drawn up by a Short

Time Committee. But it was sincerely spoken and felt, for as Blincoe next explained, he had higher hopes for his children. He was doing everything within his power to save them from the drudgery of the cotton mill:

> My eldest, of thirteen, has been to school, and can teach me. She now stays at home and helps her mother in the shop. She is as tall as me, and is very heavy; very different from what she would have been if she had worked in a factory. My two youngest go to school, and are both healthy. I send them every day two miles to school. I know from experience the ills of confinement.

Despite his ill-treatment as a boy and the absence of parental affection, Robert Blincoe had grown into a dutiful parent devoted to the betterment of his family. He was a living rebuke to the middle-class moralist who deemed workhouses capable of producing only fodder for antipodean colonies or the hangman's rope. He had mastered bourgeois morality and, excepting a few setbacks, his prudence, hard work and self-sacrifice had paid handsome dividends. The income from grocer's shop, workshop and waste cotton business had liberated both himself and his children, at least for the present, from a reliance on wage labour and the often callous whims of factory proprietors.[8]

Hawkins's last three questions returned to the subject of factory conditions. He asked Blincoe to comment on the 'forms of cruelty' practised. Blincoe had no trouble in recollecting the kinds of ill-treatment to which he had been subjected. He began: 'I have seen the time when two hand-vices of a pound weight each, more or less, have been screwed to my ears, at Lytton [*sic*] mill in Derbyshire.' Here he paused, leant over again towards Dr Hawkins, and pulled his ears forward. He then said: 'Here are the scars still remaining behind my ears.' Sitting back down, Blincoe continued:

> Then three or four of us have been hung at once on a cross beam above the machinery, hanging by our hands, without shirts or stockings. … we used to stand up, in a skip, without our shirts, and be beat with straps or sticks; the skip was to prevent us from

running away from the strap ... they used to tie on a twenty-eight pounds weight (one or two at once), according to our size, to hang down on our backs, with no shirts on. I have had them myself. Then they used to tie one leg up to a faller, whilst the hands were tied behind.

When Dr Hawkins asked the all-important question, 'Did the masters know of these things, or were they done only by the overlookers?', Blincoe answered crisply, his mind doubtless flooded with images of Ellis Needham's thrashings and John Needham's improprieties: 'The masters have often seen them, and have been assistants in them.'

Perhaps the most striking feature of Blincoe's testimony to Dr Hawkins is its honesty. Unlike so many short time men, he didn't try to insinuate that conditions in 1833 were as horrendous as they had been in 1803. With the decline in parish apprenticeship, the shift of most factories to less secluded areas, the advent of new technologies, and greater public pressure for masters to behave humanely, things had improved significantly. Blincoe freely admitted all this. 'Mind, we were apprentices', he said, 'without father or mother to take care of us.' And in Manchester, he explained, 'justice is always at hand'. Blincoe also conceded, without prompting, that the kinds of machine that had inflicted such appalling damage on Mary Richards were now 'old-fashioned'. Still, he had little doubt that overlookers went on thrashing boys and girls, just not so often or so severely as in those dark early days.

Blincoe might have felt ill at ease speaking to a professor of medicine and government commissioner, but the style of his answers suggests the reverse. Most workers replied to official questions in monosyllables or mere fragments of sentences, disjointed, cagey, unsure of how much or little to say. This isn't surprising. Few would have been used to open questions from their betters, and hardly any would ever have sat before a true gentleman interested in their subjective experiences of life and work. Even some expert witnesses lost their typical loquaciousness when confronted by formal panels of inquiry. Only a few, such as Robert Owen and the elder Robert Peel, thrived in this environment. Like them, however, Blincoe spoke in full paragraphs, with confidence, clarity, fluency, and even a hint of brio. His answers were also remarkably even-handed for someone so ardently committed to the short time cause.

Just before leaving, Blincoe plugged his own *Memoir*, saying: 'I have a book written about these things, describing my own life and sufferings.' Apparently not waiting for Hawkins to show any interest, he boldly added: 'I will send it to you.' He was true to his word, and Hawkins was able to add a footnote to his published report, saying: 'Enclosed for the inspection of the Central Board. It is entitled "A Memoir of Robert Blincoe, & c. Manchester." J. Doherty. 1832.' The inclusion of Doherty's name, however, would not have encouraged the Central Board to peruse its pages.[9]

At the time of giving evidence, Blincoe and his fellow short time men felt that Sadler's Bill might yet pass. On 17 June, Lord Ashley introduced the Ten Hours Bill for a second reading in the House of Commons, with an amendment – against Doherty's wiser judgement – requiring gaol terms for masters convicted of breaking the law three times. The Short Time Committees now had a month to prepare for the debate. Two weeks later, more than 15,000 (and perhaps as many as 60,000) people travelled to a meeting held on Wibsey Low Moor, near Bradford in Yorkshire, to commend Lord Ashley's efforts.[10]

Back in London, Chadwick laboured long hours. Just two months after the start of the inquiry, he issued his report. It was a masterpiece of synthesis. Having received the voluminous statements and transcripts from the different commissioners, he rendered them down into easily digestible form. To the surprise of the short time men, who were expecting a whitewashing of the masters, the final report endorsed the testimony given to Sadler's committee of the gruelling hours worked by children. Most of the commissioners found that it was far from unusual for children to labour from six in the morning to nine or ten at night. Sometimes they were bullied or bribed into working the whole night through, and over and over again the investigators heard parents complain of their children's exhaustion: 'So tired when she leaves the mill that she can do nothing'; 'Has often seen his daughter come home in the evening so fatigued that she would go to bed supperless.' The children said much the same. 'Whiles I do not know what to do with myself', remarked one, 'as tired every morning as can be.' Nor did masters and overlookers often allow the sick to go home to recover. One young witness recalled feeling too ill to work. The overlooker had been happy for him to leave, but only with the proviso that if he went he 'must not come back'. But the Benthamites were perhaps more appalled that those few children who did attend school were too tired to take anything in. Many a twenty-year-old, they discovered, couldn't read a single chapter from the New Testament. Their morals were at risk.[11]

Chadwick's report also detailed mills with disgusting sanitary conditions – 'privies situated in view' and shared by both sexes had a 'tendency to destroy shame, and conduced to immorality.' Potentially lethal machines were unguarded and the aisles between them so narrow that some tired children would inevitably lose fingers, limbs or lives. And, Chadwick noted, 'workpeople are abandoned from the moment that an accident occurs.' The report also accepted that going to work in mills at a young age led to a 'permanent deterioration of the physical constitution' and the 'production of disease often wholly irremediable'. John Drinkwater, in Yorkshire, revealed that some of Sadler's star witnesses had exaggerated the frequency of beatings, and that some children with missing fingers had lost them through games of dare involving rollers and flywheels. But that vicious physical abuse went on was not denied. Chadwick quoted from one commissioner's report: 'Hears the spinners swear very bad at their piecers, and sees 'em lick 'em sometimes; some licks 'em with a strap, some licks 'em with hand; some straps is as long as your arm; some is very thick, and some thin; don't know where they get the straps.'[12]

Yet Chadwick, like Blincoe, realised that urban mills were usually more salubrious and humane than Sadler's report suggested. 'The large factories, and those recently built, have a prodigious advantage over the old and small mills', Chadwick surmised, and only the latter were typically 'dirty; low-roofed; ill-ventilated; ill-drained; … [with] machinery not boxed in.' Beatings, too, were most common in 'the small obscure mills belonging to the smallest proprietors', in other words, the remote concerns like Lowdham and Litton. As we have seen, several leading masters from Manchester had spent years pushing for the enforcement of existing statutes so as not to be undercut by less fastidious rural mills.[13]

The commissioners also established that the kinds of deformity under which Blincoe and hundreds of others laboured were now less common. Most deformities had been induced by Arkwright's water-frame, which had required asymmetrical movements of the child's body. This machine was now obsolete and soon to be phased out. Blincoe had admitted this, too. But if children were less often bludgeoned with billy rollers in central Manchester, and if their limbs now grew straighter than before, they still worked hours that Chadwick's team, despite its instinctual aversion to interference in the market, considered patently excessive. And here the Central Board made the crucial admission that child workers were 'not free agents, but are let to hire, [their] wages ... being received and appropriated by their parents and guardians.' Their own precondition for legislative reform had been met. The children could be protected because they weren't free to choose if or where they worked. As many an adult operative noted, this was a curious principle since they too were under a compulsion to work, and if they walked out on one master following ill-treatment, they risked being refused employment by all the others. Chadwick turned a blind eye to this fact, but he did at least feel that he had a mandate to act.[14]

Now he caught the Ten Hours men off-guard. Chadwick said that their Bill was inadequate because it meant working young boys and girls *too long*. He had an ulterior motive, however, which emerged as his argument against Lord Ashley's Bill unfolded: 'its operations, if it could be carried into effect', he wrote, 'would be to restrict the labour of adults, as well as that of children, to ten hours.' Without any real inquiry, Chadwick accepted the claim that reducing operating hours would compromise England's lead over the textile firms of France, Germany, America, Switzerland and India. So he set himself the task of finding a means of relieving the distress of young children while keeping the adults hard at work. There was only one way to reduce the child's hours without touching those of adults. It involved introducing a relay system. Chadwick agonised over whether children should work six or eight hours, and finally settled for the longer of the two. With the children divided into two groups, each working for eight hours, while the adults laboured for the full sixteen, factories could be kept running from early morning until late at night with the minimum of fuss and disruption. And while adults continued to work long shifts, the children would have time to attend school without being too fatigued to learn the duties of their station.[15]

As Chadwick drafted the government's Bill, Lord Ashley soldiered on with the Ten Hours Bill. He stood no chance, however, with MPs awaiting the publication of the Royal Commission report. On 18 July 1833, the Ten Hours Bill went down in a heavy defeat. This was Chadwick's cue. On 9 August, the government minister Lord Althorp introduced a Bill largely devised by Chadwick. What became known as Althorp's Act stipulated that no one under nine years of age was to be employed in any kind of textile factory; children aged nine to thirteen were limited to eight-hour days; and those between thirteen and eighteen couldn't be worked for more than twelve hours a day. The youngest workers were also to attend school for at least two hours each day, and provide evidence that they had done so. Moreover, before children could be hired, parents had to produce certificates proving their age, authenticated by a doctor and countersigned by a magistrate. In addition, four inspectors were appointed to ensure the mill owners' compliance. The Bill delighted most MPs. It extended the state's protection to the youngest and most vulnerable, while in no way compromising the productivity of textile mills. The basic tenets of political economy were upheld without upsetting the market in either textiles or adult toil.[16]

The short time movement had been outflanked. Lord Ashley was now faced with the invidious choice of either conceding defeat or arguing that children aged between nine and thirteen should work *ten* hours rather than *eight*. After expressing some objections, he did the former, and *Hansard* recorded his admission that 'the noble Lord [Althorp] had completely defeated him.' On 29 August the government Bill received royal assent. Doherty, Oastler, and the other short hours men were left jaded by defeat. They complained that the Act reflected the interests of masters, not men. And the Bradford Short Time Committee was convinced that '[t]he Central Board had a Committee of large Factory Proprietors at their elbows. These Gentlemen suggested to the Central Board much of what had been passed into an Act.' This wasn't quite correct, but it had some validity. While plenty of masters did fume at the invasive powers of the new inspectorate, some were indeed pleased with Althorp's Act, though not for the reasons given by Doherty and Oastler. The masters who welcomed the Act tended to own steam-powered mills in larger towns and cities like Manchester, Salford, Stockport and Bradford. The Act's most implacable critics, in contrast, were those like the Lamberts and Needhams who operated mills in remote valleys alongside streams using waterwheels. These mills, because of their remote locations, were far more reliant on child labour, and often depended on working into the early hours of the morning to make up for time lost during dry spells when streams became shallow and languid. Urban bosses knew their business well enough to realise this, and they presumably also saw that Althorp's Act would hurt their rural competitors so badly that it would more than compensate for the inconvenience of having to organise a complex system of relays. By ensuring that the clause prohibiting night work for children was enforced, the 1833 Act promised to benefit urban mill owners very nicely indeed.[17]

In the event, Althorp's Act enjoyed fair success. It was hard for inspectors to maintain a vigilant watch over thousands of mills; but even with patchy surveillance, Ashley calculated that by the end of 1835, one in eleven mill owners had been convicted under the 1833 Act. Those bosses who had been penalised acquired a vested interest in making sure that the Act was applied universally, hence convictions and compliance increased rapidly. Yet what Chadwick gave with one hand he then unwittingly confiscated with the other. The gains accrued to the labouring classes from the 1833 Act were soon to be forfeited with the New Poor Law in 1834.[18]

In a vast and selectively compiled report written by Chadwick and another leading Benthamite, Nassau Senior, in 1834, the blame for the escalation in levels of beggary was laid squarely on the poor themselves and the Elizabethan Poor Law which had helped to degrade them. The authors received plenty of evidence to the contrary, numerous informants telling of a sudden surge in the rural population. This they blithely ignored or attributed to the old Poor Law 'improperly' keeping paupers alive long enough to reproduce. Chadwick and Senior then outlined their preconceived plan for tackling the pauper crisis, a proposal which quickly became law. The Poor Law Amendment Act of 1834 slashed outdoor relief and wage allowances. Anyone who wanted parish help now had to go to the workhouse to get it, and in order to stop workhouses silting up with the able-bodied, it was stipulated that they should be made so unpleasant that only the genuinely needy would suffer to enter. The 'less eligibility' clause meant that the regime inside had to be maintained at a level below that which the most wretched labourer could tolerate. In effect, so as to deter the idle, those in genuine need were deprived of all of life's comforts. Husbands and wives were split up, served bland food and little of it, housed in drab surroundings, and subjected to long hours of tedious labour. Over the following years, dozens of new 'union' workhouses appeared, into which thousands of forlorn men, women and children were herded.[19]

The writer Thomas Carlyle disparaged the new union workhouses as 'poor men's bastilles'. Many Tory squires also objected. One Oxford JP fumed about the 'Ministerial pack of Malthusian barbarians' and the 'cold-blooded, heartless ignorance' of the 1834 Poor Law report. But the Benthamites, articulate, analytical, irrepressibly confident, and with reams of data at their fingertips, easily trounced Radical opponents and romantic Tories in parliamentary debate. The Act's critics were reduced to facile whingeing, powerless to annul the Act or overturn the ideology of political economy. What Chadwick and Senior didn't anticipate, however, was that the 1833 Factory Act and 1834 Poor Law Amendment Act would work at cross-purposes. Failing to see that the explosion in poverty had more to do with a shortage of jobs in rural England than with laziness, viciousness or drink, they were alarmed to find that depriving poor families of outdoor relief drove more and more of them to find their children work in mills. And as parish aid was withdrawn, so the incentive increased for them to procure forged certificates of age for their young children and to make them work more than one shift every day, often in different factories.[20]

By the end of 1833, Robert Blincoe had achieved all he could for the short time cause. He had told his story often, forcefully and with commendable honesty. This wasn't all. He had also gone out of his way and risked his hard-earned savings to liberate John Doherty, the leader of Lancashire's short time movement, from gaol. In the follow-ing years he observed from the sidelines as momentum for factory reform gathered again. Working men's associations continued the fight for the Ten Hours Bill, arguing that, given the impracticalities of children and adults working different hours, those of all mill workers should be reduced. At a giant meeting in Preston, Lancashire, on 23 August 1833, they warned that unless they were heard, 'the sequel ... will be written in blood.' Richard Oastler chose words no less vitriolic. 'You are laying the foundation', he raged, 'upon which to build a nation of slaves, or a nation of criminals ... it has been reserved for the [mill owner] to out Herod Herod, in Tyranny and Cruelty! ... [their victims] have a RIGHT to take advantage of their numbers, and by force, to deprive you of your property, or of your lives!'[21]

Bitterly disappointed by the failure of Ashley's Ten Hours Bill, as Oastler's violent speech implies, within months the short time leaders were toying with more militant tactics. They conceived the plan of securing an eight-hour day by way of staging a general strike. It was a hugely ambitious proposal, but Doherty's success in bringing together the nation's spinners, and Owen's short-lived Grand National Consolidated Trades Union, did suggest that mass collective action might be possible. Owen himself began to talk of the demise of capitalism and the erection in its place of co-operative harmony between masters and men. This was all too much for Tory paternalists like Richard Oastler. He wanted social harmony, but on the terms of the landed elites. And in the event, perhaps because memories of the 1829 debacle were still too fresh in the workers' minds, the proposed strikes never came to pass.[22]

Instead, the war of words intensified. In 1835 Andrew Ure brought out his paean to the capitalist classes, *The Philosophy of Manufactures*. It was a bizarre rag-bag comprising angry polemics against short time men, dewy-eyed reflections on the paternal kindness of mill bosses, detailed descriptions of factory processes and machines, even a chapter on the microscopic structures of cotton, flax, wool and silk. Ure poured scorn on factory workers and their leaders, arguing that they complained only because their 'high wages' enabled them to 'pamper themselves into nervous ailments by a diet too rich and exciting for their in-door occupations.' As for the children, they were blessed indeed. 'They seemed to be always cheerful and alert', he wrote, 'taking pleasure in the light play of their muscles ... The work of these lively elves seemed to resemble a sport, in which habit gave them a pleasing dexterity. Conscious of their skill, they were delighted to show it off to any stranger.' As Karl Marx later pointed out, Ure's credulity when talking about the humanity of mill owners had no apparent limits.[23]

This was typical, however, of Ure's complex character. He was a man who either loved or loathed. Desperate for the public's esteem, he was in the habit of lashing out at anyone who stood in his way, and talking down to those who would stand for it. His *Philosophy of Manufactures* was produced in a spirit of keen gratitude after Ure had turned to writing about the textile industry when suffering from 'anxiety of mind and bodily fatigue', and had found several of the mill owners he visited to be most solicitous hosts. Ure's prose had little of John Brown's seething emotionality, but both men were driven by deep-seated instability to take up violently extreme positions. What Marx called Ure's 'apotheosis of large-scale industry' embarrassed even some political economists with its abject refusal to accept that mill owners might ever have overstepped the boundaries of decency.[24]

The following year, 1836, a new leader of the short time movement, John Fielden, penned a rebuttal. The owner of a mill outside Manchester and an energetic Radical MP, Fielden said it all with the title of his book, *The Curse of the Factory System*. He told of the long hours and the cruel ill-usage of children, and he refuted the suggestion that mill labour was physically undemanding for grown men and women. 'These men', he wrote, 'never rest for an instant during the hours of working … it must be obvious to every one, that it is next to impossible for any human being … to sustain this exertion for any length of time, without permanently injuring his constitution.' Fielden had investigated claims about how far a young piecer walked every day. He reckoned on about twenty miles. How many of the upper class, he wondered, would allow a 'a damsel of sixteen' to dance at a ball for more than a few hours?[25]

Doherty weighed in here too. He estimated that piecers had to walk 25 miles a day, expending as much energy as a mail-horse. This issue now assumed inordinate importance. Lord Ashley called in an actuary to make proper measurements and calculations. He settled on a distance of between 18 and 32 miles, depending on the thickness of the thread. There was nothing comical in this endeavour for the short time leaders, and Ashley risked much on being vindicated. 'If I be refuted', he announced in Parliament, 'my career as a public man is over; I could never again make a speech in the House of Commons or elsewhere. I should be proved to be as near a liar as a man can well be, short of actually dealing in falsehoods.' In this matter, at least, he carried the day.[26]

Fielden's *The Curse of the Factory System* was among the first attempts to write a proper history of the movement for factory reform. And in talking of the pioneering days of water-powered spinning, Fielden did what so many were to do after him: he discussed Blincoe's *Memoir*. 'I wish every man and woman in England', Fielden reflected, 'would see and read this pamphlet. It is published at Manchester, where the crippled subject of the memoir now lives to testify the truth of all that I have said above.' From that point onwards, Blincoe's place in the pantheon of the short time movement was assured.[27]

33

Fact into fiction

In late 1836, Charles Dickens began sketching the plot and themes of his second novel, *Oliver Twist*. The first instalment appeared in the periodical *Bentley's Miscellany* in February 1837 and the story ran for 24 months. In some ways, it's not hard to understand why Dickens wrote a book in which the action skipped from a union workhouse to a thieves' den and the drawing rooms of London's well-to-do. Dickens was drawing deeply upon his own troubled childhood. As a youth of twelve, he had been forced to labour as a poor apprentice just off the Strand, sticking labels on bottles of boot-blacking. He never overcame the 'secret agony' of the humiliating decline in his family's fortunes – caused by his father's reckless spending – which led to this grim employment; only a close friend and his wife were ever told the details of an episode that blighted his early life and left him with a deep sense of stigma.[1]

But *Oliver Twist* was far more than an exercise in literary catharsis. It was also intensely and bitingly topical. This isn't surprising, for during the mid-1830s, Dickens was employed as a parliamentary reporter for a series of newspapers: the *True Sun*, the *Mirror of Parliament*, and then the *Morning Chronicle*. Sitting up in the gallery of the House of Commons recording the debates verbatim in his famously accurate shorthand, Dickens spent long days and evenings immersed in the major social and political issues of the day. The new Poor Law, the privations of chimney sweeps, the rapacity of Poor Law officers, and the rising mendacity of the lower orders were recurrent issues, as old-school Radicals and romantic Tories battled it out with Whigs and 'liberal' Tories on the floor of the House. Dickens also observed as Sadler's Ten Hours Bill flared into prominence every few weeks from early February 1832 until the passage of Lord Althorp's

Act in 1833; and he was in all likelihood seated in the gallery on 27 June 1832 as Lord Morpeth unfurled the 'important and immense petition from the county of York', 800 yards long, despatched by Oastler and the Yorkshire short time men; as well as on numerous occasions when Michael Sadler, and later Lord Ashley, told of the unspeakable treatment of young boys and girls in factories; on the evening of 5 July 1833 when Sir Samuel Whalley declared that 'in the English factory, everything that is valuable to manhood is sacrificed in childhood', and when Joseph Brotherton pointedly asked: 'would not the Members of this House feel it a great hardship if all were required to remain in their seats during the whole day?'; and during dozens of sessions in late summer and early autumn 1833, when a series of MPs rose to their feet and quoted, with disgust, from the Royal Commission report of 1833 describing the terrible hours and abuse inflicted on so many children.[2]

Had Dickens perused a copy of Dr Hawkins's section of Chadwick's report, he would almost certainly have come across not only Blincoe's testimony, but also explicit reference to his *Memoir*. We cannot prove that he did so, but that Dickens was familiar with the matter of child labour in textile mills is revealed by several passages in his first novel, *Pickwick Papers*. Here he struck a note strongly redolent of the *Memoir*, pointing out the hypocrisy of those who expressed concern for the welfare of African slaves while being callously indifferent to the sufferings of children in mills. Lampooning the commercial classes of Muggletown, Dickens wrote: 'no fewer than one thousand four hundred and twenty petitions' had been presented to Parliament 'against the continuation of negro slavery abroad, and an equal number against any interference with the factory system at home.' Dickens also highly approved of Lord Ashley's efforts, writing in 1838: 'With that nobleman's most benevolent and excellent exertions, and with the evidence which he was the means of bringing forward, I am well acquainted.' It may be that the reports of the early 1830s, including the *Memoir*, initiated this education. And had he read of Blincoe's life, the themes of parochial brutality, sweated labour and the horror of poor apprenticeships would have spoken directly to his own experiences.[3]

We cannot, though, assume that Dickens needed Blincoe's *Memoir* in order to be able to write *Oliver Twist*. A pre-existing loathing for the 1834 Poor Law certainly encouraged him to write a literary censure of the cruelties it unleashed. And, politically speaking, Dickens would have had little truck with free-thinking Paineites such as Richard Carlile or fiery trades unionists like John Doherty. Nevertheless, the parallels between the early chapters of *Oliver Twist* and Blincoe's story are too strong to be casually passed over. The abandonment of a child to a workhouse, a parish orphan with genteel forbears, a close shave with a master sweep, and a flight from apprentice masters – these aren't wholly singular themes in novels of the day, but it's striking that in both *Oliver Twist* and Blincoe's *Memoir* they are all brought within the compass of a single work. In many ways, *Oliver Twist* reads as an embellishment of a true account of a parish boy's progress written over a decade before by a journalist of Radical hue.

If Charles Dickens did take ideas and inspiration from the *Memoir*, we are left with the question of why he did not set the later parts of Oliver Twist's life in a secluded cotton-spinning mill alongside a fictional river in northern England. Assuming that he did read the *Memoir*, this isn't hard to account for. In 1836 Dickens had only a meagre knowledge of manufacturing towns and of the technological revolution of the previous half-century. And yet he was a novelist who nearly always carried out scrupulous research. Fanciful as some of the coincidences in his novels may have been, when it came to matters of fact, Dickens was a harsh self-disciplinarian. Needing a bad-tempered magistrate for *Oliver Twist*, he went to Hatton Garden court to observe a notorious example in action. When the writing of *Hard Times* called for a detailed description of a strike, he travelled to Preston to witness one. Similarly, Squeers, the pedagogical monster in *Nicholas Nickleby*, was closely based on a schoolmaster found during a fact-finding mission to Yorkshire. So, given that he lacked the time to travel to remote mills in the Peak District in 1836 and 1837, even had Dickens read the *Memoir*, it would not have been his style to follow his parish orphan there.[4]

It was only in 1838, encouraged by Lord Ashley's efforts, that Dickens ventured into some of Manchester's cotton mills. After a journey through 'miles of cinder paths, and blazing furnaces, and roaring steam engines, and such a mass of dirt, gloom, and misery as I never before witnessed', he then decided to 'strike the heaviest blow in my power for these unfortunate creatures.' That Dickens never fulfilled this promise – except in a watered-down form in *Hard Times* – was probably due to the fact that he felt too great a pride in the achievements of English manufacturers to bear mill owners the same malice as he did parish beadles, master sweeps or senile magistrates. He was, as the artist and critic John Ruskin said, a member of the 'steam-whistle party'. Feelings of ambivalence towards the factory age would also have led Dickens to shy away from incorporating the later sections of the *Memoir* into *Oliver Twist*. He wanted villains whose come-uppances couldn't be seen to jeopardise national prosperity.[5]

Dickens chose not to satirise rich manufacturers. But there were plenty of other writers for whom Britain's status as the world's leading economic power could not be enjoyed so long as it depended on the forced sacrifices of thousands of innocent children. Dickens had, moreover, created a vogue for stories of the vulnerable child deprived of the warmth of family and the safeguards of gentility. It was now only a matter of time before a story like *Oliver Twist* was set in the factory milieu. The moment came in late 1837.

In February of that year, just as the serialisation of *Oliver Twist* began, the Short Time Committees of Lancashire and Yorkshire mounted a new drive to get a Ten Hours Bill through Parliament. Their efforts soon miscarried. The younger Robert Peel, having little of his father's sympathy for factory reform, pressured Lord Ashley into abandoning his Bill, at least for the present. So, instead, his lordship devoted his time to extra-parliamentary campaigns. He helped those injured by unfenced machines to gain redress in courts of law, and he gave whatever assistance he could to those willing to expose the evils of child labour. One of those he assisted was a talented essayist and novelist called Frances Trollope.[6]

'Fanny' hadn't intended to be a writer, but she had married a lacklustre barrister who threw away the family's money on a crazy farming venture, and in 1827 the Trollopes were holed up in a run-down farmhouse in Hertfordshire. At this point, determined to do her best by her children, Fanny sailed for America with her eldest son and two daughters to help them make a new life in a utopian community in Tennessee. Four years later they returned to England. The trip had been a disaster. Disappointed but boundlessly energetic, at the age of 50 Fanny wrote a book entitled *Domestic Manners of the Americans*. It ridiculed Americans as hypocrites, full of lofty talk of liberty and rights, but in reality little more than selfish and uncouth money-grubbers. Outrageous and unfair yet funny and entertaining, the book was a huge publishing success. Fanny became a 'literary lioness' and the family's finances revived. Within a few years, however, they had to flee the country to escape a new set of creditors. In Europe, both Fanny's husband and eldest son died.[7]

In 1836 Fanny moved back to England and resumed writing. *Jonathon Jefferson Whitlaw* and *The Vicar of Wrexhill* were both highly successful. As novels they were lightly written and melo-dramatic – Fanny aimed to appeal to the low-brow subscribers to circulating libraries – but they weren't the romantic throwaways of much female fiction of the period. Fanny Trollope insisted on dealing with divisive themes like slavery and evangelical religion, and she did so with such creativity and wit that Dickens reckoned her to be serious competition. William Makepeace Thackeray later noted: 'I do not care to read ladies' novels, except those of Mesdames Gore and Trollope.' Backhanded or not, it was high praise.[8]

With a journalistic eye for the topic of the moment, in early 1837 Fanny followed as the short hour movement flickered into life again, only to be doused by the younger Robert Peel. Fanny, as her son Tom later recalled, had taken 'a great interest in the then-hoped for factory legislation, and in Lord Shaftesbury's [Lord Ashley's] efforts in that direction' and she seized on the idea of writing 'a novel on the subject with the hope of doing something towards attracting the public mind to the question.' Having resolved to do so, Fanny made arrangements for visiting Lancashire and its mills, 'for the purpose of obtaining accurate information and local details.' Lord Ashley, forgiving Fanny her slights against evangelicals in *The Vicar of Wrexhill*, agreed to meet her and Tom. A short while later, the Trollopes travelled north by mail train, 'incognito', with 'a number of introductions from Lord Shaftesbury to a rather strange assortment of persons ... energetic agitators in favour of legislation.' His lordship parted with the words: 'They will show you the secrets of the place, as they showed them to me.' For, despite Southey's warnings, Ashley too had now visited a cotton-spinning mill. The experience, while heart-rending, had fortified his belief in the short hours campaign.[9]

Having toured the Manchester district, Fanny and Tom then headed eastwards for neighbouring Yorkshire. There, Oastler's height and bearing prompted Tom to dub him 'the Danton of the movement'. Parson Bull escorted them round the mills and slums of Bradford, and they drove out to 'a miserable little chapel, filled to suffocation', where restless workers heard the Methodist preacher Joseph Rayner Stephens sermonise on the iniquities of the factory system. Stephens's fiery rhetoric, seditious and violent, was soon to land him in Chester gaol; but it was great copy for a southern novelist who had never heard its like.[10]

While in Lancashire, Fanny and Tom had invited John Doherty for dinner in their opulent Manchester hotel. He was at first reluctant to enter a place of such conspicuous privilege. In getting him to accept, the Trollopes had to assuage his fears that he would be out of place or that his critics would call him a class apostate. Perhaps through nervous excitement, Doherty then spoke volubly and passionately from the first to last course, hardly touching his meal. Tom didn't record what Doherty said, but in all likelihood he spent some of his time discoursing on the horrors of Robert Blincoe's existence at Lowdham and Litton mills. It's even possible that Fanny and Tom tracked Blincoe down to his Turner Street address during their stay in Manchester. What's certain is that they left the city with a copy of Blincoe's *Memoir* in Doherty's pamphlet form. We know this because large swathes of the novel that Fanny now wrote derived their inspiration from this real-life parish boy's experiences.[11]

Back in London, Fanny contracted with Henry Colburn, owner and publisher of the *New Monthly Magazine*, to write twelve instalments of an industrial novel, each of which would sell for a shilling. In return, she received a hefty £800. Fanny's prose was evidently in very high demand, for few other contemporary authors ever commanded such sums. The first part of Fanny's novel, *The Life and Adventures of Michael Armstrong, the Factory Boy*, came out in March 1839. As Blincoe surely learned, *Michael Armstrong* was profoundly indebted to his very own *Memoir*.[12]

The novel begins at the rural mansion of a wealthy cotton magnate,

Sir Michael Dowling, whose burning ambition is to be accepted by the local gentry. To this end, he plays down the shabby source of his fortune and lives some miles from his cotton-spinning factory. Although married, he also relishes the opportunity of flirting with any heiresses willing to accept his overdone hospitality. During a brief turn in his park with a titled but penniless Scot, Lady Clarissa Shrimpton, they encounter a harmless old cow in their path. Acting the white knight, Dowling pretends that they are in mortal danger. Seeing the commotion, a ragged young boy, who turns out to be Michael Armstrong, one of Dowling's ill-paid mill hands, shoos the cow away. Lady Clarissa proclaims him a hero and Dowling, determined to impress her ladyship, promises to bring up Michael as if he were a son of his own.

The nine-year-old Michael leaves his sick mother and crippled brother, Edward, and moves into the Dowling mansion. There, he's treated with utter contempt. A wealthy neighbour, Mary Brotherton, whose deceased father had also been a factory owner, perceives Michael's sufferings and, through her eyes, the reader discovers what Wordsworth called 'bondage lurking under shape of good'. Sick of having to play the benefactor, Dowling eventually apprentices Michael to a cotton mill in Deep Valley, where he is entrusted to the care of Ellgood Sharpton, a wicked master who beats, starves and overworks his apprentices. Knowing that there's always a ready supply of work'us children, Ellgood thinks nothing of letting them die of basic wants. After a long search, Mary discovers that Michael has been sent to Deep Valley. When she locates the mill, however, she is misinformed that he has died from fever. So Mary instead rescues his young companion, a fellow factory slave called Fanny Fletcher. She then also adopts Michael's crippled brother Edward and takes both him and Fanny across to the continent.

In Germany Michael, alive after all, eventually tracks them down, and within a few years all three children grow into educated and polished gentlefolk. The novel ends with a pair of marriages: not only do Michael and Fanny tie the knot, but despite the disparity in their ages, so do Edward and Mary. To complete the tidying up, we also learn that Dowling's mill went bust and that, his cruel master having died a bankrupt, Michael uncynically offered to pay for a decent burial.[13]

Fanny Trollope had been deeply moved by the weeks she spent in the north, but some of the pain she had witnessed there had a familiar aspect. One of the book's central themes is the tragedy of a mother being unable to protect her own offspring. Fanny saw that this applied to many a labouring family, and, having feared for her own children during times of poverty and sickness, she readily identified. In this sense, *Michael Armstrong* contains plenty of unconscious self-reflection which lends the novel a heavy and rather earnest tone. The novel has more obvious flaws: its plot is often absurd, some lead characters are mere caricatures, and few mills of the decade were quite as wretched as Deep Valley. There are, however, plenty of powerful scenes, and Fanny wrote movingly of a factory system which was 'horribly destructive of every touch of human feelings' and led to the exploitation of the 'low-priced agony of labouring infants'. *Michael Armstrong* was also richly illustrated. Most of the drawings were from the pen of a French artist and close family friend, Auguste Hervieu. His gruesome pictures complemented the often lurid descriptions of conditions at Deep Valley's mill.[14]

When Charles Dickens heard of Fanny's latest offering he seethed with annoyance. His trip to the industrial north around Christmas 1838 had probably been designed to supply him with material for *Nicholas Nickleby*, of which he still had nearly two-thirds left to write. Having been revolted by the interiors of cotton mills, Dickens wrote to a friend saying that he would turn his fury on mill owners in 'the "Nickleby", or wait some other opportunity.' *Michael Armstrong* scotched any possibility of his talking of the darker side of factory labour in *Nicholas Nickleby*, and he settled instead for presenting the Cheeryble brothers as model factory employers. But Dickens clearly disliked the direction of his novels being determined by third parties, and he wrote to a friend in the highest dudgeon: 'if Mrs Trollope were even to adopt Ticholas Tickleby as being a better-sounding name than Michael Armstrong, I don't think it would cost me a wink of sleep, or impair my appetite in the smallest degree.' Dickens was a famous man, but he feared that *Michael Armstrong* would undercut the sales of *Nicholas Nickleby*. Still aggrieved several weeks later, Dickens wrote to another friend: 'I will express no further opinion of Mrs Trollope, than that I think Mr Trollope must have been an old dog and chosen his wife from the same species.'[15]

Wider reaction to Fanny's latest novel was predictably extreme. Whatever they thought of the book's literary qualities, advocates of factory and political reform relished it. *Michael Armstrong* brought the hardships of child labour and the greed of the capitalist classes into tens of thousands of middle-class drawing rooms in a way that no parliamentary report ever could. Innumerable respectable ladies and gentlemen found themselves reading of English children, Christians all, fighting for turnip scraps, working obscene hours, and being subjected to gratuitous violence. This wasn't usual fare for serialised stories, least of all those written by women. Fanny managed to place before well-to-do readers an unremitting attack on the mill-owning *arriviste*, or what one of her characters damned as 'base-born spinning spiders!'[16]

Two generous reviews appeared in the *New Monthly Magazine*. This was, not coincidentally, owned by the book's publisher, Henry Colburn. The few other journals that reviewed it were less than gushing. The reviewer for the *Athenaeum* could wait only for the sixth episode before going on the offensive. Seditious tracts like *Michael Armstrong* belonged in the gutter, not in the homes of the decent, he claimed; it had to be condemned before it demoralised and corrupted. And this reviewer genuinely feared that Fanny's novel would fan the flames of political disaffection. The timing of the book's publication is significant. Large sections of the working classes in 1839 initiated a massive campaign, dubbed Chartism after the 'charter' of demands that its leaders drew up, calling for the extension of the electoral franchise to all free-born Englishmen. To Fanny's many critics, this was no time for literary ladies to start pouring fuel on the fire. The upper classes might dislike 'incurably ill-bred' self-made men every bit as much as Fanny Trollope did, but a master was a master and a servant had to accept his lot. From their point of view, she was encouraging working-class unrest, even insurrection.[17]

As its many readers appreciated, *Michael Armstrong* was a frontal attack on the factory system itself. It laid the blame for the deaths and cruel treatment of innocents squarely at the feet of the industrialists themselves. Thus Fanny made Sir Michael Dowling an utterly irredeemable torturer of children. Talking of his harsh treatment of young Michael, he says: 'The long and the short of it is, that I can't keep my hands off him.' Only the strong arm of the law would have any effect on a human being aptly described by Mary Brotherton as a 'MONSTER!' Furthermore, where most middle-class essayists and novelists, and even many Radicals, argued that the onus was on poor men and women to rise above their hardships through temperance and hard graft, Fanny implied that doing one's best simply wasn't enough. It required legislative action, she argued, to protect young children from lucre-loving capitalists. Hence *Michael Armstrong* was seen as a serious threat to an embattled social order. The *Athenaeum* warned that the book was 'scattering firebrands among the people', with every prospect of over-excited workers setting 'fire to the four quarters of the kingdom'. Fanny was sensitive to these rebukes, and she was perturbed to learn that the Chartists were the book's biggest fans. Unsettled, she soon ditched her planned sequel.[18]

R.H. Hone, author of *A New Spirit of the Age*, turned his caustic wit upon her. 'Mrs Trollope', he wrote, 'takes a strange delight in the hideous and revolting. Nothing can exceed the vulgarity of Mrs Trollope's mob of characters. We have heard it urged on behalf of Mrs Trollope that her novels are, at all events, drawn from life. So are sign paintings.' This was mild compared to the *Bolton Free Press*, whose readers, many of them either mill owners or investors in mills, stood to lose most from the sympathies which *Michael Armstrong* had whipped up among the metropolitan middle classes. Its reviewer railed:

> The author of Michael Armstrong deserves as richly to have eighteen months in Chester Gaol as any that are now there for using violent language against 'the monster cotton mills'.

But what most stuck in the craw of the Bolton reviewer were Hervieu's picaresque illustrations. One in particular caught his attention:

> [I]f the text be bad, still worse are the plates that illustrate it. What, for instance, must be the effect of the first picture in No. VI (mill children competing with pigs for food), on the heated imaginations of our great manufacturing towns, figuring as they do in every book-seller's window.

Figure 21. An illustration from Frances Trollope's novel *Michael Armstrong*, showing the pauper apprentices of a cotton mill struggling over scraps left for the owner's pigs. This scene was based directly on Blincoe's experiences at Litton Mill.

What had been for Robert Blincoe a secret and degrading battle with Ellis Needham's well-fed pigs had graduated to the pages of a widely-read narrative of shocking factory abuse.[19]

The parallels between Blincoe and Armstrong run deep. The novel begins with Dowling's announcement that Michael 'is to be made a gentleman of' and taught the trade of 'stocking weaving', falsehoods with strong overtones of the sham promises used to win the acquiescence of Blincoe and his fellow work'us children in 1799. But Fanny also lifted a number of episodes directly from John Brown's account. She includes a scene, based on Blincoe's first evenings at Lowdham and Litton mills, in which a rank dinner of water porridge and sour, musty 'oaten cake' is interrupted by 'a master of ceremonies' brandishing 'a huge horsewhip', followed by the entrance of dozens of 'filthy, half-starved wretches' who lap up the food that the newcomers can't stomach. The passage in *Michael Armstrong* in which its hero approaches Deep Valley mill, on his way to a spot 'effectually hidden from the eyes of all men', is clearly based on Brown's gothic account of Blincoe's arrival at Litton Mill. And where Brown told of the starving apprentices eating oatmeal doled out as a substitute for soap, Fanny describes how 'the coarse meal' given out to the apprentices of Deep Valley in place of soap is 'invariably swallowed, being far too precious in the eyes of the hungry children to be applied to the purpose for which it was designed.' Likewise, Blincoe's war of wits with the pigs, strikingly portrayed by Hervieu, inspired in *Michael Armstrong* a long and graphic account of 'the contest between the fierce snouts of angry pigs, and the active fingers of the wretched crew.'

Perhaps most strikingly, Fanny plucked from the *Memoir* its description of how a 'contagious fever' tore through the mill. Here the novel is little but an elaboration of the *Memoir*. Fanny tells of how vinegar is sprinkled on the floor of the 'prentice house; a local physician recommends nothing but decent food; and the canny Ellgood Sharpton allays suspicions by dividing the burials between the graveyards of 'Tugswell [i.e. Tideswell] and Meddison'. And later in the story, Michael is restored to health thanks to plenty of 'kitchen physic', Blincoe's own choice phrase. In addition, Deep Valley itself is obviously inspired by Miller's Dale. Ellgood Sharpton is quite clearly Ellis Needham, and the denouement involving Dowling's bankruptcy is also based on Needham's fate. Indeed, it was almost certainly with the *Memoir*, its subject, Robert Blincoe, and publisher, John Doherty, in mind that Fanny wrote in her account of Deep Valley:[20]

The real name of this valley (which most assuredly is no creation of romance) is not given, lest an action for libel should be the consequence. The scenes which have passed there, and which the few following pages will describe, have been stated to the author on authority not to be impeached.[21]

Even if many of Fanny's own class detested her evocation of factory life, her publisher Henry Colburn had nothing to regret when he reviewed his yearly accounts. In both serial and book form, *Michael Armstrong* fully justified the 'long price' of £800 he had paid. Unlike *Oliver Twist*, Fanny's novel did soon disappear from view. Her *Domestic Manners of the Americans* is the only one of her books to have survived the vagaries of fashion. But at the time, *Michael Armstrong* made a loud and violent splash, and it also helped to inspire an entire genre of industrial fiction. In 1828 and then 1832, Blincoe's *Memoir* had not travelled far beyond the working-men's libraries, tenements and two-up-two-downs of the industrial north. But courtesy of Fanny Trollope, some of his harshest experiences now reached tens of thousands of readers spread across the country. Few were aware that they were reading episodes from Blincoe's life, but in fictional form his story helped to galvanise public outrage about the treatment of young children in textile factories. And the moral authority invoked by novelists, politicians, Short Time Committees, working men and women, newspapers, free-thinkers, trades unionists, plus a sizeable number of capitalists and clergymen, helped to ensure that on 8 June 1847 Parliament finally passed Sadler's and Ashley's Ten Hours Bill.[22]

34

A pleasant retirement

By a cruel twist of fate, Lord Ashley had lost his seat in Parliament by the time that the Ten Hours Bill passed into law. This in no way diminished his joy on hearing the news. 'Praised be the Lord, praised be the Lord, in Christ Jesus', he enthused to his diary. After more than 30 years of campaigning, all within Robert Blincoe's lifetime, the Short Time Committees had finally pulled off their coup. Both adults and children would now labour in the nation's thousands of textile mills for no more than ten hours per day. Times had truly changed. Attempts by the mill owners' faction to derail Ashley's Bill had been successful as recently as 1844. Then, just three years later, opposition to factory reform had been trounced by Commons and Lords alike. Despite mill owners having predicted the demise of the textile trade in 1802, 1816, 1819, 1825 and 1833, orders for fabrics and yarn had only increased. Not even wages had fallen. Unsurprisingly, the manufacturers' well-rehearsed arguments looked rather threadbare by the 1840s, and in June 1847 Parliament signalled its impatience. Confounding the mill owners' dire predictions, the textile industry survived once more.[1]

By then, Lord Ashley had also managed to secure legislative protection for chimney sweeps and young children labouring down mines. And in his later years, as the seventh Earl of Shaftesbury, he would advance schemes for reducing homelessness among young boys and tackling the unsanitary conditions of England's cities. Despite a long series of successes, he never shed the personal doubts and insecurities of his youth, and the early deaths of three of his six children intensified his private grief. Yet Lord Ashley remained politically active until the end. Admired and celebrated as the 'poor man's earl', he was buried with due pomp and ceremony in Westminster Abbey in October 1885.

John Doherty's moment passed far sooner. He played a key role in establishing the Grand National Consolidated Trades Union of February 1834. Thereafter he receded from public view. For another decade he remained active in working-class movements, and he maintained the shop on Withy Grove. But when he died in 1854, he had been largely forgotten. His decision to reprint the *Memoir* had lifted Robert Blincoe out of obscurity. Paradoxically, now Doherty was to be remembered, if at all, as the publisher of this timeless work.[2]

Richard Oastler lived on far longer in the minds of friends and foes, but his personal life deteriorated. As the violence of his rhetoric intensified, his employer, the squire of Fixby Hall, dismissed him from his post and sued him for running up debts. From December 1840, Oastler spent three-and-a-half years in the misery of the Fleet gaol. Eventually his friends and admirers set up an 'Oastler liberation fund', which raised an enormous £2,500 by the end of 1843. John Fielden then chipped in the outstanding sum, and Oastler walked free. Living on a small income provided through the generosity of his friends, for several years Oastler went on expounding his vision of 'Christian Tory Democracy', but gaol had sapped his earlier confidence and élan. He died in 1861, not forgotten but now remote from the main currents of popular radicalism.[3]

As for Blincoe, his period of political activism had come to a close soon after he gave evidence to Dr Hawkins in the York Hotel. In 1839, albeit in the guise of a fictional character, he had again risen to public prominence. It was to be the last time. Over the remaining 21 years of his life, Blincoe left few recoverable traces. Trade directories do, though, give us a sense of his increasing prosperity. He continued to run his waste cotton business in Turner Street, but the Blincoes soon moved to 23 Garden Street in Ardwick, 'an elegant suburb' with a smattering of parks and fields. Here they joined the nightly exodus of those who could afford to escape the grime and odours of the great city itself. By 1843 they had moved again, this time to nearby Bellevue Street on Hyde Road, close to the new zoological gardens. These were no slum properties; in fact, the Blincoes were living in some comfort.

But the 1843 reference is the last mention of the family in the city's directories. It seems that around the age of 50, Blincoe retired. His crooked limbs and damaged lungs would probably no longer suffer him working long hours bent over machines.[4]

Parish bastards who beat the odds by living to old age invariably worked until they dropped, or finished their lives amid the calculated squalor of one of the new union workhouses. Blincoe, as he had striven so hard to do, had broken the cycle. He spent his last years an independent man who could look back with considerable pride on a successful business career. Knock-knees and scars were now the only signs to strangers that Blincoe had not always known what it was to eat until full, to live in a warm house, or to wear more than rags and coarse shirts.

By great good fortune, a photograph of Blincoe has survived from his last years. It's an enlightening portrait. What little hair he had left was combed down over his ears. A rather wiry beard fringed his face, and his head – as in Keeling's 1832 woodcut – was out of proportion to his diminutive upper body. Blincoe's slender shoulders likewise indicated a history of severe childhood malnutrition. But, again as in Keeling's cruder portrait, we see here a man of modest affluence. Photographic portraits weren't cheap, and so Blincoe wore his Sunday best to the sitting. It says much that he could now afford a black silk cravat and a clean, starched white shirt under an expensive-looking black double-breasted suit, presumably tailored to fit his distorted physique.[5]

Even though exposure time had now been reduced to two or three seconds, greatly lessening the risk of blurring, smiling still wasn't deemed appropriate for portraits. Blincoe's face, however, has a care-worn look rather than the blank expressions assumed by most sitters of the age. His mouth set straight, his gaze unfocused and his left hand clasping his ear, Blincoe looks awkwardly out of place. It's not hard to guess why. His body wore too many traces of abuse, alienation and neglect for him to relish having his likeness taken with a 'warts and all' technology like photography. With a reflex movement, perhaps, he raised his hand to one of his ears as the photographer exposed his plate, hiding the heavy scarring dating from Litton Mill days.

The position of Blincoe's hand helps us to date his portrait. Before the early 1850s, commercial photographers took daguerreotypes or calotypes, both of which involved long exposure times. The fact that Blincoe's arm is unblurred in the photograph shows that it was taken using the collodion, or wet-plate, process, devised by Englishman Frederick Archer in 1851. This method produced a negative image in seconds as opposed to minutes. Blincoe must therefore have been in his late 50s or early 60s when his portrait was taken. It was a memento for posterity of a man who knew his days were running out.

These were years in which, having progressed as far as he was able, Blincoe transferred his hopes and aspirations to his children; and so the conclusion to his story leads us into the lives of Ruth, Martha and Robert junior. Their successes were the consummation of his own. Of the three, Ruth's life was the least remarkable. Aside from a period of time spent with her brother in London, she ran the grocer's along-side her mother and later established a coffee-house or tea-room. Martha's fortunes make a dramatic contrast. At the age of sixteen she wed George Parker, Esquire, the owner of a local cotton mill. One assumes that George was a humane employer, but it was an excep-tional match from a dynastic point of view. It catapulted Martha from the modest comfort of the petit bourgeoisie to the opulence of the upper middle class. An oil painting of 1854 gives an idea of the pros-perity she had married into. In approved style, Martha and George are pictured in their drawing room with their three young children close by. A large satin drape hangs behind, setting off the richness of the furnishings and the fine dresses of the two daughters, both dainty and demure in white. Presumably hung in the Parkers' drawing room, the painting was an emblem of their wealth and respectability.[6]

By 1860, Martha, George and the children had moved into Bank House on Gunco Lane in Macclesfield. A contemporary photograph of their new abode shows a plain but expansive house, painted white, with several ladies, all attired in high Victorian fashion, sitting outside on a winter or early spring day, as a maid rocks a baby in a pram. Even the wildest of imaginations would have found it hard to believe that the elegant lady of the house was the daughter of a parish bastard. One supposes that Martha seldom volunteered information about her genealogy, but it would seem that she did at least tell her own children. We can't say if she did so with a sense of awe at what he had accomplished, but in this branch of the family Robert's childhood became part of their oral heritage. When writing his autobiography at the end of a long and distinguished career, Martha's grandson, the Shakespeare scholar G.B. Harrison, spoke of Blincoe's story with conspicuous pride.[7]

Of Blincoe's three children, the life of his son Robert is the best documented and the most revealing. Robert's life had, of course, begun inauspiciously. Immediately before or after his birth, his father was confined in a debtors' gaol. There followed a period of extreme privation, but the Blincoes got through it, and by the time his father was giving evidence to Dr Hawkins in 1833, Robert the younger was attending day school. Not until the 1870s did schooling become compulsory for all children in Britain; before at least mid-century, many offspring of labouring parents never saw the inside of a school-room. If they received any instruction at all, it tended to take place once a week at Sunday School. What little they learned there fitted them for reflex obedience and sweated labour, and not much besides. Manchester, by now the nation's second city, also had scores of third-rate or worse schools run by clergymen, poor spinsters or men with dubious qualifications. Such schools were tailored to working-class families with aspirations for their children to work somewhere more salubrious than mills, foundries, mines and forges, and who had a few pence to spare each week. Sons of small manufacturers like Robert Blincoe might be sent there before being apprenticed to a local trade at the age of twelve or thirteen.

But the Blincoes aimed higher, and thanks to the profits from their shop and cotton businesses, they could afford to give their son a better start. Robert obviously excelled at the school he attended in the out-skirts of Manchester, for during the late 1830s his father secured for him a place at Manchester's Free Grammar School, situated in Long Millgate on the banks of the River Irk in the heart of the old city. From then onwards, as he settled into a comfortable retirement, Blincoe observed with profound satisfaction as his son Robert achieved social and intellectual successes beyond anything he could have hoped for. Robert Blincoe's story leads us into a world utterly beyond his father's experience or comprehension.[8]

PART 6

The View from Retirement

The intentions of the founder had been altered, or at all events amplified, and instead of educating the 'poore of my home', he now educated the upper middle classes of England.

E.M. Forster, *The Longest Journey* (1907)

[T]he greatest felicity that age and worth can know – the contemplation of the happiness of those on whom the warmest affections and tenderest cares of a well-spent life have been unceasingly bestowed.

Charles Dickens, *Oliver Twist* (1837–8)

35

Another world

Manchester Grammar School had been established in 1515 by Hugh Oldham to fulfil his hope that the 'pregnant wit' of children born into Lancashire's unruly lower and middle orders could be converted into 'virtue, cunning, erudition, literature, and … good manners.' This laudable scheme was funded by a tax levied on malt ground in Manchester's mills, so that, for every sip of beer paid for by the locals, a small sum went towards maintaining the school and paying its masters. In return, the Grammar School had an open-door policy, and to ensure that poor boys like Robert Blincoe didn't feel too out of place among the sons of the gentry, Oldham wisely forbade any distinction in dress. He also provided scholarships for hard-up boys. In practice, it wasn't possible to abolish caste completely from the school. Since the children of impecunious labouring families arrived at the school with low levels of literacy, they had to spend their first years being taught by a 'poor scholar', presumably paid a pittance for the task. Even so, for centuries the school provided an entrée into a respectable vocation for some local boys. Among them was Joshua Brookes, the irascible cleric who had joined Robert and Martha in matrimony.[1]

By the early 1800s, the school comprised a subterranean Lower School, teaching elementary literacy to boys from humbler families who would quit education at the age of eleven or twelve, and a well-lit Upper School, over which the Usher and High Master presided. The boys in the Upper School learned mostly Latin and Greek grammar, poetry and prose, essential for those hoping to attend university or to acquire the polish that marked out the gentleman. Many of these boys were boarders who lodged in the Master's house. And since it cost money to board, most of them were the sons of well-heeled families from rural Lancashire and surrounding counties. By 1800 the social gap between the Lower and Upper Schools was such that Thomas De Quincey reminisced: 'As the access to [the] plebeian school lay downwards through long flights of steps, I never found surplus energy enough [to visit it].' The boys in the Upper School, if this famous opium eater is a reliable guide, relished a sense of social superiority over the poor boys in the vault below.[2]

By the early 1800s, however, an institution that reflected the social order of old England, and had become a bastion of Toryism, found itself uncomfortably out of place in the heartland of the new industrial economy. As capitalists and skilled artisans assumed more authority in city affairs, the running of the school came under heavy fire. The sons of the city's multitude of masters, artisans, tradesmen and shop-keepers needed a free education, but instead most of the money derived from the malt tax went on fitting up rich boys, often from outside the county, for the 'learned professions'. The school that Robert entered in the 1830s was a battleground in the bitter feud between Manchester old and new, a conflict which pitted the city's burgeoning commercial class, led by men of talent, drive and frustrated political ambition, against the traditional elites, families with their prestige invested in land, inherited money and genteel bloodlines. The school's governors, or feoffees, were hopelessly out of step with the entrepreneurial spirit of a great industrial city. Old-school Tories and Anglicans, they found industry distasteful, and several had applauded the slaughter of Peterloo in 1819.[3]

In 1833, after a long legal wrangle, the Master and feoffees bowed to pressure and set up a Commercial School, where a teacher provided free instruction in 'English, Arithmetic, Mathematics and French' to the sons of local artisans and small manufacturers. The idea was that children from the lower middle classes would receive a rudimentary but useful education over two or three years before embarking on an apprenticeship in their early teens. The Commercial School promised to make the sons of spinners into clerks in banks and counting houses. But the city's Radicals weren't appeased. As they pointed out, the majority of school funds were still being expended on providing a few already well-off boys with a virtually free education, plus handsome scholarships to Oxford or Cambridge universities. As the Wigan MP Richard Potter said in 1833, for the amount spent on 'teaching 150 boys Latin and Greek' the school could 'have been teaching 3,000 children more useful subjects.'[4]

Against the grain of social expectations, young Robert Blincoe was sent not to the new Commercial School but to the Upper School, where he would receive a classical schooling alongside the sons of respectable farmers, professionals and clergymen. Going to the Upper School meant that he would receive a privileged education at little cost, but a knowledge of Homer, Sophocles and Cicero would be of no use to him if he needed to find work as a clerk. Robert and Martha were taking a heavy gamble on him managing to go on from grammar school to university. They perhaps didn't realise what a parlous state the school had fallen into. With the income from the local malt mills declining steeply as more and more merchants did their grinding out of town to avoid the school tax, a decision in the Court of Chancery in the 1830s then forbade the granting of university scholarships or exhibitions to boarders. This reduced the number of rich boys going to the school, in turn slashing the masters' salaries and sapping their morale. Three High Masters resigned in five years.[5]

Robert received most of his instruction from two men: the High Master, the Reverend Nicholas Germon, and his Usher, Richard Thompson. The quality of their pedagogy left much to be desired. Germon's imposing figure and stern manner won obedience and a fair amount of respect, but 'Old Tommy' Thompson was so short-sighted that he could see only through a thick, square-shaped eye-glass. For most of the lesson time, 'the doings of the boys were quite outside his ken.' Many slipped out of the schoolroom and into the playground.[6]

It can't have been easy for boys of modest means like Robert to assume the relaxed air of social superiority that came naturally to the sons of gentlemen. The school magazine of the period, *The New Microcosm*, brims with the conceit of the landed class. In poems and short stories, manufacturers were portrayed as boorish tyrants, and the aristocracy as the natural leaders and protectors of the poor. Perhaps it was in order for Robert to feel less alien in such company that in 1840 his father gave him a gold watch, an emphatic symbol of worldly success. But if Robert did experience angst about his social roots, it in no way detracted from his studies.[7]

Every year the pick of the crop from the Upper School went to either Oxford or Cambridge universities. Most of these boys – usually the sons of doctors, lawyers, clergymen and sundry government officials – were destined to take holy orders, after which they would spend long careers shimmying up the greasy pole of the ecclesiastical hierarchy. These scholarships usually went to the Master's boarders, but that was before middle-class politicians turned on the school's feoffees. Among their sworn detractors was Mark Philips, MP. Arch-advocate of the bourgeois ethos of 'letting-things-alone', Philips inveighed against everything that the elder Blincoe stood for. Any suggestion that hours of factory labour for children be shortened he had condemned as an unconscionable blow against English trade and commercial freedom. But Philips was to do Blincoe junior a rather good turn. It was largely through his politicking that the Court of Chancery had denied scholarships to the school's boarders. While this caused a drop in the standard of teaching as masters fretted about the drop in their incomes, it also provided opportunities for day boys in the Upper School. Many of Robert's richer peers were put out of the running.[8]

The procedure for assigning scholarships was for a master, in this case Richard Thompson, to examine students following guidelines laid down by the relevant university. The master would then confer the school's one remaining scholarship on the young man who showed the greatest learning and intellectual virtuosity. In 1844 just two students went on to university from Manchester Grammar School. Only one was judged fit both to attend Cambridge University and to receive the school's scholarship. This was the younger Robert Blincoe.[9]

In late 1844, Robert exchanged the smog, grime and frenetic energy of industrial Manchester for the cloistered calm of Queens' College, Cambridge. He was destined to become an Anglican clergyman, a member of the most serious of the Victorian age's 'higher profes-sions'. There was to be no mill work or even bank clerking for him. Robert was to embrace a gentleman's calling, and over the next four years at Cambridge he was to rub shoulders with future prime ministers, statesmen, archbishops and leading scientific thinkers. For the son of a work'us bastard to find his way into an elite university was so rare a phenomenon as almost to defy belief. One can scarcely imagine the intensity of the delight experienced by Robert senior and Martha. Perhaps they also felt anxiety that their son would no longer respect his uneducated parents; but for weeks following Robert's acceptance by Queens', and when they provided the several shillings he needed to buy copies of *Ajax* by Sophocles, Cicero's works and Euclid's *Geometry*, pride must surely have thrust aside all other emotions.[10]

As Robert was to discover, Cambridge University was no levelling institution. It made few concessions to those of low birth, and in various ways it strived, proudly and often self-consciously, to uphold the distinctions of rank. Except for the highest-performing students, or 'wranglers', status at Cambridge in the 1840s still had more to do with birth than ability. At the apex of the students' pyramid of rank sat the sons of noblemen, who ate with the college dons on high table, were permitted to wear distinctive hats rather than academic caps, and could leave with an MA degree after two years of residence, having attended no lectures and sat no exams. Fellow commoners came next down in the hierarchy. They were typically from wealthy but untitled families. As such, when they left after two years of socialising, they could take only the less prestigious BA degree. Many of them saw no point in taking any degree at all. Most of the university's students were lowlier scholars or pensioners, the former receiving college scholarships, the latter paying a modest amount every term for tuition. These young men tended to come from genteel but not overly wealthy families. On an even lower rung, however, perched the 'sizars'. Robert was among their number. Poor students who paid reduced fees, sizars had in earlier times made their way through university by acting as servants to noblemen or fellow commoners. At some colleges they had been allowed to eat only after the other students had finished their meals, and sometimes they could consume only what their superiors had left. By the 1840s, cleaning duties had been abolished, but on the eve of Robert's arrival some colleges had only just permitted sizars to wear the same gowns and eat in hall at the same times as other students. In spite of these concessions, sizars retained their lowly status.[11]

Robert wasn't alone at the bottom of the pecking order. In his year at Queens' there were about fifteen other sizars studying alongside about 75 pensioners and fellow commoners. It wasn't easy for the sons of small manufacturers to adapt to such a world. Queens' did, however, look favourably on the unconventional student, partly because it provided a home for evangelicals. A keen exponent of evangelicalism and President of Queens' in the early 1800s, Isaac Milner had loudly attacked the dry theology of orthodox Anglicanism and praised the simple piety of 'the lower orders'. No friend of the rich and titled, Milner went so far as to claim that 'the great and the high have ... forgotten that they have souls.' Evangelicals like Milner were seeking to re-energise Christianity by taking it into the slums, the mining valleys, and the hovels of the lower orders. They were driven to do so by the belief that, in order to prove their own worthiness for God's grace, they had to minister to the needs of others. This missionary zeal often made evangelicals socially less aloof than their more restrained brethren. Vehemently low-church, most also rejected the showy rituals, ostentatious vestments and 'bells and smells' of High Anglicanism, declaring them to be hollow distractions. Quite a few proscribed church music.[12]

The evangelical tradition of Queens' College perhaps attracted Robert there. He may have felt that it would offer a more congenial home to the son of a 'small manufacturer' than one of the more traditional colleges. Unfortunately, no records survive to tell us whether or not he managed to thrive despite his lowly status. There is only one indication as to how Robert coped with his humble birth amid the privilege of his Cambridge peers. When he gave his first sermon many years later in a Lancashire parish, he felt the need to explain to the congregation that he had been born and bred in the county. Evidently, since 1844 he had cultivated a higher-class accent, more suitable to his aspirations than the Lancashire brogue acquired growing up in Manchester.[13]

In January 1848, Robert Blincoe received his BA degree and began scouring the pages of the *Ecclesiastical Gazette* in search of vacant posts. In late spring he assumed his first position as second curate in St George's parish, Wolverhampton. As a curate, Robert received a modest stipend, but not until he became a vicar, responsible for his own parish, would his salary be sufficient for raising a family.

Regardless, he had entered a noble profession. Secularising science was on the rise in Victorian England, but orthodox religion remained a powerful and dynamic social force. Less corrupt, more energetic and better led than it had been for well over a century, Anglicanism had serious clout and considerable prestige.[14]

Wolverhampton wasn't the most sought-after place for curates who wanted to cut their clerical teeth, but it lay reasonably close to Robert's parents in Manchester, and it was to him a familiar landscape. Wolverhampton lacked the giant mills of Robert's native city – it was dominated by forges and foundries which made 'coarser articles' like 'tools, files, nails, screws, hinges, hollow-ware, gun-locks' and the like – but it shared with Manchester the woes of overcrowding, poor sanitation, disease and unemployment. In the year of Robert's ordination, Friedrich Engels described Wolverhampton in his book *The Condition of the Working-class in England*. Engels spoke of its wretched workers eating 'meat from diseased animals', and of children who 'usually do not get enough to eat' and 'have rarely other clothing than their working rags.' A government survey of living and sanitary conditions said much the same. The average lifespan was a mere nineteen years, with as many as one in six of the town's children succumbing to infectious and respiratory maladies. Roughly 26,000 people lived without proper sewage disposal, tens of thousands of gallons of effluent annually seeping into nearby ditches or 'soil-tanks' excavated beneath their houses. From the latter, the health inspector recorded, 'liquid manure may be seen oozing through to the surface and stinking horrible.' Not surprisingly, the report noted that 'in 1832 cholera raged with extreme violence'.[15]

Wolverhampton's troubles weren't only those of hygiene. For in such towns and cities, social deference seemed to be a declining commodity. In 1844, Engels cited a recent government report which found that many local boys 'had never heard the name of the Queen nor other names, such as Nelson, Wellington, Bonaparte; but … were very well instructed as to the life, deeds, and character of Dick Turpin.' One sixteen-year-old, when asked who Christ was, hazarded the guess: 'He was a king of London long ago.' Engels wondered why those 'ignored and cast out by the class in power' didn't rise up in violent revolution. The ruling classes were already asking the same question, with greater urgency in 1848 as political revolt engulfed much of continental Europe. For, as many realised, those who were lost to the Church and who revered highwaymen over Christ were easy pickings for socialistic demagogues.[16]

The building of Wolverhampton's St George's Church in 1830 was part of a nationwide campaign to turn the tide against atheism, Chartism and socialism. The disillusioned lower orders were to be won back to the established Church, and St George's needed a curate with zeal, stamina and sympathy with the proletariat. Robert had these qualities aplenty. A few years later, an admirer described him as 'holding the evangelical doctrines, and teaching them to the people.' Robert had been deeply influenced by the evangelical tradition at Queens'. So, whereas most recent BAs would have recoiled at the idea of a curacy in working-class Wolverhampton, for Robert this was a sterling opportunity to prove his missionary spirit. To the sincere evangelical, there was nothing to be gained by taking up a post among upstanding church-goers. His place was in the front line, fighting for the Almighty amid ignorance, godlessness and vice. More personally, Robert probably felt more comfortable among men of his own station and below than with the urbane squires and well-to-do farmers of rural parishes. In Wolverhampton, he wouldn't need to defer apologetically to those of equal ability but of superior rank.[17]

In the event, Robert had every opportunity to demonstrate his piety and kindred spirit. In 1848 and 1849, as it had in 1832, cholera struck Wolverhampton with savage force. Thousands of sick and dying men, women and children were confined to quarantine wards in the union workhouse or carted out to tents erected on a hill a couple of miles out of town. Within a year, more than 500 people perished. Many of the dead were laid to rest in a vast unmarked pit in the graveyard of Robert's own church. And while epidemics in the 19th century often put both doctors and clergymen to flight, Robert stayed in the parish to help in any way he could, bringing spiritual comfort to the dying, saying prayers for the dead, and conducting services to pray for the still living. Many a clergyman felt embarrassed in these years by the visitation of epidemic disease. It was hard for them to believe that cholera could have reached English shores without God's sanction, and yet He was supposed to be benevolent in all things. We don't know how Robert rationalised the onset of cholera, but he clearly went far beyond the call of duty in aiding its victims and thereby won the respect and gratitude of his congregation. A few years later, he received an anonymous £13 donation from a parishioner with the stipulation that he use it to buy a Bible with the inscription:

> Presented to the Rev. Robert Blincoe, BA, late Curate of St George's, Wolverhampton, by an unknown friend, as a testimony of personal esteem, and an appreciation of his courageous and devoted conduct during the cholera of 1849.

His honourable performance during this terrible outbreak of cholera is the first clear indication we have that Robert shared his father's exceptional humanity and resolve.[18]

Robert wasn't, however, a stranger to worldly ambition. While St George's suited his evangelicalism, he must have realised that preaching in a far-off industrial parish wouldn't get him noticed by those with the clout to advance his career. In 1853 Robert applied for the position of curate and Sunday Evening Lecturer at St Luke's Church, Old Street, in London's East End. Competing against twenty or so others, Robert secured the post. His selection boded well for his prospects of gaining his own rectorship in the not-too-distant future.[19]

Moving to London, Robert rented a few rooms above a japanner's shop at 78 Bunhill Row, close to the church. Receiving a less than generous curate's stipend, he couldn't afford any better. Robert nevertheless threw himself into the life of his new parish. As in Wolverhampton, many of his parishioners fell into the lowest social classes. Here, too, he had a mission to rejuvenate the Anglican religion among the poor. The Bishop of London, Charles Blomfield, had begun the initiative to penetrate the godless lanes, alleys and arches of the capital's East End, bringing back into the fold those masses of low-skilled workers, hawkers of fish and rank meat, flower girls, beggars, thieves, crooks, fences and prostitutes who, like Wolverhampton's iron-workers, were finding the message of socialism alarmingly seductive. To this end he had several new churches built, outposts in the midst of 'outcast London'. To the bishop's deep disappointment, however, few of them drew more than a sprinkling of worshippers. His successor, Archibald Tait, tried the common touch. He took the gospel out of doors, preaching to costermongers in Covent Garden and to porters on station platforms. This may have been rather outré for the churchwardens of St Luke's, but they did feel the need for a powerful speaker. Robert Blincoe answered their prayers.[20]

Testimonials written over the following years by fellow clerics in London, Manchester, Macclesfield and Wolverhampton all lavished Robert with praise. They complimented him on his 'zeal and devotedness', his 'ministerial talent and efficiency', his 'highly-cultivated mind' and his 'very superior talents as a preacher'. Several commented on his stunning success at drawing parishioners in to hear his evening lectures. W.M. Grist of St John's College, Cambridge, expressed astonishment that, in a far from favourable locality, Robert had managed to increase attendance every year. 'I have known few more calculated to promote the spread of the Gospel than yourself', Grist wrote. We also know that Robert spent much of his time 'visiting the sick and troubled'. It 'behoved' a minister of the Church, he later said, 'to be up and doing'.[21]

Robert remained fairly poor, despite his Cambridge degree and genteel occupation, but he was fast becoming a clerical celebrity. Preaching from St Luke's elaborate oak pulpit, he drew large crowds eager to hear his pious reflections on local, national and world events. In 1855, as a token of his growing prestige, an artist was commissioned to produce a lithographic portrait of this 'able, energetic, and accomplished divine'. Autographed copies were advertised for sale in the *Illustrated London News* for twelve shillings and sixpence. The portrait shows a man in his prime. Without even a hint of the diffidence that his father had shown before the photographer, Robert looks supremely confident and at ease, attired in a silk cravat and a set of robes presented to him by his parishioners earlier in the year. His hair is carefully coiffured, with the sides combed ostentatiously forward. The elder Robert and Martha, closely following their son's career, must have been ecstatic to receive a copy. They were entitled to feel delight. Their son had fought his way into the gentlemanly classes of Victorian society. At this point, of course, he could have become distant from his parents; but if Robert did feel embarrassed by their beginnings, it was never enough to cause an estrangement. Most comfortable preaching to tradesmen and labourers, Robert took pride in possessing the common touch. Even when he was appointed honorary chaplain of St Luke's workhouse, an event of poetic significance in itself, it seems unlikely that he berated and bullied the inmates as so many others did.[22]

With his evening lectures full to capacity and so many divines admiring his pulpit skills, Robert had every reason to expect to be appointed rector of his own parish, in which position he could begin to earn a decent salary. In 1857 he felt sufficiently confident of his prospects to become engaged to Charlotte Louisa Field Tripp, the daughter of a local publican. They agreed to postpone their marriage until Robert had secured his first rectorship. In the meantime, his popularity as a preacher went on rising. An article in the *Finsbury Herald* of 12 December 1857 testifies to this fact, telling how, 'as a most graceful proof of the very high esteem entertained by the parishioners who form part of Mr BLINCOE'S congregation, for their pastor', they had collected the very large sum of £60 to defray the expenses of his taking up his MA degree at Cambridge. 'London might be searched throughout in vain', said the *Herald*, 'for a minister who performs his duty in a more trustworthy and honourable manner.' When Blincoe finally left St Luke's he compiled a list of all the gifts he had received from grateful, but far from wealthy, parishioners. It included a 'beautifully engraved' silver tea and coffee service, a dressing case, a book slide, and a diamond ring. In addition, Robert reckoned that in total he had been given 'the noble amount' of 1,000 guineas. 'Let my descendants bear this in remembrance', he later wrote in his scrapbook, 'if ever they can aid that Parish.' By any measure, he was a much-loved pastor.[23]

News of the striking munificence of St Luke's towards its curate travelled far beyond London. Such effusive praise was not often earned by men of his lowly ecclesiastical rank, and places where Robert had previously studied or preached were quick to remind readers of their connections with the celebrated London preacher. In December 1857, the *Wolverhampton Chronicle* carried a report on the St Luke's testimonial, its editor claiming indirect credit for the town on the basis that Robert 'was previously curate of St George's Church'.

But what must have pleased his parents most of all was that the 'high esteem entertained by the parishioners of St Luke's ... for their evening lecturer, the Rev. Robert Blincoe' was announced in the pages of the *Manchester Courier* on 5 December 1857. The Blincoes' friends and acquaintances now all heard of his success. Robert was acquiring a public reputation – he even had two of his evening sermons summarised in the pages of *The Times*.[24]

Then, in 1859, Robert received the unhappy news that his mother had died at the Gunco Lane address of her daughter, Martha, and son-in-law, George Parker. A few days after her demise, she was laid to rest in the graveyard of the chapel of St Christopher in the quiet countryside of Pott Shrigley, a few miles from the silk town of Macclesfield. Robert no doubt felt the loss keenly. Illiterate at the time of her marriage, Martha inevitably struggled to comprehend her son's intellectual accomplishments. Yet a stronger connective tissue seems to have held them together: on her side, immense pride in her son's spectacular ascent to Cambridge University and then a thriving London parish; and for his part, a steadfast emotional bond born of having been lavished, emphatically, with his mother's love, encouragement and praise. A decade after his mother's death, sermonising to his St Luke's congregation on the eve of his departure from London, Robert spoke movingly of his mother's gifts to him. As the *Finsbury Free Press* recorded, Robert told of how he had 'preached his first sermon at the mature age of four (laughter), – a sermon that met with the unqualified approbation of his mother.' The report went on: 'If he had been useful as a minister of the Lord Jesus Christ, it was mainly due to the deep religious feelings imbued in him by the early teaching he had received at a mother's knee.' Martha's passing must have been the hardest of blows for her much-favoured son.[25]

The elder Robert also took it hard. Within a little over a year of his wife's death, in December 1860, he followed her into the grave. Having survived malnutrition, overwork, beatings and terrible poverty, Robert Blincoe died after a bout of bronchitis while living at his daughter's house on Gunco Lane. He had reached the grand age of 68. Few who had known Blincoe at Litton Mill, as a small-time capitalist in Manchester in the 1820s, or as an insolvent debtor in

Lancaster Castle gaol, could have imagined that he would die on clean sheets, in a warm house, and with physicians in attendance. But Blincoe's past sufferings had exacted a price. It's likely that 40 years spent inhaling the airborne flue of cotton mills had rendered him susceptible to lung disorders. Even so, his had been a long life for anyone living in Victorian Britain. Monarchs lived on average for only four years more, and Blincoe had greatly surpassed the mean age of death for industrial towns horribly prone to epidemics.[26]

A few days after his demise, Blincoe was buried beside his wife in the family's Pott Shrigley plot. Robert and Martha would eventually be joined there by Ruth, Martha (the younger) and her husband George. As befitting a man who had enjoyed several years of fame, Blincoe's death did not go unmarked by the wider community. The *Macclesfield Courier* of 15 December 1860 carried the following obituary:

> On the 12th instant at the residence of his son-in-law, George Parker, Esq., Sutton Mills, Macclesfield, aged 68, Mr Robert Blincoe, late of Manchester, and father of the Rev. R. Blincoe, MA of St Luke's, Old Street, London.

As the notice implied, this parish orphan passed away a proud man. Comfortable if not rich, he was able to reflect with the deepest satisfaction on both his own and his son's progress. The vicar who delivered the eulogy at Blincoe's funeral could hardly have done better than to quote from St Paul's Epistle to the Galatians: 'We reap what we sow.' These words do not contain an invariable truth, but to anyone who reflects on this parish boy's progress they ring very true indeed.[27]

Robert had much for which to thank his deceased father. Even on the eve of his death, the elder Blincoe was still helping to clear the path he trod. In early 1860, Robert junior paid £2,260 to purchase the clerical living of the village of Swettenham in the Cheshire countryside, a sum almost certainly obtained from his father. Blincoe had presumably hoped that his son would move back north from London, closer to where he himself lived. Bereft of his wife of 40 years, Blincoe doubtless wanted to see more of Robert and his young family. Swettenham's vicarage already had an incumbent at the time of the purchase, but he was an old man who was expected soon to retire. In the event, Blincoe died nine years before his son could take up the Swettenham living. But it was a happy state of affairs that he left behind. As deaths go, Blincoe's was a notably good one.[28]

36

Reputations

When, after a prolonged bout of melancholy and delusion, John Brown renewed contact with Robert Blincoe in 1824, he still hoped to finish the *Memoir* on an upbeat note. In the previous years, his subject had married and set up his own business, and seemed to be thriving. In 1823, Brown had spoken of Blincoe as having fulfilled at least part of the rosy prophecy for which he had paid a shilling to Old Beckkà at Chapel-en-le-Frith. But in 1824, Brown learned of the fire in Ormrod's mill and the sudden reversal in Blincoe's fortunes. He decided to include these developments in the final version of the *Memoir*, perhaps feeling that such disasters only underscored the terrible iniquities of the cotton trade. The effect of doing so, however, was to make the ending a dismal anti-climax. Eventually, of course, Blincoe recovered. Long before 1860, Old Beckkà's prophecy had been realised. Robert Blincoe died with his head raised higher than those who had once abused him, and his son's career seems to cap a stirring tale of triumph facing down adversity.[1]

Yet, as John Brown discovered in 1824, life rarely follows a straight and narrow path. After more than a decade at St Luke's in London, Robert began to despair of ever securing the clerical appointment he felt to be his due. Robert's congregation admired him, and his evening lectures went on attracting bumper audiences, but still every parish he applied to for a rectorship rejected him. After Robert and Charlotte's marriage in 1864, it became harder than ever to get by on a curate's stipend. It was all but impossible by 1869, with three children born (Robert, William Harry and Edward Harold) and another on the way. Eventually the Blincoes decided to quit St Luke's. On the retirement of its incumbent, Robert took up his rectorship in Swettenham.[2]

St Luke's obviously grieved to see him depart. On 9 March 1869, in the parish's vestry hall, a 'large number of ladies and gentlemen' gathered to provide Robert with a 'handsome testimonial' in recognition of seventeen years of dedicated service. A marble slab was unveiled bearing his name. The churchwardens then presented him with a 'beautifully engraved, silver salver, tea and coffee service', to which 300 parishioners had contributed. It was, churchwarden Jeal announced, 'a valuable gift given to a valuable man.' He also received a purse containing 50 gold sovereigns. Robert spoke graciously in reply, offering up thanks to his deceased mother for her nurturing encouragement, and going on to praise the warmth of the parishioners towards the needy of the parish, acknowledging 'their many acts of kindness'. He 'resumed his seat amid loud applause.' The ostentation of Robert's farewell from a hard-up parish demonstrates that he had been no common curate. At the bottom of the clerical pile, curates were known for being overworked and underpaid dogsbodies. Soon recognised to be a preacher of rare talent, the Reverend Blincoe had won his congregation's firm loyalty.[3]

Quiet, serene and undemanding, for many a vicar Swettenham was far closer to the ideal parish than St Luke's. But Robert had no desire for the kind of peaceful living in which so many rectors let their callings ossify. He felt himself to be living in a 'critical history of the Church of England', during which clergymen must be 'up and doing'. And while Swettenham's parishioners may, as he put it in 1869, 'have been much neglected', they certainly weren't brutish heathens who needed reclaiming for Christ. There was nothing heroic for Robert in persuading slack squires and farmers to come to church. He had wanted to win his spurs fighting the good fight where the odds were long and the rewards were high. Swettenham represented the graveyard of all his professional aspirations; the brave missionary seemed set to become a dog-collared Don Quixote. After leaving London, a request was made for him to sit for a photographic portrait for a published series on 'Distinguished Clergymen'. Robert wrote on the invitation: 'as I have no desire to come again into public life I have declined this.' He had taken his final bow from the heady ambitions that had seemed so realisable a few years before.[4]

Robert did maintain some of his earlier drive. In private, however, he had lost most of that confidence he exuded in his portrait of 1855.

In about 1872 he began a scrapbook which he intended to pass on to his children. It became a rather haphazard cache of dull parish paper-work, including gamekeeping licences and harvest home tickets, as well as newspaper clippings referring to himself and his sermons, copies of testimonials, several jottings and explanatory notes in his own hand, plus a few letters. It's clear that from the early 1850s Robert had been saving newspaper articles recording the gifts he had received and the sermons he had given. He evidently craved positive publicity. Later pasted into his scrapbook, the excerpts from the 1850s and 60s seemed to tell the story of a coming man. Ultimately, however, Robert's efforts had led not to a high rank in the Anglican Church, but to an obscure Cheshire rectory only a short train journey from where he had grown up. Robert felt his failure to secure a preferment in London acutely. It led him, in moments of melancholy, to reproach himself and bitterly to defame those he felt had held him back. Holed up in his new parish, dark clouds closed in.[5]

The income from the Swettenham parish was only about £300 a year, so Robert and his family had to live thriftily. As their real prospects of a genteel income slipped away, they resorted to other means of assert-ing the social dignity to which they aspired. The first three children of Robert and Charlotte had received unexceptional names: Robert, William Harry and Edward Harold. But their next two sons, born after their move from London, were given the far more ostentatious names of Evelyn Swettenham and Reginald St George Alleyne (sadly, both Evelyn and Reginald died young). While they sounded like the heirs to extensive country estates, the young Blincoes would not have elite educations to match. They were schooled at Macclesfield Grammar School, receiving free lessons courtesy of a Tudor bequest, just as Robert had himself.[6]

After a few years at Swettenham, Robert's health deteriorated. At the age of 50, in August 1876, he sent a letter to his wife, affectionately called 'Charlie', from a nursing home in Southport, an elegant middle-class resort on the coast just north of Liverpool. Robert was taking the 'water cure', a course of treatment of which Dr Joseph Denman would heartily have approved. At the head of this particular letter, for obvious reasons, he wrote 'Burn This'. Confessing to being 'very miserable', Robert proceeded to list the insults he had received from his brother-in-law, George, when he and his sons stayed with the Parkers in Southport. 'I neither speak, eat, write, talk refer or anything to plague him', he explained, 'and he admonishes me before the whole company. I am held up to ridicule and contempt.' Robert closed the letter on a note unflattering to George Parker but adoring of his wife Charlotte:

> Be sure if anything fatal happens to me – let him [not] nor any of the Parkers have the slightest inkling of your affairs, they can assist you in no way. ... Bring up your children, if you are left to bring them up, in your own way and heed nobody. You have more good sense by far than any of them. I think you have all we need for both of us. ... Farewell my blessed love, kiss my children, I have no real happiness but in my home where I am loved and in my Parish respected.[7]

These are words laden with a deep unhappiness. It might be that he wrote this letter in a rare fit of melancholy, but the demise of his earlier ambitions must surely have taken a heavy toll. That his state of mind remained depressed back in Swettenham is suggested by the fact that, within a year, he had moved to another parish.[8]

In late 1877 a friend, Major Tipping, offered Robert the living of All Saints' Church in Little Bolton. The stipend was lower than in Swettenham, but the move did have its advantages, for the sale of his previous living brought in some ready cash. But this may not have been Robert's primary motivation; for here in Little Bolton there were colliers, textile operatives, bleach workers, and other tradespersons to whom he could bring the gospel. When the parish threw him a welcome in early January 1878, Robert sincerely explained that he was 'not new to the work of a large and thickly-populated parish, and preferred a town "cure" to a country parish.' He went on to say that he was a 'Lancashire man, born and bred', a statement which 'evoked warm plaudits'. Robert stressed that he would devote due time to all in the parish, 'whatever their condition in life'. There are clear echoes here of the Robert Blincoe of St Luke's days. All Saints' lacked the prestige of a London parish, but he was once more to be preaching among those who had traditionally been ignored or alienated by the established Church. There was work to be done here for a man with zeal and devotion to the cause. Robert may never have learned that he would be preaching in the town from which John Brown, the man who had made his father briefly famous, had hailed a century or so before.[9]

Robert entered into the life of his new parish with some of his youthful verve. He chaired various meetings and promoted education among the parish's poorer children. But in March 1879 he had a 'severe attack of illness'. Incapacitated for several weeks, he recovered sufficiently to resume his ecclesiastical duties. Then in November he attended an evening meeting at the All Saints' School, together with the parish's churchwardens. Having seemed rather unwell, Robert retired to bed and 'during the night … was seized with a paralytic attack and remained in a speechless condition.' Notwithstanding the efforts of Dr Livy and Dr Settle, he shortly after died at his residence, Vernon House, on St George's Road in Little Bolton. Robert had had a severe stroke. He was 53 years old. A few days later his coffin was sent by train to Swettenham, where it was laid to rest. He left behind five young children.[10]

On 19 November, a local newspaper eulogised the Reverend Blincoe's ministerial career. In each of the parishes in which he served, the obituary ran, he had 'become a great favourite with his parishioners, not only for his good personal qualities, but also for his pulpit abilities.' This was all perfectly true, but many a reader would have wondered why a man who weekly preached to 'congregations seldom numbering less than 2,000 persons' in the capital should have then descended to a small Cheshire parish, and then a still less renowned Lancashire living. Those who knew the family and its history might also have reflected on how much went unsaid in the bald description of his father as a 'Manchester merchant'.[11]

Robert's had been a life of mixed fortunes. He had been a young man of immense talent and promise, but in the years following the deaths of his parents, his grand hopes had been shattered by a failure to secure a decent preferment. In his scrapbook, Robert felt the need to justify the way in which his career, once so rich in potential, had ground to a desultory halt. In October 1872 he wrote: 'It may be to some of my sons, a marvel why I remained so long unpreferred in the church in London. It was owing, so I now think, partly to myself, the other to the rector of St Luke's and the Bishop of London Tait.' The rector at St Luke's, Robert explained, 'is still, and perhaps unhappily will continue to the end, what I found him for 17 years: without principle, without honour, without religion and without God.' This was an extreme sentiment. Yet he had plenty of bile left for Archibald Tait, Bishop of London during the 1860s while Robert preached at St Luke's, and then Archbishop of Canterbury from 1869 until his death in 1882. 'The bishop Tait was a man courting influence to get the primacy', Robert fumed:

> All his preferments were given under the dictates of powerful personages whether in the state or commerce, and having none of these, I was utterly neglected.

On a later page, beneath a press cutting referring to Tait, he added: 'He was a wretched time-server of no ability himself, he hated it in others. He broke many a poor curate's heart.'[12]

A combination of envy, incompetence and greed on the parts of both rector and bishop, Robert believed, had wrecked his prospects. Bishop Tait, he asserted, was so bent on becoming Archbishop of Canterbury that he granted preferments only to the sons of men who might one day return the favour and lubricate his own ascent of the Church hierarchy. Robert had had only his talent to offer.

These allegations against Tait smack of the dyspeptic whingeing of a disappointed man. Any suggestion that the bishop had a jealous dislike for Robert is hard to credit. Tait lacked creativity and charisma, but all acknowledged him to be intellectually formidable. Nor did Tait push hard for high honours. When offered the archbishopric of Canterbury, he was as shocked as nearly everyone else. And while he had been born into a respectable land-owning family, it still took great ability for a Scotsman to rise to the Canterbury see. Robert did an able man a disservice.[13]

There is a strong indication, however, that Tait's attitude did help to scupper Robert's chances. In 1864, when applying for a London living, Robert compiled three pages of testimonials. All were highly complimentary, except for one. He had apparently applied to Bishop

Tait for an endorsement on a previous occasion, and in this application he made the best of the bishop's cool response: 'The BISHOP of
LONDON ... replied, while unable to meet his views, "I know that
you have worked acceptably and faithfully in St Luke's, Old Street."'
This was faint praise indeed for a man whose sermonising packed out
a large church in a district not known for its ready piety. Alas, we don't
know what 'views' Tait felt unwilling to concur with. Maybe they
were theological. Determined to temper the centrifugal forces that
threatened to break up the Anglican Church, Tait strove to rein in all
extreme factions, like evangelicalism. On the other hand, he would
have approved of Robert's energetic sermonising. For him, the most
important thing was that the message of Anglican Christianity got
across to the godless. Doctrinally, he and Blincoe differed, but in style
and drive they wore the same vestments.[14]

Another possibility is suggested by an article that appeared in *The
Times* of 8 October 1857. It reported on the Reverend Blincoe's
sermon at St Luke's of the previous evening. The pious words of mere
curates weren't often printed in national newspapers, but Robert had
caught the mood of many of the paper's readers. He had delivered a
scathing attack on 'the idolatrous nation of India' and the tens of
thousands of Muslims and Hindus who had joined forces to remove
all trace of British rule or influence from the Himalayas in the north to
Ceylon in the south. The 'Indian Mutiny', soon notorious for the
barbarities perpetrated by both sides, had been sparked into life by
rumours that the gun cartridges of the native troops, or sepoys, were
greased with proscribed animal fats. In using their teeth to open the
cartridges, the sepoys felt that they were violating religious taboos.
The East India Company, which ruled India in Britain's name,
quickly switched to beeswax and vegetable oils. But the real damage
had been done over decades of high-handed misrule by 'John
Company', combined with the insensitive behaviour and doctrinaire
attitudes of hundreds of evangelical missionaries for whom local
faiths were fit only to be crushed by aggressive proselytising. In May
1857, the disaffected Indian population rose up.[15]

Robert had risen to address the congregation of St Luke's as Britons
were still steadying themselves from the shock of the mutiny and were
baying for the blood of its perpetrators. Sensing the national mood,

The Times had already called for the execution of every mutineer in India. The Reverend Blincoe likewise took a firm line. He called for a concerted effort to 'Christianise' India, and urged that 'an entire change ... take place in the Government of that country.' Robert hoped that the British Crown would assume complete charge in India and that it would help push back the tide of idolatry. In the meantime, however, he demanded that the mutineers pay a heavy 'recompense of their error'. These were the views of an evangelical Christian for whom there was only one way to salvation and many routes to Hell. But the Reverend Blincoe's views no doubt delighted a patriotic congregation still reeling with hurt pride after what nearly everyone had supposed to be an inferior race had humbled British arms and nearly robbed the country of its finest and richest imperial possession. Bishop Tait, however, was probably less than impressed.

A man of moderate views who found extremism distasteful and dangerous to the integrity of the Church, it's unlikely that Tait approved of Robert's sentiments. Nor could he have relished one of his own curates wading so unabashedly into the political sphere. While Robert's views were hardly unusual, in his sermon he had made a provocative political statement, and the entire country had heard of it. Perhaps after the report in *The Times*, Tait saw Robert as a loose cannon, a man with more zeal than moderation who might seriously embarrass the Church if given the status to get noticed more often. This might explain why he praised his curate with such devastating reserve.

Robert had many of his father's personal qualities. In speaking his mind so openly and forcefully, he displayed the same outspoken determination and courage in following the dictates of his conscience which his father showed in tramping to the halls of Henry Bache Thornhill and Marmaduke Middleton and to the justices' bench at the Bull's Head Inn back in 1812. Throughout his life, the elder Blincoe had challenged authority and ridden his luck. In business he had gambled repeatedly, often falling hard but always recovering and learning from his mistakes. His son, however, entered a world in many ways quite unlike the market-place. As Anthony Trollope showed, competition for marginal advantage among the clergy could be every bit as intense and bitterly fought out as among retailers, artisans or cotton-spinners. Yet there was an important difference. Errors of judgement in business were severely punished, but the survivors typically had the option of trying again. After the fire at Ormrod's mill and his subsequent insolvency, Blincoe recovered his fortunes. In the Church, a curate who upset his bishop might never have a chance to redeem himself. Reputations were less easily salvaged or renewed than business prospects. Had Robert fallen foul of Tait as a result of his assertive political pronouncements, it may have been enough to destroy him.

There was another difference between the worlds of father and son. The subtle game of good turns and reciprocal favours prevailed in both commerce and the Church, yet in the latter, appointments were far more nepotistic. Even if the market was anything but free and fair, it provided many an opportunity for men of genuine talent. But the system of clerical appointments, in so many ways a hangover from the old society, could make advancement tortuous and uncertain for curates of low birth. Sons of small manufacturers, like Robert, were severely hindered by the inability of their parents to scratch the backs of those sitting upon the committees of clerics, churchwardens, overseers and squires who had the power to reward or refuse clerical promotion. The gratitude of a retired Mancunian cotton merchant had no intrinsic value to a London peer, rector or churchwarden. Nor would the plebeian roots of the Blincoes have helped Robert secure the favour of an influential patron. Where a 'word in season' from a powerful supporter still meant so much, Robert's prospects surely suffered every time he applied for the same living as the son of a local banker, politician or large retailer. We may never know if this is why Robert's career stalled at St Luke's. Perhaps Tait's disapproval was enough. It is, however, certain that a highly talented, if opinionated, clergyman had fallen short of his true potential.

Robert's modest wealth, his social standing, and his humble origins seem to have caused him growing disquiet. Doubtless he felt gratitude towards his father for the sacrifices he had made in sending him to school and allowing him to go on to university, but Robert's children seem to have grown up knowing nothing at all of their grandfather's remarkable progress from parish workhouse to cotton business. This wasn't unusual for the times. Few Victorians looked back with anything other than horror on their poorer antecedents. The obscure and the mediocre tended to be quietly removed from family trees, while spurious connections were often asserted to eminent generals, lords, intellects or clerics. Men like Blincoe, who beat fantastic odds to rise from workhouse and parish apprenticeships to relative comfort, won few accolades for all their pains. A person's origins still counted for as much as the road they travelled, and the Reverend Blincoe certainly had not achieved the genteel heights from which he could reflect on his roots with either indifference or satisfaction. And so, rather than telling of his own father's ultimately successful struggle, he inserted into his scrapbook a Hyde family crest and motto said to belong to his wife's maternal line. Robert probably didn't know that the Hyde family referred to in the crest had nothing to do with his own wife's ancestors. It was a cheap affectation adopted by one of her relations to give some aristocratic polish to an otherwise unprepossessing family line. But Robert wasn't likely to inquire too deeply into its provenance, for the same reason that he became highly circumspect in telling of his own. Robert's gentlemanly status as a poor rector was too insecure for him to risk allowing his father's history to be widely broadcast.[16]

And so, for perhaps most of his grandchildren, the elder Blincoe had been a mere manufacturer of cotton goods. The truth was, of course, quite different. Blincoe died in relative obscurity in 1860, but his life had been anything but conventional or bland. Small, crooked and ungainly, on sight alone he had been easy to underestimate. But those who got to know him, like John Doherty and John Brown, saw far more than a mere victim of circumstance. Blincoe was one of life's battlers, and his refusal to accept ill-treatment, low wages and poor conditions, despite decades of shameless exploitation, had impelled him to claw his way out of the hand-to-mouth existence of England's industrial poor. But perhaps most creditably, Blincoe's last years were spent charting the ascent of his children through that vast hierarchy of ranks and degrees which the St Pancras workhouse chaplain had so confidently asserted to be immutable and divinely ordained. And even if the younger Robert died a disappointed man, it remains truly remarkable that the son of a parish bastard earned a scholarship to Cambridge, was ordained a clergyman, and preached for seventeen years to hundreds of admiring Londoners. The Reverend Blincoe's story is still an extraordinary one, and it stands as eloquent testimony to his father's outstanding achievement.

For understandable reasons, the scale of the elder Blincoe's successes went unrecognised by most of his descendants. But others kept his memory alive. The Ten Hours man John Fielden had already recommended the *Memoir* in his campaigning history of the short time movement published in 1836, and during the 1840s and beyond, Blincoe lived on in the minds of those at the fore of the humanitarian lobby as it extended its efforts to protect children working in mines, fields, workshops and chimneys. Victorian chroniclers of the struggle over factory reform nearly all referred to him in their accounts of the early industrial age when terrible cruelties were inflicted in obscure, inaccessible valleys. Among them was Samuel ('Alfred') Kydd, at one time Richard Oastler's personal secretary. Author of the classic two-volume work *The History of the Factory Movement*, published in 1857, Kydd spoke at length of Blincoe's servitude at Lowdham and Litton mills, and he remarked with the air of one who had made Blincoe's acquaintance that he was now 'a comparatively prosperous man'. For many such writers, this parish orphan's early life exemplified the horrors which Oastler, Sadler and Lord Ashley had taken on and eventually defeated. As late as 1888, when a query about Robert Blincoe was sent in to the periodical *Manchester Notes and Queries*, it elicited a flurry of letters from people who had read his *Memoir* and knew 'Bobby's' story well.[17]

For their contributions to the short time cause and allied movements, statues were erected to both Oastler and Lord Ashley. Blincoe was never honoured in this way, but in 1904 a road was named after him in the village of Urmston, a few miles south-east of Manchester. John Doherty's son Austin had become a property developer, and he built a cluster of streets in Urmston, naming them after people who had played significant roles in his father's life. Blinco [*sic*] Road was built alongside Allen Road, Allen having been a character in Harriet Martineau's novel *A Manchester Strike*, said to have been based on John Doherty. A third street was dubbed, one assumes ironically, Gilpin Road, after the libelled Stockport reverend. Blincoe would have taken comfort from the fact that, as duplicitous parish officials and brutal factory masters receded from view, he had been granted an accolade which in Victorian Britain was largely reserved for those who profited from the system which had so callously exploited his and many other young bodies.[18]

During the early 20th century, the memory of Robert Blincoe still did not fade. The *Memoir* continued to feature in accounts of the factory reform movement. Paul Mantoux, for instance, discussed 'the well-known catalogue of the sufferings of the factory apprentice, Robert Blincoe' at length in his 1928 account of the early factory system. And then in 1966 the English historians Albert Musson and Owen Ashmore republished Blincoe's life story from John Doherty's original 1832 pamphlet with the support of the Derbyshire Archaeological Society. Within a decade, the *Memoir* had been reprinted again by both American and British publishers. For those studying social or economic history during the late 1960s and 70s, it became a 'must read', a key text in the debate between those who believed factory labour to have been shamefully hard (the 'pessimists') and those who felt that its evils had been wildly exaggerated by trades unionists like Doherty and Tory romantics like Richard Oastler and Michael Sadler (the 'optimists'). In the post-Second World War political ferment, these two rival camps both found it easy to recruit.[19]

Blincoe's *Memoir* provided the 'pessimist' school with a potent weapon. Musson and Ashmore admitted that his case represented the extreme end of the spectrum of ill-treatment, 'one of the blackest examples of child slavery'. But they insisted that disgracefully long hours, bullying and poor diets were the norm in the first-generation textile mills. It wasn't long, however, before the 'optimists' started to question the authenticity of Blincoe's narrative. The English historian Stanley Chapman concluded in a 1967 book that it was 'written by a gullible sensationalist, whose statements must be treated with the utmost caution.' If Chapman's sceptical outlook is a sensible one, his analysis in this instance was far from sound. He was surely right to highlight the philanthropy of certain factory masters and the overblown nature of many of the accusations lodged against them but, hell-bent on exculpating the pioneer cotton-, flax- and wool-spinners from any slight or suspicion, Chapman missed what is perhaps most singular and impressive about the *Memoir*.[20]

Despite having been written by a mentally unstable propagandist, it was emphatically and demonstrably honest. Blincoe erred in talking of the scale of fatalities at Litton Mill, but in every other respect independent sources serve only to confirm what the *Memoir* said. His account of conditions at Litton is borne out not only by other children employed there – 'Orphan John' and John Joseph Betts – but by two magistrates, neither of whom had anything to gain by finding fault with Needham's mill. Even the question of deaths to fever in Miller's Dale speaks in Blincoe's favour. Ellis Needham did, as he said, divide the burials among different graveyards to hide the unusually high rate of mortality caused by feeding growing children water-porridge and working them for fifteen or more hours a day. Furthermore, it goes a long way towards establishing Blincoe's reliability that he freely admitted that conditions for child and adult operatives had been vastly better at Thomas Oldknow's Mellor Mill than at either Lowdham or Litton. And his account of serving under John Clayton accords with dozens of others, including the reports of Dr Denman and Marmaduke Middleton. Robert Blincoe was evidently cautious, fair and discriminating when laying charges against mill bosses.

In smaller matters of detail, the *Memoir* was also unfailingly accurate. The fellow St Pancras children whom Blincoe mentions along the way – Mary Richards, Fanny and Mary Collier, and James Cooper – all appear in the surviving parish apprenticeship registers. The same documents confirm that St Pancras' overseers were in the habit of indenturing young boys to master sweeps. They even corroborate the unlikely-sounding story of Blincoe crossing paths with a party of parish beadles and overseers at Oldknow's mill in June 1814. Blincoe told his tale over a decade after leaving Litton, and twenty years after the closure of the Lamberts' mill, but the sort of treatment to which he had been subjected was not easily forgotten. And conditions in both places had been so ineffably bad that he had absolutely no need to embellish or invent.

Over the last two decades, scholars writing on the recent history of childhood, labour movements, parish apprenticeship, and factory reform in Britain have almost invariably alluded to Blincoe's *Memoir*. The debate between optimists and pessimists rumbles on, but most scholars accept the integrity of the story Blincoe told, and his experiences are now enshrined within scores of accounts of the industrial age. The *Memoir* stands, as one modern scholar puts it, as 'perhaps the most savage indictment of the [early factory] system.' Historians of all stripes acknowledge that while many came close, few mills of the early 1800s were quite as bad as Lowdham or Litton. But it's equally appreciated that Blincoe's *Memoir* provides posterity with valuable insights. It tells us of the horrors that are liable to be inflicted on the weak where capitalism is unrestrained by either law or human decency, where politicians prefer not to get involved, and where those who profit most from sweated labour are allowed to excuse the suffering of others with a vague and speculative promise of future riches for all. Whether Blincoe's story is now being re-enacted on a global scale in the sweatshops of the world's developing countries is a matter for debate, but perhaps, as we survey the bonanza of cheap cotton goods in our shops, we too should reflect on the full price of their provision.

In some ways, solely emphasising Blincoe's appalling childhood does him a disservice, for he made his own history to a far greater extent than most of his contemporaries who had much more auspicious starts in life. The fuller story of Blincoe's progress, following on from where the *Memoir* peters out, sheds light on some of the more positive social conditions that arose as a direct consequence of industrialisation and the demise of a relatively static old society. Furthermore, Blincoe's early suffering underscores, and should not be allowed to efface, the achievements of his adult life. To repeat the words of one of his descendants, the scholar G.B. Harrison, he was 'a most remarkable young man'.[21]

But it wouldn't be fitting to end Blincoe's story on so uplifting a note. His life story was truly exceptional, and for this very reason it's useful to remember that few other parish apprentices, whether idle or energetic, resourceful or helpless, ambitious or defeatist, won any kind of respite at all. Mary Richards lived what years were left to her as a cripple in a parish that didn't want her, 130 miles from whatever family she still had. Sarah Heeley, having been carted from Derbyshire to London and back again, passed away no doubt in great loneliness and distress in the parish of Tideswell. And there were thousands of others just like Mary and Sarah, but only a fraction of their injuries and indignities were documented in committee and commission reports in 1816, 1818, 1819, 1832, and beyond. The Tory evangelical William Busfeild Ferrand told of one tragic incident unrecorded by Peel, Sadler, Ashley or Chadwick. Ferrand became converted to the short time cause in the early 1830s, having risen early one morning to 'shoot wild fowl' in his native Yorkshire. Instead of his usual brace, he returned to his hall carrying the body of a small girl, a 'little factory slave half-buried in a snow-drift fast asleep', moments from death. Ferrand saved her life.[22]

Plenty of others died far too young. Some were killed outright by fast-moving machinery. Others bled to death after rollers or flywheels tore limbs and crushed flesh. Many more succumbed to passing maladies after years of overwork and malnutrition had shattered their already feeble constitutions. It's true that the mills provided poor families with work just as a population explosion began to place intolerable demands on the labour market and food supplies. The rise of industry helped to avert a Malthusian nightmare. Even so, the hopeless lack of regulation by either conscience or legislation which characterised the early stages of industrialisation unleashed suffering, exploitation and abuse on a scale in no way necessary for the success of English manufactures. Nor, as Manchester's Dr Thomas Percival and many others pointed out, was it good management to give jobs requiring concentration and stamina to children whose limbs drooped through tiredness and whose eyes bleared over towards late afternoon due to severe sleep deprivation.

Although Blincoe's achievements were dazzling, it would be a mistake to infer that all those other work'us children could have done as much if they had only pushed harder or refused the easy relief of the gin-shop and ale-house. Blincoe's life does, however, contain an important political message, one which John Brown instinctively perceived back in early 1822. Giving the lie to the prejudices of the Victorian elites, his *Memoir* revealed that virtue, talent, guts and pride are to be found anywhere, from the lowliest hovel and grimiest workhouse to the stateliest mansion and bishop's palace. If Dickens had wanted a counter-example with which to silence the *Quarterly Review* critic who asserted that 'workhouse boys are not born with original virtue', he could hardly have done better than cite Blincoe's

Memoir. For whatever his parentage, lowly or genteel, here was a boy raised in a workhouse who had succeeded spectacularly. Workhouses were said to be receptacles for worthless children who, on leaving, 'dropped almost automatically into the ranks of pauperism and crime.' In dying a 'comparatively well off' man, Blincoe hinted at a deeper truth: that the brutal pessimism of such attitudes crushed the spirits and kept from rising innumerable other young men and women of exceptional ability. There had never been so many opportunities for the poor to improve their lot, but the obstacles were still insuperable to most. Blincoe was extremely lucky as well as highly able. Even in success, his biography serves to recall the moving lines of Thomas Gray:[23]

> Full many a gem of purest ray serene
>   The dark unfathom'd caves of ocean bear;
> Full many a flower is born to blush unseen,
>   And waste its sweetness on the desert air.

The End

Notes

Introduction

1 For detailed accounts of this event, see Samuel ('Alfred') Kydd, *The History of the Factory Movement* (New York: Kelley, 1966 reprint), p. 255; The *Manchester Guardian*, 1 September 1832; and Raymond George Kirby and A.E. Musson, *The Voice of the People: John Doherty, 1798–1854: Trade Unionist, Radical and Factory Reformer* (Manchester: Manchester University Press, 1975), pp. 376–7.

2 Alan J. Kidd, *Manchester Illustrated from the Archives and with Contemporary Photographs by Ian Beesley* (Keele, Staffs: Ryburn, 1993); Asa Briggs, *Victorian Cities* (London: Oldhams Press, 1963); Samuel Bamford, *Passages in the Life of a Radical,* preface by Tim Hilton (Oxford: Oxford University Press, 1984 reprint).

3 George Eliot, *Felix Holt the Radical* (London: William Blackwood and Sons, 1864), p. 12; Alexis de Tocqueville, *Journeys to England and Ireland,* translated by George Lawrence and K.P. Mayer, edited by J.P. Mayer (New Haven: Yale University Press, 1958), pp. 107–8; Evidence of Dr Bisset Hawkins, *Second Report of the Central Board of His Majesty's Commissioners appointed to collect information in the manufacturing districts, as to the employment of children in factories, and as to the propriety and means of curtailing the hours of their labour* (London: The House of Commons, 15 July 1833), p. 607.

4 Sir James Kay-Shuttleworth, *The Moral and Physical Condition of the Working Classes Employed in the Cotton Manufacture in Manchester* (London: J. Ridgway, 1832), p. 12; Briggs, *Victorian Cities,* p. 90.

5 Briggs, *Victorian Cities,* p. 89.

6 For general accounts of the campaign, see: Betty Leigh Hutchins and A. Harrison, *A History of Factory Legislation,* with a preface by Sydney Webb (London: Frank Cass, 1966); Peter Kirby, *Child Labour in Britain, 1750–1870,* Social History in Perspective series (Basingstoke: Palgrave Macmillan, 2003); and Maurice Walton Thomas, *The Early Factory Legislation: a Study in Legislative and Administrative Evolution* (Westport, CT: Greenwood Press, 1970).

7 Robert Benton Seeley, *Memoirs of the Life and Writings of Michael Thomas Sadler, Esq.* (London: R.B. Seeley and W. Burnside and sold by L. and G. Seeley, 1842); and *Report from the Select Committee on the 'Bill to Regulate the labour of children in the mills and factories of the United Kingdom' ... 1831–2* (Shannon: Irish University Press, 1968–9).

8   See Cecil Herbert Driver, *Tory Radical: The Life of Richard Oastler* (New York: Oxford University Press, 1946).

9   Driver, *The Life of Richard Oastler*, pp. 118–24. Adolphus Trollope, *What I Remember* (second edition, 1887), pp. 7–13, cited in Pamela Neville-Sington, *Fanny Trollope: the Life and Adventures of a Clever Woman* (London: Viking, 1997), p. 273.

10 J.C. Gill, *The Ten Hours Parson: Christian Social Action in the Eighteen-Thirties* (London: SPCK, 1959).

11 *Manchester Guardian*, 1 September 1832.

12 Noted by the *Leeds Intelligencer*'s reporter, quoted in Kydd, *History of the Factory Movement*, p. 255.

13 Kydd, *Factory Movement*, p. 256.

14 *Manchester Guardian*, 1 September 1832.

15 For this common theme in Radical circles, see Robert Q. Gray, *The Factory Question and Industrial England, 1830–1860* (New York: Cambridge University Press, 1996).

16 All references in the text are to the following edition: John Brown, *A Memoir of Robert Blincoe ...* (Firle, Sussex: Caliban Books, 1977).

17 *Memoir of Robert Blincoe*, p. 14.

18 *Memoir of Robert Blincoe*, pp. 15–16; H.M. Mackenzie, 'Cressbrook and Litton Mills, 1779–1835. Part 1', *Derbyshire Archaeological Journal*, vol. 88, 1968, p. 79.

19 Adam Smith, *An Inquiry into the Nature and Causes of the Wealth of Nations* (London: printed for W. Strahan and T. Cadell, 1776), conclusion to Book 1; Karl Marx, *The Eighteenth Brumaire of Louis Bonaparte. Translated from the German for the People, Organ of the Socialist Labour Party, by Daniel De Leon* (New York: International Publishing Co., 1898), p. 106.

20 For more on this genre, see John Burnett, David Vincent and David Mayall (eds), *The Autobiography of the Working Class: an Annotated Critical Bibliography* (Brighton: Harvester, 1984–9).

21 There were accounts of working-class life published before the *Memoir*. None of them, however, is as detailed or substantial as Blincoe's story. Nor are they so exclusively concerned with the nature of life and work for the labouring orders. The autobiographies of Robert Barker, Benjamin Starkey, James Downing, John Gibbs, William Huntington, Thomas Holcroft, Thomas Preston and Mary Saxby are closest in style to the *Memoir* (see Bibliography). However, the first two provide few details of working life, the following two are mostly concerned with showing how the authors underwent personal conversion experiences and were saved from vice, Holcroft was first and foremost a well-known criminal, Preston a leading Radical politician, and Saxby spent much of her life as a vagrant. See Burnett et al., *Autobiography of the Working Class*.

22 See Albert E. Musson, 'Robert Blincoe and the Early Factory System', in his *Trade Union and Social History* (London: Cass, 1974), pp. 195–206.

23 *The Lion*, vol. 1, nos 4–8, 25 January–22 February 1828. For Charles Dickens' childhood and the stigma of his early working years, see J. Forster, *The Life of Charles Dickens*, ed. J.W.T. Ley (1928), p. 26; Peter Ackroyd, *Dickens* (London: Sinclair-Stevenson, 1990).

Chapter 1

1 *Memoir of Robert Blincoe*, pp. 6–11.
2 Jonas Hanway, *An Earnest Appeal for Mercy to the Children of the Poor, particularly those belonging to the parishes within the Bills of Mortality, appointed by an Act of Parliament to be registered, being a general reference to the deserving conduct of some parish officers, and the pernicious effects of the ignorance and ill-judged parsimony of others …* (London: J. Dodsley, 1766), p. 12; *Memoir of Robert Blincoe*, p. 9.
3 Nathaniel Hawthorne's novel *The Scarlet Letter* wonderfully dramatises the reluctance of an adulterous cleric to admit his guilt.
4 See Marton Gloria Liddall, *The St Pancras Vestry: a Study in the Administration of a Metropolitan Parish 1760–1835* (unpublished Ph.D thesis, Rutgers University, 1981), p. 181.
5 John Brown tells us that the story made him 'painfully agitated'. If so, it seems unlikely that he would have so freely confided in Brown and, later, John Doherty. Brown was probably trying to reassure 'respectable' readers that Blincoe felt appropriate shame in his ancestry. See *Memoir of Robert Blincoe*, p. 9.
6 Cited in R. Percival, *A Collection Illustrative of the History and Topography of the Parish of Saint Pancras* (London: 1729–1830). For the gratuitous use of Godfrey's Cordial, see James Walvin, *A Child's World: a Social History of English Childhood, 1800–1914* (Harmondsworth: Penguin, 1982), p. 26.
7 Roger A.E. Wells, *Wretched Faces: Famine in Wartime England, 1793–1801* (Gloucester: A. Sutton, 1988), pp. 36–8. For the heightened mortality of these years in London, see Dorothy M. George, *London Life in the Eighteenth Century* (London: Kegan Paul, Trench, Trubner and Co., 1925), chapter 1.
8 K.H. Strange, *Climbing Boys: a Study of Sweeps' Apprentices, 1773–1875* (New York: Allison and Busby, 1982), p. 50.
9 *Memoir of Robert Blincoe*, p. 15.
10 Gillian Wagner, *Thomas Coram, Gent.* (Woodbridge, Suffolk: The Boydell Press, 2004); *Memoir of Robert Blincoe*, pp. 8–9.
11 *Memoir of Robert Blincoe*, p. 9.
12 Anthony Brundage, *The English Poor Laws, 1700–1930*, Social History in Perspective series (Basingstoke: Palgrave, 2001).
13 Vestry Minutes, no. 406, 6 July 1795; Norman Longmate, *The Workhouse* (London: Temple Smith, 1974), p. 36; Walter E. Brown, *The St Pancras Poor: a Brief Record of their Treatment, etc., from 1718 to 1904* (London, 1905), p. 11.
14 After 1662, there were six main ways of gaining an all-important settlement: by being born in the parish; by marriage and parentage (wives were automatically granted settlement in their husband's parish, legitimate children also took their father's settlement, but illegitimate offspring had settlement in the parish in which they were born); by being apprenticed in a parish; by being employed there for a year; by paying poor rates; or by serving in a parish office. In 1795, the government proposed doing away with most of the settlement laws as a hindrance to the mobility of labour. The St Pancras vestry was promptly convened. Terrified lest the parish be flooded by poor migrants, it elected to 'join the opposition to the Bill'. The Act passed anyway, though it remained legal to eject pregnant, unwed women (see Vestry Minutes, no. 403, 4 April 1795).

15 After 1692, a poor labourer could move to another parish if he or she had a special permit granted by his or her parish; but these were granted with extreme reluctance. See Richard Burn, *The History of the Poor Laws: with Observations* (London: printed by H. Woodfall and W. Strahan, for A. Millar, 1764).

16 The London tailor and politician Francis Place told of many a successful master ruined by subtle changes in taste or fashion. His first boss was a leather breeches-maker called Mr France whose once thriving business was destroyed by a growing preference for 'cottons, corduroys and velvateens'. The Frances were reduced to making cheap breeches out of off-cuts which they then sold to workhouse masters. Before long they had followed their breeches into the workhouse, where they died shortly afterwards. See Francis Place, *The Autobiography of Francis Place (1771–1854)* (Cambridge: Cambridge University Press, 1972), pp. 70–9; Lynn Hollen Lees, *The Solidarities of Strangers: the English Poor Laws and the People, 1700–1948* (Cambridge: Cambridge University Press, 1998), p. 57.

17 Jonathan David Chambers, *Nottinghamshire in the Eighteenth Century: a Study of Life and Labour under the Squirearchy* (London: P.S. King and Son, 1932), p. 225; Brown, *St Pancras Poor*, p. 54. In 1793, Esther Herbert, a Fulham parishioner, fell pregnant with the child of a rather dissolute Samuel Gillingham. The overseers, alarmed lest she give birth to a bastard child likely to be chargeable on the parish for a decade or more, threatened her with gaol if she didn't marry her child's father. Gillingham too was threatened with imprisonment if he didn't do the decent thing. In a calculated fit of generosity, the parish paid for the marriage licence, a ceremony at the local church, and even a celebratory dinner. Unfortunately for the overseers, having had his fill of roast beef and ale, Gillingham fled straight after the proceedings. He never returned. So the parish received the bill for both the day's festivities and the child's upkeep for the next decade. See Lees, *Solidarities of Strangers*, p. 57.

18 Chambers, *Nottinghamshire in the Eighteenth Century*, p. 225. Marylebone parish, bordering St Pancras to the west, paid an inspector a huge £50 per annum to work out who did or did not have a settlement right. And he received a commission of seven shillings and sixpence for every father of a bastard child he apprehended. See Alan R. Neate, *The St Marylebone Workhouse and Institution, 1730–1965* (London: St Marylebone Society, 1967), p. 12.

19 Vestry Minutes, 16 October 1793.

20 Vestry Minutes, 1 January 1796; the 1601 Act had recommended that 'necessary places of habitation' be provided for the very poorest. Many of those who established workhouses cited this as a precedent. See Sir Frederic Morton Eden, Bart., *The State of the Poor* (London, 1784), p. 271.

21 Vestry Minutes, 21 October 1730. See also Brown, *St Pancras Poor*, pp. 10–11.

Chapter 2

1 James Frederick King, *The Kentish Town Panorama* (The London Topographical Society in conjunction with The London Borough of Camden, Libraries and Arts Department, 1986), panel 16.

2 Quoted in Eden, *The State of the Poor*, p. 457.

3 Vestry Minutes, no. 415, 22 September 1796; Liddall, *St Pancras Vestry*, p. 333.

4 Vestry Minutes, 30 May 1775; Vestry Minutes, 11 July 1809. See also Liddall, *St Pancras Vestry*, pp. 183–5 and Brown, *St Pancras Poor*, p. 13.

5 George, *London Life*, chapter 3, and Place, *Autobiography*, p. 30.

6 Vestry Minutes, 10 December 1802. See also Liddall, *St Pancras Vestry*, p. 184 and Brown, *St Pancras Poor*, p. 13; for John Howard, see L. Baumgartner, 'John Howard (1726–1790), Hospital and Prison Reformer: a Bibliography', *Bulletin of the History of Medicine*, 7 (1939), 486–626.

7 Longmate, *Workhouse*, chapter 2.

8 Pamela Horn, *Children's Work and Welfare, 1780–1880s,* Studies in Economic and Social History series (Basingstoke: Macmillan, 1994); Daniel Defoe, *A Tour Through the Whole Island of Great Britain* (London: Everyman edn, 1974), vol. 1, p. 17; Horn, *Children's Work and Welfare*, p. 1. See also Ann Kussmaul, *A General View of the Rural Economy of England, 1538–1840* (Cambridge: Cambridge University Press, 1990).

9 See Rev. R.G. Bouyer, *An Account of the Origin, Proceedings, and Intentions of the Society for the Promotion of Industry: in the Southern District of the Parts of Lindsey, in the County of Lincoln. Published at the desire, and with the approbation of the standing committee of the said Society; in which the Society's accounts, and the lists of benefactors, subscribers, and trustees, are continued to the audit in 1789* (Louth: R. Sheardown, 1789), p. 74; Gilbert J. French, *The Life and Times of Samuel Crompton*, 3rd edn (1862), p. 58; Hugh Cunningham, 'The Employment and Unemployment of Children in England c. 1680–1851', *Past and Present*, no. 126 (February 1990), 115–150, p. 137.

10 See Harold Perkin, *Origins of Modern English Society* (London: Routledge, 1991), early chapters.

11 Quoted in Horn, *Children's Work and Welfare*, p. 2.

12 Quoted in Horn, *Children's Work and Welfare*, p. 53.

13 Vestry Minutes, 22 September 1775.

14 Neate, *St Marylebone Workhouse*, p. 14; Brown, *St Pancras Poor*, p. 55; Geoffrey Harris, 'The Humanity of Hampstead Workhouse', *Camden History Review*, vol. 4 (1976), 28–31, p. 30.

15 Vestry Minutes, 16 December 1803; Liddall, *St Pancras Vestry*, pp. 190–5; *Memoir of Robert Blincoe*, p. 23.

16 Liddall, *St Pancras Vestry*, p. 193.

17 Vestry Minutes, 16 December 1803.

18 Vestry Minutes, 16 December 1803.

19 James Stephen Taylor, 'Philanthropy and Empire', *Eighteenth-Century Studies*, vol. 12, no. 3 (Spring 1979), 285–305, p. 290. See also James Stephen Taylor, *Hanway: Founder of the Marine Society: Charity and Policy in Eighteenth-Century Britain* (Berkeley, CA: Scolar Press, 1985).

20 Jonas Hanway, *An Earnest Appeal*; John L. and Barbara Hammond, *The Town Labourer, 1760–1832: the New Civilisation* (London: Longmans, Green, 1917), p. 101.

21 Peter Gay, *The Enlightenment: an Interpretation* (New York: Norton, 1977), p. 43; for medical care in St Pancras in the 1790s, see Samuel Bagster, *Samuel*

Bagster of London, 1772–1851: an Autobiography (London: Bagster, 1972), p. 16.

22 Vestry Minutes, 4 May 1781; *The Times*, 27 November 1799, p. 2, issue 4651.

23 Liddall, *St Pancras Vestry*, p. 248.

24 Bagster, *Samuel Bagster*, p. 145.

Chapter 3

1 See Gillian Tindall, *The Fields Beneath: the History of One London Village* (London: Phoenix Press, 2002), chapter 1.

2 Vestry Minutes, 17 July 1766; see Liddall, *St Pancras Vestry*, p. 96.

3 See several newspaper cuttings in Percival, *History and Topography of the Parish of Saint Pancras*. The well-heeled inhabitants living in the north of the parish complained regularly of burglaries. 'Robings we heare of all most every day', moaned one Hampstead resident in a glum letter to her sister. See Hazel Brothers, 'Fear of Crime in Eighteenth-century Hampstead', *Camden History Review*, vol. 23 (1999), 10–13; Tindall, *Fields Beneath*, p. 103; Liddall, *St Pancras Vestry*, p. 11. See also *The Times*, Saturday 29 June 1793, p. 3, issue 2713; *The Times*, Tuesday 11 June 1799, p. 3, issue 4506.

4 Marian Kamlish, 'Before Camden Town 1745–1795', *Camden History Review*, vol. 21 (1997), 20–22; Tindall, *Fields Beneath*, chapters 6 and 7.

5 Dorothy M. George, *London Life in the Eighteenth Century* (London: Kegan Paul, Trench, Trubner and Co., 1925), chapter 1.

6 Kamlish, 'Camden Town', p. 22.

7 Tindall, *Fields Beneath*, pp. 90–3, 112.

8 J.T. Coppock and Hugh C. Prince (eds), *Greater London* (London: Faber and Faber, 1964), pp. 87–90; Tindall, *Fields Beneath*, p. 90.

9 William Poole, *The Life and Death of St Pancras, a Young Martyr of the Early Christian Church: with notes and appendix, containing a letter to the young on persecution, and thoughts on the commemoration of departed friends* (London: William Poole, 1882). See also Charles Henry Denyer, *St Pancras Through the Centuries* (London: LePlay House Press, 1935), p. 11.

10 Bagster, *Samuel Bagster*, p. 43; Norden quoted in Tindall, *Fields Beneath*, pp. 31–2.

11 From a 1730 handbill quoted in Percival, *History and Topography of the Parish of Saint Pancras*; William Maitland, *History and Survey of London from its Foundation to the Present Time* (London: T. Osborne, J. Shipton and J. Hodges, 1756), p. 1379; Place, *Autobiography*, p. 29, fn. 1; Warwick Wroth, *The London Pleasure Gardens of the Eighteenth Century* (London: Macmillan, 1896).

12 Samuel Palmer, *St Pancras: Being Antiquarian, Topographical, and Biographical Memoranda, relating to the extensive metropolitan parish of St Pancras, Middlesex; with some account of the parish from its foundation* (London: S. Palmer, 1870), pp. 204–6.

13 Frederick Miller, *St Pancras Past and Present* (London: Heywood, 1874), p. 152; newspaper reports pasted into Percival, *History and Topography of the Parish of Saint Pancras*. In April 1793, Robespierre's Jacobin government declared: 'The émigrés are banished in perpetuity from French territory; they are civilly dead;

their property is acquired by the Republic.' The Bishop of Coutances, the Bishop of Tréguier, the Bishop of Noyon, the Comte de Montboissier, the Grand Senechal de Quercy, the Marquis de Bouillé, and the Comtesse de Polastron all found final peace in this corner of the parish. See Kirsty Carpenter, *Refugees of the French Revolution: Emigrés in London, 1789–1802* (Basingstoke: Macmillan, 1999).

14 Hugh C. Prince, 'North-west London 1814–1863', chapter 4 of Coppock and Prince, *Greater London*, p. 80. See also newspaper reports pasted into Percival, *History and Topography of the Parish of Saint Pancras*. That men continued to duel despite its illegality is unsurprising given that in 1789 the Prime Minister himself rose before dawn to meet a political foe.

15 Bagster, *Samuel Bagster*, p. 16; Colquhoun quoted in Eden's *The State of the Poor*, p. 466. In one case from the 1760s, prospective buyers of a city property stumbled across two old women starved to death in the upper rooms and an emaciated girl and old woman downstairs (see George, *London Life*, p. 174).

16 See G.C. Cook, 'Dr William Woodville (1752–1805) and the St Pancras Smallpox Hospital', *Journal of Medical Biography*, vol. 4, no. 2 (May 1996), pp. 75–6.

17 Quoted in C.W. Dixon, *Smallpox* (London: J. and A. Churchill, 1962), p. 512.

18 William Woodville, *The History of the Inoculation of the Small-pox in Great Britain*, vol. 1 (London: printed and sold by James Phillips, 1796), pp. 151–6.

19 Woodville, *History of the Inoculation of the Small-pox*, p. 379; *Memoir of Robert Blincoe*, p. 16.

20 *Memoir of Robert Blincoe*, p. 16.

Chapter 4

1 *Memoir of Robert Blincoe*, p. 13.

2 See Joan Lane, *Apprenticeship in England, 1600–1914* (London: UCL Press, 1996) and George, *London Life*, chapter 5.

3 Prior to 1774, apprentices were bound until the age of 24 unless – in the case of young women – they were married before this age. See Lane, *Apprenticeship in England*. Place, *Autobiography*, p. 71.

4 *An Account of Several Work-Houses for Employing and Maintaining the Poor*, second edition (London, 1732), p. ix. Burn, *Poor Laws*, p. 212.

5 See George, *London Life*, pp. 223–34 and Mary B. Rose, 'Social Policy and Business: Parish Apprenticeship and the Early Factory System 1750–1834', *Business History*, vol. 31, no. 4 (1989), 5–33. See also Wagner, *Thomas Coram*.

6 St Pancras parish register of apprentices, 1778–1801, vol. no. P90 PAN1 361 (London Metropolitan Archives).

7 Rose, 'Social Policy and Business', p. 7.

8 George, *London Life*, pp. 224, 228; Lane, *Apprenticeship*, p. 229; minutes of meeting on 22 June 1805 of the St Pancras Directors of the Poor.

9 *Memoir of Robert Blincoe*, p. 13.

10 W.W. Rostow, 'Business Cycles, Harvests, and Politics: 1790–1850', *Journal of Economic History*, vol. 1, no. 2 (November 1941), 206–221, p. 211. Vestry Minutes, no. 404, 7 April and 15 July 1795; Vestry Minutes, 10 March 1796.

11 Liddall, 'St Pancras Vestry', p. 333, esp. appendix V.A.

12 See Eden, *The State of the Poor*, p. 467.

13 Eden, *The State of the Poor*, p. 458; not until 1809 was the third parish workhouse built near Battle Bridge. It quickly became notorious for its squalid conditions. See Richard Conquest, 'The Black Hole of St Pancras', *Camden History Review*, vol. 3 (1975), pp. 19–25.

14 Quoted in John and Barbara Hammond, *The Town Labourer*, pp. 158, 160–1.

15 See Anne Stott, *Hannah More: the First Victorian* (Oxford: Oxford University Press, 2003), chapters 5 and 6; and Anthony Brundage, *The English Poor Laws, 1700–1930*, Social History in Perspective series (Basingstoke: Palgrave, 2001).

16 Defoe quoted in Eden, *The State of the Poor*, p. 262; see Eric J. Evans, *The Forging of the Modern State: Early Industrial Britain, 1783–1870* (London: Longman, 1983), chapters 15 and 16. See also Mark Blaug, 'The Myth of the Old Poor Law and the Making of the New', *Journal of Economic History*, vol. 23 (1963), 151–80, and Mark Blaug, 'The Poor Law Report Re-examined', *Journal of Economic History*, vol. 24 (1964), 229–45.

17 Eden, *The State of the Poor*, p. xxv; Thomas Ruggles, *The History of the Poor, their Rights, Duties, and the Laws Respecting Them: in a Series of Letters* (London: printed for J. Deighton, 1793–4), p. 45; Edmund Gillingwater, *An Essay on Parish Workhouses: Containing Observations on the Present State of English Workhouses; with Some Regulations Proposed for their Improvement* (Bury St Edmunds, 1786). For general discussions of Poor Law practice and strategies, see Sidney and Beatrice Webb, *English Poor Law History. Part 1: The Old Poor Law* (London: Frank Cass and Co., 1963 reprint), chapter 4. See also Brundage, *English Poor Laws*, chapters 2 and 3.

18 Reverend Thomas Malthus, *An Essay on the Principle of Population as it Affects the Future Improvement of Society* (London, 1798).

19 A law of 1723 had denied relief to anyone unless they went into the workhouse. The idea, to be resurrected in the 1830s, was that paupers would be stung into finding work if faced by the threat of entering its stark interior. In contrast, during the later 1700s, hundreds of parishes across the country adopted the 'roundsman' system: billeting poor men and women on local farmers and manufacturers, and paying all or some of their wages from the parish kitty. See Brundage, *English Poor Laws*, pp. 56–7. The Webbs called the Speenhamland system 'calamitous'. Mark Blaug and more recent historians have largely invalidated their case (see Blaug, 'The Myth of the Old Poor Law').

20 From newspaper cuttings pasted into Percival, *History and Topography of the Parish of St Pancras*.

21 See Strange, *Climbing Boys*, pp. 21, 64; James Montgomery, *The Chimney-Sweeper's Friend, and Climbing-Boy's Album. ... Arranged by J.M.* (London, 1824), p. 25; Minutes of evidence taken before the Lords Committee concerning an 'Act for the Better Regulation of Chimney Sweeps', March 1818.

22 Quoted in Montgomery, *Chimney-Sweeper's Friend*, p. 144. See also Robert Holden, *Orphans of History: The Forgotten Children of the First Fleet* (Melbourne, Australia: Text Publishing, 2000), chapter 3.

23 Quoted in Montgomery, *Chimney-Sweeper's Friend*, p. 83.

24 Sophie de la Roche, quoted in Strange, *Climbing Boys*, p. 99; William Buchan, *Advice to Mothers, on the Subject of Their Own Health; and on the Means of Promoting the Health, Strength, and Beauty of their Off-spring* (London, 1803), p. 70; Percivall Pott, *Chirurgical Observations Relative to the Cataract, the Polypus of the Nose, the Cancer of the Scrotum, ... Ruptures, and the Mortification of the Toes, etc.* (London, 1775), p. 12.

25 Jonas Hanway, *A Sentimental History of Chimney-sweepers in London and Westminster, Shewing the Necessity of Putting them Under Regulations. ... With a Letter to a London Clergyman on Sunday Schools, etc.* (London, 1785); see also George, *London Life*, pp. 239–43, 377, and Strange, *Climbing Boys*, pp. 35–8, 51.

26 Charles Dickens, *Oliver Twist, or, the Parish Boy's Progress* (London: Penguin, 2002; originally published in serial form 1837–8), p. 25.

27 *Memoir of Robert Blincoe*, p. 14.

28 *Memoir of Robert Blincoe*, p. 14.

29 Dickens, *Oliver Twist*, pp. 24–5.

30 *Memoir of Robert Blincoe*, p. 15.

31 *Memoir of Robert Blincoe*, pp. 14–16.

32 For the parish's financial woes, see Liddall, *St Pancras Vestry*, chapter 4.

Chapter 5

1 Stanley D. Chapman, *The Early Factory Masters: the Transition to the Factory System in the Midlands Textile Industry* (Newton Abbot: David and Charles, 1967), pp. 82–3, 177–8; S.M. Worrall, 'Water Power on the Dover Beck' (unpublished thesis, Nottingham University, 1994).

2 See minutes of the meeting of Directors of the Poor, 22 June 1805; Liddall, *St Pancras Vestry*, pp. 202–5; Brown, *St Pancras Poor*, pp. 36–7; Rose, 'Social Policy and Business', p. 14.

3 Paul Carter, 'Poor Relief Strategies: Women, Children and Enclosure in Hanwell, Middlesex, 1780 to 1816', *Local Historian*, vol. 25, no. 3 (1995), 164–77; Marjorie Cruickshank, *Children and Industry: Child Health and Welfare in North-west Textile Towns During the Nineteenth Century* (Manchester: Manchester University Press, 1981), p. 13; Owen Ashmore, 'The Early Textile Industry in the Derwent Valley', part one of John Brown, *A Memoir of Robert Blincoe*, Derbyshire Miscellany series, supplement 10 (Duffield: Derbyshire Archaeological Society, Local History Section, 1966), p. 16.

4 Rose, 'Social Policy and Business'; John Farey, *General View of the Agriculture and Minerals of Derbyshire* (London: Sherwood, Neely and Jones, 1815), vol. 3, pp. 501–2. See also Chapman, *Early Factory Masters*, p. 169.

5 Andrew Ure, *The Philosophy of Manufactures, or, An Exposition of the Scientific, Moral, and Commercial Economy of the Factory System of Great Britain*, second edition (London: C. Knight, 1835), p. 15; Richard K. Fleischman, *Conditions of Life Among the Cotton Workers of Southeastern Lancashire, 1780–1850* (New York: Garland, 1985), p. 77. See also Chapman, *Early Factory Masters*, p. 156.

6 See Neil J. Smelser, *Social Change in the Industrial Revolution: an Application of Theory to the Lancashire Cotton Industry 1770–1840* (London: Routledge and

Kegan Paul, 1959), and Chapman, *Early Factory Masters*, chapter 9; Sydney Pollard, 'The Factory Village in the Industrial Revolution', *English Historical Review*, vol. 79, no. 312 (July 1964), 513–31.

7 Evidence of James Pattison, Esq., in *Report of the Minutes of Evidence Taken Before the Select Committee on the State of the Children Employed in the Manufactories of the United Kingdom, 25 April–18 June 1816* (London: The House of Commons, 28 May and 19 June 1816), p. 77; Ure, *Philosophy of Manufactures*, p. 16.

8 Jonathan David Chambers, *Nottinghamshire in the Eighteenth Century: a Study of Life and Labour under the Squirearchy* (London: P.S. King and Son, 1932), p. 230; *Manchester Mercury*, 19 October 1784, quoted in Rose, 'Social Policy and Business', p. 15.

9 Rose, 'Social Policy and Business', p. 22; Brown, *St Pancras Poor*, p. 37; Lane, *Apprenticeship*, p. 88; Sidney and Beatrice Webb, *English Poor Law History*, pp. 204–5.

10 *Memoir of Robert Blincoe*, pp. 16–17.

11 Henri Misson, *Memoirs and Observations of Travels over England* (London, 1719), pp. 310–11. See Ben Rogers, *Beef and Liberty: Roast Beef, John Bull and the English Nation* (London: Chatto and Windus, 2003), p. 13.

12 Quoted in Rogers, *Beef and Liberty*, p. 7.

13 Pehr Kalm, *Kalm's Account of his Visit to England on his Way to America in 1748*, translated by Joseph Lucas (London, 1892), p. 34; Misson, *Memoirs and Observations*, p. 17.

14 'Orphan John', *Ashton Chronicle*, May 1849.

15 Blincoe estimated the number sent to the Lamberts at 80. This is much too high, but a pardonable error given that he was only seven at the time. *Memoir of Robert Blincoe*, pp. 18–19; St Pancras parish register of apprentices, 1778–1801, vol. no. P90 PAN1 361 (London Metropolitan Archives).

16 Smith, *Wealth of Nations*, book IV, chapter V, section IV.

17 Norman Gash, *Mr Secretary Peel: the Life of Sir Robert Peel to 1830* (London: Longman, 1985), p. 23; Perkin, *Origins of Modern English Society*, p. 94.

18 *Memoir of Robert Blincoe*, pp. 17–19.

19 *Memoir of Robert Blincoe*, p. 19.

20 *Memoir of Robert Blincoe*, p. 19.

Chapter 6

1 George Unwin, *Samuel Oldknow and the Arkwrights* (Longmans, 1924), p. 171; *Memoir of Robert Blincoe*, pp. 19–20.

2 *Memoir of Robert Blincoe*, p. 19.

3 Rosamond Bayne-Powell, *Travellers in Eighteenth-Century England* (London: John Murray, 1951), chapter 2.

4 Eric Pawson, *Transport and Economy: the Turnpike Roads of Eighteenth-Century Britain* (London: Academic Press, 1977), pp. 330–1; Bayne-Powell, *Travellers in Eighteenth-Century England*, p. 14; Arthur Young, *A Six Months Tour Through the North of England, containing an account of the present state of agriculture, manufactures and population, in several counties of this Kingdom* ...

interspersed with descriptions of the seats of the nobility and gentry, and other remarkable objects ... (London: printed for W. Strahan, W. Nicoll, ... B. Collins, ... J. Balfour ..., 1770), vol. 4, pp. 431–5; Liddall, *St Pancras Vestry*, p. 109.

5 John Beckett (ed.), *A Centenary History of Nottingham* (Manchester: Manchester University Press, 1997), p. 200; *Memoir of Robert Blincoe*, p. 20.

6 *Memoir of Robert Blincoe*, p. 20.

7 *Memoir of Robert Blincoe*, p. 20.

8 John Blackner, *The History of Nottingham: Embracing its Antiquities, Trade, and Manufactures, from the earliest authentic records, to the present period* (Nottingham: printed by Sutton and Son, 1815), p. 13.

9 J. Holland Walker, 'An Itinerary of Nottingham', *Transactions of the Thoroton Society*, 29 (1925); Blackner, *History of Nottingham*, pp. 14, 22, 29; quoted in Chambers, *Nottingham in the Eighteenth Century*, p. 80; Beckett, *Centenary History of Nottingham*, p. 197.

10 Beckett, *Centenary History of Nottingham*; Sheila A. Mason, *Nottingham Lace, 1760s–1950s: the Machine-made Lace Industry in Nottinghamshire, Derbyshire and Leicestershire* (Ilkeston, Derbyshire: Sheila A. Mason, 1994), pp. 72–80; Stanley D. Chapman, 'The Transition to the Factory System in the Midlands Cotton-spinning Industry', *Economic History Review*, vol. 18, no. 3 (1956), 526–43.

11 Land Tax Records, Nottinghamshire Record Office. See also Chapman, *Early Factory Masters*, pp. 82–3, 177–8.

12 *Memoir of Robert Blincoe*, p. 20; Blackner, *History of Nottingham*, pp. 238, 243.

13 Bernard Mandeville, *The Fable of the Bees; or, Private Vices, Publick Benefits* (originally published in 1714, Harmondsworth: Penguin, 1970), motto on title page; this phrase is widely attributed to Adam Smith.

14 Chambers, *Nottingham in the Eighteenth Century*, p. 190.

15 Blackner, *History of Nottingham*, p. 393; William Felkin, *An Account of the Machine-wrought Hosiery Trade: its Extent, and the Condition of the Framework-knitters, etc.* (London, 1845), pp. 115–20. See also Wells, *Wretched Faces*, pp. 37–8, 120–5.

16 *Memoir of Robert Blincoe*, p. 20.

17 *Memoir of Robert Blincoe*, p. 21; Chapman, *Early Factory Masters*, pp. 82–3.

18 Blackner, *History of Nottingham*, pp. 31, 41, 45.

Chapter 7

1 Felkin, *Machine-wrought Hosiery Trade*, p. 51. See also Edward Baines, *History of the Cotton Manufacture in Great Britain: with a notice of its early history in the East, and in all the quarters of the globe, a description of the great mechanical inventions, which have caused its unexampled extension in Britain, and a view of the present state of the manufacture, and the condition of the classes engaged in its several departments* (London: Fisher, Fisher and Jackson, 1835).

2 Baines, *History of the Cotton Manufacture*, p. 79; R.S. Fitton and A.P. Wadsworth, *The Strutts and the Arkwrights, 1758–1830: A Study of the Early Factory System* (Manchester: Manchester University Press, 1958), p. 68; Geoffrey Timmins, *Four Centuries of Lancashire Cotton*, chapter 2.

3 Felkin, *Machine-wrought Hosiery Trade*, p. 100; William Turner, *Riot! The Story of the East Lancashire Loom-breakers in 1826* (Preston: Lancashire County Books, 1992), p. 26; Sheila Masson, *Nottingham Lace*, p. 3.

4 Chapman, *Early Factory Masters*, pp. 22, 37–9, 42.

5 Chapman, 'The Transition to the Factory System', p. 528.

6 Felkin, *Machine-wrought Hosiery Trade*, pp. 110–20.

7 *Bailey's Western and Midland Directory* (1783–4); Chapman, *Early Factory Masters*, pp. 82–3. See also *Universal British Directory*, 1791–8; Abstract of Title of Messrs Lamberts: messuage, water-corn mill on the Dover Beck called Cliff Mill alias Clewles Mill, DDF 7/1 (Nottinghamshire Archives).

8 Baines, *History of the Cotton Manufacture*, chapter 8; William Thom, *Rhymes and Recollections of a Hand Loom Weaver* (London: Smith, Elder and Co., 1845).

9 Some weavers spent the morning walking three, four or more miles, calling in on single spinners seeking extra yarn; see Baines, *History of the Cotton Manufacture*, pp. 114, 117.

10 Baines, *History of the Cotton Manufacture*, pp. 119–46 and chapter 9.

11 Baines, *History of the Cotton Manufacture*, pp. 171–5.

12 Quoted in Fitton and Wadsworth, *The Strutts and the Arkwrights*, p. 199; Baines, *History of the Cotton Manufacture*, p. 148; Chapman, *Early Factory Masters*, p. 67.

13 Baines, *History of the Cotton Manufacture*, chapter 10.

14 Baines, *History of the Cotton Manufacture*, p. 152; Fitton and Wadsworth, *The Strutts and the Arkwrights*, p. 139.

15 See Baines, *History of the Cotton Manufacture*, p. 193.

Chapter 8

1 *Memoir of Robert Blincoe*, p. 23; S.M. Worrall, 'Water Power on the Dover Beck', p. 143.

2 *Memoir of Robert Blincoe*, p. 23.

3 *Memoir of Robert Blincoe*, p. 23.

4 *Memoir of Robert Blincoe*, pp. 24–5; William Ashley, 'The Place of Rye in the History of English Food', *Economic Journal*, vol. 123, no. 31 (September 1921), 285–308, p. 288. Arthur Young, *The Farmer's Letters to the People of England*, third edition (Dublin: printed for J. Millikin, 1768), p. 207.

5 *Memoir of Robert Blincoe*, p. 24.

6 *Memoir of Robert Blincoe*, p. 25.

7 *Memoir of Robert Blincoe*, pp. 26–7.

8 *Memoir of Robert Blincoe*, p. 27.

9 *Memoir of Robert Blincoe*, p. 27.

10 *Memoir of Robert Blincoe*, p. 28.

11 *Memoir of Robert Blincoe*, p. 29; John and Barbara Hammond, *The Town Labourer*, p. 109.

12 *Memoir of Robert Blincoe*, p. 30.

13 Evidence of John Moss and William Sidgwick in *Select Committee on the State of the Children ... 1816*, pp. 179, 115.

14 *Memoir of Robert Blincoe*, pp. 30–2.
15 *Memoir of Robert Blincoe*, p. 31.
16 *Memoir of Robert Blincoe*, pp. 33–4.
17 Quoted in Clifford Morsley, *News from the English Countryside, 1750–1850* (London: Harrap, 1979), p. 27; and Chambers, *Nottingham in the Eighteenth Century*, p. 330.
18 *Memoir of Robert Blincoe*, p. 35.

Chapter 9

1 Baines, *History of the Cotton Manufacture*, pp. 181–2. My thanks to Dr Alan Crosby for help in clarifying Blincoe's probable role.
2 *Memoir of Robert Blincoe*, pp. 28–9.
3 *Memoir of Robert Blincoe*, p. 35.
4 *Memoir of Robert Blincoe*, pp. 35, 29.
5 Robert Southey, *Sir Thomas More, or, Colloquies on the Progress and Prospects of Society* (London: John Murray, 1829), vol. 1, p. 171; Robert Southey, *Letters from England* (London: Cresset Press, 1951); David Eastwood, 'Robert Southey and the Intellectual Origins of Romantic Conservatism', *English Historical Review*, vol. 104 (1989), 307–21, p. 316; Asa Briggs, *Essays in Labour History, 1918–1939* (London: Croom Helm, 1977); David Roberts, *Paternalism in Early Victorian England* (London: Croom Helm, 1979).
6 Ashmore, 'The Early Textile Industry in the Derwent Valley', p. 4; John Dinwiddy, *From Luddism to the First Reform Bill: Reform in England, 1810–1832* (Oxford: Blackwell, 1987), pp. 26–7; Baines, *History of the Cotton Manufacture*, p. 160.
7 Hugh Cunningham, *Children and Childhood in Western Society since 1500* (Harlow: Pearson/Longman, 2005); Horn, *Children's Work and Welfare*; Kirby, *Child Labour*; Kussmaul, *Rural Economy of England*; Clark Nardinelli, *Child Labor and the Industrial Revolution* (Bloomington, IN: Indiana University Press, 1990); Ivy Pinchbeck and Margaret Hewitt, *Children in English Society* (London: Routledge and Kegan Paul, 1969–73); Cunningham, 'The Employment and Unemployment of Children; Clark Nardinelli, 'Child Labor and the Factory Acts', *Journal of Economic History*, vol. 40, no. 4 (1980), 739–55; Carolyn Tuttle, 'A Revival of the Pessimist View: Child Labor and the Industrial Revolution', *Research in Economic History*, 18 (1998), 53–82.
8 Defoe quoted in Lane, *Apprenticeship*, p. 98; David Hume quoted in Christopher Lawrence and Steven Shapin (eds), *Science Incarnate: Historical Embodiments of Natural Knowledge* (London: University of Chicago Press, 1998), p. 67; the poet, historian and politician Thomas Babington Macaulay had a point when he observed that the 1800s ushered in not so much greater cruelty as the 'intelligence which discerns it'. See Cunningham, 'The Employment and Unemployment of Children', p. 110.
9 Early in the 1700s, brandy shops and geneva shops thrived in London, selling poisonous and highly intoxicating liquors. Responsible locals pointed to the sickening destruction of adult life that they caused, the orphaning of children on a vast scale, and the neglect of infants 'starved and naked at home', not to

mention the damage done to foetuses by mothers imbibing large quantities of gin. But landowners were making too much money selling grain to distillers to entertain scruples. When the government tried to restrict licences for the sale of spirits, aristocrats cried foul and joined forces with gin retailers to stymie the legislation. It took the combined efforts of city authorities, philanthropists, physicians, and the urban middle classes, all rightly convinced that cheap gin was destroying the metropolis, to force the landed interest to back down. The peerage might have held out even longer had a rise in grain prices not made them less reliant on the income from distillers. See George, *London Life*, pp. 41–55.

10 Sidney and Beatrice Webb wrote: 'It is characteristic of the country gentlemen that it was not to the love of money that their judicial impartiality and intellectual integrity succumbed, but to their overmastering desire to maintain their field sports and protect the amenity of their country seats.' Quoted in Chambers, *Nottingham in the Eighteenth Century*, p. 74.

11 Place, *Autobiography*, p. 34 and Rod Morgan, 'John Howard (1726?–1790)', *Dictionary of National Biography* (Oxford: Oxford University Press, 2005).

12 Quoted in James Walvin, *A Child's World: a Social History of English Childhood, 1800–1914* (Harmondsworth: Penguin, 1982), p. 48; Blackner, *History of Nottingham*, p. 123. John Blackner was incensed at this kind of treatment. A Radical humanitarian, he deemed it 'unbecoming severity' (p. 126).

13 See E.P. Thompson, *The Making of the English Working Class* (London: Gollancz, 1963), pp. 366–70 and Tuttle, 'A Revival of the Pessimist View', pp. 72–3.

14 Engels cited in John T. Ward's *The Factory System* (New York: Barnes and Noble, 1970), vol. 1, p. 67. See also Cruickshank, *Children and Industry*, p. 11 and John and Barbara Hammond, *The Town Labourer*, chapter 8.

15 Pollard, 'The Factory Village', p. 515; Sir James Kay-Shuttleworth, *The Moral and Physical Condition of the Working Classes Employed in the Cotton Manufacture in Manchester* (London: J. Ridgway, 1832), p. 12.

16 *Memoir of Robert Blincoe*, p. 29.

17 Ure, *Philosophy of Manufactures*, p. 290.

18 Evidence of Thomas Bennett, *Select Committee on the State of the Children … 1816*, p. 103.

19 Cited in Cruickshank, *Children and Industry*, p. 9.

20 Fitton and Wadsworth, *The Strutts and the Arkwrights*, pp. 92–9; Cruickshank, *Children and Industry*, pp. 15–20; for an accessible summary of their labour practices, see James Cooper, *Transformation of a Valley: the Derbyshire Derwent* (London: Heinemann, 1981), chapter 9.

21 Margaret Cole, *Robert Owen of New Lanark* (New York: A.M. Kelley, 1969); Ian Donnachie, *Robert Owen: Owen of New Lanark and New Harmony* (East Linton: Tuckwell, 2000); Fitton and Wadsworth, *The Strutts and the Arkwrights*, pp. 234–5.

22 Pollard, 'The Factory Village', p. 529.

23 *Memoir of Robert Blincoe*, p. 41.

Chapter 10

1 *Memoir of Robert Blincoe*, p. 36. Parish apprenticeship registers (London Metropolitan archives).

2 Gregory Claeys, 'Owen, Robert (1771–1858)', *Dictionary of National Biography* (Oxford: Oxford University Press, 2005). A particularly gruesome example of death caused by spinning machinery was reported by *The Times* on 7 February 1826. An eight-year-old girl 'had her head entirely cut off from her body' after her clothes became entangled in the shaft. Her headless body was discovered 'revolving, at a most frightful speed, with the shaft'. *The Times*, p. 3, issue 12884, col. D.

3 Rose, 'Social Policy and Business', p. 22. Evidence of Theodore Price, Esquire, *Select Committee on the State of the Children ... 1816*, p. 123.

4 See A.G.E. Jones, 'The Putrid Fever at Robert Peel's Radcliffe Mill', *Notes and Queries*, January 1958, 26–35, p. 34.

5 Lord Stanley's copy letter book, 1802–3, DDK box 168 (Lancashire Record Office).

6 See Thomas, *Early Factory Legislation*, pp. 7–17.

7 See evidence of Nathaniel Gould, *Select Committee on the State of the Children ... 1816*, p. 328.

8 John and Barbara Hammond, *The Town Labourer*, pp. 167–9 and p. 23, fn. 7.

9 Letter from Reverend Sir William Henry Clark to Lord Stanley, 24 May 1802, from Lord Stanley's copy letter book (1802–3), DDK box 168 (Lancashire Record Office).

10 Chapman, *Early Factory Masters*, p. 175.

11 Evidence of William Sidgwick, *Select Committee on the State of the Children ... 1816*, p. 115; Ursula R.Q. Henriques, *Before the Welfare State: Social Administration in Early Industrial Britain* (London: Longman, 1979), pp. 68–70; *Memoir of Robert Blincoe*, pp. 37–8.

12 *Memoir of Robert Blincoe*, p. 37; St Pancras Vestry Minutes, no. 450, 1 January 1801.

13 *Memoir of Robert Blincoe*, p. 37.

14 *Memoir of Robert Blincoe*, pp. 38–9.

15 Robert Owen, *Crisis*, vol. 3, no. 21, 18 January 1834; John Throsby, *The History and Antiquities of the Town and County of the Town of Nottingham: containing the whole of Thoroton's account of that place, and all that is valuable in Deering* (Nottingham: sold by Burbage and Stretton, Tupman, Wilson and Sutton, 1795), p. 70; Blackner, *History of Nottingham*, pp. 393–5. Eventually, the sheriff and county gentlemen leaned on the millers and bakers to lower the price of flour. But alarmed lest this be seen as rewarding rioters, the Home Office insisted that price restrictions be lifted. Reinforcements were sent in and nightly curfews imposed. The poor of Nottingham continued to make their resentment felt through posters, letters and graffiti. When a soup kitchen ran dry on Christmas Day, riots erupted once more. See Wells, *Wretched Faces*, pp. 58–63.

16 Blackner, *History of Nottingham*, p. 396.

17 *Memoir of Robert Blincoe*, p. 39.

18 See Chapman, *Early Factory Masters*, chapter 11.
19 To make matters worse, during the first years of the new century the unthinkable happened. Stockings fell gradually out of vogue. In part due to the earnest moralising of the evangelical movement, with the advent of the new century, clothing in general became far more restrained. In this sterner cultural milieu, silk stockings were associated with hedonism and effeminacy. So, in preference to knee-breeches worn with stockings, men increasingly wore ankle-length pantaloons. Hence William and Francis Lambert were producing yarn for a slowly vanishing market.
20 *Memoir of Robert Blincoe*, pp. 39–40; Liddall, appendix V.A., p. 333.
21 *Memoir of Robert Blincoe*, p. 40.
22 *Memoir of Robert Blincoe*, p. 41.
23 Evidence of John Moss and William Travers, *Select Committee on the State of the Children ... 1816*, pp. 179–85 and pp. 288–93, p. 291.
24 *Memoir of Robert Blincoe*, p. 32.

Chapter 11

1 *Memoir of Robert Blincoe*, pp. 44–5.
2 Fitton and Wadsworth, *The Strutts and the Arkwrights*, pp. 100–3; Reverend David P. Davies, *A New Historical and Descriptive View of Derbyshire from the Remotest Period to the Present Time* (Belper, Derbyshire: S. Mason, 1811), p. 29. See also Cooper, *The Transformation of a Valley*, pp. 243–5.
3 *Memoir of Robert Blincoe*, pp. 44–5.
4 *Memoir of Robert Blincoe*, p. 45; John Byng quoted in Fitton and Wadsworth, *The Strutts and the Arkwrights*, p. 97.
5 *Memoir of Robert Blincoe*, p. 45; William Bray, *Sketch of a Tour into Derbyshire and Yorkshire: including part of Buckingham, Warwick, Leicester, Nottingham, Northampton, Bedford, and Hertford-shires* (London: printed for B. White, 1778), p. 102; James Pilkington, *A View of the Present State of Derbyshire; with an Account of its most Remarkable Antiquities, etc.* (Derby: J. Drewry, 1789), p. 57. For Brown's description, see Robert Gray, *The Factory Question and Industrial England, 1830–1860* (New York: Cambridge University Press, 1996), p. 139 and Cooper, *The Transformation of a Valley*, pp. 227–8.
6 William Adam, *The Gem of the Peak: or, Matlock Bath and its Vicinity ...* (London: Longman and Co., 1843), pp. 67–9; Cooper, *The Transformation of a Valley*, pp. 222–4; *Memoir of Robert Blincoe*, p. 45; John B. Firth, *Highways and Byways in Derbyshire, with illustrations by Nelly Erichsen* (London: Macmillan, 1905), p. 230; *Pigot and Co.'s Directory of Derbys, Herefs ...*, 1835. See also M.H. Mackenzie, 'Cressbrook and Litton Mills, 1779–1835. Part 1', *Derbyshire Archaeological Journal*, vol. 88 (1968), 1–25, pp. 2–3.
7 *Memoir of Robert Blincoe*, p. 45.
8 *Memoir of Robert Blincoe*, pp. 45–6. For a picture of the entrance to the 'prentice house, see Cooper, *Transformation of a Valley*, p. 224. It seems that the gateposts no longer survive.
9 *Memoir of Robert Blincoe*, p. 48; [Joseph Rayner Stephens], *Ashton Chronicle*, 19 May 1849, p. 6 (reproduced in Martin Hulbert (ed.), *Orphan Child Factory*

Workers at Litton and Cressbrook Mills (unpublished pamphlet, no date), pp. 4–11).

10 *Ashton Chronicle*, p. 9.

11 *Memoir of Robert Blincoe*, p. 43.

12 See Mackenzie, 'Cressbrook and Litton Mills', pp. 12–13. I am grateful here for the research conducted by Helen Mycock; 'Valuation of Hill and Hargate Wall Estates, 29th April 1795' (Bagshawe MSS, John Rytlands Library, Manchester). See also Chapman, *Early Factory Masters*, pp. 200–1 and p. 229, fn. 51.

13 Mackenzie, 'Cressbrook and Litton Mills', p. 13. The decline in the family's fortunes was such that the codicil to Hannah Hague's will, dated January 1792, worried that her sons would not be able to pay the annuity promised to her daughter, also called Hannah.

14 Pilkington, *Derbyshire*, pp. 409–10. Pilkington counted 52 stocking frames in Litton and a 'few hand machines or jennies for spinning cotton' in Tideswell. See Helen Harris, *The Industrial Archaeology of the Peak District* (Newton Abbot: David and Charles, 1971), p. 105.

15 Baines, *History of the Cotton Manufacture*, p. 90 and pp. 166–9; Fitton and Wadsworth, *The Strutts and the Arkwrights*, p. 86.

16 Fitton and Wadsworth, *The Strutts and the Arkwrights*, p. 86; Mackenzie, 'Cressbrook and Litton Mills', p. 6; the relationship of Newton and Seward is described in Joseph Tilley, *The Old Halls, Manors, and Families of Derbyshire, vol. 1, The High Peak Hundred* (London: Simpkin, Marshall, Hamilton, Kent, and Co. Ltd, 1892), p. 144.

17 Mackenzie, 'Cressbrook and Litton Mills', p. 13; *Nottingham Journal*, 11 February 1786; *Derby Mercury*, 10 August 1786. See also J.M.J. Fletcher, *Tideswell in the Days of Parson Brown* (reprinted from 1927 pamphlet by Tideswell Women's Institute, 1977, and republished by S.J. Books, 1986), p. 7.

18 Mackenzie, 'Cressbrook and Litton Mills', pp. 17, 22; *Derbyshire Deeds* (Matlock: Derbyshire Record Office), MSS 3566, 7 June 1819; MSS 3541, 1 February 1819; MSS 3560, 3 June 1819. See also Chapman, *Early Factory Masters*, p. 201.

19 See Cooper, *Transformation of a Valley*, pp. 224–5. The advert added, not altogether truthfully, 'Litton Mill is … well supplied with Hands from the neighbouring Villages at Low Wages.'

20 *Derbyshire Deeds*, MSS 3541. Farey, *Derbyshire*, vol. 3, p. 503.

21 Farey, *Derbyshire*, p. 504; Mackenzie, 'Cressbrook and Litton Mills', p. 17. *Derbyshire Deeds* (Derbyshire Public Library), MSS 3560/38, 23 February 1816. Ellis Needham's handwriting can be seen on the churchwarden's account books for Wormhill.

22 Wills of Hannah Hague (Lichfield diocesan record office).

23 Jurors' Books, 1784–1815 (Derbyshire County Record Office). Ellis and Sarah wed on 25 January 1787, and their son John was born on 9 September 1787. Helen Mycock has reconstructed the Ellis family tree (unpublished MS). See also Mackenzie, 'Cressbrook and Litton Mills', p. 13.

24 'The Diary of Parson Brown of Tideswell' (University of Birmingham Library). For Brown's taste for ale see, for example, 13 and 14 January 1796. Canon

Fletcher quotes extensively from the diaries – see 'Tideswell in the Days of Parson Brown'.

25 Fletcher, 'Parson Brown', pp. 1–3, 3–4.
26 Firth, *Highways and Byways in Derbyshire*, p. 239; Mackenzie, 'Cressbrook and Litton Mills', p. 18; *Derbyshire Deeds* (Derbyshire Public Library), MSS 3547.
27 See Parson Brown's diary for 26 September 1791 and 9 June 1796. See also Fletcher, 'Parson Brown', pp. 3–4.
28 Parson Brown's diary, 16 September 1797; Fletcher, 'Parson Brown', p. 7; *Derbyshire Deeds* (Derbyshire Public Library), MSS 3560, 3 June 1819; Mackenzie, 'Cressbrook and Litton Mills', p. 19.

Chapter 12

1 *Memoir of Robert Blincoe*, pp. 49, 75; *House of Lords Account of Cotton and Woollen Mills and Factories in the United Kingdom of Great Britain and Ireland, 1803–1818 (Parliamentary Papers*, 1819, CVIII, Lords' Sessional Papers), pp. 48–9, 50.
2 *Memoir of Robert Blincoe*, pp. 47, 67.
3 *Ashton Chronicle*, p. 9; *Memoir of Robert Blincoe*, p. 63; for the magistrates' reports, see following chapter and *House of Lords Account of Cotton Mills*, pp. 48–9, 50.
4 *Poor Man's Advocate*, Saturday 9 June 1832, p. 1; Peter Gaskell, *Artisans and Machinery: the Moral and Physical Condition of the Manufacturing Population Considered with Reference to Mechanical Substitutes for Human Labour* (London, 1836), pp. 147–8.
5 *Memoir of Robert Blincoe*, pp. 46–8, 62, 63.
6 *Memoir of Robert Blincoe*, pp. 47, 63, 67.
7 *Memoir of Robert Blincoe*, pp. 63–4.
8 *Memoir of Robert Blincoe*, pp. 47–8, 63; Farey, *Derbyshire*, p. 156; *Ashton Chronicle*, p. 6.
9 *Memoir of Robert Blincoe*, pp. 56–7. See *Second Report of the Central Board of His Majesty's Commissioners appointed to collect information in the manufacturing districts, as to the employment of children in factories, and as to the propriety and means of curtailing the hours of their labour* (London: The House of Commons, 15 July 1833), pp. 17–18; *Poor Man's Advocate*, Saturday 9 June 1832, p. 1.
10 *Memoir of Robert Blincoe*, pp. 56–8. Blincoe and Brown called the mule a 'spinning-frame'.
11 *Memoir of Robert Blincoe*, p. 57.
12 *Memoir of Robert Blincoe*, pp. 58–9.
13 *Memoir of Robert Blincoe*, pp. 57–8, 60–2, 71.
14 *Memoir of Robert Blincoe*, pp. 57, 70.
15 *Second Report of the Central Board of His Majesty's Commissioners … 1833*, p. 18.
16 *Ashton Chronicle*, p. 7; *Memoir of Robert Blincoe*, pp. 61–2.
17 *Memoir of Robert Blincoe*, p. 61; *Ashton Chronicle*, p. 8.
18 Chapman, *Early Factory Masters*, pp. 2, 3, 4. For the counter-view, see

Mackenzie, 'Cressbrook and Litton Mills', pp. 23–4. For the treatment of children in schools, see Walvin, *A Child's World*, especially p. 50 and Place, *Autobiography*, pp. 43–62.

19 Fletcher, 'Parson Brown', p. 12. 'Parson Brown's diary', 29 November 1790; 'Mad-Houses', *The Times*, Wednesday 4 October 1815, p. 4, issue 9643, col. A; Montgomery, *Chimney-Sweeper's Friend*, p. 16; Mackenzie, 'Cressbrook and Litton Mills', p. 18.

20 Fletcher, 'Parson Brown', p. 12; *Ashton Chronicle*, p. 14.

21 *The Lion*, 22 February 1828, p. 238; Derbyshire Quarter Sessions Order Book for 1816, pp. 290, 356–7, and Order Book for 1817, pp. 442–3 (Derbyshire Record Office).

22 *Memoir of Robert Blincoe*, pp. 48–9; burial registers of Tideswell, Wormhill and Taddington (Lichfield Diocesan Registry); Mackenzie, 'Cressbrook and Litton Mills', p. 10; Chapman, *Early Factory Masters*, p. 206; Kay-Shuttleworth, *Condition of the Working Classes*, p. 67. In seeking to discredit Blincoe's *Memoir*, Chapman counted the number of fatalities from Litton Mill in the Tideswell parish registers and compared this figure with the fatalities for Cressbrook Mill. In both mills, he reckoned, there were only six deaths between 1780 and 1810. Chapman acknowledged Blincoe's statement about others having been laid to rest in Taddington, but he brushed this off as unimportant. H.M. Mackenzie's research demonstrates the contrary: more than four times as many Litton Mill apprentices were buried in Taddington as in Tideswell. Perhaps had Chapman consulted the Taddington burial registers as well he might have revised his general conclusions. It's also important to remember that since parish apprentices weren't always recorded as such in these registers, the death rate has almost certainly been understated.

23 *Memoir of Robert Blincoe*, pp. 48, 52, 54, and Mackenzie, 'Cressbrook and Litton Mills', p. 23. I am grateful to John Palmer for drawing my attention to the Quarter Session records. They were originally transcribed by Michael Cox.

24 *Memoir of Robert Blincoe*, pp. 68–70.

25 *Memoir of Robert Blincoe*, pp. 62–3.

26 *Memoir of Robert Blincoe*, p. 68.

27 *Ashton Chronicle*, p. 7; *Memoir of Robert Blincoe*, pp. 69, 71.

28 *Memoir of Robert Blincoe*, pp. 65–7.

29 *Memoir of Robert Blincoe*, p. 64.

Chapter 13

1 *Account of the Cotton and Woollen Mills*, pp. 46–57. Details are given in Charles J. Cox, *Three Centuries of Derbyshire Annals*, vol. 2 (London: Bemrose and Sons, 1890), pp. 211–13.

2 Firth, *Highways and Byways*, pp. 156, 159; Joseph Denman, *Observations on the Effects of Buxton Water* (London: printed for J. Johnson, 1793; second edition 1801), p. 106; Ernest Axon, 'Historical Notes on Buxton, its Inhabitants and Visitors: Buxton Doctors Since 1700', *Buxton Advertiser*, 23 December 1939; memorial inscriptions of St Martin's Church in Stoney Middleton. Denman managed to make use of the warm springs in Stoney Middleton too – see *Kelly's*

Directory of the Counties of Derby, Notts, Leicester and Rutland … 1891, pp. 308–9. See also Joseph Arnould, *Memoir of Thomas, First Lord Denman, Formerly Lord Chief Justice of England* (London: Longmans, Green, and Co., 1873).

3 *Memoir of Robert Blincoe*, pp. 41, 77–8.

4 Evidence of David Evans, *Select Committee on the State of the Children … 1816*; see also Thomas, *The Early Factory Legislation*, p. 13; *Account of the Cotton and Woollen Mills*, p. 48. Denman shows some confusion regarding the stipulations of the 1802 Act – see p. 49.

5 *Account of the Cotton and Woollen Mills*, p. 48.

6 *Memoir of Robert Blincoe*, pp. 77–8.

7 John and Barbara Hammond, *The Town Labourer*, pp. 134–6 and Mackenzie, p. 19; *Derby Mercury*, 26 January 1809.

8 Pollard, 'The Factory Village', p. 526. See also John and Barbara Hammond, *The Town Labourer*, p. 16; Farey, *Derbyshire*, vol. 2, p. 27. John Farey expressed his admiration for Ellis's cultivation of potatoes and carrots (the latter were fed to horses 'with good effect'). Farey also admired his high-walled garden at Hargate Wall, and his innovative practice of 'transplanting' onions when they were about the size 'of Goose-quills at bottom, at proper distances from each other'. Farey, *Derbyshire*, vol. 2, pp. 150–1, 152, 207, 212.

9 *Account of the Cotton and Woollen Mills*, p. 48.

10 *Account of the Cotton and Woollen Mills*, p. 48.

11 See Mackenzie, 'Cressbrook and Litton Mills', p. 11; *Derbyshire Deeds* (Derbyshire Borough Library), vol. 15, MSS 3560, no. 43.

12 Mackenzie, 'Cressbrook and Litton Mills', p. 11; Hulbert, *Orphan Child Factory Workers*, pp. 11–22.

Chapter 14

1 For Ellis Needham's rise to local popularity, see Mackenzie, 'Cressbrook and Litton Mills', p. 24. The nature of the Buxton assemblies are briefly described in Firth, *Highways and Byways*, p. 160. In some towns there were separate facilities for the amusement of 'wealthy Tradesmen'; in others, steward and guests simply made them feel unwelcome. See Dorothy Marshall, *English People in the Eighteenth Century* (London: Longmans, Green, 1956), pp. 130–1. There is a possibility that the Needhams introduced school-teaching, albeit of a desultory kind, after Dr Denman's complaints.

2 Douglas Johnson, 'Anna Seward at Buxton, 1808', *Derbyshire Miscellany*, vol. 10, pt. 6 (Autumn 1985), pp. 175–6, p. 176.

3 Mackenzie, 'Cressbrook and Litton Mills', p. 12. Disruptions to trade severely affected cotton manufacturers, since not only did all the raw material come from overseas, but as much as 60% of the manufactured articles were exported to overseas markets. See Duncan Bythell, 'The Hand-loom Weavers in the English Cotton Industry during the Industrial Revolution: Some Problems', *Economic History Review*, vol. 17, no. 2 (1964), 339–53, p. 340. See also P. Deane and W.A. Cole, *British Economic Growth, 1688–1959* (Cambridge: Cambridge University Press, 1962), p. 187. For the economic difficulties of English manufacturers, see Evans, *Forging of the Modern State*, pp. 82–5.

4 Mackenzie, 'Cressbrook and Litton Mills', p. 20; *Derbyshire Deeds* (Derbyshire Borough Library), 3563/8, 22 March 1811 and MSS 3568, 11 May 1811.

5 *Account of the Cotton and Woollen Mills*, p. 50; Marmaduke Middleton, *Poetical Sketches of a Tour in the West of England* (Sheffield: printed for the author by J. Montgomery, 1822); Farey, *Derbyshire*, vol. 2, p. 205.

6 Tilley, *Halls, Manors, and Families of Derbyshire*, p. 144; William Wood, *The History and Antiquities of Eyam; with a Minute Account of the Great Plague which Desolated that Village in the Year 1666* (London, 1848), p. 27.

7 Middleton, *Poetical Sketches*, p. 43.

8 Mackenzie, 'Cressbrook and Litton Mills', p. 23; *Account of the Cotton and Woollen Mills*, p. 50. See George Unwin, *Samuel Oldknow and the Arkwrights* (London: Longmans, 1924), chapter 11.

9 *Account of the Cotton and Woollen Mills*, p. 50.

10 *Account of the Cotton and Woollen Mills*, p. 50.

11 *Account of the Cotton and Woollen Mills*, p. 50.

12 John Joseph Betts (letter), *The Lion*, 22 February 1828, p. 238.

13 Mackenzie, 'Cressbrook and Litton Mills', p. 20; deeds and letters of William Cheek relating to Ellis Needham's bankruptcy (Derbyshire Record Office); Chapman, *Early Factory Masters*, p. 202.

14 Nardinelli, *Child Labor and the Industrial Revolution*, early chapters; Rose, 'Social Policy and Business', pp. 20–2; Chapman, *Early Factory Masters*, p. 173.

15 Rose, 'Social Policy and Business', pp. 20–1. For corroborative testimony, see *Account of the Cotton and Woollen Mills*, pp. 188, 211–12; Ure, *Philosophy of Manufactures*, p. 336. Note that Ure was highlighting the suffering of the weavers as a means of diminishing the plight of the spinners.

16 Nardinelli, *Child Labor and the Industrial Revolution*, early chapters.

17 Peel cited in Rose, 'Social Policy and Business', p. 23. See also Sir Samuel Romilly, *Memoirs of the Life of Sir Samuel Romilly, Written by Himself* (London, 1840), vol. 2, pp. 372, 392.

18 John and Barbara Hammond, *The Town Labourer*, pp. 107–8.

Chapter 15

1 *Memoir of Robert Blincoe*, pp. 71–2.

2 See J.T. Ward and W.H. Fraser (eds), *Workers and Employers: Documents on Trade Unions and Industrial Relations in Britain since the Eighteenth Century* (London: Macmillan, 1980), pp. 15–19.

3 Kay-Shuttleworth, *Condition of the Working Classes*, p. 71. See also Perkin, *Origins of Modern English Society*, chapter 6, and Asa Briggs, *Essays in Labour History*, chapter 1.

4 *Memoir of Robert Blincoe*, pp. 72–3.

5 *Memoir of Robert Blincoe*, p. 72.

6 *Ashton Chronicle*, p. 10. The victim's name was James Arnott.

7 *Memoir of Robert Blincoe*, pp. 72–3.

8 *Memoir of Robert Blincoe*, pp. 72–3.

9 For details of Bakewell, see *Pigot and Co.'s Directory of Cheshire, Cumbria ..., 1828–29*; *Memoir of Robert Blincoe*, p. 73.

10 Davies, *History of Derbyshire*, p. 60; See also *Kelly's Directory of the Counties of Derby, Notts, Leicester and Rutland* (London, 1891), pp. 305–6; *Memoir of Robert Blincoe*, p. 73.

11 *Memoir of Robert Blincoe*, p. 73.

12 *Memoir of Robert Blincoe*, p. 73. Blincoe's spellings are idiosyncratic. For 'Thornhill' he wrote 'Thornelly' and he spelt 'Eyam' as 'Heam'. It should be remembered that Blincoe was all but illiterate at the time.

Chapter 16

1 See Wood, *History of Eyam*, early chapters.

2 *Memoir of Robert Blincoe*, p. 74; Wood, *History of Eyam*, p. 27.

3 *Memoir of Robert Blincoe*, p. 74.

4 *Memoir of Robert Blincoe*, p. 74.

5 See John and Barbara Hammond, *The Town Labourer*, p. 52.

6 Approximately two million Frenchmen died to satisfy the imperial ambitions of the Napoleonic regime.

7 Malcolm I. Thomis (ed.), *Luddism in Nottinghamshire* (London: Phillimore, 1972); M.I. Thomis, *Politics and Society in Nottingham, 1785–1835* (Oxford: Oxford University Press, 1969). See also Fleischman, *Conditions of Life among the Cotton Workers*, p. 200, and E.J. Hobsbawm, 'The Machine Breakers', *Past and Present*, no. 1 (February 1952), 57–70.

8 *Parliamentary Debates*, first series, vol. 20, 1811, col. 609. See also Felkin, *An Account of the Machine-wrought Hosiery Trade*, pp. 230–40.

9 See John and Barbara Hammond, *The Town Labourer*, pp. 162–3.

10 Mackenzie, 'Cressbrook and Litton Mills', p. 20; *Memoir of Robert Blincoe*, p. 74.

11 *Memoir of Robert Blincoe*, pp. 74–5.

12 *Memoir of Robert Blincoe*, p. 75.

13 *Memoir of Robert Blincoe*, p. 75.

Chapter 17

1 *Memoir of Robert Blincoe*, p. 75.

2 *Memoir of Robert Blincoe*, pp. 75–6.

3 For the appearance of Leam Hall in the early 1800s, see the drawing in Tilley, *The Old Halls, Manors, and Families of Derbyshire*, p. 142. The external appearance has hardly changed to this day. *Memoir of Robert Blincoe*, p. 76.

4 *Memoir of Robert Blincoe*, p. 76.

5 *Memoir of Robert Blincoe*, pp. 76–7.

6 *Memoir of Robert Blincoe*, pp. 77–8.

7 Cheek papers relating to the Needhams' bankruptcy (Derbyshire Record Office); Mackenzie, 'Cressbrook and Litton Mills', pp. 20–1; *Derbyshire Deeds* (Derbyshire Record Office), MSS 3563/11, 2 May–25 December 1811. Bankruptcies had already robbed Ellis and his sons of several local friends and allies. He now seems to have quarrelled with Parson Brown, who had earlier refused to support his loans. Brown ditched his erstwhile patron with the cold business logic that made him a fine usurer but a mediocre cleric. When a son

and daughter of Ellis and Sarah's married Ann and William Bass, respectively, the ceremony took place in Ashbourne Church, not in Tideswell. It's hard not to read this as a deliberate snub against the fair-weather parson. See Mackenzie, 'Cressbrook and Litton Mills', pp. 20–1.

8 *Memoir of Robert Blincoe*, p. 79. Of course, it's entirely possible that Robert was given the name 'Blincoe' at random. It's not clear if he reflected seriously on this more painful possibility.

9 *Memoir of Robert Blincoe*, p. 79.

10 John Joseph Betts (letter), *The Lion*, 22 February 1828, p. 238. For more on Betts, see Marc William Steinberg, *Fighting Words: Working-class Formation, Collective Action, and Discourse in Early Nineteenth-century England* (Ithaca, NY: Cornell University Press, 1999); *Second Report of the Central Board ... appointed to collect information in the manufacturing districts, as to the employment of children in factories*, pp. 17–18.

11 *Memoir of Robert Blincoe*, p. 79.

12 *Memoir of Robert Blincoe*, p. 79.

13 *Memoir of Robert Blincoe*, pp. 79–80; Farey, *Derbyshire*, vol. 3, pp. 625–6.

14 *Memoir of Robert Blincoe*, p. 80.

Chapter 18

1 For Paine, see Gregory Claeys, *Thomas Paine: Social and Political Thought* (Boston, MA: Unwin Hyman, 1989) and Eric Foner, *Tom Paine and Revolutionary America* (New York: Oxford University Press, 1976).

2 See Evans, *Forging of a Modern State*, pp. 66–8.

3 See John and Barbara Hammond, *The Town Labourer*, p. 72.

4 Melville W. Patterson, *Sir Francis Burdett and his Times (1770–1844): including hitherto unpublished letters of Mrs Fitzherbert, George Prince of Wales, the Duke of York and others* (London: Macmillan, 1931), vol. 1, p. 34; Marc Baer, 'Burdett, Sir Francis', *Dictionary of National Biography* (Oxford: Oxford University Press, 2005).

5 John Walter Osborne, *John Cartwright* (Cambridge: Cambridge University Press, 1972).

6 Raymond Williams, *Cobbett* (Oxford: Oxford University Press, 1983), pp. 1–4; George Spater, *William Cobbett: the Poor Man's Friend* (Cambridge: Cambridge University Press, 1982); Samuel Bamford, *Passages in the Life of a Radical* (Oxford: Oxford University Press, 1967), vol. 2, pp. 11–12; Evans, *Forging of the Modern State*, pp. 184–5.

7 Williams, *Cobbett*, pp. 25–7.

8 Williams, *Cobbett*, p. 30.

9 John Belchem, *'Orator' Hunt: Henry Hunt and English Working-class Radicalism* (Oxford: Clarendon Press, 1985).

10 See Joyce Marlow, *The Peterloo Massacre* (London: Rapp and Whiting, 1969), pp. 23, 41.

11 For the treatment of working-class Radicals, see John and Barbara Hammond, *The Town Labourer*, p. 53; Archibald Prentice, *Historical Sketches and Personal*

Recollections of Manchester: intended to illustrate the progress of public opinion from 1792 to 1832 (London: Cass, 1970 reprint), pp. 77–80.

12 Cited in Perkin, *Origins of Modern English Society*, p. 213.

Chapter 19

1 Derek Brumhead, Roger Bryant and Ron Weston, *New Mills: a Look Back at its Industrial Heritage* (New Mills, Derbyshire: New Mills Local History Society, 1997).

2 Evidence of Theodore Price, *Select Committee on the State of the Children ... 1816*, p. 122.

3 See Michael Huberman, 'Invisible Handshakes in Lancashire: Cotton Spinning in the First Half of the Nineteenth Century', *Journal of Economic History*, vol. 46, no. 4 (December 1986), 987–98, p. 990; Michael Huberman, 'Industrial Relations and the Industrial Revolution: Evidence from M'Connel and Kennedy, 1810–1840', *Business History Review*, vol. 65, no. 2 (Summer 1991), pp. 345–78.

4 George Unwin (ed.), *Samuel Oldknow and the Arkwrights* (Manchester: Manchester University Press, 1924), chapters 9–11; Roy Millward and Adrian Robinson, *The Peak District* (Eyre Methuen: The Regions of Britain series, 1975), pp. 215–18.

5 Unwin, *Samuel Oldknow and the Arkwrights*, chapter 11.

6 Unwin, *Samuel Oldknow and the Arkwrights*, pp. 172–4.

7 *Memoir of Robert Blincoe*, p. 82.

8 See the St Pancras apprenticeship registers, 1802–67, vol. no. P90 PAN1 362 (London Metropolitan Archives).

9 *Memoir of Robert Blincoe*, p. 82.

10 *Memoir of Robert Blincoe*, pp. 82–3; Unwin, *Samuel Oldknow and the Arkwrights*, p. 174.

11 *Memoir of Robert Blincoe*, p. 83.

12 Evidence of Alexander Dean, *Report from the Select Committee on the 'Bill to Regulate the Labour of Children in the Mills and Factories of the United Kingdom' ... 1831–2* (Shannon: Irish University Press, 1968–9), p. 374; *Memoir of Robert Blincoe*, p. 83.

13 Evidence of Richard Arkwright, *Select Committee on the State of the Children ... 1816*, p. 284.

14 Ian Haynes, *Stalybridge Cotton Mills* (Manchester: Neil Richardson, 1990), pp. 4–7. The population had reached 12,000 by 1825; see Cruickshank, *Children and Industry*, p. 12.

15 *Memoir of Robert Blincoe*, pp. 86–7. See Haynes, *Stalybridge Cotton Mills*, pp. 19–20.

16 *Memoir of Robert Blincoe*, p. 87; Haynes, *Stalybridge Cotton Mills*, p. 25.

17 *Memoir of Robert Blincoe*, p. 87; Haynes, *Stalybridge Cotton Mills*, p. 22.

Chapter 20

1 Bamford cited in Cruickshank, *Children and Industry*, p. 18. See also Briggs, *Victorian Cities*, chapter 1.

2 See Edward Baines, *Manchester and its Environs* [map]: *Engraved from an Actual Survey made in 1824, by William Swire, Leeds; for the History, Directory and Gazetteer of Lancashire, by Edwd. Baines. Engraved by Franks and Johnson* (Ithaca, NY: Historic Urban Plans, 1973); Briggs, *Victorian Cities*, p. 89; Mike Williams and D.A. Farnie, *Cotton Mills in Greater Manchester* (Preston: Carnegie, 1992), pp. 18–19; Roger Lloyd-Jones and M.J. Lewis, *Manchester and the Age of the Factory: the Business Structure of Cottonopolis in the Industrial Revolution* (London: Croom Helm, 1988).

3 Williams and Farnie, *Cotton Mills in Greater Manchester*, p. 19; William Cooke Taylor, *Notes of a Tour in the Manufacturing Districts of Lancashire; in a Series of Letters to His Grace the Archbishop of Dublin*, second edition (London, 1842), p. 14.

4 For Adam Smith on capitalists, see Evans, *Forging of the Modern State*, p. 39; de Tocqueville, *Journeys to England and Ireland*, p. 108.

5 *Memoir of Robert Blincoe*, pp. 87–8; St Pancras apprenticeship registers, 1802–67, vol. no. P90 PAN1 362 (London Metropolitan Archives).

6 Castlereagh cited in John Plowright, *Regency England: the Age of Lord Liverpool* (London: Routledge, 1996), p. 12.

7 See Boyd Hilton, *Corn, Cash, Commerce: the Economic Policies of the Tory Governments 1815–1830* (Oxford: Oxford University Press, 1977).

8 Prentice, *Historical Sketches and Personal Recollections*, p. 70; Evans, *Forging of the Modern State*, p. 181.

9 Belchem, *'Orator' Hunt*, p. 89.

10 John and Barbara Hammond, *The Town Labourer*, p. 108.

11 *Memoir of Robert Blincoe*, pp. 88–9; Plowright, *Regency England*, p. 14; Belchem, *'Orator' Hunt*, p. 51.

12 *Memoir of Robert Blincoe*, p. 88; Williams, *Cobbett*, p. 16; Evans, *Forging of the Modern State*, chapter 19.

13 See Marlow, *The Peterloo Massacre*, pp. 27–31; Dinwiddy, *Luddism to the First Reform Bill*, chapter 2.

14 Williams and Farnie, *Cotton Mills in Greater Manchester*, pp. 55–6, 159–62.

15 *Memoir of Robert Blincoe*, p. 88.

16 *Memoir of Robert Blincoe*, pp. 88–9.

Chapter 21

1 Francis Place cited in Cooper, *Transformation of a Valley*, p. 249.

2 *Memoir of Robert Blincoe*, pp. 88–9.

3 Steinberg, *Fighting Words*, p. 139.

4 See Evans, *Forging of the Modern State*, chapter 19; E.P. Thompson, *English Working Class*, pp. 672–5; Belchem, *'Orator' Hunt*, p. 62; Williams, *Cobbett*, p. 11.

5 E.P. Thompson, *English Working Class*, pp. 709–12; Reginald J. White, *Waterloo to Peterloo* (Harmondsworth: Penguin, 1968).

6 *Memoir of Robert Blincoe*, p. 89.

7 Kirby and Musson, *Voice of the People*, pp. 16–24; for Doherty's arrest, see esp. pp. 21–2; Kidd, *Manchester*, pp. 77–83.

8 Kirby and Musson, *Voice of the People*, p. 21.

9 *Memoir of Robert Blincoe*, p. 89.

10 *Memoir of Robert Blincoe*, p. 90.

11 Linnaeus Banks, *The Manchester Man*, pp. 20–1; W.E.A. Axon, 'Brookes, Joshua', *Dictionary of National Biography* (Oxford: Oxford University Press, 2005).

12 Banks, *The Manchester Man*, p. 23.

13 *Memoir of Robert Blincoe*, p. 90; marriage record of Robert and Martha Blincoe held by the Cathedral Collegiate and Parish Church of Manchester. For levels of literacy, see Kirby, *Child Labour*, p. 116 and R.S. Schofield, 'Dimensions of Illiteracy, 1750–1850', *Explorations in Economic History*, vol. 10 (1973), pp. 65–90.

14 Belchem, 'Orator' Hunt, p. 94.

15 Joel H. Wiener, *Radicalism and Freethought in Nineteenth-century Britain: the Life of Richard Carlile* (Westport, CT: Greenwood Press, 1983), especially pp. 40–2.

16 Marlow, *The Peterloo Massacre*, pp. 85, 125.

17 Bamford, *Life of a Radical*, vol. 2, pp. 155–6; Marlow, *The Peterloo Massacre*; E.P. Thompson, *English Working Class*, pp. 745–60.

18 Marlow, *The Peterloo Massacre*, especially pp. 160–4; Belchem, 'Orator' Hunt, p. 115.

19 Belchem, 'Orator' Hunt, pp. 115–20.

20 E.A. Smith, *A Queen on Trial: the Affair of Queen Caroline* (Phoenix Mill, Glos: A. Sutton, 1994).

21 John Dinwiddy, *Luddism to the First Reform Bill*, pp. 37–9; Radcliffe cited in Fleischman, *Conditions of Life*, p. 50.

Chapter 22

1 Kirby and Musson, *Voice of the People*, p. 346; Thomas, *The Early Factory Legislation*, chapter 2, especially pp. 17–20.

2 *Select Committee on the State of the Children … 1816*, in particular the evidence of Robert Peel, pp. 132–45, and Robert Owen, pp. 20–40.

3 Evidence of Joseph Mayer, James Pattison, Esq., and William Sidgwick, *Select Committee on the State of the Children … 1816*, pp. 54, 79, 114.

4 Evidence of Charles Pennington, Gilbert Blane and Kinder Wood, *Select Committee on the State of the Children … 1816*, pp. 222, 46–8, 191–208; Lloyd-Jones and Lewis, *Manchester and the Age of the Factory*, pp. 106–7; and John and Barbara Hammond, *The Town Labourer*, pp. 111–12. For Gilbert Blane and scurvy, see Kenneth J. Carpenter, *The History of Scurvy and Vitamin C* (Cambridge: Cambridge University Press, 1986).

5 Gaskell quoted in Cooper, *Transformation of a Valley*, p. 248; Steinberg, *Fighting Words*, p. 137; *Mirror of Parliament*, 5 July 1833, p. 2799.

6 Walvin, *A Child's World*, p. 62; evidence of Anthony Carlisle, *Select Committee on the State of the Children … 1816*, p. 42; Kirby and Musson, *Voice of the People*, p. 348; Horn, *Children's Work and Welfare*, p. 42; Thomas, *Early Factory Legislation*, p. 21; Henriques, *Before the Welfare State*, p. 81.

7 Letter from William Simmons, *Select Committee on the State of the Children ... 1816*, pp. 286–7; Henriques, *Before the Welfare State*, pp. 81–2. See also Mary MacKinnon and Paul Johnson, 'The Case Against Productive Whipping', *Explorations in Economic History*, vol. 12, no. 2 (April 1984), pp. 218–23.

8 Kirby and Musson, *Voice of the People*, p. 348.

9 Thomas, *The Early Factory Legislation*, pp. 23–5; John and Barbara Hammond, *The Town Labourer*, pp. 113–14.

10 Evidence of Henry Hardie, *House of Lords Account of Cotton Mills*, p. 50; John and Barbara Hammond, *The Town Labourer*, pp. 113–14.

11 John and Barbara Hammond, *The Town Labourer*, p. 115.

12 Kirby and Musson, *Voice of the People*, p. 351; [Robert Southey], *Letters from England*, edited and introduced by Jack Simmons (London: Cresset Press, 1951), p. 198; this work purported to be the reflections of a Spanish nobleman who had toured England.

13 Kirby and Musson, *Voice of the People*, p. 349.

Chapter 23

1 *Memoir of Robert Blincoe*, p. 7; J. Gee, 'Robert Blincoe, the Parish Apprentices in a Factory', *Manchester Notes and Queries*, 7 July 1888, p. 218.

2 Richard Ford (review of *Oliver Twist*), *Quarterly Review*, vol. 64 (June 1839), reproduced in Michael Hollington (ed.), *Charles Dickens: Critical Assessments* (Mountfield, E. Sussex: Helm Information, 1995), vol. 1, pp. 83–102.

3 *Charles Dickens: Critical Assessments*, vol. 1, p. 86.

4 *Memoir of Robert Blincoe*, p. 7.

5 John Brown, *The Mysteries of Neutralization, or, The British Navy Vindicated from the Charges of Injustice and Oppression towards Neutral Flags* (London: printed for the author, 1806), p. 1. Brown showed how well organised the system of deception had become. He quoted from original documents and conversations with alleged perpetrators.

6 Reverend Charles Gillespie, 'The Life of a Parish Apprentice: Robert Blincoe', *Manchester Notes and Queries*, 30 June 1888, pp. 214–15; John Brown, *The Northern Courts, Containing Original Memoirs of the Sovereigns of Sweden and Denmark since 1766* (London, 1818), p. viii. Some of the dates in *The Northern Courts* also suggest that Brown may have visited Sweden in 1803; see Brown, *Northern Courts*, p. 231.

7 These are probably Brown's mis-spellings of two of the leaders of the aristocratic reform party, Hans Jaerta and General Adlercreutz. See Brown, *Northern Courts*, pp. 244, 340, 335, 348–52.

8 John Brown, *Anecdotes and Characters of the House of Brunswick, Illustrative of the Courts of Hanover and London from the Act of Settlement to the Youth of George the Third; including an original memoir of the Electress Sophia and a journal said to have been written by ... the Princess Sophia Dorothea* (London: T. and J. Allman, 1821), pp. 3, 6, 209–15, 217, 244–6, 265.

9 Kirby and Musson, *Voice of the People*, p. 349. They convincingly attribute to Smith and Brown an advertisement for the *Manchester Examiner* signed

enigmatically 'XYZ'. See *Manchester Gazette*, 2 and 30 November 1822. *Memoir of Robert Blincoe*, p. 10.

10 *Memoir of Robert Blincoe*, p. 10.

Chapter 24

1 *Memoir of Robert Blincoe*, p. 90.

2 Betts, *The Lion*, 22 February 1828, p. 238.

3 Mackenzie, 'Cressbrook and Litton Mills', p. 21; deeds and letters of William Cheek relating to Ellis Needham's bankruptcy (Derbyshire Record Office).

4 George Eliot, *The Mill on the Floss* (Harmondsworth: Penguin, 2002; first published in 1880) p. 230. The Derbyshire county records show that Ellis Needham still had some lands to sell over the following decade. He was, however, a ruined man. See *Derbyshire Deeds* (Derbyshire Record Office), D504/142/3/3–4, bond between Matthew Roberts, Richard White, William Bagshaw, Joseph Braddock, William Wilkinson and Robert Wright, proprietors of estates at Taddington and Priestcliffe, Derbyshire, re. joint purchase of estate of Ellis Needham at Priestcliffe Nether Lees and Litton, Derbyshire, 21 December 1821.

5 Mackenzie, 'Cressbrook and Litton Mills', pp. 21–2; *Derbyshire Deeds* (Derbyshire Record Office), MSS 3560, 23 February 1816; figures on Taddington's population derived from the website of Liz Sparkes.

6 Hulbert, *Orphan Child Factory Workers*, pp. 28–9; Edmund and Ruth Frow, *The Dark Satanic Mills: Child Apprentices in Derbyshire Spinning Factories* (Manchester: Manchester Free Press, 1985); Mackenzie, 'Cressbrook and Litton Mills', pp. 21–2.

7 Mackenzie, 'Cressbrook and Litton Mills', p. 21.

8 Mackenzie, 'Cressbrook and Litton Mills', p. 21; *Derbyshire Deeds* (Derbyshire Record Office), MSS 3560, 23 February 1816.

9 *Directory of the County of Derby* (1829), p. 22 (contains a reference to 'Needham Mesdames (ladies' boarding)' in Chapel-en-le-Frith); *Pigot's Commercial Directory of Derbyshire* (1830); Adam, *Geology of Derbyshire*, p. 30; probate documents of Ellis Needham (Lichfield Record Office), P/C/11, sworn on 19 January 1831.

10 Chapman, *Early Factory Masters*, chapter 10; Stanley D. Chapman, 'Cressbrook and Litton Mills: an Alternative View', *Derbyshire Archaeological Journal*, vol. 89 (1969); H.M. Mackenzie, 'Cressbrook and Litton Mills: a Reply', *Derbyshire Archaeological Journal*, vol. 90 (1970); Mackenzie, 'Calver Mill and its Owners', *Derbyshire Archaeological Journal*, vol. 83 (1963), 22–34.

11 John and Barbara Hammond, *The Town Labourer*, p. 139.

12 *Memoir of Robert Blincoe*, p. 90.

Chapter 25

1 *Memoir of Robert Blincoe*, p. 91.

2 Lloyd-Jones and Lewis, *Manchester and the Age of the Factory*, pp. 104–5; A. Musson, *The Growth of British Industry*, p. 14.

3 For an example of a more serious fire in a cotton mill, see *Manchester Guardian*,

16 October 1824; *Manchester Guardian*, 30 October 1824; *The Times*, 24 May 1825, p. 2, issue 12661, col. A.

4 *Memoir of Robert Blincoe*, p. 91.

5 John Brown, *The History of Great and Little Bolton* (Manchester: printed by C.W. Leake; published by Kell, Bolton, Clarke, Manchester, 1824), p. 321 and back cover of issues from no. 3 onwards.

6 Gilbert French, *Life and Times of Samuel Crompton* (London, 1859), pp. 71, 205–11; Baines, *History of the Cotton Manufacture*, chapter 10; Stanley Chapman, 'Cotton', *Chambers' Encyclopaedia* (London, 1918), 3.510.

7 French, *Samuel Crompton*, pp. 209, 281–7. Brown may have left Bolton somewhat later, in early 1826.

8 Richard Carlile's preface to the *Memoir of Robert Blincoe*, p. 3.

Chapter 26

1 Carlile's preface, *Memoir of Robert Blincoe*, p. 4.

2 Anthony Trollope, *An Autobiography*, introduced by John Sutherland (London: Trollope Society, 1999), pp. 30–1.

3 William Thom, *Rhymes and Recollections of a Hand Loom Weaver* (London: Smith, Elder and Co., 1845), p. 28. See also William Turner, *Riot! The Story of the East Lancashire Loom-breakers in 1826* (Preston: Lancashire County Books, 1992), chapter 1.

4 John Champness, *Lancaster Castle: a Brief History* (Preston: Lancashire County Books, 1993), pp. 37–9; Turner, *Riot!*, pp. 83–5.

5 Quoted from 34, 35 Henry VIII, c. 4, s. 1, in Ian P.H. Duffy, 'English Bankrupts, 1571–1861', *American Journal of Legal History*, vol. 24, no. 4 (October 1980), 283–305, p. 285; E. Welbourne, 'Bankruptcy Before the Era of Victorian Reform', *Cambridge Historical Journal*, vol. 4, no. 1 (1932), 51–62; Hugh Barty-King, *The Worst Poverty: a History of Debt and Debtors* (Wolfeboro Falls, NH: Alan Sutton Publishing, 1991).

6 Duffy, 'English Bankrupts', p. 296.

7 Barty-King, *The Worst Poverty*, pp. 132–4.

8 Duffy, 'English Bankrupts', p. 300; Prinny's profligacy at the state's expense did, however, disgust many a humble taxpayer. It 'redoubles the odium in which the Prince is held', said a contemporary, and 'excites ... disgust at monarchy'. Quoted in Barty-King, *The Worst Poverty*, pp. 101–2.

9 Turner, *Riot!*, chapters 7 and 9, especially pp. 31, 77–8.

10 Turner, *Riot!*, chapters 10 and 13.

11 E. Slack, 'Sketches of the Debtor's Prison at Lancaster Castle by a Briefless Barrister, designed and drawn on stone by E. Slack' (Lancaster Borough Library); Barty-King, *The Worst Poverty*, pp. 110–13, 116, 143.

12 Information obtained from Lancaster Castle website.

13 Letter from George Bradley, debtor held in Lancaster Castle for debt, 19 November 1825 (Lancashire Record Office).

14 The Reverend Robert Blincoe's scrapbook (Blincoe family papers); *Pigot and Co.'s Directory to Lancashire ... 1828–9*; Blincoe is described here as a 'shopkeeper'.

Chapter 27

1 Wiener, *Radicalism and Freethought*, chapter 8.

2 French, *Samuel Crompton*, p. 209.

3 French, *Samuel Crompton*, p. 211; Fred Leary, 'Robert Blincoe, the Parish Apprentice', *Manchester Notes and Queries*, 14 July 1888, p. 222.

4 Wiener, *Radicalism and Freethought*, chapters 5 and 6.

5 Cobbett, *Political Register*, 20 November 1824; Kirby and Musson, *Voice of the People*, pp. 350–1.

6 Marc Baer, 'Burdett, Sir Francis, fifth Baronet (1770–1844)', *Dictionary of National Biography* (Oxford: Oxford University Press, 2005); Kirby and Musson, *Voice of the People*, pp. 351–3; Thomas, *The Early Factory Legislation*, pp. 27–8.

7 Kirby and Musson, *Voice of the People*, p. 352.

8 Richard Carlile, *Jail Journal: Prison Thoughts and Other Writings. Edited and selected by Guy A. Aldred* (Glasgow: Strickland Press, 1942), p. 11.

9 Carlile's preface, *Memoir of Robert Blincoe*, p. 3.

10 *Memoir of Robert Blincoe*, p. 3.

11 Carlile's preface, *Memoir of Robert Blincoe*, pp. 3–4.

12 *Memoir of Robert Blincoe*, pp. 4–5.

13 Joseph Johnson, 'The Life of a Parish Apprentice: Robert Blincoe', *Manchester Notes and Queries*, 23 June 1888, p. 211.

14 For the success of *The Lion*, see Wiener, *Radicalism and Freethought*, p. 147; the issuing of a pamphlet of the *Memoir* was announced in *The Lion*, vol. 1, no. 13, 28 March 1828, p. 401.

15 *Memoir of Robert Blincoe*, p. 99; *The Lion*, vol. 1, no. 13, 28 March 1828, p. 401.

16 John Joseph Betts, *The Lion*, 24 February 1828; *Memoir of Robert Blincoe*, pp. 92–3.

17 *The Lion*, vol. 1, no. 11, 14 March 1828, p. 339; *Memoir of Robert Blincoe*, pp. 98–9.

18 Letter of Samuel Davy, *The Lion*, vol. 1, no. 9, 1 March 1828; *Memoir of Robert Blincoe*, pp. 93–4.

19 Trollope, *What I Remember*, vol. 2, p. 7.

20 Kirby and Musson, *Voice of the People*, chapter 10.

Chapter 28

1 *Pigot and Co.'s Directory of Yorks, Leics ..., 1841*, p. 114; the family had previously been living at 407 Oldham Road in Manchester; see *Pigot and Co.'s Directory of Ches, Cumb ..., 1828–29*, p. 57; *Second Report of the Central Board of His Majesty's Commissioners ... 1833*, pp. 17–18.

2 For brief mentions of Blincoe's *Memoir* in the *Poor Man's Advocate* (*PMA*), see 14 April and 28 April 1832; Kirby and Musson, *Voice of the People*, especially chapters 2–6 and chapter 10.

3 Kirby and Musson, *Voice of the People*, chapters 1 and 10.

4 Kirby and Musson, *Voice of the People*, pp. 353–7, 358–9.

5 Kirby and Musson, *Voice of the People*, pp. 356, 358.

6 Kirby and Musson, *Voice of the People*, pp. 53, 58, 362–4, 66.

7 Kirby and Musson, *Voice of the People*, chapter 3, especially pp. 59, 87–100. In the midst of the Lancashire strike, Doherty also sought to strengthen the fighting power of the working man by forming a union that combined cotton operatives in hundreds of towns, cities and counties. A meeting of the Grand Union of Cotton Spinners, with delegates from all around the country, met on the Isle of Man in 1829. It was smoothly organised and coolly pulled off, and the island's magistrates had no idea what had occurred in their midst. Home Secretary Peel was left in considerable doubt as to whether a meeting had taken place. Doherty would later work hard to establish a National Association for the Protection of Labour, uniting different trades and localities. Both attempts were to be wrecked by provincial separatism and the differing interests of the groups involved. See Kirby and Musson, *Voice of the People*, chapters 5–7.

8 Kirby and Musson, *Voice of the People*, p. 364.

9 Sadler quoted in Driver, *Tory Radical*, p. 108.

10 Driver, *Tory Radical*, p.108; Peter Mandler, 'Cain and Abel: Two Aristocrats and the Early Victorian Factory Acts', *Historical Journal*, vol. 27, no. 1, March 1984, 83–109, p. 90.

11 Driver, *Tory Radical*, chapter 4, p. 41.

12 Quoted in Ward, *The Factory System*, p. 74; Driver, *Tory Radical*, pp. 45–8, 53.

13 Driver, *Tory Radical*, chapter 5.

14 Karl W. Schweizer and John Osborne, *Cobbett in His Times* (London: Leicester University Press, 1990), p. 7 and chapter 3; Belchem, *'Orator' Hunt*, pp. 216–20.

15 Kirby and Musson, *Voice of the People*, pp. 364–7; Thomas, *Early Factory Legislation*, pp. 27–33; *Hansard*, second series, XIII, p. 451.

16 Kirby and Musson, *Voice of the People*, p. 367; Driver, *Tory Radical*, p. 115.

17 Driver, *Tory Radical*, pp. 125–9; Henriques, *Before the Welfare State*, p. 74.

18 See, for example, *PMA*, 28 April 1832, pp. 113–17; Kirby and Musson, *Voice of the People*, pp. 368–70.

19 Driver, *Tory Radical*, p. 136.

20 *Hansard*, second series, XI, pp. 340–85; Samuel Kydd, *The History of the Factory Movement: From the Year 1802, to the Enactment of the Ten Hours' Bill in 1847* (London: Simpkin, Marshall and Co., 1857), vol. 1, pp. 152–90.

21 *Hansard*, second series, XI, pp. 340–85; Driver, *Tory Radical*, p. 167.

22 *The Times*, quoted in Driver, *Tory Radical*, pp. 167–8.

23 *PMA*, 21 April 1832. In the next week's issue, brief mention was also made of Robert Blincoe's servitude at Litton.

24 *PMA*, 5 May 1832, pp. 121–9; Driver, *Tory Radical*, chapter 14.

25 Albert Nicholson (revised by Anne Pimlott Baker), 'Keeling, William Knight (1807–1886)', *Dictionary of National Biography* (Oxford: Oxford University Press, 2005); *PMA*, 26 May, 9 June, 16 June and 23 June 1832.

26 *PMA*, 9 June 1832, pp. 161–2.

Chapter 29

1 *PMA*, 9 June 1832, pp. 161–2.

2 *Memoir of Robert Blincoe*, p. 100.

3 See evidence of William Cooper, pp. 6–10; James Kirk, p. 15; David Bywater, p.

27; and Elizabeth Bentley, p. 51, in *Report from the Select Committee ... 1831–2*. See also Henriques, *Before the Welfare State*, p. 75 and Thomas, *Early Factory Legislation*, pp. 39–42.

4 Evidence of Peter Smart, p. 338; William Swithenbank, p. 75; and William Cooper, pp. 6–10, in *Report from the Select Committee ... 1831–2*.

5 Evidence of Alexander Dean, p. 373, and James Paterson, p. 389, in *Report from the Select Committee ... 1831–2*.

6 Evidence of Thomas Bennett, p. 103; Samuel Downe, p. 55; Matthew Crabtree, p. 97; Alexander Dean, pp. 373–5 and 383; and Joshua Drake, p. 42, in *Report from the Select Committee ... 1831–2*.

7 Driver, *Tory Radical*, p. 176.

8 See, for example, W.H. Hutt, 'The Factory System of the Early Nineteenth Century', in F.A. Hayek (ed.), *Capitalism and the Historians* (Chicago: University of Chicago Press, 1954), pp. 156–84.

9 Evidence of William Lutener, p. 270; C.T. Thackrah, p. 514; and James Blundell, p. 546, in *Report from the Select Committee ... 1831–2*.

Chapter 30

1 See, for example, *PMA*, 28 April 1832, p. 116.

2 See *PMA*, Saturday 14 April 1832, pp. 97–9; Kirby and Musson, *Voice of the People*, pp. 339, 368–78, 433–58.

3 Kirby and Musson, *Voice of the People*, p. 436; *PMA*, 9 June 1832; *PMA*, 18 August 1832; *PMA*, 15 September 1832, pp. 243–4, 248 (Blincoe's name is recorded in this issue as an individual subscriber); *PMA*, 22 September 1832, p. 8.

4 See Ruth Richardson, *Death, Dissection and the Destitute* (London: Penguin, 1988); Helen Macdonald, *Human Remains: Episodes in Human Dissection* (Carlton, Victoria: Melbourne University Press, 2005); *Manchester Guardian*, 21 February 1824.

5 See William F. Bynum, *Science and the Practice of Medicine in the Nineteenth Century* (Cambridge: Cambridge University Press, 1994), especially chapter 2.

6 Mrs Pemper Reeves quoted in Walvin, *A Child's World*, p. 40.

7 See *PMA*, 11 and 18 August 1832; Kirby and Musson, *Voice of the People*, p. 437.

8 *PMA*, 1 December 1832; *PMA*, 5 January 1833, pp. 391–6; Kirby and Musson, *Voice of the People*, p. 437.

9 *PMA*, 21 July 1832, pp. 214–15.

10 *PMA*, 5 January 1833, p. 395.

11 John and Barbara Hammond, *The Town Labourer*, p. 166; Kirby and Musson, *Voice of the People*, p. 437; *PMA*, 5 January 1833, p. 396.

12 Edward Pearce, *Reform: the Fight for the 1832 Reform Act* (London: Jonathan Cape, 2003); Evans, *Forging of the Modern State*, chapter 23; Michael Brock, *The Great Reform Act* (London: Hutchinson, 1973); Norman Gash, *Aristocracy and People: Britain 1815–1865* (London: Edward Arnold, 1979).

13 Driver, *Tory Radical*, p. 180; Evans, *Forging of the Modern State*, p. 212; and Brock, *Great Reform Act*, p. 319.

14 *Manchester Guardian*, 31 August 1832.

15 *PMA*, 25 August 1832.

16 Ure, *Philosophy of Manufactures*, p. 300.

17 Driver, *Tory Radical*, p. 188; Richard Oastler, *Eight Letters to the Duke of Wellington, a Petition to the House of Commons, and a Letter to the Editor of the Agricultural and Industrial Magazine* (London: J. Cochrane, 1835).

18 Ure, *Philosophy of Manufactures*, p. 277.

19 *Manchester Guardian*, 1 September 1832; Sarah Lloyd, 'Cottage Conversations: Poverty and Manly Independence in Eighteenth-century England', *Past and Present*, vol. 184 (2004), pp. 69–108. See also Taylor, *Notes of a Tour*, p. 26 and Geoffrey B.A.M. Finlayson, *The Seventh Earl of Shaftesbury, 1801–1885* (London: Eyre Methuen, 1981), pp. 200, 211–20.

20 See John and Barbara Hammond, *The Town Labourer*, chapter 7 and Horn, *Children's Work and Welfare*, pp. 27–34. Not even Humphry Davy's safety lamp improved matters; it simply meant that colliers could be sent even deeper into the earth. The level of risk remained essentially the same.

Chapter 31

1 Belchem, *'Orator' Hunt*, p. 248; Driver, *Tory Radical*, chapter 17.

2 Eastwood, 'Robert Southey', p. 330; Edwin Hodder, *The Life and Work of the Seventh Earl of Shaftesbury* (London: Cassell, 1888), vol. 1, pp. 146–8; Mandler, 'Cain and Abel', p. 92; Finlayson, *Shaftesbury*, pp. 211–20.

3 Finlayson, *Shaftesbury*, p. 15. School brought Lord Ashley no relief. The Reverend Dr Thomas Horne's school in Chiswick had much in common with Dotheboys Hall in Charles Dickens' *Nicholas Nickleby*, except that at Horne's school the boys being beaten and neglected were from among the wealthiest families in the land. Since the master suffered from insomnia, classes frequently began at four in the morning. The boys were supposed to be hardened into men by a regime of unrelenting harshness. In this respect, the school did at least provide a good preparation for Eton, where Ashley's brother Francis was killed after a two-hour fist-fight in 1825.

4 See Mandler, 'Cain and Abel', pp. 83–4.

5 Mandler, 'Cain and Abel', p. 93. Oastler was by now so preoccupied with the cause that he had no time for his estate business; to keep up appearances, his wife took over and learned to use his handwriting to maintain the ruse.

6 Driver, *Tory Radical*, chapter 18; Mandler, 'Cain and Abel', p. 94.

7 *Manchester Guardian*, 18 December 1844, quoted in Henriques, *Before the Welfare State*, pp. 80–1.

8 Evidence of Richard Wilson, p. 128, in *Report from the Select Committee … 1831–2* (Wilson's brother was now dead, and the father had been killed by a spinning machine); Carlile's preface to the *Memoir of Robert Blincoe*, p. 4.

9 For discussion about the wages of factory hands, see Ure, *Philosophy of Manufactures*, pp. 298–320; Smelser, *Social Change in the Industrial Revolution*, p. 197; Kirby and Musson, *Voice of the People*, pp. 146–8.

10 See evidence of William Swithenbank, p. 76; C.T. Thackrah, p. 516; and Daniel Kenworthy, p. 83, in *Report from the Select Committee … 1831–2*. See also Ure, *Philosophy of Manufactures*, p. 279, and Kirby and Musson, *Voice of the People*, p. 384.

Chapter 32

1 Edward C. Tufnell, *Second Report of the Central Board of His Majesty's Commissioners ... 1833*, pp. 210–11.

2 Henriques, *Before the Welfare State*, pp. 83–7; Kirby and Musson, *Voice of the People*, pp. 381–3.

3 Thomas, *Early Factory Legislation*, p. 49; Driver, *Tory Radical*, pp. 225–36, p. 236 fn.

4 See Henriques, *Before the Welfare State*, p. 85.

5 Chadwick's introduction to the *Second Report of the Central Board of His Majesty's Commissioners ... 1833*, p. 13; Tufnell, *Second Report of the Central Board of His Majesty's Commissioners ... 1833*, p. 194.

6 Chadwick's introduction to the *Second Report of the Central Board of His Majesty's Commissioners ... 1833*, p. 6; Francis Bisset Hawkins, *Germany: the Spirit of her History, Literature, Social Condition, and National Economy, illustrated by reference to her physical, moral, and political statistics, and by comparison with other countries* (London: J.W. Parker, 1838).

7 Evidence of Robert Blincoe, *Second Report of the Central Board of His Majesty's Commissioners ... 1833*, pp. 17–18.

8 Evidence of Robert Blincoe, *Second Report of the Central Board of His Majesty's Commissioners ... 1833*, pp. 17–18.

9 Evidence of Robert Blincoe, *Second Report of the Central Board of His Majesty's Commissioners ... 1833*, p. 18.

10 See Hutchins and Harrison, *A History of Factory Legislation*, pp. 53–4; Kirby and Musson, *Voice of the People*, p. 383; Driver, *Tory Radical*, pp. 239–41.

11 *First Report of His Majesty's Commissioners Appointed to Collect Information in the Manufacturing Districts, as to the Employment of Children in Factories, session 29 January–29 August 1833* (London, 1833), pp. 13, 26–7, 30.

12 *First Report of His Majesty's Commissioners*, pp. 18–19, 32. See also Henriques, *Before the Welfare State*, pp. 87–9.

13 *First Report of His Majesty's Commissioners*, p. 16.

14 Tufnell's evidence, *Second Report of the Central Board of His Majesty's Commissioners ... 1833*, p. 200; *First Report of His Majesty's Commissioners*, p. 32.

15 See Tufnell's report, *Second Report of the Central Board of His Majesty's Commissioners ... 1833*, p. 203; Henriques, *Before the Welfare State*, pp. 87–8.

16 Sir James Mackintosh, eminent philosopher and economist, had commented that, while a convert to political economy, 'he would not allow even the principles of political economy to be accessory to the infliction of torture.' With Althorp's Act he didn't need to sacrifice the one for the other. Henriques, *Before the Welfare State*, pp. 88–9; Driver, *Tory Radical*, p. 243; Thomas, *Early Factory Legislation*, chapter 5; Mark Blaug, 'The Classical Economists and the Factory Acts – A Re-Examination', *Quarterly Journal of Economics*, vol. 72 (1958), 211–26.

17 Driver, *Tory Radical*, pp. 246–8; Howard P. Markel, 'Factory Regulation: a Reinterpretation of Early English Experience', *Journal of Law and Economics*, vol. 20, no. 2 (October 1977), 379–402.

18 Markel, 'Factory Regulation', p. 387.

19 Brundage, *The English Poor Laws*, chapter 4.

20 See David Eastwood, *Governing Rural England: Tradition and Transformation in Local Government 1780–1840* (Oxford: Clarendon Press, 1994), pp. 181–6.

21 Richard Oastler, *Serious Address to the Millowners, Manufacturers, and Cloth-Dressers of Leeds* (Huddersfield, Yorkshire, 1834), p. 7.

22 Kirby and Musson, *Voice of the People*, p. 384.

23 Ure, *Philosophy of Manufactures*, pp. 298–301; W.V. Farrar, 'Andrew Ure, FRS, and the Philosophy of Manufactures', *Notes and Records of the Royal Society of London*, vol. 27, no. 2 (February 1973), 299–324.

24 Farrar, 'Andrew Ure, FRS', pp. 309–11; Ure, *Philosophy of Manufactures*, preface.

25 John Fielden, *The Curse of the Factory System; or, A Short Account of Factory Cruelties* (London, 1836), pp. 35, 43.

26 For this debate, see Fielden, *Curse of the Factory System*, pp. 39–43.

27 Fielden, *Curse of the Factory System*, p. 6.

Chapter 33

1 Forster, *The Life of Charles Dickens*, chapter 2.

2 *Mirror of Parliament*, 1 February 1832, p. 414; 27 June 1832, pp. 2782–4; 5 July 1833, pp. 2794–9.

3 Dickens to Edward Marlborough Fitzgerald, 29 December 1838, *The Letters of Charles Dickens*, ed. Madelaine House and Graham Storey, 2 vols (Oxford: Clarendon Press, 1965–9), vol. 1, pp. 483–4; see also Patrick Brantlinger, 'Dickens and the Factories', *Nineteenth-Century Fiction*, vol. 26, no. 3 (December 1971), 270–85, p. 274.

4 See the *Spectator*'s review of *Oliver Twist* in Hollington, *Charles Dickens: Critical Assessments*, vol. 1, pp. 78–81.

5 To Mrs Charles Dickens, 1 November 1838, *Letters*, vol. 1, p. 447; Brantlinger, 'Dickens and the Factories', p. 274; Charles Dickens to E.M. Fitzgerald, 29 December 1838, *Letters*, vol. 1, pp. 483–4.

6 Neville-Sington, *Fanny Trollope*.

7 Neville-Sington, *Fanny Trollope*, chapters 7–10.

8 *Fraser's Magazine*, vol. 18 (1843), p. 350, cited in Pamela Neville-Sington, 'Trollope [*née* Milton], Frances', *Dictionary of National Biography* (Oxford: Oxford University Press, 2005).

9 Trollope, *What I Remember*, pp. 7–8; Finlayson, *Shaftesbury*, p. 124; W.H. Chaloner, 'Mrs Trollope and the Early Factory System', *Victorian Studies*, vol. 4, no. 2 (December 1960), pp. 159–66, 180.

10 For Stephens, see M.S. Edwards, *Purge this Realm: a Life of Joseph Rayner Stephens* (London: Epworth, 1994).

11 Trollope, *What I Remember*, pp. 9–13; Chaloner, 'Mrs Trollope and the Early Factory System', pp. 159–66.

12 See Neville-Sington, *Fanny Trollope*, pp. 276–7.

13 For a good summary of the plot and an astute analysis of the novel, see Priti Joshi, '*Michael Armstrong*: Rereading the Industrial Plot', in Brenda Ayres (ed.),

Frances Trollope and the Novel of Social Change (London: Greenwood Press, 2002), pp. 35–51; Ivanka Kovacevic, *Fact into Fiction*, pp. 85–9.

14 Neville-Sington, *Fanny Trollope*, p. 275 and Kovacevic, *Fact into Fiction*, p. 99.

15 Dickens cited in Neville-Sington, *Fanny Trollope*, pp. 276–7.

16 Trollope, *Michael Armstrong*, p. 27.

17 Reviews cited in Neville-Sington, *Fanny Trollope*, pp. 278–9.

18 Neville-Sington, *Fanny Trollope*, p. 277; Joseph Kestner, *Protest and Reform: The British Social Narrative by Women 1827–1867* (London: University of Wisconsin Press, 1985), pp. 30–9; Trollope, *Michael Armstrong*, p. 117. Fanny's representation of mill owners was also more strident than anything her readers were accustomed to. They were more familiar with the ardent political economy of Harriet Martineau, whose tract-like novels expressed plenty of pity for those pauperised by the advent of machines or led by low factory wages to go out on strike. But Martineau made her view quite clear that new technologies must be accepted and that strikers had to conform to 'the natural course of things'. The subtitle to her 1829 novel *The Turn-out* said it all: *Patience the Best Policy*. She reassured readers that, while things looked bad among the working masses, state intervention would only make matters worse. Fanny heartily disagreed. See Harriet Martineau, *The Hill and the Valley: a Tale* (Series: Illustrations of Political Economy), (London: Charles Fox, 1832) and Kovacevic, *Fact into Fiction*, p. 101.

19 Neville-Sington, *Fanny Trollope*, pp. 277–8.

20 Trollope, *Michael Armstrong*, pp. 44, 143, 180–1, 182–3, 212, 216, 279.

21 Trollope, *Michael Armstrong*, pp. 182–3. See also Kestner, *Protest and Reform*, p. 53.

22 *Mary Ashley, the Factory Girl*, written by barrister Frederic Montagu, was perhaps the most forgettable of this new genre. Written in 1839 as a direct counterpoint to *Michael Armstrong*, it followed the career of a young girl from an inner-city slum to the 'happiness' of life in a cotton mill under a benevolent master. Montagu's novel ends with 'the sweet voice' of a factory girl 'singing the last verse of a psalm'. More in keeping with Fanny's belief that the factory age had to be humanised were Elizabeth Gaskell's novels *Mary Barton* (1848) and *North and South* (1855). In terms of literary quality, these stand way ahead of the field, though Benjamin Disraeli also told candidly and memorably of the hardships of mill life in his novel *Sybil, or the Two Nations* (1845). See Gray, *The Factory Question*, p. 148; Frederic Montagu, *Mary Ashley, the Factory Girl: or Facts Upon Factories* (London, 1839).

Chapter 34

1 Thomas, *Early Factory Legislation*, pp. 290–301.

2 Kirby and Musson, *Voice of the People*, pp. 4–7.

3 Driver, *Tory Radical*, chapter 40.

4 *Pigot and Co.'s Directory of Yorks, Leics ... 1841*, p. 114; Musson, *Trade Union and Social History*, pp. 204–5.

5 This photograph is in the possession of the descendants of the Reverend Robert Blincoe. I am grateful to Edward Blincoe for providing me with a copy.

6 Ruth Blincoe is listed in *Slater's Directories of Important English Towns, 1847*, at 26 Deansgate; for Martha Blincoe and George Parker, see G.B. Harrison, *One Man in his Time: the Memoirs of G.B. Harrison 1894–1984* (Palmerston North, NZ: Dunmore Press, 1985), pp. 35–6.

7 Harrison, *One Man in his Time*, p. 35.

8 The only published source on the Reverend Blincoe is Edward Blincoe, 'Robert Blincoe, a Child of the Industrial Revolution', in Jack Blencowe (ed.), *The Blencowe Families of Cumbria and Northamptonshire and their Descendants* (London: The Blencowe Families' Association, 2001), pp. 329–36.

Chapter 35

1 See Alfred Alexander Mumford, *The Manchester Grammar School, 1515–1915: a Regional Study of the Advancement of Learning in Manchester Since the Reformation* (London: Longmans, Green and Co., 1919), pp. 2, 197.

2 Quoted in Mumford, *The Manchester Grammar School,* p. 27.

3 The school's High Master, the Reverend Jeremiah Smith, was just the man for them. He had joined the Tory Pitt Club, gave evidence to help send Orator Hunt down following Peterloo, and gladly signed a petition against the Great Reform Bill. Manchester's capitalists ensured, however, that Master and Usher appreciated the scale of the transformation in the streets outside the school. In 1824 a local manufacturer converted a warehouse next door to the Usher's house into a power-loom factory. The Usher fled the 'unbearable' noise of shuttles and rollers. In doing so, he joined a general exodus of 'respectable' people from Long Millgate as heavy industry encroached ever closer, and poor Irish labourers, fleeing extreme poverty, made it their home. But the school itself couldn't be moved. It sat next to the Irk as increasingly revolting smells rose up from 'the slime and refuse accumlat[ing] and rot[ting] in thick masses behind the weirs'. In 1845, Friedrich Engels would describe the area with horrified disgust. See Mumford, *The Manchester Grammar School*, chapter 3, p. 32 and p. 256; James Bentley, *Dare to be Wise: a History of the Manchester Grammar School* (London: James and James, 1990), pp. 48–55.

4 Mumford, *The Manchester Grammar School*, pp. 34–6 and Bentley, *Dare to be Wise*, p. 49. In a scathing pamphlet of 1837, the Unitarian minister J.R. Beard lamented: 'Standing at the end of three centuries we behold that which was designed for the poor either rendered inoperative or possessed by the rich.' He revealed that nearly all of the school's university exhibitions went to the Master's well-off boarders. More perceptively, Beard commented that there were all manner of ways in which a 'free school may be worked so as to repel the poor'. See J.R. Beard's *The Abuses of the Manchester Free Grammar School Considered by a Friend of Popular Education* (London: Simpkin, Marshall and Co., 1837), p. 9.

5 Mumford, *The Manchester Grammar School*, p. 276; Bentley, *Dare to be Wise*, p. 52.

6 Bentley, *Dare to be Wise*, pp. 52–4.

7 *The New Microcosm. Edited by the Senior Class of the Manchester School. From June 1839, to June 1840* (Manchester: printed by Cave and Sever, 1840). A

typical satire concerns a fictional Mr Coddle, a man of 'low birth' who makes a fortune and becomes a tyrant (pp. 22–38).

8 Mumford, *The Manchester Grammar School*, p. 276; Bentley, *Dare to be Wise*, p. 50.

9 Brief biographical sketch by the Reverend Robert Blincoe in his scrapbook. This item is in the possession of the Blincoe family, though some papers have been copied and lodged with the Islington Local History Centre. For statistics of MGS boys going on to university and receiving scholarships, see Mumford, *The Manchester Grammar School*, p. 281 and appendices.

10 Robert Blincoe's scrapbook contains the original letter sent by Queens' College detailing the books he would need for his first term of study.

11 Denys Arthur Winstanley, *Unreformed Cambridge: a Study of Certain Aspects of the University in the Eighteenth Century* (Cambridge: Cambridge University Press, 1935), pp. 197–8; Peter Searby, *A History of the University of Cambridge* (Cambridge: Cambridge University Press, 1977), pp. 68–71.

12 John Twigg, *A History of Queens' College, Cambridge 1448–1986* (Woodbridge, Suffolk: Boydell, 1987), pp. 134–8. A year after Robert left, the college welcomed Alexander Crummell, one of the first black clergymen ordained in America. See Twigg, *Queens' College*, p. 136.

13 'All Saints' Schools: Welcome to the Rev. R. Blincoe, MA', *Bolton Chronicle*, 5 January 1878. This passage was noted by Edward Blincoe, 'Reverend Robert Blincoe 1826–79', unpublished manuscript.

14 J.A. Venn, *Alumni Cantabrigienses: a Biographical List of all Known Students, Graduates and Holders of Office at the University of Cambridge, from the Earliest Times to 1900* (Cambridge: Cambridge University Press, 1940), p. 298; scrapbook of the Reverend Robert Blincoe (Blincoe family).

15 Friedrich Engels, *The Condition of the Working-class in England in 1844. With a Preface Written in 1892 by Frederick Engels. Translated by Florence Kelley Wischnewetzky* (London: Swan Sonnenschein and Co., 1892), p. 112; Robert Rawlinson, *Report to the General Board of Health on a Preliminary Inquiry into the Sewerage, Drainage, and Supply of Water, and the Sanitary Condition of the Inhabitants of the Borough of Wolverhampton, and the townships of Bilston, Willenhall, and Wednesfield* (London: W. Clowes and Sons for HMSO, 1849).

16 Engels, *Working-class in England*, p. 113.

17 Testimonial from the Reverend W.R.B. Arthy, in scrapbook of the Reverend Robert Blincoe (Blincoe family).

18 Scrapbook of the Reverend Robert Blincoe (Blincoe family); for attempts by the clergy to rationalise the appearance of cholera, see Reverend Samuel Arnott, *An Address to the Inhabitants of the District of St Luke's, Berwick Street, and Particularly to those Attending the Church, on the Late Visitation of Cholera* (London, 1854), pp. 8–9. See also Charles E. Rosenberg, *The Cholera Years, the United States in 1832, 1849, and 1866* (Chicago: University of Chicago Press, 1962), pp. 6, 13, 17–22.

19 It presumably helped that at least one churchwarden was of an evangelical bent; a few years before, he had upbraided the organist for playing a selection from a Mozart Mass, for choosing 'such jiggy stuff'. See Charles R. Simpson, *St Luke's*

Church 1733–1933: a Short Summary of its History (unpublished pamphlet, 1933), p. 11. See also Blincoe's testimonials in the scrapbook of the Reverend Robert Blincoe (Blincoe family).
20 See Peter T. Marsh, *The Victorian Church in Decline: Archbishop Tait and the Church of England, 1868–1882* (London: Routledge and Kegan Paul, 1969).
21 That several of Robert's admirers were clerics in northern cities, including Manchester and Macclesfield, suggests that on occasion he saved enough from his stipend to travel up to see his ageing parents. Robert's oldest sibling, Ruth, also lived with him for some time at 78 Bunhill Row. See testimonials in scrapbook of the Reverend Robert Blincoe (Blincoe family); *Finsbury Free Press, and General Advertiser*, 13 March 1869; Blincoe, 'Reverend Robert Blincoe', unpublished manuscript.
22 *Illustrated London News*, 28 July 1855.
23 *Finsbury Herald*, 19 December 1857; testimonials in scrapbook of the Reverend Robert Blincoe (Blincoe family); Blincoe, 'Reverend Robert Blincoe', unpublished manuscript.
24 *Manchester Courier*, 5 December 1857; *The Times*, 8 October 1857, p. 5, issue 22806, col. A; newspaper cuttings (including the *Wolverhampton Chronicle* and *The Times*) pasted into scrapbook of the Reverend Robert Blincoe (Blincoe family). Blincoe was also mentioned in *The Times* of 7 October 1858.
25 *Finsbury Free Press, and General Advertiser*, 13 March 1869.
26 See F.B. Smith, *The People's Health, 1830–1910* (London: Croom Helm, 1979).
27 Blincoe, 'Reverend Robert Blincoe', unpublished manuscript; *Macclesfield Courier*, 15 December 1860; *Memoir of Robert Blincoe*, p. 100. I am grateful to Julian Blincoe for information on Blincoe's burial and death.
28 Venn, *Alumni Cantabrigienses*, p. 298; Blincoe, 'Reverend Robert Blincoe', unpublished manuscript.

Chapter 36
1 *Memoir of Robert Blincoe*, pp. 90–1.
2 Blincoe, 'Reverend Robert Blincoe', unpublished manuscript.
3 Even his wife Charlotte was honoured. The congregation presented her with a set of gold earrings and brooch, a work box, a cheque book, a gold chain and a photograph album. See scrapbook of the Reverend Robert Blincoe (Blincoe family).
4 *Finsbury Free Press, and General Advertiser*, 13 March 1869; scrapbook of the Reverend Robert Blincoe (Blincoe family).
5 Scrapbook of the Reverend Robert Blincoe (Blincoe family).
6 Blincoe, 'Reverend Robert Blincoe', unpublished manuscript.
7 Robert Blincoe to Charlotte Blincoe, scrapbook of the Reverend Robert Blincoe (Blincoe family).
8 Blincoe, 'Reverend Robert Blincoe', unpublished manuscript.
9 *Bolton Chronicle*, 5 January 1878.
10 Blincoe, 'Reverend Robert Blincoe', unpublished manuscript; scrapbook of the Reverend Robert Blincoe (Blincoe family).
11 Scrapbook of the Reverend Robert Blincoe (Blincoe family).

12 Written in October 1872 and stuck into the scrapbook of the Reverend Robert Blincoe (Blincoe family).

13 For Tait, see Marsh, *The Victorian Church in Decline*.

14 Marsh, *The Victorian Church in Decline*, early chapters; testimonials included in the scrapbook of the Reverend Robert Blincoe (Blincoe family).

15 *The Times*, 8 October 1857, p. 5, issue 22806, col. A. For the Indian Mutiny, see Lawrence James, *Raj: the Making and Unmaking of British India* (London: Little, Brown, 1997).

16 Edward Blincoe, great-grandson of the Reverend Blincoe, writes: 'I am quite sure that my own grandfather knew nothing of his grandfather's origins.' See Blincoe, *The Blencowe Families*, p. 336.

17 Kydd, *History of the Factory Movement*, pp. 17–27, cited in Hutt, 'The Factory System', p. 175; *Manchester Notes and Queries*, 16 June 1888, pp. 208–9; 23 June 1888, pp. 211–12; 30 June 1888, pp. 214–15; 7 July 1888, pp. 218–20; 14 July 1888, p. 222.

18 Kirby and Musson, *Voice of the People*, p. 5; I am grateful to several contributors to the website www.urmston.net for assistance with dating the building of Blinco Road.

19 Paul Joseph Mantoux, *The Industrial Revolution in the Eighteenth Century: an Outline of the Beginnings of the Modern Factory System in England*, translated by Marjorie Vernon (London: Jonathan Cape, 1928); Thomas, *Early Factory Legislation*, p. 7, n. 19; Thompson, *English Working Class*, p. 374. For an analysis of the debate between optimists and pessimists, see Fleischman, *Conditions of Life*, especially chapter 3 and Conclusion.

20 Chapman, *Early Factory Masters*, pp. 208–9.

21 Harrison, *One Man in his Time*, p. 35.

22 Ferrand's experiences cited in Ward, *The Factory System*, p. 82.

23 Quotation from Pinchbeck and Hewitt, *Children in English Society*, vol. 2, p. 499.

Bibliography

Books

Ackroyd, Peter, *Dickens* (London: Sinclair-Stevenson, 1990).

Adam, William, *Brief Remarks on the Geology of Derbyshire. A Catalogue of the Rocks, Marbles and Minerals of the County ... The History of the Fluor Spar ... and the Botany of the High and Low Peak* (London: Longman and Co., 1846).

Adam, William, *The Gem of the Peak: or, Matlock Bath and its Vicinity: an Account of Derby, a Tour from Derby to Matlock, Excursions to Chatsworth, Haddon, Monsal Dale, Dovedale, Ilam, Alton Towers, Hardwick, Wingfield, Ashbourne, Buxton, and Castleton, Historical and Geological: Brief History of the Fluor Spar, from the Earliest Period, Down to the Present Time, a Review of the Geology of Derbyshire, Catalogue of Minerals and Rocks, and of the Flora of the High and Low Peak: Illustrated with Maps and Numerous Engravings* (London: Longman and Co., 1843).

Aikin, J., *Description of the Country for Thirty to Forty Miles Round Manchester* (London: printed for John Stockdale, 1795).

Anonymous, *A Brief Account of the Charity School of St Pancras, for Instructing, Cloathing, Qualifying for Useful Servants and Putting Out to Service, the Female Children of the Industrious Poor. Instituted in the year M.DCC.LXXVI* (London: printed by S. Law, 1796).

Anonymous, *An Account of Several Work-houses for Employing and Maintaining the Poor: Setting Forth the Rules by Which They Are Governed, Their Great Usefulness to the Publick, and in Particular to the Parishes Where They Are Erected: as Also of Several Charity Schools for Promoting Work and Labour. The Second Edition Very Much Enlarged* (London: Printed by Jos. Downing, 1732).

Anonymous, *The New Microcosm. Edited by the Senior Class of the Manchester School. From June, 1839, to June 1840* (Manchester: printed by Cave and Sever, 1840).

Arnott, Samuel, *An Address to the Inhabitants of the District of St Luke's, Berwick Street, and Particularly to Those Attending the Church, on the Late Visitation of Cholera* (London, 1854).

Arnould, Joseph, *Memoir of Thomas, First Lord Denman, Formerly Lord Chief Justice of England* (London: Longmans, Green and Co., 1873).

Ashton, John, *The Fleet* (London: T. Fisher Unwin, 1888).

Ayres, Brenda (ed.), *Frances Trollope and the Novel of Social Change* (Westport, CT: Greenwood Press, 2001).

Bagster, Samuel, the Elder, *Samuel Bagster of London, 1772–1851: an Autobiography* (London: Bagster, 1972).

Baines, Edward, *History of the Cotton Manufacture in Great Britain: With a Notice of its Early History in the East, and in All the Quarters of the Globe, a Description of the Great Mechanical Inventions, which Have Caused Its Unexampled Extension in Britain, and a View of the Present State of the Manufacture, and the Condition of the Classes Engaged in Its Several Departments* (London: Fisher, Fisher and Jackson, 1835).

Bamford, Samuel, *Passages in the Life of a Radical* (Oxford: Oxford University Press, 1967).

Bamford, Samuel, *Passages in the Life of a Radical*, preface by Tim Hilton (Oxford: Oxford University Press, 1984 (reprint)).

Barker, Robert, *The Genuine Life of Robert Barker, Dictated by Himself While in a State of Total Darkness … Containing a Clear Account of his Remarkable Travels, etc.* (London: for the author, 1809).

Barty-King, Hugh, *The Worst Poverty: a History of Debt and Debtors* (Wolfeboro Falls, NH: Alan Sutton Publishers, 1991).

Bayne-Powell, Rosamond, *Travellers in Eighteenth-century England* (London: J. Murray, 1951).

Beard, R.J., *The Abuses of the Manchester Free Grammar School Considered by a Friend of Popular Education* (London: Simpkin, Marshall and Co., 1837).

Beckett, John (ed.), *A Centenary History of Nottingham* (Manchester: Manchester University Press, 1997).

Belchem, John, *'Orator' Hunt: Henry Hunt and English Working-class Radicalism* (Oxford: Clarendon Press, 1985).

Bentley, James, *Dare to Be Wise: a History of the Manchester Grammar School* (London: James and James, 1990).

Blackner, John, *The History of Nottingham: Embracing Its Antiquities, Trade, and Manufactures, from the Earliest Authentic Records, to the Present Period / by John Blackner* (Nottingham: printed by Sutton and Son, 1815).

Blake, Robert, *Disraeli* (London: Eyre and Spottiswoode, 1966).

Blencowe, J.W. (ed.), *The Blencowe Families of Cumbria and Northamptonshire and their Descendants* (London: The Blencowe Families' Association, 2001).

Bouyer, Revd R.G., *An Account of the Origin, Proceedings, and Intentions of the Society for the Promotion of Industry: in the Southern District of the Parts of Lindsey, in the County of Lincoln. Published at the Desire, and with the*

Approbation of the Standing Committee of the said Society; in which the Society's Accounts, and the Lists of Benefactors, Subscribers, and Trustees, are Continued to the Audit in 1789 (Louth: R. Sheardown, 1789).

Bray, William, *Sketch of a Tour into Derbyshire and Yorkshire: Including Part of Buckingham, Warwick, Leicester, Nottingham, Northampton, Bedford, and Hertford-shires* (London: printed for B. White, 1778).

Briggs, Asa, *Essays in Labour History, 1918–1939* (London: Croom Helm, 1977).

Briggs, Asa, *Victorian Cities* (London: Odhams Press, 1963).

Brock, Michael, *The Great Reform Act* (London: Hutchinson, 1973).

Brown, John, *A Memoir of Robert Blincoe* (Firle: Caliban Books, 1977).

Brown, John, *A Memoir of Robert Blincoe, an Orphan Boy Sent from the Workhouse ... to ... a Cotton-mill, etc.* (Manchester: J. Doherty, 1832).

Brown, John, *A Memoir of Robert Blincoe, an Orphan Boy, Sent at Seven to Endure the Horrors of a Cotton-mill* (Series: British Labour Struggles: Contemporary Pamphlets 1727–1850), (New York: Arno, 1972).

Brown, John, *A Memoir of Robert Blincoe. With: A Brief Account of the Early Textile Industry in Derbyshire by Owen Ashmore. And: An Introductory Note on Robert Blincoe and the Early Factory System by A.E. Musson* (Series: Derbyshire Miscellany, Supplement: 10), (Duffield: Derbyshire Archaeological Society, Local History Section, 1966).

Brown, John, *Anecdotes and Characters of the House of Brunswick, Illustrative of the Courts of Hanover and London from the Act of Settlement to the Youth of George the Third; Including an Original Memoir of the Electress Sophia and a Journal Said to Have Been Written by ... the Princess Sophia Dorothea* (London: T. and J. Allman, 1821).

Brown, John, *The Historical Gallery of Criminal Portraitures, Foreign and Domestic: Containing a Selection of the Most Impressive Cases ... in Modern History* (Manchester: J. Gleave, 1823).

Brown, John, *The History of Great and Little Bolton* (Manchester: printed by C.W. Leake; published by Kell, Bolton, Clarke, 1824).

Brown, John, *The Mysteries of Neutralization, or, The British Navy Vindicated from the Charges of Injustice and Oppression Towards Neutral Flags* (London: printed for the author, 1806).

Brown, John, *The Northern Courts: Containing Original Memoirs of the Sovereigns of Sweden and Denmark Since 1766* (London, 1818).

Brown, Walter E., *The St Pancras Poor: A Brief Record of Their Treatment, etc., from 1718 to 1904* (London, 1905).

Brumhead, Derek, Roger Bryant and Ron Weston, *New Mills: A Look Back at its Industrial Heritage* (New Mills: New Mills Local History Society, 1997).

Brundage, Anthony, *The English Poor Laws, 1700–1930* (Series: Social History in Perspective), (Basingstoke: Palgrave, 2001).

Brundage, Anthony, *The Making of a New Poor Law: The Politics of Inquiry, Enactment and Implementation, 1832–39* (London: Hutchinson, 1978).

Buchan, William, *Advice to Mothers, on the Subject of Their Own Health; and on the Means of Promoting the Health, Strength, and Beauty of their Offspring* (London, 1803).

Burn, Richard, *The History of the Poor Laws: With Observations* (London: printed by H. Woodfall and W. Strahan, for A. Millar, 1764).

Burnett, John, David Vincent and David Mayall (eds), *The Autobiography of the Working Class: An Annotated Critical Bibliography* (Brighton, Sussex: Harvester, 1984–1989).

Bynum, W.F., *Science and the Practice of Medicine in the Nineteenth Century* (Cambridge: Cambridge University Press, 1994).

Carlile, Richard, *Jail Journal: Prison Thoughts and Other Writings. Edited and Selected by Guy A. Aldred* (Glasgow: Strickland Press, 1942).

Carpenter, Kenneth J., *The History of Scurvy and Vitamin C* (Cambridge: Cambridge University Press, 1986).

Carpenter, Kirsty, *Refugees of the French Revolution: Emigrés in London, 1789–1802* (Houndmills, Hampshire: Macmillan, 1999).

Chambers, Jonathan David, *Nottinghamshire in the Eighteenth Century: A Study of Life and Labour under the Squirearchy* (London: P.S. King and Son, 1932).

Champness, John, *Lancaster Castle: A Brief History* (Preston: Lancaster County Books, 1993).

Chapman, Stanley D., *The Early Factory Masters: The Transition to the Factory System in the Midlands Textile Industry* (Newton Abbot, Devon: David and Charles, 1967).

Claeys, Gregory, *Thomas Paine: Social and Political Thought* (Boston: Unwin Hyman, 1989).

Clinch, George, *Marylebone and St Pancras: Their History, Celebrities, Buildings, and Institutions* (London: Truslove and Shirley, 1890).

Cole, Margaret, *Robert Owen of New Lanark* (New York: A.M. Kelley, 1969).

Cook, Gordon Charles, *From the Greenwich Hulks to Old St Pancras: A History of Tropical Disease in London* (London: Athlone Press, 1992).

Cooper, James, *Transformation of a Valley: The Derbyshire Derwent* (London: Heinemann, 1981).

Coppock, J.T., and Hugh C. Prince (eds), *Greater London* (London: Faber and Faber, 1964).

Coull, Thomas, *The History and Traditions of St Pancras* (London: T. and W. Coull, 1861).

Cox, J. Charles, *Three Centuries of Derbyshire Annals: As Illustrated by the Records of the Quarter Sessions of the County of Derby from Queen Elizabeth to Queen Victoria* (London: Bemrose, 1890).

Cruickshank, Marjorie, *Children and Industry: Child Health and Welfare in North-west Textile Towns During the Nineteenth Century* (Manchester: Manchester University Press, 1981).

Cunningham, Hugh, *Children and Childhood in Western Society Since 1500* (Harlow: Pearson/Longman, 2005).

Davies, David Peter (Reverend), *A New Historical and Descriptive View of Derbyshire from the Remotest Period to the Present Time* (Belper: S. Mason, 1811).

Deane, P. and W.A. Cole, *British Economic Growth, 1688–1959* (Cambridge: Cambridge University Press, 1962).

Deering, Charles, *Nottinghamia Vetus et Nova: Or an Historical Account of the Ancient and Present State of the Town of Nottingham. ... Adorn'd with ... Copper-plates with an Appendix, ... By Charles Deering, M.D.* (Nottingham: printed by and for George Ayscough and Thomas Willington, 1751).

Defoe, Daniel, *A Tour Through the Whole Island of Great Britain* (London: Everyman, 1974).

Defoe, Daniel, *Parochial Tyranny* (London: J. Roberts, 1724).

Denman, Joseph, *Observations on Buxton Water ... Second Edition, Corrected and Enlarged* (London: J. Johnson, 1801).

Denman, Joseph, *Observations on the Effects of Buxton Water* (London: J. Johnson, 1793).

Denyer, Charles Henry, *St Pancras Through the Centuries* (London: LePlay House Press, 1935).

Dinwiddy, John Rowland, *From Luddism to the First Reform Bill: Reform in England, 1810–1832* (Oxford: B. Blackwell, 1987).

Dixon, C.W., *Smallpox* (London: J. and A. Churchill, 1962).

Donnachie, Ian, *Robert Owen: Owen of New Lanark and New Harmony* (East Linton: Tuckwell, 2000).

Dorling, William, *Henry Vincent, a Biographical Sketch and Life of Joseph Rayner Stephens by George Jacob Holyoake* (New York: Garland Publishing, 1986).

Downing, James, *A Narrative of the Life of James Downing ... Composed by Himself in Easy Verse ... Third Edition* (London: printed for the author, 1815).

Driver, Cecil Herbert, *Tory Radical: The Life of Richard Oastler* (New York: Oxford University Press, 1946).

Dunlop, O. Jocelyn, *English Apprenticeship and Child Labour: A History* (London: T. Fisher Unwin, 1912).

Eachard, John, *Dr Eachard's Works, Viz. I. The Grounds and Occasions of the Contempt of the Clergy and Religion Enquir'd into ... II. Observations on an Answer to the Enquiry ... III. Mr Hobbs's State of Nature Considered ... To Which Are Added Five Letters, andc. By John Eachard* (London: printed for J. Phillips ... H. Rhodes ... and J. Taylor ..., 1705).

Eastwood, David, *Governing Rural England: Tradition and Transformation in Local Government 1780–1840* (Oxford: Clarendon Press, 1994).

Eden, Sir Frederic Morton, Bart., *The State of the Poor* (London, 1784).

Edwards, Michael S., *Purge This Realm: A Life of Joseph Rayner Stephens* (London: Epworth, 1994).

Eliot, George, *Felix Holt the Radical* (London: William Blackwood and Sons, 1864).

Eliot, George, *The Mill on the Floss* (London: Penguin, 2002).

Engels, Friedrich, *The Condition of the Working-class in England in 1844. With a Preface Written in 1892 by Frederick Engels*, trans. Florence Kelley Wischnewetzky (London: Swan Sonnenschein and Co., 1892).

Evans, Eric J., *The Forging of the Modern State: Early Industrial Britain, 1783–1870* (London: Longman, 1983).

Farey, John, *General View of the Agriculture and Minerals of Derbyshire: With Observations on the Means of Their Improvement / Drawn Up for the Consideration of the Board of Agriculture and Internal Improvement by John Farey* (London: Sherwood, Neely and Jones, 3 vols, 1811–1815).

Felkin, William, *An Account of the Machine-wrought Hosiery Trade: Its Extent, and the Condition of the Framework-knitters, etc.* (London, 1845).

Fielden, John, *The Curse of the Factory System; or, A Short Account of Factory Cruelties* (London, 1836).

Finlayson, Geoffrey B.A.M., *The Seventh Earl of Shaftesbury, 1801–1885* (London: Eyre Methuen, 1981).

Firth, John Benjamin, *Highways and Byways in Derbyshire, with Illustrations by Nelly Erichsen* (London: Macmillan, 1905).

Fissell, Mary Elizabeth, *Patients, Power, and the Poor in Eighteenth-century Bristol* (Cambridge: Cambridge University Press, 1991).

Fitton, R.S., and A.P. Wadsworth, *The Strutts and the Arkwrights, 1758–1830: A Study of the Early Factory System* (Manchester: Manchester University Press, 1958).

Fleischman, Richard K., *Conditions of Life Among the Cotton Workers of Southeastern Lancashire, 1780–1850* (New York: Garland Publishing, 1985).

Fletcher, Canon J.M.J., *Tideswell in the Days of Parson Brown* (reprinted from 1927 pamphlet by Tideswell Women's Institute, 1977, and republished by S.J. Books, 1986).

Fletcher, Canon, *Tideswell in the Days of Parson Brown: and More Particularly During the Years 1785–1800* (Litton: Hilltop Press, 1977).

Foner, Eric, *Tom Paine and Revolutionary America* (New York: Oxford University Press, 1976).

Forster, John, *The Life of Charles Dickens ... Edited and Annotated, with an Introduction, by J.W.T. Ley* (London: Cecil Palmer, 1928).

French, Gilbert J., *Life and Times of Samuel Crompton* (London, 1859).

Frow, Edmund, and Ruth Frow, *The Dark Satanic Mills: Child Apprentices in Derbyshire Spinning Factories* (Manchester: Manchester Free Press, 1985).

Furneaux, Robin, *William Wilberforce* (London: Hamilton, 1974).

Gash, Norman, *Aristocracy and People: Britain 1815–1865* (London: Edward Arnold, 1979).

Gash, Norman, *Mr Secretary Peel: The Life of Sir Robert Peel to 1830* (London: Longman, 1985).

Gaskell, P., *Artisans and Machinery: The Moral and Physical Condition of the Manufacturing Population Considered with Reference to Mechanical Substitutes for Human Labour* (London, 1836).

Gay, Peter, *The Enlightenment: An Interpretation* (New York: Norton, 1977).

George, M. Dorothy, *London Life in the Eighteenth Century* (London: Kegan Paul, Trench, Trubner and Co., 1925).

Gibbs, John, *The Life and Experience of the Author and Some Traces of the Lord's Gracious Dealings Towards the Author J.G., etc.* (Lewes, 1827).

Gill, J.C., *The Ten Hours Parson: Christian Social Action in the Eighteen-thirties* (London: SPCK, 1959).

Gillingwater, Edmund, *An Essay on Parish Workhouses: Containing Observations on the Present State of English Workhouses; with Some Regulations Proposed for Their Improvement* (Bury St Edmunds, 1786).

Glover, Stephen, *The Peak Guide, Containing the Topographical, Statistical, and General History of Buxton, Chatsworth, Edensor, Castleton, Bakewell, Haddon, Matlock, and Cromford; with an Introduction Giving a Succinct Account of the Trade and Manufactures of the County; an Alphabetical List of Noblemen and Gentlemen's Seats, and Several Road Sketches* (Derby: printed for the publisher by H. Mozley and Son, 1830).

Gray, Robert Q., *The Factory Question and Industrial England, 1830–1860* (New York: Cambridge University Press, 1996).

Guest, Richard, *A Compendious History of the Cotton-manufacture: With a Disproval of the Claim of Sir Richard Arkwright to the Invention of Its Ingenious Machinery* (Manchester, 1823).

Hammond, John and Barbara, *The Town Labourer, 1760–1832: The New Civilisation* (London: Longmans, Green, 1917).

Hanway, Jonas, *A Sentimental History of Chimney-sweepers in London and Westminster, Shewing the Necessity of Putting Them Under Regulations. … With a Letter to a London Clergyman on Sunday Schools, etc.* (London, 1785).

Hanway, Jonas, *An Earnest Appeal for Mercy to the Children of the Poor, Particularly Those Belonging to the Parishes Within the Bills of Mortality, Appointed by an Act of Parliament to be Registered, Being a General Reference to the Deserving Conduct of Some Parish Officers, and the*

Pernicious Effects of the Ignorance and Ill-judged Parsimony of Others ... (London: J. Dodsley, 1766).

Harris, Helen, *The Industrial Archaeology of the Peak District* (Newton Abbot: David and Charles, 1971).

Harrison, George Bagshawe, *One Man in his Time: The Memoirs of G.B. Harrison 1894–1984* (Palmerston North, NZ: Dunmore Press, 1985).

Hawkins, Francis Bisset, *Germany: The Spirit of Her History, Literature, Social Condition, and National Economy, Illustrated by Reference to Her Physical, Moral, and Political Statistics, and by Comparison with Other Countries* (London: J.W. Parker, 1838).

Hayek, F.A. (ed.), *Capitalism and the Historians* (Chicago: University of Chicago Press, 1954).

Haynes, Ian, *Stalybridge Cotton Mills* (Manchester: Neil Richardson, 1990).

Hazlitt, William, *A Reply to the Essay on Population by the Rev. T.R. Malthus. In a Series of Letters* (London: Longman, Hurst, Rees and Orme, 1807).

Henriques, Ursula R.Q., *Before the Welfare State: Social Administration in Early Industrial Britain* (London: Longman, 1979).

Hilton, Boyd, *Corn, Cash, Commerce: The Economic Policies of the Tory Governments 1815–1830* (Oxford: Oxford University Press, 1977).

Hodder, Edwin, *The Life and Work of the Seventh Earl of Shaftesbury* (London: Cassell, 1888).

Holcroft, Thomas, *Memoirs: Written by Himself, and Continued to the Time of His Death, from His Diary, Notes and Other Papers by W. Hazlitt* (London, 1816).

Hollington, Michael (ed.), *Charles Dickens: Critical Assessments* (Mountfield: Helm Information, 1995).

Horn, Pamela, *Children's Work and Welfare, 1780–1880s* (Series: Studies in Economic and Social History), (Basingstoke: Macmillan, 1994).

Huberman, Michael, *Escape from the Market: Negotiating Work in Lancashire* (New York: Cambridge University Press, 1996).

Hulbert, Martin (ed.), *Orphan Child Factory Workers at Litton and Cressbrook Mills* (unpublished pamphlet).

Huntington, William, *Memoirs of the Reverend William Huntington, S.S., the Coal-heaver ... Interspersed with Various Anecdotes from his Writing* (London, 1813).

Hutchins, Betty Leigh and A. Harrison, *A History of Factory Legislation* (London: Frank Cass, 1966).

James, Lawrence, *Raj: The Making and Unmaking of British India* (London: Little, Brown, 1997).

Kalm, Pehr, *Kalm's Account of His Visit to England on His Way to America in 1748*, trans. Joseph Lucas (London, 1892).

Kay-Shuttleworth, Sir James, *The Moral and Physical Condition of the Working*

Classes Employed in the Cotton Manufacture in Manchester (London: J. Ridgway, 1832).

Kestner, Joseph A., *Protest and Reform: The British Social Narrative by Women, 1827–1867* (London: Methuen, 1985).

Kidd, Alan J., *Manchester Illustrated from the Archives and with Contemporary Photographs by Ian Beesley* (Keele, Staffordshire: Ryburn, 1993).

Kirby, Peter, *Child Labour in Britain, 1750–1870* (Series: Social History in Perspective), (Houndmills, Basingstoke: Palgrave Macmillan, 2003).

Kirby, Raymond George, and A.E. Musson, *The Voice of the People: John Doherty, 1798–1854: Trade Unionist, Radical and Factory Reformer* (Manchester: Manchester University Press, 1975).

Kovacevic, Ivanka (ed.), *Fact into Fiction: English Literature and the Industrial Scene, 1750–1850* (Leicester: Leicester University Press, 1975).

Kussmaul, Ann, *A General View of the Rural Economy of England, 1538–1840* (Cambridge: Cambridge University Press, 1990).

Kydd, Samuel, *The History of the Factory Movement* (New York: Kelley, 1966).

Kydd, Samuel 'Alfred', *The History of the Factory Movement: From the Year 1802, to the Enactment of the Ten Hours' Bill in 1847* (London: Simpkin, Marshall and Co., 1857).

Lane, Joan, *Apprenticeship in England, 1600–1914* (London: UCL Press, 1996).

Lavalette, Michael (ed.), *A Thing of the Past? Child Labour in Britain in the Nineteenth and Twentieth Centuries* (Liverpool: Liverpool University Press, 1999).

Lawrence, Christopher, and Steven Shapin (eds), *Science Incarnate: Historical Embodiments of Natural Knowledge* (London: University of Chicago Press, 1998).

Lees, Lynn Hollen, *The Solidarities of Strangers: The English Poor Laws and the People, 1700–1948* (Cambridge: Cambridge University Press, 1998).

Liddall, Marton Gloria, *The St Pancras Vestry: A Study in the Administration of a Metropolitan Parish 1760–1835* (unpublished Ph.D thesis, Rutgers University, 1981).

Lloyd-Jones, Roger, and M.J. Lewis, *Manchester and the Age of the Factory: The Business Structure of Cottonopolis in the Industrial Revolution* (London: Croom Helm, 1988).

Longenbach, James, *Fleet River* (Chicago: University of Chicago Press, 2003).

Longmate, Norman, *The Workhouse* (London: Temple Smith, 1974).

Lovell, Percy W., and W. Marcham, *The Parish of St Pancras* (Series: Survey of London; vols 17, 19, 21, 24), (London: London County Council, 1936–1952).

Lysons, Daniel, *The Environs of London*, 4 vols (London: A Strahan, 1792–6).

Maitland, William, *History and Survey of London from its Foundation to the Present Time* (London: T. Osborne, J. Shipton and J. Hodges, 1756).

Malthus, Revd Thomas, *An Essay on the Principle of Population as it Affects the Future Improvement of Society* (London, 1798).

Mandeville, Bernard, *The Fable of the Bees; or, Private Vices, Publick Benefits* (originally published in 1714; Harmondsworth: Penguin, 1970).

Mantoux, Paul Joseph, *The Industrial Revolution in the Eighteenth Century: An Outline of the Beginnings of the Modern Factory System in England*, trans. Marjorie Vernon (London: Jonathan Cape, 1928).

Marlow, Joyce, *The Peterloo Massacre* (London: Rapp and Whiting, 1969).

Marsh, Peter T., *The Victorian Church in Decline: Archbishop Tait and the Church of England, 1868–1882* (London: Routledge and Kegan Paul, 1969).

Marshall, Dorothy, *English People in the Eighteenth Century* (London: Longmans, Green, 1956).

Martineau, Harriet, *The Hill and the Valley: A Tale* (Series: Illustrations of Political Economy), (London: Charles Fox, 1832).

Marx, Karl, *The Eighteenth Brumaire of Louis Bonaparte, Translated from the German for the People, Organ of the Socialist Labor Party, by Daniel De Leon* (New York: International Publishing Co., 1898).

Mason, Sheila A., *Nottingham Lace, 1760s–1950s: The Machine-made Lace Industry in Nottinghamshire, Derbyshire and Leicestershire* (Ilkeston: Sheila A. Mason, 1994).

Middleton, Marmaduke, *Poetical Sketches of a Tour in the West of England* (Sheffield: printed for the author by J. Montgomery, 1822).

Miller, Frederick, *St Pancras Past and Present* (London: Heywood, 1874).

Millward, Roy, and Adrian Robinson, *The Peak District* (Series: The Regions of Britain), (London: Eyre Methuen, 1975).

Misson, Henri, *Memoirs and Observations of Travels over England* (London, 1719).

Montagu, Frederic, *Mary Ashley: or Facts upon Factories* (London, 1839).

Montgomery, James, *The Chimney-Sweeper's Friend, and Climbing-Boy's Album. ... Arranged by J.M.* (London, 1824).

More, Hannah, *Village Politics; With, The Shepherd of Salisbury Plain* (Oxford: Woodstock Books, 1995).

Morsley, Clifford, *News from the English Countryside, 1750–1850* (London: Harrap, 1979).

Morton, Arthur Leslie, *The Life and Ideas of Robert Owen* (London: Lawrence and Wishart, 1962).

Mumford, Alfred Alexander, *The Manchester Grammar School, 1515–1915: A Regional Study of the Advancement of Learning in Manchester since the Reformation* (London: Longmans, Green, and Co., New York, 1919).

Musson, Albert Edward, *The Growth of British Industry* (New York: Holmes and Meier, 1978).

Musson, Albert Edward, *Trade Union and Social History* (London: Cass, 1974).

Nardinelli, Clark, *Child Labor and the Industrial Revolution* (Bloomington: Indiana University Press, 1990).

Nash, Thomas, *The Works of Thomas Nashe*, ed. from the original texts by Ronald B. McKerrow; reprinted from the original edition with corrections and supplementary notes, ed. F.P. Wilson (Oxford: B. Blackwell, 1966).

Neate, Alan R., *The St Marylebone Workhouse and Institution, 1730–1965* (London: St Marylebone Society, 1967).

Neville, Sylas, *The Diary of Sylas Neville, 1767–1788*, ed. Basil Cozens-Hardy (London: Oxford University Press, 1950).

Neville-Sington, Pamela, *Fanny Trollope: The Life and Adventures of a Clever Woman* (London: Viking, 1997).

Oastler, Richard, *Eight Letters to the Duke of Wellington, a Petition to the House of Commons, and a Letter to the Editor of the Agricultural and Industrial Magazine* (London: J. Cochrane, 1835).

Oastler, Richard, *Richard Oastler: King of Factory Children; Six Pamphlets, 1835–1861* (New York: Arno Press, 1972).

Olsen, Kirstin, *Daily Life in Eighteenth-century England* (Westport, CT: Greenwood Press, 1999).

Osborne, John Walter, *John Cartwright* (Cambridge: Cambridge University Press, 1972).

Owen, Robert, *A New View of Society or, Essays on the Formation of the Human Character …* (London: printed for Longman, Hurst, Rees, etc., 1817).

Palmer, Samuel, *St Pancras: Being Antiquarian, Topographical, and Biographical Memoranda, Relating to the Extensive Metropolitan Parish of St Pancras, Middlesex; with Some Account of the Parish from its Foundation* (London: S. Palmer, 1870).

Patterson, Melville W., *Sir Francis Burdett and His Times (1770–1844): Including Hitherto Unpublished Letters of Mrs Fitzherbert, George Prince of Wales, the Duke of York and Others* (London: Macmillan, 1931).

Pawson, Eric, *Transport and Economy: The Turnpike Roads of Eighteenth-century Britain* (London: Academic Press, 1977).

Pearce, Edward, *Reform: The Fight for the 1832 Reform Act* (London: Jonathan Cape, 2003).

Percival, R., *A Collection Illustrative of the History and Topography of the Parish of Saint Pancras, Formed by Mr R. Percival, Comprising Engraved Views and Portraits, Coloured and Pencil Sketches and MS. Notes; with Cuttings from Books and Newspapers Printed Between the Dates 1729 and 1829* (London: 1729–1830).

Perkin, Harold, *Origins of Modern English Society* (London: Routledge, 1991).

Picard, Liza, *Dr Johnson's London: Life in London, 1740–1770* (London: Weidenfeld and Nicolson, 2000).

Pilkington, James, *A View of the Present State of Derbyshire; with an Account of its Most Remarkable Antiquities, etc.* (Derby: J. Drewry, 1789).

Pinchbeck, Ivy, and Margaret Hewitt, *Children in English Society* (London: Routledge and Kegan Paul, 1969–73).

Place, Francis, *The Autobiography of Francis Place (1771–1854)*, edited with an introduction and notes by Mary Thale (Cambridge: Cambridge University Press, 1972).

Plowright, John, *Regency England: The Age of Lord Liverpool* (London: Routledge, 1996).

Pool, Daniel, *What Jane Austen Ate and Charles Dickens Knew: From Fox Hunting to Whist: The Facts of Daily Life in Nineteenth-century England* (New York: Simon and Schuster, 1993).

Poole, William, *The Life and Death of St Pancras, a Young Martyr of the Early Christian Church: with Notes and Appendix, Containing a Letter to the Young on Persecution, and Thoughts on the Commemoration of Departed Friends* (London: William Poole, 1882).

Poor Law Commissioners, *The Poor Law Report of 1834*, edited with an introduction by S.G. and E.O.A. Checkland (Harmondsworth: Penguin, 1974).

Porter, Roy, and Lindsay Granshaw (eds), *The Hospital in History* (London: Routledge, 1989).

Pott, Percivall, *Chirurgical Observations Relative to the Cataract, the Polypus of the Nose, the Cancer of the Scrotum, … Ruptures, and the Mortification of the Toes, etc.* (London, 1775).

Prentice, Archibald, *Historical Sketches and Personal Recollections of Manchester: Intended to Illustrate the Progress of Public Opinion from 1792 to 1832* (London: Frank Cass, 1970 (reprint)).

Preston, Thomas, *The Life and Opinions of Thomas Preston, Patriot and Shoemaker* (London, 1817).

Rawlinson, Robert, *Report to the General Board of Health on a Preliminary Inquiry into the Sewerage, Drainage, and Supply of Water, and the Sanitary Condition of the Inhabitants of the Borough of Wolverhampton, and the Townships of Bilston, Willenhall, and Wednesfield* (London: W. Clowes and Sons for HMSO, 1849).

Richardson, John, *A History of Camden: Hampstead, Holborn, St Pancras* (London: Historical Publications in association with the London Borough of Camden, 1999).

Richardson, Ruth, *Death, Dissection and the Destitute* (London: Penguin, 1988).

Roberts, David, *Paternalism in Early Victorian England* (London: Croom Helm, 1979).

Rogers, Ben, *Beef and Liberty: Roast Beef, John Bull and the English Nation* (London: Chatto and Windus, 2003).

Romilly, Sir Samuel, *Memoirs of the Life of Sir Samuel Romilly, Written by Himself* (London, 1840).

Rose, Michael E. (ed.), *The English Poor Law, 1780–1930* (Newton Abbot: David and Charles, 1971).

Rosenberg, Charles E., *The Cholera Years: The United States in 1832, 1849, and 1866* (Chicago: University of Chicago Press, 1962).

Ruggles, Thomas, *The History of the Poor, Their Rights, Duties, and the Laws Respecting Them: In a Series of Letters* (London: printed for J. Deighton, 1793–4).

Saxby, Mary, *Memoirs of Mary Saxby: a Female Vagrant. To Which Are Added, Directions for the Recovery of Persons Apparently Drowned* (London: printed by Tilling and Hughes, …, Chelsea; and sold by F. Collins, …, London; and J. Nisbet, 1806).

Scheuermann, Mona, *In Praise of Poverty: Hannah More Counters Thomas Paine and the Radical Threat* (Lexington: University Press of Kentucky, 2002).

Schweizer, Karl W., and John Osborne, *Cobbett in his Times* (London: Leicester University Press, 1990).

Searby, Peter, *A History of the University of Cambridge* (Cambridge: Cambridge University Press, 1977).

Seeley, Robert Benton, *Memoirs of the Life and Writings of Michael Thomas Sadler* (London: R.B. Seeley and W. Burnside, sold by L. and G. Seeley, 1842).

Sheppard, Francis, *Local Government in St Marylebone, 1688–1835: A Study of the Vestry and the Turnpike Trust* (London: University of London, Athlone Press, 1958).

Sheppard, Francis, *London, 1808–1870: The Infernal Wen* (Berkeley: University of California Press, 1971).

Simpson, Charles R., *St Luke's Church 1733–1933: A Short Summary of Its History* (unpublished pamphlet, 1933).

Smelser, Neil J., *Social Change in the Industrial Revolution: An Application of Theory to the Lancashire Cotton Industry 1770–1840* (London: Routledge and Kegan Paul, 1959).

Smith, Adam, *An Inquiry into the Nature and Causes of the Wealth of Nations* (London: printed for W. Strahan and T. Cadell, 1776).

Smith, E.A., *A Queen on Trial: The Affair of Queen Caroline* (Phoenix Mill: A. Sutton, 1994).

Smith, Francis Barrymore, *The People's Health, 1830–1910* (London: Croom Helm, 1979).

Southey, Robert, *Letters from England* (London: Cresset Press, 1951).

Southey, Robert, *Sir Thomas More, or,: Colloquies on the Progress and Prospects of Society* (London: John Murray, 1829).

Spater, George, *William Cobbett: The Poor Man's Friend* (Cambridge: Cambridge University Press, 1982).

Starkey, Benjamin, *Memoirs of the Life of Benjamin Starkey ... Written by Himself* (Newcastle, 1818).

Steinberg, Marc William, *Fighting Words: Working-class Formation, Collective Action, and Discourse in Early Nineteenth-century England* (Ithaca, NY: Cornell University Press, 1999).

Stone, Lawrence, *The Family, Sex and Marriage in England, 1500–1800* (Harmondsworth: Penguin, 1979).

Stott, Anne, *Hannah More: The First Victorian* (Oxford: Oxford University Press, 2003).

Strange, K.H., *Climbing Boys: A Study of Sweeps' Apprentices, 1773–1875* (New York: Allison and Busby, 1982).

Stuckey, Thomas, *A Narrative of the Proceedings at the General Meeting of the London Corresponding Society, Held on Monday, July 31, 1797, in a Field, Near the Veterinary College, St Pancras, in the County of Middlesex* (London: printed for the society and published by Symonds, 1797).

Taylor, James Stephen, *Hanway: Founder of the Marine Society: Charity and Policy in Eighteenth-century Britain* (Berkeley, CA: Scolar Press, 1985).

Taylor, William Cooke, *Notes of a Tour in the Manufacturing Districts of Lancashire; in a Series of Letters to ... the Archbishop of Dublin ... Second edition, etc.* (London, 1842).

Thackrah, Charles Turner, *The Effects of Arts, Trades and Professions, and of Civic States and Habit of Living, on Health and Longevity: with Suggestions for the Removal of Many of the Agents which Produce Disease, and Shorten the Duration of Time* (London: Longman, Rees, Orme, Brown, Green and Longman, Simpkin and Marshall, 1832).

Thom, William, *Rhymes and Recollections of a Hand Loom Weaver* (London: Smith, Elder and Co., 1845).

Thomas, Maurice Walton, *The Early Factory Legislation: A Study in Legislative and Administrative Evolution* (Westport, CT: Greenwood Press, 1970).

Thomis, Malcolm I. (ed.), *Luddism in Nottinghamshire* (London: Phillimore, 1972).

Thomis, Malcolm I., *Politics and Society in Nottingham, 1785–1835* (Oxford: Oxford University Press, 1969).

Thompson, Edward Palmer, *The Making of the English Working Class* (London: Gollancz, 1963).

Thrale, Mary (ed.), *Selections from the Papers of the London Corresponding Society 1792–1799* (Cambridge: Cambridge University Press, 1983).

Throsby, John, *The History and Antiquities of the Town and County of the Town of Nottingham: Containing the Whole of Thoroton's Account of that*

Place, and All that is Valuable in Deering (Nottingham: sold by Burbage and Stretton, Tupman, Wilson, and Sutton, 1795).

Tilley, Joseph, *The Old Halls, Manors, and Families of Derbyshire, Vol. 1, The High Peak Hundred* (London: Simpkin, Marshall, Hamilton, Kent, and Co. Ltd, 1892).

Timmins, Geoffrey, *Four Centuries of Lancashire Cotton* (Preston: Lancashire County Books, 1996).

Tindall, Gillian, *The Fields Beneath: The History of One London Village* (London: Temple Smith, 1977).

Tocqueville, Alexis de, *Journeys to England and Ireland*, trans. George Lawrence and K.P. Mayer, ed. J.P. Mayer (New Haven: Yale University Press, 1958).

Townsend, Joseph, *A Dissertation on the Poor Laws by a Well-wisher to Mankind*, 2nd edn (London: printed for C. Dilly, 1786).

Trollope, Anthony, *An Autobiography*, with an introduction by John Sutherland (London: Trollope Society, 1999).

Trollope, Frances, *Life and Adventures of Michael Armstrong, the Factory Boy, etc.* (London, 1840).

Trollope, Thomas Adolphus, *What I Remember* (London: Richard Bentley and Son, 1887).

Turner, William, *Riot! The Story of the East Lancashire Loom-breakers in 1826* (Preston: Lancashire County Books, 1992).

Tuttle, Carolyn, *Hard at Work in Factories and Mines: The Economics of Child Labor During the British Industrial Revolution* (Boulder, CO: Westview Press, 1999).

Twigg, John, *A History of Queens' College, Cambridge 1448–1986* (Woodbridge: Boydell, 1987).

Unwin, George, *Samuel Oldknow and the Arkwrights* (London: Longmans, 1924).

Ure, Andrew, *The Philosophy of Manufactures, or, An Exposition of the Scientific, Moral, and Commercial Economy of the Factory System of Great Britain*, 2nd edn (London: C. Knight, 1835).

Venn, J.A., *Alumni Cantabrigienses: A Biographical List of All Known Students, Graduates and Holders of Office at the University of Cambridge, from the Earliest Times to 1900* (Cambridge: Cambridge University Press, 1940).

Wagner, Gillian, *Thomas Coram, Gent.* (Woodbridge: Boydell Press, 2004).

Walvin, James, *A Child's World: A Social History of English Childhood, 1800–1914* (Harmondsworth: Penguin Books, 1982).

Ward, J.T., and W.H. Fraser (eds), *Workers and Employers: Documents on Trade Unions and Industrial Relations in Britain Since the Eighteenth Century* (London: Macmillan, 1980).

Ward, John Towers, *The Factory System*, 2 vols (New York: Barnes and Noble, 1970).

Webb, Sydney and Beatrice, *English Poor Law History, Part 1: The Old Poor Law* (London: Frank Cass and Co. Ltd, 1963 reprint).

Wells, Roger A.E., *Wretched Faces: Famine in Wartime England, 1793–1801* (Gloucester: A. Sutton, 1988).

White, Reginald J., *Waterloo to Peterloo* (Harmondsworth: Penguin, 1968).

Wiener, Joel H., *Radicalism and Freethought in Nineteenth-century Britain: The Life of Richard Carlile* (Westport, CT: Greenwood Press, 1983).

Wilberforce, William, *A Practical View of the Prevailing Religious System of Professed Christians in the Higher and Middle Classes in this Country, Contrasted with Real Christianity* (London: reprint of original from SCM Press, 1958).

Williams, Mike, and D.A. Farnie, *Cotton Mills in Greater Manchester* (Preston: Carnegie, 1992).

Williams, Raymond, *Cobbett* (Oxford: Oxford University Press, 1983).

Winstanley, Denys Arthur, *Unreformed Cambridge: A Study of Certain Aspects of the University in the Eighteenth Century* (Cambridge: Cambridge University Press, 1935).

Winstanley, Michael (ed.), *Working Children in Nineteenth-century Lancashire* (Preston: Lancashire County Books, 1995).

Wood, William, *The History and Antiquities of Eyam; with a Minute Account of the Great Plague which Desolated that Village in the Year 1666* (London, 1848).

Woodville, William, *The History of the Inoculation of the Small-pox: in Great Britain*, vol. 1 (London: printed and sold by James Phillips, 1796).

Worrall, S.M., *Water Power on the Dover Beck* (unpublished thesis, Nottingham University, 1994).

Wroth, Warwick, *The London Pleasure Gardens of the Eighteenth Century* (London: Macmillan, 1896).

Young, Arthur, *A Six Months Tour Through the North of England, Containing an Account of the Present State of Agriculture, Manufactures and Population, in Several Counties of this Kingdom … : Interspersed with Descriptions of the Seats of the Nobility and Gentry, and Other Remarkable Objects …* (London: printed for W. Strahan, W. Nicoll, … B. Collins, … J. Balfour …, 1770).

Young, Arthur, *The Farmer's Letters to the People of England*, 3rd edn (Dublin: printed for J. Millikin, 1768).

Articles, book chapters and biographical entries

Anderson, Michael, 'The Sociological History and the Working-class Family: Smelser Revisited', *Social History*, Vol. 3 (1976), 317–34.

Ashley, William, 'The Place of Rye in the History of English Food', *The Economic Journal*, Vol. 123, No. 31 (September 1921), 285–308.

Ashmore, Owen, 'The Early Textile Industry in the Derwent Valley', Part One of John Brown, *A Memoir of Robert Blincoe*, Series: Derbyshire Miscellany, Supplement: 10 (Duffield: Derbyshire Archaeological Society, Local History Section, 1966).

Axon, Ernest, 'Historical Notes on Buxton, Its Inhabitants and Visitors: Buxton Doctors Since 1700', *Buxton Advertiser*, 23 December 1939.

Baer, Marc, 'Burdett, Sir Francis, Fifth Baronet (1770–1844)', *Dictionary of National Biography* (Oxford: Oxford University Press, 2005).

Bartrip, P.W.J., 'Success or Failure: The Prosecution of the Early Factory Acts', *Economic History Review*, 38 (1985), 423–36.

Baugh, D.A., 'The Cost of Poor Relief in South-East England, 1790–1834', *Economic History Review*, Vol. 28, No. 1 (February 1975), 50–68.

Baumgartner, L., 'John Howard (1726–1790), Hospital and Prison Reformer: A Bibliography', *Bulletin of the History of Medicine*, 7 (1939), 486–626.

Blaug, Mark, 'The Classical Economists and the Factory Acts – A Re-Examination', *Quarterly Journal of Economics*, Vol. 72 (1958), 211–26.

Blaug, Mark, 'The Myth of the Old Poor Law and the Making of the New', *Journal of Economic History*, Vol. 23 (1963), 151–80.

Blaug, Mark, 'The Poor Law Report Re-examined', *Journal of Economic History*, Vol. 24 (1964), 229–45.

Brothers, Hazel, 'Fear of Crime in Eighteenth-century Hampstead', *Camden History Review*, Vol. 23 (1999), 10–13.

Bythell, Duncan, 'The Hand-loom Weavers in the English Cotton Industry During the Industrial Revolution: Some Problems', *Economic History Review*, Vol. 17, No. 2 (1964), 339–53.

Carter, Paul, 'Poor Relief Strategies: Women, Children and Enclosure in Hanwell, Middlesex, 1780 to 1816', *Local Historian*, Vol. 25, No. 3 (1995), 164–77.

Chaloner, W.H., 'Mrs Trollope and the Early Factory System', *Victorian Studies*, Vol. IV, No. 2 (December 1960), 159–66.

Chapman, Stanley D., 'Peel, Sir Robert, First Baronet (1750–1830)', *Dictionary of National Biography* (Oxford: Oxford University Press, 2005).

Chapman, Stanley D., 'The Transition to the Factory System in the Midlands Cotton-spinning Industry', *Economic History Review*, Vol. 18, No. 3 (1956), 526–43.

Claeys, Gregory, 'Owen, Robert (1771–1858)', *Dictionary of National Biography* (Oxford: Oxford University Press, 2005).

Clark, Gregory, 'Factory Discipline', *Journal of Economic History*, Vol. 54, No. 1 (March 1994), 128–63.

Cochran, Peter, 'Hobhouse, John Cam', *Dictionary of National Biography* (Oxford: Oxford University Press, 2005).

Conquest, Richard, 'The Black Hole of St Pancras', *Camden History Review*, Vol. 3 (1975), 19–25.

Cook, Gordon C., 'Dr William Woodville (1752–1805) and the St Pancras Smallpox Hospital', *Journal of Medical Biography*, Vol. 4, No. 2 (May 1996), 71–8.

Cornish, Rory T., 'Cartwright, John (1740–1824)', *Dictionary of National Biography* (Oxford: Oxford University Press, 2005).

Corrigan, P.R.D., 'Tufnell, Edward Carleton', *Dictionary of National Biography* (Oxford: Oxford University Press, 2005).

Cunningham, Hugh, 'The Employment and Unemployment of Children in England c. 1680–1851', *Past and Present*, No. 126 (February 1990), 115–50.

Duffy, Ian P.H., 'English Bankrupts, 1571–1861', *American Journal of Legal History*, Vol. 24, No. 4 (October 1980), 283–305.

Eastwood, David, 'Robert Southey and the Intellectual Origins of Romantic Conservatism', *English Historical Review*, Vol. 104 (1989), 307–21.

Farnie, D.A., 'Crompton, Samuel (1753–1827)', *Dictionary of National Biography* (Oxford: Oxford University Press, 2005).

Felkin, William, 'The Lace and Hosiery Trades of Nottingham', *Journal of the Statistical Society of London*, Vol. 29, No. 4 (December 1866), 536–41.

Fell-Smith, Charlotte, 'Newton, William (1750–1830)', *Dictionary of National Biography* (Oxford: Oxford University Press, 2005).

Gee, J., 'Robert Blincoe, the Parish Apprentices in a Factory', *Manchester Notes and Queries* (7 July 1888), 218.

Gillespie, Revd Charles, 'The Life of a Parish Apprentice: Robert Blincoe', *Manchester Notes and Queries* (30 June 1888), 214–15.

Harris, Geoffrey, 'The Humanity of Hampstead Workhouse', *Camden History Review*, Vol. 4 (1976), 28–31.

Hobsbawm, E.J., 'The Machine Breakers', *Past and Present*, No. 1 (February 1952), 57–70.

Howe, A.C., 'Oldknow, Samuel (1756–1828), *Dictionary of National Biography* (Oxford: Oxford University Press, 2005).

Huberman, Michael, 'Industrial Relations and the Industrial Revolution: Evidence from M'Connel and Kennedy, 1810–1840', *Business History Review*, Vol. 65, No. 2 (Summer 1991), 345–78.

Huberman, Michael, 'Invisible Handshakes in Lancashire: Cotton Spinning in the First Half of the Nineteenth Century', *Journal of Economic History*, Vol. 46, No. 4 (December 1896), 987–98.

Hutt, W.H., 'The Factory System of the Early Nineteenth Century', in F.A. Hayek (ed.), *Capitalism and the Historians* (Chicago: University of Chicago Press, 1954), 156–84.

Johnson, Douglas, 'Anna Seward at Buxton 1808', *Derbyshire Miscellany*, Vol. 10, Pt. 6 (Autumn 1985), 175–6.

Johnson, Joseph, 'The Life of a Parish Apprentice: Robert Blincoe', *Manchester Notes and Queries* (23 June 1888), 211.

Jones, A.G.E., 'The Putrid Fever at Robert Peel's Radcliffe Mill', *Notes and Queries* (January 1958), 26–35.

Kamlish, Marian, 'Before Camden Town 1745–1795', *Camden History Review*, Vol. 21 (1997), 20–22.

Landau, Norma, 'The Regulation of Immigration, Economic Structures and Definitions of the Poor in Eighteenth-century England', *Historical Journal*, Vol. 33, No. 3 (September 1990), 541–71.

Lloyd, Sarah, 'Cottage Conversations: Poverty and Manly Independence in Eighteenth-century England', *Past and Present*, Vol. 184 (2004), 69–108.

Mackenzie, M.H., 'Calver Mill and Its Owners', *Derbyshire Archaeological Journal*, Vol. 83, 1963, 22–34.

Mackenzie, M.H., 'Cressbrook and Litton Mills, 1779–1835, Part 1', *Derbyshire Archaeological Journal*, Vol. 88, 1968, 1–25.

Mackenzie, M.H., 'Cressbrook and Litton Mills: A Reply', *Derbyshire Archaeological Journal*, Vol. 90, 1970, 56–9.

Mackenzie, M.H., 'Cressbrook Mill, 1810–1835', *Derbyshire Archaeological Journal*, Vol. 90, 1970, 60–70.

MacKinnon, Mary, and Paul Johnson, 'The Case against Productive Whipping', *Explorations in Economic History*, Vol. 12, No. 2 (April 1984), 218–23.

Mandler, Peter, 'Cain and Abel: Two Aristocrats and the Early Victorian Factory Acts', *Historical Journal*, Vol. 27, No. 1 (March 1984), 83–109.

Markel, Howard P., 'Factory Regulation: A Reinterpretation of Early English Experience', *Journal of Law and Economics*, Vol. 20, No. 2 (October 1977), 379–402.

Martin, Philip W., 'Richard Carlile (1790–1843)', *Dictionary of National Biography* (Oxford: Oxford University Press, 2005).

Melikan, R.A., 'Romilly, Sir Samuel (1757–1818)', *Dictionary of National Biography* (Oxford: Oxford University Press, 2005).

Morgan, Rod, 'John Howard (1726?–1790)', *Dictionary of National Biography* (Oxford: Oxford University Press, 2005).

Musson, A.E., 'Robert Blincoe and the Early Factory System', Part Two of John Brown, *A Memoir of Robert Blincoe*, Series: Derbyshire Miscellany, Supplement: 10 (Duffield: Derbyshire Archaeological Society, Local History Section, 1966).

Musson, Albert E., 'Robert Blincoe and the Early Factory System', in Albert Musson, *Trade Union and Social History* (London: Cass, 1974), 195–206.

Nardinelli, Clark, 'Child Labor and the Factory Acts', *Journal of Economic History*, Vol. 40, No. 4 (1980), 739–55.

Neville-Sington, Pamela, 'Trollope [née Milton], Frances (1779–1863)', *Dictionary of National Biography* (Oxford: Oxford University Press, 2005).

Pollard, Sydney, 'The Factory Village in the Industrial Revolution', *English Historical Review*, Vol. 79, No. 312 (July 1964), 513–31.

Porter, Roy, 'The Gift Relation: Philanthropy and Provincial Hospitals in Eighteenth-century England', in Roy Porter and Lindsay Granshaw (eds), *The Hospital in History* (London: Routledge, 1989).

Roberts, David, 'Tory Paternalism and Social Reform in Early Victorian England', *American Historical Review*, Vol. 63, No. 2 (January 1958), 323–37.

Rose, Mary B., 'Social Policy and Business: Parish Apprenticeship and the Early Factory System 1750–1834', *Business History*, Vol. 31, No. 4 (1989), 5–33.

Rostow, W.W., 'Business Cycles, Harvests, and Politics: 1790–1850', *Journal of Economic History*, Vol. 1, No. 2 (November 1941), 206–21.

Schofield, R.S., 'Dimensions of Illiteracy, 1750–1850', *Explorations in Economic History*, Vol. 10 (1973), 65–90.

Slater, Michael, John Greaves and Malcolm Holmes, 'Dickens in Camden', *Camden History Review*, Vol. 3 (1975), 11–13.

Smith, D.F., 'Workhouse Children', *Historian: a Journal of History*, Vol. 61, No. 4 (1999), 949–50.

Taylor, James Stephen, 'Philanthropy and Empire', *Eighteenth-century Studies*, Vol. 12, No. 3 (Spring 1979), 285–305.

Taylor, James Stephen, 'The Impact of Pauper Settlement', *Past and Present*, No. 73 (November 1976), 42–74.

Tuttle, C., 'A Revival of the Pessimist View: Child Labor and the Industrial Revolution', *Research in Economic History*, Vol. 18 (1998), 53–82.

Walker, J. Holland, 'An Itinerary of Nottingham', *Transactions of the Thoroton Society*, Vol. 29 (1925).

Welbourne, E., 'Bankruptcy Before the Era of Victorian Reform', *Cambridge Historical Journal*, Vol. 4, No. 1 (1932), 51–62.

Archival sources
Parliamentary Papers

Minutes of evidence taken before the Lords Committee concerning an 'Act for the Better Regulation of Chimney Sweeps' (March 1818).

'Report of Select Committee on Parish Apprentices', *Hansard*, April 11, 1815, 533–41.

Report of the Minutes of Evidence taken before the Select Committee on the State of the Children Employed in the Manufactories of the United Kingdom, 25th April–18th June, 1816 (London: House of Commons, 28 May and 19 June 1816).

'House of Lords Account of Cotton and Woolen Mills and Factories in the

United Kingdom of Great Britain and Ireland, 1803–1818', *Parliamentary Papers*, Vol. 108, 1819, House of Lords' Sessional Papers.

Report of the Select Committee on the 'Bill to Regulate the Labour of Children in the Mills and Factories of the United Kingdom' … 1831–2 (Shannon, Ireland: Irish University Press, 1968–9 (reprint)).

Second Report of the Central Board of His Majesty's Commissioners Appointed to Collect Information in the Manufacturing Districts, as to the Employment of Children in Factories, and as to the Propriety and Means of Curtailing the Hours of their Labour (London: House of Commons, 15 July 1833).

Parish records

Minutes of the St Pancras Vestry meetings (1718–1836), Camden Local Studies Library.

Minutes of the St Pancras Directors of the Poor meetings, Camden Local Studies Library.

Index to the Minutes of the St Pancras Vestry, Camden Local Studies Library.

The Heal Collection (maps, engravings, and photographs), Camden Local Studies Library.

James Frederick King, *The Kentish Town Panorama* (The London Topographical Society in conjunction with the London Borough of Camden, Libraries and Arts Department, 1986).

Derbyshire Deeds (Derby Borough Library).

Land tax records (Nottinghamshire Record Office).

Land tax records (Derbyshire Record Office).

Miscellaneous records

Two letters from George Bradley, a debtor held in Lancaster Castle, to Mr Birch and Mr Darnborough, Innkeepers at Clitheroe, 1825, 1826, M0122889LC (Burnley Library, Lancashire).

File relating to Revd Robert Blincoe (Islington Record Office).

Scrapbook of Revd Robert Blincoe (held by the Blincoe family).

Probate records of the Needham family (Lichfield Record Office).

Cheek papers relating to Ellis Needham's bankruptcy (Derbyshire Record Office).

The diary of Parson Brown (Birmingham University Library).

Lord Stanley's copy letter book 1802–1803, DDK box 168 (Lancashire Record Office).

Newspapers and periodicals

Ashton Chronicle
Bolton Chronicle
Derby Mercury

Macclesfield Observer
Manchester Gazette
Manchester Guardian
Manchester Mercury
Manchester Notes and Queries
Nottingham Journal
The Conciliator
The Lion
The Poor Man's Advocate
The Poor Man's Guardian
The Times

Trade directories

Bailey's Western and Midland Directory … 1783–4
Directory of the County of Derby (Glover) … 1829
Kelly's Directory of the Counties of Derby, Notts, Leicester and Rutland … 1891
Morris and Co.'s Directory and Gazetteer of Cheshire, 1874
Pigot and Co.'s Directory of Cheshire, Cumbria …, 1828–9
Universal British Directory, 1791–8
White's Directory of Derbyshire … 1857

Acknowledgements

Reconstructing the life and times of the parish apprentice Robert Blincoe has required the generous assistance and insights of a considerable number of people. I am very grateful to my colleagues in the Department of History and Philosophy of Science and the Centre for Health and Society at the University of Melbourne for their support and advice; in particular, Cecily Hunter, Janet McCalman, Neil Thomason, Anthony La Montagne, Lynn Gillam and Matthew Klugman. Academics from various universities have provided essential information and advice, including Jason Edwards, Alan Crosby, Simon Skinner, Peter Marsh and Mary B. Rose. Richard and Penny Graham-Yooll, Alison and Darian Stibbe, and Alan Ogden have also all provided incisive editorial comments along the way.

In addition, I am indebted to many librarians and archivists: Richard Knight of Camden's Local Studies Centre, Martin Banham of the Islington Local History Centre, Mark Dorrington of the Nottinghamshire Archives, John Benson, John Convey and Andrew Thynne of the Lancashire County Record Office, Sue Ashworth of Lancaster's City Museum, Paul Stebbing, Neil Bettridge, Judith Philips and their colleagues at the Derbyshire Record Office, Lisa Bates and Sue Band of Matlock's Local Studies Library, Graeme Siddall of the Sheffield Libraries Archives and Information Services, Jennifer Loveridge and Susan Wilson of Lancaster Reference Library, Jacqueline Cox of the University Archives of Cambridge University Library, Richard Palmer and Gabriel Lineham of the Church of England's Lambeth Palace Library, Christopher Hunwick and Geoffrey Robinson of Manchester Cathedral, Anne Marie Clarkson of The John Rylands University Library, Sally Rogers and Carole Pemberton of Manchester Grammar School, Gayle M. Richardson, Jill Cogen and Sue Hodson of the

Huntingdon Library, Bridget Howlett of the London Metropolitan Archives, Malcolm Mercer of the National Archives, and the staffs of Tideswell and Burnley libraries. Many other archivists and librarians, in Britain and Australia, have helped in smaller but important ways. I also profited from conversations with the staff of the Masson Mills textile museum in Matlock.

Several other people have contributed vital information or helped me obtain copies of articles, books and archival records from overseas. Helen Mycock provided me with lots of useful material, including a photograph of the Needhams' Old Hall, in addition to useful reflections on the history of the hamlet of Wormhill. Other contributors include: Gloria Rees of the Lowdham Historical Society, Jack Blencowe, John Palmer, George H. Toulmin, Bruce Calvert-Toulmin, David Hayes, Steve King and Peter Razzell. Simon Skinner's teaching helped ignite my enthusiasm for 19th-century British history. And several researchers have made it possible for me to complete this book while living in Australia: I am especially indebted to Michael and Susan Waller, Alan Crosby, Graham Paul, Maurice Dunman and Vreni Schoenenberger. For their intrepid and skilful photography I am grateful to Brian and Joan Lloyd and to Jules Hill-Landolt. I'd also like to thank Jane, Jason and Georgina Zibarras for their generosity. The trustees of the Symonds Bequest provided funds for research assistance. In addition, three historians warrant a mention here: M.H. Mackenzie, Raymond Kirby and A.E. Musson. All three died some years ago, and I never made their acquaintance, but their rigorous and ground-breaking research into the early industrial age made this book possible.

The team at Icon Books have been a genuine pleasure to work alongside. This book has benefited enormously from Simon Flynn's belief, right from the outset, in the value of the story it tells; his enthusiasm and his advice along the way have been invaluable. And the manuscript has been most fortunate to pass under the scrupulous editorial gaze of Icon Books' Duncan Heath. I'd also like to acknowledge the hard work of Icon's Ruth Tidball.

But to two families I owe the most gratitude. First, the Blincoes. Edward, Julian, Brian and Freda have very kindly made available to me the oral traditions of their family, as well as surviving photographs and the Reverend Blincoe's scrapbook. Edward Blincoe's written account of Robert's life has proved particularly useful. Second, the Wallers. My father, Michael, has been a constant teacher, mentor and guide, and my mother, Susan, a wonderful source of support. My wife, Abigail, has helped me greatly in understanding Blincoe's character and has shown exceptional patience in coping with her husband's obsessive desire to tell his story.

Index